Praise for  net b

"**T**hanks to Wolff and friends, the cyberswamp may just have become a little less murky." —*Entertainment Weekly*

"*NetGuide* is the computer world's online *TV Guide*®."—*Good Morning America*

"*NetGuide* will keep you from wandering around aimlessly on the Internet, and is full of good ideas for where to pull over."—*Forbes FYI*

"*NetGuide* is the liveliest, most readable online guide yet."—*USA Today*

"What you need to connect."—*Worth Magazine*

"*NetGuide* is the *TV Guide*® to Cyberspace!" —Louis Rossetto, publisher/editor, *Wired*

"One of the more complete, well-organized guides to online topics. From photography to the Church of Elvis, you'll find it here." —*PC Magazine*

"The best attempt yet at categorizing and organizing all the great stuff you can find out there. It's the book people keep stealing off my desk." —Joshua Quittner, *New York Newsday*

"It's changed my online life. Get this book!" —Mike Madson, "Computer Bits," Business Radio Network

"My favorite for finding the cool stuff." —*The Louisville Courier-Journal*

"*NetGuide* focuses on the most important aspect of online information—its content. You name it, it's there—from erotica to religion to politics." —Lawrence J. Magid, *San Jose Mercury News*

"Not only did all the existing Net books ignore Cyberspace's entertaining aspects, but they were process-oriented, not content-oriented. Why hadn't someone made a *TV Guide*® for the Net? Wolff recognized an opportunity for a new book, and his group wrote *NetGuide*." —Mark Frauenfelder, *Wired*

"Couch potatoes have *TV Guide*®. Now Net surfers have *NetGuide*." —*Orange County Register*

"*NetGuide* is one of the best efforts to provide a hot-spot guide to going online." —*Knoxville News-Sentinel*

"Assolutamente indispensabile!" —*L'Espresso*, Italy

"A valuable guide for anyone interested in the recreational uses of personal computers and modems." —Peter H. Lewis, *The New York Times*

"*NetGames* is a good map of the playing fields of Netdom."—*Newsweek*

"This guide to games people play in the ever-expanding Cyberspace shows you exactly where to go."—*Entertainment Weekly*

"The second book in a very good series from Wolff and Random House." —Bob Schwabach, syndicated columnist

"Hot addresses!"—*USA Weekend*

"Move over Parker Brothers and Nintendo— games are now available online. There's something in *NetGames* for everyone from crossword-puzzle addicts to Dungeons & Dragons fans." —*Reference Books Bulletin*

"Whether you're a hardened game player or a mere newbie, *NetGames* is the definitive directory for gaming on the Internet."—*.net*

"A wide and devoted following." —*The Wall Street Journal*

"*NetMoney* is a superb guide to online business and finance!" —*Hoover's Handbook of American Business*

"[*NetChat*] is...the best surfer's guide out there." —*Entertainment Weekly*

"A product line of guidebooks for explorers of the Internet."—*Inside Media*

In bookstores now!

NetSpy

Become an online sleuth! Now the ordinary computer user can tap into the information and data that credit agencies, lawyers, research companies, government departments, and other investigative and "snooping" firms have used for decades. Leave no relevant Web page unscrolled as you locate lost family members and check out potential employers.

ISBN
0-679-77029-1
US: $12.95
Canada: $17.50
200 pages

NetCollege

NetCollege gives you a crash course on how to get into the college of your choice—the online way! Visit virtual campuses. Stop by cyber-admissions offices. Get some SAT practice. Sort through financial aid info online. And, soon enough, find out the good (or bad) news via email.

ISBN 0-679-77380-0
US: $19.95
Canada: $27.00
400 pages

NetStudy

Where can I get help with my algebra homework? My English paper's due tomorrow and the library's closed. I don't understand frog anatomy. From the beginner studying astronomy to the math whiz taking AP calculus, *NetStudy* can help students get an education online. Includes Internet resources for teachers and parents.

ISBN 0-679-77381-9
US: $22.00
Canada: $30.00
400 pages

NetDoctor

NetDoctor offers a powerful cure for medical ignorance—the Internet! Packed with thousands of sites that let you diagnose your own maladies and lead you to the latest research on ailments ranging from AIDS to cancer to the common cold, this is the only book you'll ever need to stay healthy.

ISBN 0-679-77173-5
US: $22.00
Canada: $30.00
400 pages

Fodor's NetTravel

Fodor's NetTravel—from Fodor's and the creators of *NetGuide* and the Net-Books Series—tells you how to find the best online travel sites. Find your way to brilliant travelogues and wonderful travel secrets—plus subway maps, restaurant and hotel guides, movie listings, and train schedules.

ISBN 0-679-77033-X
US: $22.00
Canada: $30.00
400 pages

NetMarketing

NetMarketing is the first book that spells out strategies for how corporate marketers and mom-and-pop businesses can use the Net to powerful advantage. It includes hundreds of successful Web sites, a primer for getting started, and a directory of more than 1,000 marketing sites.

ISBN 0-679-77381-9
US: $22.00
Canada: $30.00
400 pages

NetGames 2

NetGames 2 is the all-new, updated edition of the original bestseller. It covers more than 4,000 games, including *Doom*, *Marathon*, *Harpoon II*, *Myst*, and more than a hundred MUDs, MUSHes, and MOOs, plus demos, tips, and free upgrades!

ISBN 0-679-77034-8
US: $22.00
Canada: $30.00
400 pages

NetSci-Fi

The ultimate guide for science fiction fanatics! *NetSci-Fi* covers topics from *Aliens* to *The X-Files* and everything in between. Want to work on a *Battlestar Galactica* revival campaign or learn about the value of those old *Star Wars* trading cards? *NetSci-Fi* will unlock a new universe of sci-fi trivia and fandom.

ISBN 0-679-77322-3
US: $22.00
Canada: $30.00
400 pages

Instant

Visit Your Personal Net at

Updates.

http://www.ypn.com

Your Guide to
Total Financial Success
Using the Internet
and Online Services

A MICHAEL WOLFF BOOK

For free updates visit Your Personal Net at http://www.ypn.com

New York

WOLFF NEW MEDIA

The NetBooks Series is published by Wolff New Media LLC, 520 Madison Avenue, 11th Floor, New York, NY 10022, and distributed by National Book Network, 4720 Boston Way, Lanham, MD 20706, as agent for Wolff New Media LLC.

NetMoney 2nd Edition has been wholly created and produced by Michael Wolff & Company, Inc. and Wolff New Media LLC. *NetMoney, NetLove, NetKids, NetShopping, NetSci-Fi, NetSpy, NetCollege, NetStudy, NetDoctor, NetMarketing, NetVote, NetJobs, NetGames2, Net-Travel, NetTaxes, NetMusic, NetGames, NetChat, NetTech, NetSports,* Your Personal Net, the Your Personal Net Logo, NetBooks, NetHead, NetSpeak, NetBest, and CyberPower are trademarks of Wolff New Media LLC. The Net Logo, What's On In Cyberspace, and YPN are registered trademarks of Wolff New Media LLC. All design and production has been done by means of desktop-publishing technology. The text is set in the typefaces Champion, Century 725, EclecticOne, Eldorado, and Zapf Dingbats.

Microsoft is a registered trademark of the Microsoft Corporation. The Microsoft Money logo is used with the permission of the Microsoft Corporation.

Published simultaneously in the U.S. and Canada by Wolff New Media LLC

0 9 8 7 6 5 4 3 2 1

ISBN 1-889670-22-7

The authors and publisher have used their best efforts in preparing this book. However, the authors and publisher make no warranties of any kind, express or implied, with regard to the documentation contained in this book, and specifically disclaim, without limitation, any implied warranties of merchantability and fitness for a particular purpose with respect to listings in the book, or the techniques described in the book. In no event shall the authors or publisher be responsible or liable for any loss of profit or any other commercial damages, including but not limited to special, incidental, consequential, or any other damages in connection with or arising out of furnishing, performance, or use of this book.

All of the photographs and illustrations in this book have been obtained from online sources, and have been included to demonstrate the variety of work that is available on the Net. The caption with each photograph or illustration identifies its online source. Text and images available over the Internet and other online services may be subject to copyright and other rights owned by third parties. Online availability of text and images does not imply that they may be reused without the permission of rights holders, although the Copyright Act does permit certain unauthorized reuse as fair use under 17 U.S.C. §107. Care should be taken to ensure that all necessary rights are cleared prior to reusing material distributed over the Internet and other online services. Information about reuse is available from the institutions that make their materials available online.

Trademarks

A number of entered words in which we have reason to believe trademark, service mark, or other proprietary rights may exist have been designated as such by use of initial capitalization. However, no attempt has been made to designate as trademarks or service marks all personal-computer words or terms in which proprietary rights might exist. The inclusion, exclusion, or definition of a word or term is not intended to affect, or to express any judgment on, the validity or legal status of any proprietary right which may be claimed in that word or term.

Manufactured in the United States of America.

New York

WOLFF NEW MEDIA

Michael Wolff
Publisher and Editor in Chief

Kelly Maloni
Executive Editor

Dina Gan
Editor

Stephen Gullo
Creative Director

Research Editor: Kristin Miller
Managing Editor: Donna Spivey

Associate Art Director: Eric Hoffsten
Assistant Art Director: Jay Jaffe

Associate Editors: Deborah Cohn, Lev Grossman
Assistant Editor: Wendy Nelson
Staff Writer: Henry Lam
Copy Editor: Sonya Donaldson
Editorial Assistant: Vicky Tsolomytis
Research Assistants: Max Greenhut, Rachel Kleinman
Production Assistants: Alex Fogarty, Gary Gottshall
Contributing Writers: Jonathan Bellack, Iris Finkel, Ben Greenman, Stevan Keane, Jennifer Levy

Vice President, Marketing: Jay Sears
Advertising Director: Michael Domican
Advertising Sales: Eric Oldfield
Marketing Coordinator: Amy Winger
Marketing Assistant: Joanna Harper

YPN Development Producer: Jonathan Bellack
YPN Managing Editor: Mila Shulkleper
YPN Directory Editor: Hylton Jolliffe
YPN Producers: Molly Confer, Rachel Greene, Alison Grippo, Jonathan Spooner
YPN Photo Editor: Jackie Fugere

Systems Administrator: Jonathan Chapman
Database Administrator: Graham Young
Database Technician: Toby Spinks

Administrative Assistant: Ann Peters

WOLFF NEW MEDIA LLC

Michael Wolff
President

James M. Morouse
Executive Vice President

Alison Anthoine
Vice President

Joseph Cohen
Chief Financial Officer

Special thanks:

NetResponse—Tom Feegel, Richard Mintz, Adam Behrens, Luis Babicek, Bob Bachle, Cheryl Gnehm, Paul Hinkle, Larry Kirk, Chris Quillian, Jonathan Rouse, Brent Sleeper, and Pete Stein

And, as always, Aggy Aed

The editors of *NetMoney* can be reached at Wolff New Media LLC, 520 Madison Avenue, 11th Floor, New York, NY 10022, or by voice call at 212-308-8100, fax at 212-308-8837, or email at editors@ypn.com.

CONTENTS

CONTENTS

PART 5: Finance Your Life

PART 6: **Spend Your Money**

Appendix

FOREWORD

THE WAY YOU MANAGE your personal finances has changed. Nearly half of all U.S. households now have a personal computer, and most are connected to the Internet, a medium that has truly come of age. Now, you can get accurate and timely information about any subject you can imagine—including personal finance—and you can act on that information quickly. With a PC and Internet access, you can budget your income, track your spending, invest online, find out about new opportunities, plan for a secure financial future, and carry out your total financial plan—faster and easier than ever before.

The Internet provides a new way to deliver financial information with unprecedented speed and convenience. Financial institutions with online banking services enable you to access your account balances, review recent transactions, and pay bills without writing paper checks—any time, day or night, from the comfort of your home PC.

Online brokers and investment Web sites let you get stock and mutual fund quotes on demand and even automatically track your portfolio value for you. And online delivery is changing the cost dynamics for this information—you can now get more timely and accurate data that impacts your finances at a lower cost than ever.

You can then bring the information into your personal finance software for a more complete picture of your financial health. You can create your personal financial plan and execute it today—online. Clearly, where money and personal finance is concerned, the PC and Internet user is at a distinct advantage.

But making sense of the explosion of information available to you brings its own challenges. Easy-to-use, authoritative resource guides such as the Net-Book series are invaluable tools that will help you make the best choices. That's why we on the Microsoft Money team are happy to be working with Your Personal Net to bring you this second edition of *NetMoney*.

FOREWORD

What will the future hold for personal finance online? In many ways, it's up to those who use it. Successful companies listen to their customers, and in the world of personal finance, the entire industry is listening. Software companies, financial institutions, and online content providers are all working together to bring you better tools and information that will make your personal finances easier to manage. So keep talking to us. We're listening. The future of personal finance is up to you, the PC user. And the future begins right now.

—Lewis Levin,
   Vice President, Microsoft's Desktop Finance Division

FAQ

"Frequently Asked Questions" about the Net and NetMoney

I. Why do I need *NetMoney*?

YOU'RE WORRIED ABOUT MONEY. It's not that you don't make enough; you're just a little disorganized. All you have to show for your paycheck at the end of the month is movie ticket stubs, empty takeout cartons, and what seems like an inordinately high dry-cleaning bill. You've never gone hungry, but you've grown weary of bounced checks and sheepishly mooching off friends because your credit card is maxed out. Your idea of personal finance is to resolve not to tip the waiter so much when you dine out. What you need is a plan. *Net-Money* is that plan. This book will show you the way toward financial health using the Internet's vast resources. If you're looking for a specific topic, just turn to the *NetMoney* index. If you are of a more systematic leaning, then you may wish to read the book, section by section. Accordingly, *NetMoney* is divided into six parts:

- **Get Your Bucks in a Row**
  If your personal finance plan amounts to counting the spare change in your pocket at the end of the day, the first chapter in this part gives you a crash course on the virtues of organizing your finances. You'll also learn the benefits of banking online, the ins and outs of credit and debt, and how to pinch a pretty penny.

- **Make Money**
  We give you three ways: Get a job, start a business, and—just for fun—win the lottery. In this part, you'll find instructions for everything from creating an electronic resume to running your startup from home to picking lucky numbers online.

- **Pay Your Taxes**
  It doesn't have to be a chore anymore. Once you discover how easy it is to use tax preparation software, get free advice from the Internet, and file electronically, you'll stop letting your accountant have all the fun.

FREQUENTLY ASKED QUESTIONS

- **Invest Your Money**

  You don't have to go to Spain to run with the bulls. In this part, we'll take you from zero to 60 on investment fundamentals. You'll learn how to talk like a trader, play simulated stock games, get free investment advice, and make the most of mutual funds, discount brokers, and IPOs.

- **Finance Your Life**

  As you know, money makes the world go 'round. This part explains the best ways to finance all of life's goals, from college to marriage to that leisurely stretch of life before death, otherwise known as retirement. You'll also learn how to get the best deals on life's big purchases—cars, computers, houses, and the like. There's even a section on how to teach the kids about money. (Even if you don't have kids, you might learn something, too.)

- **Spend Your Money**

  What good is money unless you can spend it? If you've worked hard at getting your finances in shape, you should have plenty of disposable cash. In this part, you'll find suggestions on where to spend a little of your hard-earned dough, as well as resources to help you become a smart consumer.

Other bells and whistles to watch out for:

Simple Steps • In these time-tested, user-friendly, step-by-step methods of accomplishing specific goals, we'll hold your hand through doing everything from finding a job to filing your taxes—all online.

Cash Register • Your hot links to total financial success. Every feature in *NetMoney* includes a list of the essential Web sites discussed within it.

 Click Picks • If you want to take a rapid tour of the book and only look at the sites we have deemed the very best in any category, look for the target symbol.

2. I get it. This book will make me a financial genius with the help of the Internet! So, what exactly is the Internet?

THE INTERNET IS THE PRESENT AND FUTURE of communications, the global, noncommercial system that has more than 30 million computers communicating through it. The World Wide Web, email, Usenet, FTP, telnet, and IRC are all part of the Internet, also known as the Net.

Most other Net traffic passes through the commercial online services, such as America Online and CompuServe. Running on their own networks, commercial services are generally more secure than the Internet and some people are more comfortable using them for online financial transactions. You can also use them for email, and most offer gateways to the Internet.

The Net is most commonly used to exchange email, and unless you have spent the last two years in an ashram on Venus, you will know that the second most commonly used area of the Net is the World Wide Web.

3. Ah, the World Wide Web. How does it work?

THINK OF A WORD, ANY WORD. Prefix it with a "www." and suffix it with a ".com". Chances are you will have come up with a functioning Web address. The Web is the hypertext-based information structure that now dominates Internet navigation. In its early days, people described it as being like a house in which every room has doors to a number of other rooms. Today, most people recognize that a computer screen invariably has an option in which words, icons, and pictures on a page are connected to elements on other pages not only on the same machine, but anywhere in the world. If you know exactly where you want to go on the Net and don't want to wade through Net directories and indexes, you can type a Web address, known as a URL (uniform resource locator). The URL for Your Personal Net, for example, is www.ypn.com. Unless you have WebTV, you will need a computer and a modem to get online and find your way around.

4. What computer and modem do you recommend?

OPEN A NEWSPAPER AND YOU will see endless advertisements for powerful home computers with built-in modems and extraordinary processing power. Wait six months and you will see the same package for much less money. It's infuriating, but eventually you will have to take the plunge, and the standard advice to anyone buying a computer is: Decide what you want it for. You will likely want the fastest processor you can afford and a fast CD-ROM. If you want a computer for design, you may want a Mac. Either way, you will want a 28,800 modem—which transfers data at speeds up to 28,800 bits per second (bps)—built into your system or plugged in externally. You should be able to pick one up for about $100, if you shop around. Finally, you'll want a telephone line. If that's still not fast enough, you could install an ISDN line, which conveys data up to five times the speed.

5. And what kind of account?

A COUPLE OF YEARS AGO the easiest way to play online was to sign up with one of the big services, usually America Online, CompuServe or Prodigy. These days most people know that a free-standing online service can't give you the diversity of information and entertainment you will find on the World Wide Web. As a result, all online services are now repurposing themselves as Internet gateways with bells and whistles. For now, the most popular way to access the Net is through an Internet Service Provider, and the simplest way to find the nearest one to you is, oddly enough, to look them up online. At www.thelist .com you'll find a directory of many of the ISPs in the country. Most will provide you with a basic package of software you wil need; if not, you can get the friend who showed you the list's Web site to download it for you.

For your information, here are some of your current access choices:

Email Gateway

This is the most basic access you can get. It lets you send and receive messages to and from anyone, anywhere, anytime on the Net. Keep your eye open for free (i.e., ad-sponsored) services like Juno.

Online Services

Online services are cyber city-states. The large ones have more "residents" (members) than most U.S. cities—enough users, in other words, to support lively discussions and games among their membership, and enough resources to make a visit worthwhile. They generally require special start-up software, (Hint: Look for the inescapable starter-kit giveaways.).

Internet Providers

As explained in question 4, there are many full-service Internet providers. Dial-up SLIP (serial line Internet protocol) and PPP (point-to-point protocol) accounts are currently the most popular types of Internet connections. Even faster connection methods like ISDN, ASDL, and cable modems are hovering on the horizon).

BBSs

BBSs range from mom-and-pop, hobbyist computer bulletin boards to large professional services. What the small ones lack in size they often make up for in affordability and homeyness. Unfortunately, the scenic byroads off the infobahn are becoming obsolete. On the other hand, many of the largest BBSs are almost as rich and diverse as the commercial online services. BBSs are easy to get started with. If you find one with Internet access or an email gateway, you'll get the best of local color and global reach at once. You can locate local BBSs through the Usenet discussion groups alt.bbs.lists and comp.bbs.misc, the BBS forums of the commercial services, and regional and national BBS lists kept in the file libraries of many BBSs. Many, if not most, local BBSs now offer Internet email, as well as live chat and file libraries.

Direct Network Connection

The direct network connection is the fast track of college students, computer scientists, and a growing number of employees of high-tech businesses. It puts the user right on the Net, bypassing phone connections. In other words, it's a heck of a lot faster.

6. Email? Will it replace the telephone?

WITH EMAIL, YOU CAN WRITE to anyone on a commercial service, Internet site, or Internet-linked BBS, as well as to those people on the Net via email gateways, SLIPs, and direct-network connections.

An Internet address is broken down into four parts: the user's name (e.g., wolff), the @ symbol, the computer and/or company name, and what kind of Internet address it is: **net** for network, **com** for a commercial enterprise—as with Your Personal Net (ypn.com) and America Online (aol.com)—**edu** for educational institutions, **gov** for government sites, **mil** for military facilities, and **org** for nonprofit and other private organizations. For instance, the address for our executive vice president, who schmoozes faster than a speeding bullet, leaps tall corporate bureaucrats in a single bound, and actually bears a striking resemblance to Clark Kent, would be jmorouse@ypn.com.

7. What about these newsgroups?

THERE ARE MANY PLACES in cyberspace where netsurfers can post their opinions, questions, and comments, but the most widely read bulletin boards are a group of over 10,000 "newsgroups" collectively known as Usenet. Usenet newsgroups are global, collecting thousands of messages a day from whomever wants to "post" to them. Everything is discussed here. Check out www .dejanews.com for comprehensive lists and searchable archives. To cut back on repetitive questions, newsgroup members often compile extensive lists of answers to frequently asked questions (FAQs). Many FAQs have grown so large and so comprehensive that they are valuable resources in their own right, informal encyclopedias (complete with hypertext links) dedicated to the newsgroup's topic.

8. Mailing lists?

MAILING LISTS ARE LIKE NEWSGROUPS, except that they are distributed by Internet email. The fact that messages show up in your mailbox tends to make the discussion group more intimate, as does the proactive act of subscribing. Mailing lists are often more focused, and they're less vulnerable to irreverent and irrelevant contributions.

To subscribe to a mailing list, send an email to the list's subscription address. You will often need to include very specific information, which you will find in this book. To unsubscribe, send another message to that same address. If the mailing list is of the listserv, listproc, or majordomo variety, you can usually unsubscribe by sending the command **unsubscribe ‹listname›** or **signoff ‹listname›** in the message body. If the mailing list instructs you to "write a request" to subscribe ("Dear list owner, please subscribe me to..."), you will probably need to write a request to unsubscribe.

9. And telnet, FTP, gopher? Can you explain?

Telnet

When you telnet, you're logging on to another computer somewhere else on the Internet. You then have access to the programs running on the remote computer. If the site is running a library catalog, for example, you can search the catalog. If it's running a live chat room, you can communicate with others logged on. Telnet addresses are listed as URLs, in the form **telnet://domain .name:port number**. A port number is not always required, but when listed, it must be used.

FTP

FTP (file transfer protocol) is a way to copy a file from another Internet-connected computer to your own. Hundreds of computers on the Internet allow "anonymous FTP". Since the advent of Web browsers, netsurfers can transfer files without using a separate FTP program. In this book, FTP addresses are listed as URLs, in the form **ftp://domain.name/directory/filename.txt**. And here's a bonus—logins and passwords aren't required with Web browsers.

Gopher

A program that turns Internet addresses into menu options. Gophers perform many Internet functions, including telnetting and downloading but have now been superceded by the Web. Any gopher addresses you might access through the addresses in this book will be accessible via your Web browser.

10. So the addresses will look how exactly?

ALL ENTRIES IN *NETMONEY* have a name, review, and address. The site name appears first in boldface, followed by a review of the site. After the review, complete address information is provided. The name of the service appears first: **WEB** to designate the World Wide Web, and so on. The text following the service tells you what you need to do to get to the site. When you see an arrow ($\rightarrow$), this means that you have another step ahead of you. Bullets separate multiple addresses.

If the item is a Web site, an FTP site, telnet, or gopher, it will be displayed in the form of a URL. FTP and gopher sites will be preceded by **URL**, while telnet sites, which cannot be launched directly through a browser, will be preceded by **TELNET**. If the item is a mailing list, the address will include an email address and instructions on how to subscribe. IRC (Internet Relay Chat) addresses indicate what you must type to get to the channel you want once you've connected to the IRC server. Entries about newsgroups are always followed by the names of the newsgroups.

In an online service address, the name of the service is followed by the keyword (also called "go word"). Additional steps are listed where necessary. In addition, there are a few special terms used in addresses. *Info* indicates a supplementary informational address. *Archives* is used to mark collections of past postings for newsgroups and mailings lists. And *FAQ* designates the location of a "frequently asked questions" file for a newsgroup.

11. Great! What else can I do?

WE AT NETBOOKS ARE CHARTING the whole range of human existence as it is represented online, and we probably have exactly what you're looking for. Try one of these for size: *NetChat, NetGames, NetSports, NetMusic, Fodor's NetTravel, NetVote, NetJobs, NetMarketing, NetTech, NetDoctor, NetStudy, NetCollege, NetSpy, NetShopping, NetKids, NetLove,* and *NetSci-Fi.* Lined up for the future we have *NetFix-It,* and *NetWine.* Just around the corner, look out for *NetTravel USA* and *NetOut.* Happy hunting!

PART I

Get Your Bucks in a Row

SOUND FINANCIAL LIVING starts with breaking out of a paycheck-to-paycheck lifestyle, and the Net has all the tools you need. In this part, you'll find out how to: Examine your spending habits and use software to help you keep better track of them. Get rid of debt and make sure your credit history remains clean. Pay your bills online and never get charged another late-payment fee again. Above all, save money. Experts agree that your immediate goal should be to maintain at least three to six months worth of living expenses in cash savings. We'll take you step-by-step through accomplishing this goal using the Internet and online services. Women will find a special section addressing their specific financial planning needs. So don't worry. Your money problems will soon be over.

Even if you're not rich, you can still have your financial health

PICTURE YOURSELF kicking back someday, somewhere sunny, enjoying a life of financial ease. You'd be there now, except that you spend your waking hours at a nine-to-whenever job reading the **Dilbert Zone** to keep your mind off money matters. Now picture this: Financial health is within your reach, right now, if you know where to find it. You don't need to spend what little you have on the latest **Profit Prophet** either. All you need is the Net.

A Beginner's Guide

A Penny Saved

Are you carrying too much insurance? Do you refuse to bury your dead stocks? Are you abandoning your financial strategy because you're hitting some economically hard times? If so, join the party. These are some of the **Top 10 Money Mistakes of 1996**, according to financial consultants Ernst & Young. But don't beat yourself up over the error of your ways. Just admit you have a lot to learn.

First, take a look at **Your Life**, which takes the scrapbook approach to personal finance. There you are on the home page, sitting on the edge of a pier and staring at your future. Turn the page and you're windsurfing, thinking, "It's only money. When you're young and carefree, who's got time to worry about money?" Like an older, wiser (Canadian) sibling, this site advises you to get serious about your financial life. Start saving now, when it's easier. If you're in your twenties, you might be planning to begin putting away the pennies only when you "start making the big bucks." But by that time you'll probably have bigger

to Personal Finance

financial concerns, like a family and a mortgage. The lesson? Save now. Once you've learned the virtues of saving, Your Life moves on to the rudiments of credit, interest, and inflation, and offers basic advice on planning for retirement and buying a car or home.

Ready to learn more? Head to **Get a Financial Life**, where bestselling author Beth Kobliner dispenses her wisdom to twenty- and thirtysomethings. Kobliner's **Financial Crash Course** provides instant answers to questions you may not even have thought to ask, such as "Should I take the money in my savings account and use it to pay off my credit card debt?" and "How can I

Set sail on your financial future
http://www.yourlife.com

CASH REGISTER

The Dilbert Zone
WEB http://www.unitedmedia.com
/comics/dilbert

Profit Prophet
WEB http://alpha.netaccess.on.ca
/~biron/WealthCoach/index.html

Top Ten Money Mistakes of 1996
WEB http://www.cnnfn.com/your
money/9611/08/yomo_money/

Your Life
WEB http://www.yourlife.com/

Get a Financial Life
WEB http://www.simonsays.com
/3715106211143710/titles/0684812134
/index.html

Financial Crash Course
WEB http://www.simonsays.com
/3715106211143710/titles/0684812134
/qanda.html

MoneyWhiz Forum
AMERICA ONLINE *keyword* moneywhiz

A fool and his money don't have to be parted
http://fool.web.aol.com/

make sure that I don't spend my golden years in poverty?" Plus, there's a worksheet to assess your monthly financial health, as well as a glossary of financial terms and, of course, excerpts from Kobliner's book.

If you want to become a true financial genius, head to America Online's **MoneyWhiz** forum, which was founded by independent financial journalist Christy Heady. She's made a career out of chronicling real-life folks and their financial problems, and believes that everyone has the same goal: "to make their money work as hard for them as they do for it." But those who find themselves facing an ever-increasing load of financial obligations—from credit card bills to college tuition—can easily get sidetracked. The MoneyWhiz site will help you stay on top. Start with the site's "10 Very Basic Tips" about personal finance. They include common sense admonitions about organizing, setting goals, and planning personal finance strategies. If you find yourself losing sight of the light at the end of the tunnel, seek encouragement and advice from the site's populous message board and the nightly MoneyWhiz chat show, where you can talk about everything from insurance to taxes with expert insiders.

Another popular AOL forum, **The Motley Fool**, which is on the Web in full force (jester's hat and all), provides an even more lighthearted approach to personal finance with its segment about **Fools & Their Money.** The "foolish" advice is anything but: Settle your personal finances, set up a plan for regular savings, erase your credit card debt, take a look at the big picture, and above all, try to have fun.

A Penny Earned

Part of personal finance, of course, is personal investing. We'll take you step-by-step through your first investing moves in Part 4 of this book, but to whet your appetite, stop first at the **Beginner's Investment Checklist**, where the first words of advice are, "Whenever you get investment advice (or any advice for that matter), you should always consider its source. The Internet has no shortage of free advice, and much of it is worth what you pay for it." The webmaster himself admits, in fact, that he has no special qualifications to offer advice except that he is "old enough to have made some mistakes, and young enough to expect to make many more." The goal here is merely to "stimulate your thinking" about investing and help you avoid "or at least knowingly choose" the more common mistakes. Begin with "Money and Investing," which answers the questions "What is money?" and

Learn from the error of your ways
http://www.cnnfn.com/yourmoney/9611
/08/yomo_money/

"What is investing?" Then read the half-dozen other articles including "Good Books for Beginners," "Asset Allocation for Absolute Beginners," and "Beginner's Guide to Investment Newsletters." You'll feel all the wiser.

Right about now, you might be overwhelmed with the feeling that investing is too big a topic for you to tackle alone. You might be overcome by the urge to call your nearest full-service broker. Don't pick up the phone

" Right now, you might be overwhelmed with the feeling that investing is too big a topic for you to tackle alone. "

just yet. Instead, visit **InvestorGuide's Learning** section, where you will learn "Why You Can Do It Yourself" (because the Web has all the tools you'll need) and "Why You Should Do It Yourself" (because others may not always put your financial interests first). *Research Magazine* has some tips on **Getting Started**. Its primer, Investing 101, answers the question conservative minds want to know: "Given the existence of risk, why invest at all?" The level-headed reply goes beyond the platitude "nothing ventured, nothing gained," but if you've learned your lesson about considering the source of information, you'll note that the advice comes from a securities firm. To its credit, however, the same site also provides a link to **"What Every Investor Should Know"** a consumer handbook issued by the U.S. Securities and Exchange Commission. It includes information about laws that protect individual investors, which can come in handy if you decide to use a commercial brokerage and it squanders your life savings. Of course, now that you know the basics of personal finance, you'll be much too smart for that.

▼ Starting points

Interactive Nest Egg "Tools for building prosperity," runs the subtitle, and who couldn't do with a little prosperity? It sounds a lot nicer than plain old filthy lucre, doesn't it? This online magazine specializes in personal finance advice slanted toward the private investor. The site is divided into several self-explanatory departments—the Equity Center, the IPO Center, the Mutual Fund Center, and Planning Your Future (fun retirement calculator!). For focused mini-articles, head straight to the Fast Track, which has answers to such burning questions as "What's Better: A 15- or 30-year Mortgage?" and "A Simple Formula for Picking Bonds?" This is all in addition to the online issue of *Nest Egg*, which carries sensible articles in such areas as tax, insurance, college, real estate, retirement, and other financial topics.
WEB http://nestegg.iddis.com/nestegg.html

Personal Finance Center A cache of information conveyed in a reassuring tone. Features include the Budget Doctor, a.k.a Lesley Alderman, a staff writer for *Money* magazine, who doles out "prescriptions" in response to emailed questions from CompuServe subscribers about personal finance and budgeting issues. In Your Goals, topics include ways to cut down on the food bill and find out a used car's worth. One recent saving-for-college feature included a list of 75 mutual funds in which to invest while the kids grow up. Chat areas and current market information are also included.
COMPUSERVE *go* finance

Personal Finance Network Feature articles on subjects like retirement planning, pensions, 401(k) plans, personal savings, and changes to Social Security are the order of the day here. The contents are slanted toward older readers, and, interestingly, they're presented in a half-text, half-audio format. The site is divided into eight or nine separate sections, with titles like Financial Tips and Women and Pensions. There's a section devoted to tracking developments in Washington that could affect the way you invest and save. The site hosts virtual town meetings with public officials and finance experts.
WEB http://www.wwbroadcast.com/pfn

The Quicken Financial Network Quicken is rapidly expanding from a mere personal finance application to an entire institution in its own right. Now Intuit, the company that makes Quicken, has created a financial news and advice Web site as part of the Quicken franchise. The Quicken Financial Network consists of six departments: Investments, News, Library, Insurance, Banking, and Intuit Products. Some of the more appealing features include a daily financial newsletter, which you can personalize by choosing the industries you need it to focus on, links to

---

Don't put all your eggs in one basket, even if it's interactive
http://nestegg.iddis.com/nestegg.html

Quicken has the answers... whatever the financial questions may be
http://www.qfn.com/

current stock and mutual fund information, a free insurance shopping service, and Intuit product support.
WEB http://www.qfn.com/

▼ News & advice

American Express Financial Advisors Do you have questions about your insurance policy? Need some advice about nest eggs and retirement plans, but aren't really familiar with all the financial lingo used by most heavy duty economics experts? No problem. Just hum the the tune, "We're off to see the The Advisor," tap your mouse three times, and you'll find yourself in the Emerald City of personal finance advice. Look over the Hot Topics section, where you'll find tips on how to do your taxes and plan a small business. Check out Market Watch to get the recent stock recommendations, and look up the latest stock quotes. Get advice on how to assess your financial goals and select investments. Look into all the information available on small businesses, tax planning, and education payments. When you're tired of reading over

information, create your own personal financial profile using the interactive tools provided.
WEB http://www.americanexpress.com/advisors/

Bloomberg Personal Even though Bloomberg Personal is decidedly a personal finance magazine, rather than a hard-core investment news service, it can be a little terrifying at first: The first thing you see is the current date and time, to the minute. The focus here is on the market: stocks, bonds, mutual funds, the works. Unless you speak the language like a native, you may not get much out of this site. If you do, however, you'll be getting a wealth of breaking financial news and up-to-date market information.
WEB http://www.bloomberg.com

Bonehead Finance If this site is for you, you probably know it. Bonehead Finance is a professional financial planning consultancy, but it's got some free wisdom online, like a tutorial that provides you with some simple steps, formulas, and guidelines for budget planning. There's also a handy glossary of financial terms, and a wonderful page of links and downloadable files such as "Money Tips for Newlyweds."
WEB http://ourworld.compuserve.com/homepages
/Bonehead_Finance/

Center for Financial Well-Being The plugs for books by Grady Cash, a financial author and speaker, may have you wondering whether this site is more concerned about his financial well-being than yours. But Cash (a pseudonym perhaps?) offers a few pearls of financial wisdom for free. The colloquial prose here is readable, even if it's a little bit common-sensical at times: Check out the tip of the week, or chapters from Cash's *7 Deadly Money Mistakes*.
WEB http://www.ns.net/cash/index.html

CNNfn—Your Money Surprisingly, CNNfn is a lot sassier and funnier than its buttoned-up parent, and its personal finance section presents the visitor with solid advice in readable and innovative formats. The articles are a mixture of daily financial news, often with a focus on online events, and financial advice that covers the traditional topics—the top ten home finance mistakes, how to pay for college, how to refinance your mortgage—as well as some more specialized interests, like advice for laid-off workers and trends in corporate raise schedules. There's also a mortgage calculator, stock and mutual fund information, and gossip about CNN financial reporters. Who could ask for more?
WEB http://cnnfn.com/yourmoney/

Financenter Financenter has accumulated loads of information on the best way to buy, finance, or refinance major assets such as cars and houses, all presented in a clean, handsome format. Credit cards are another major focus: Comparisons are displayed that clarify the many options out there and suggest ways to manage cumbersome debts. The site includes financial decision calculators that help you decide whether it's better to buy or rent, or how much money you should put down on a house. You can even apply online for loans from various finance companies, some of which offer discounts and special deals to Financenter users.
WEB http://www.financenter.com

The Financial Electric Library The Electric Library is an archive of news stories and articles drawn from more than 500 books, magazines, newspapers, news wires, and even TV and radio transcripts. A sample search for "Quicken" turned up 30 articles. The Electric Library also maintains a Q&A forum, which answers queries like, "What is dis-saving?" "What is the Wilshire 5000?" and "Should I

THE SEVEN DEADLY MONEY MISTAKES

You may wonder: "How can there be only seven money mistakes? There must be thousands of reasons why people make money mistakes!" To understand how all money mistakes can fall into one of only seven patterns, imagine a long chain. Each of the events leading up to a spending mistake is a link in that chain. Some links, like habits learned from parents, go all the way back to childhood. Other links are more current, like advertising hype, keeping up with the Joneses, job stress, or an argument with a spouse. Regardless of the number of links in the chain, the most critical link is the last one—the spending decision itself. It is at this moment that all these previous life events come together to affect thes pending decision. If the decision is a mistake, it will always result from one of the seven subconscious patterns you are about to learn.

THE SPENDING MISTAKE CHAIN
The bonds of the spending mistake chain imprison its victims in economic slavery by lowering standards of living and preventing people from getting ahead. Since the spending mistake chain takes a lifetime to build, it would seem impossible to address every link. Fortunately, it isn't necessary. Regardless of the number of events in the chain, breaking just the final link—the spending personality mistake—breaks the chain and prevents the mistake from occurring. Of course, those other links may be causing problems in other life dimensions, but it is not necessary to resolve them first to stop yourself from making spending mistakes. All you must do is recognize and stop the spending pattern itself. What's your spending pattern? Read on to find out.

—from Center For Financial Well-Being

consider investing in ValueJet now?" For each question, the Library assembles a group of articles that help answer it.
WEB http://www.elibrary.com/intuit/

Fine Ants Get it? Like fin-ance? *Fine Ants* is an email newsletter: You subscribe ($12 for a year's subscription), and the Ants email you 52 weekly issues with tips and advice on such topics as: how to retire and earn what you do now, for the rest of your life; how to properly plan for your child's college without any added income; legal secrets that save you money on your taxes; how to get out of debt completely; and both long- and short-term financial planning goals. Sound too good to be true? Some of them may be—*Fine Ants* is a grab bag of tips and schemes that promise a lot. But for $12 a year, it might be worth it. And remember: Those subscription costs are tax-deductible.
WEB http://www.prismnet.com/~andrew/

On Finances *On Finances* is one of a growing number of online personal finance newsletters sponsored by large financial institutions, in this case Crestar, a DC-area bank. But even though *On Finances* is mostly a PR device, it has a wealth of useful information and advice on a range of topics—small-business finance, investment, loans, banking, and insurance. There's also a Q&A column ("Ask 'Dr. Finance'") and an email newsletter you can personalize to meet your particular financial needs.
WEB http://www.crestar.com/cbmm_onfmenu.html

The Personal Finance Network This is something a little unusual: Using the (free, download-able) RealAudio software, this Web site brings you five broadcasts a week on a variety of personal finance topics such as current personal finance news, investment tips, retirement plans, pensions, women and finance, and a number of others. Getting the broadcasts to play is quite simple, and the "sound" advice is clear and concise.
WEB http://wwbroadcast.com/pfn

▼ Magazines

Financial Counseling and Planning Journal If you're interested in the academic slant on financial planning, you can get selected articles from this scholarly journal. Its goal is disseminate some of the loftier academic research currently being done on issues related to financial planning in a form that we, the little people, can understand. "Why do men invest differently than women?" and other burning questions are considered.
WEB http://www.hec.ohio-state.edu/hanna/index.htm

Green *Green* is slacker-bait: a personal finance magazine directed at recent college grads who are just too alternative to deal with that whole money scene, man. This plucky startup's Web page is really just an advertisement for the print magazine ($10 for four issues per year), but there are current articles here (you only

"Sound" financial advice
http://wwbroadcast.com/pfn

get to read about half of the full piece) as well as an archive of past issues. The articles seem to be divided into two categories: the serious, plain-talking, worth-reading kind ("How to Buy Life Insurance") and the joking, content-free, please-read-this-magazine kind ("How to Look Busy at Work").

WEB http://members.aol.com/greenzine/INDEX.I.HTM

Live both as a sensible capitalist and an ecologically responsible human.

GreenMoney On-Line Guide Green-Money has a motto: "Responsibility from the Supermarket to the Stock Market!" GreenMoney generally has a little more to say about the latter than the former, but its heart is in the right place: The online guide's professed goal is to "educate and empower individuals and businesses to make informed financial decisions through aligning their corporate and financial principles." But how, you ask? Two ways: by giving you articles on how to shop, invest, and live both as a sensible capitalist and an ecologically responsible human, and by directing you to other resources that can help you do the same. GreenMoney's strong writing and refreshingly realistic outlook help, too.

WEB http://www.greenmoney.com

Kiplinger's Personal Finance Magazine As far as financial magazines go, *Kiplinger's* offers you the best of both worlds: a reliable, long-standing (since 1920) offline reputation combined with free in-depth information online. The magazine specializes in serious financial news and advice delivered in clear, readable prose. A sample issue might run feature articles covering

investment software reviews, insurance tips, advice on how to buy a vacation home, and an article on prominent twentysomething financial figures. And this is only part of the enormous *Kiplinger's* site, which brings you breaking financial news, stock picks, mutual fund info, financial FAQs, retirement advice, a section for kids—it's endless. A must-book-mark.

WEB http://www.kiplinger.com/magazine/maghome.html

Money The people at *Money* magazine have obviously made an effort to prevent their site from becoming just another print magazine slapped onto the Web. Articles incorporate such interactive treats as calculators and a worksheet to determine your chances of getting audited by the IRS. There's a daily audio report from money editors giving a rundown of the day's top business stories; you can also sign up for a free subscription to *Money Daily*, which will be rushed to you via email every evening, complete with a quick recap of the day's market activity.

WEB http://pathfinder.com/money/

The Wall Street Journal Interactive Edition One of the most successful of the online news sites, the *Wall Street Journal* has found loyal online readers, and will undoubtedly find more. The *Journal's* excellent writing and Bible-like reputation for reliability would be enough. But the editors have built some special interactive features into their online edition that could prove extremely useful, particularly for people who follow the market. Perhaps the most useful is the Personal Journal, a computerized clipping service that will not only email you articles that meet your particular needs—specified by newspaper section, word, and company—but will even let you set up a clipping file for later retrieval. But take note: In contrast to the free (for now) *New York Times*, a subscription

HOW TO RETIRE AT AGE 35

I'm 30 years old, have about 100K in the bank, and want to retire at 35 because I hate nothing as much as thinking about stuff that I don't want to think about (i.e.: working).

If you continue as you have for 5 more years, you should easily get to having 200K to 250K saved by the time you are 35. Suppose that you could set aside 200K and not touch it for five to seven years. The 200K could easily double. Investing in a mix of a diversified fund and a couple of agressive funds should do the trick with only moderate risk. One tack you might take at age 35 would be to live as frugally as possible for a few years while not touching either your "nest egg"nor its accumulated interest. You seem like the adventurous type, soyou might explore the ways you could live virtually for free for a few years.

Examples that come to mind: House-sitting; moving to an extremely low-cost-of-living place like some parts of India; take a series of jobs where you can can paid basically just to show up & then be free to "think" all you want to on the job (night-clerk at a small hotel, security guard at a place where there is minimal risk like at some sleepy midwestern factory); or spend a few years in academia as a 'professional student'/teaching assistant.

Try skimming through the book *Your Money or Your Life*. Its authors seem to agree with your basic premise/goals... I didn't feel that it contained many new ideas, but it might help you to look through it. Of course, you should BORROW the book from a library rather than BUYING it :-).

—from misc.invest.financial-plan

here will cost you $49 for a year (if you have a print subscription, it's just $29).
WEB http://www.wsj.com

▼ Q&A

Health, Home, Family One of the most persistent pitfalls is time: How can you juggle the demands of a toddler and a full-time job? Cook dinner and still have time to pay the bills? What to do when there aren't enough hours in the day? One answer is to make time to visit this conference to learn the organizational strategies of other harried adults.
AMERICA ONLINE *keyword* exchange→Health, Home, Family

misc.invest.financial-plan The emphasis here is more on the financial planning than on the investing, although it's a healthy mix: You'll find questions about college planning, tax credits, credit histories, and trust funds alongside more investment-oriented topics: IRAs, 401(k)s, and mutual funds. The questions are always earnest, the answers usually well-informed. The thread titled, "I Don't Want to Work" is taken quite seriously.
USENET misc.invest.financial-plan

Money Matters The Exchange is a network of bulletin boards that covers everything under the sun, but come to the Money Matters for home budgeting and consumer chatter. The forum advocates down-to-earth economic responsibility. Members praise frugality and exchange cost-cutting hints, worry over the safety of safe deposit boxes, struggle to patent their inventions, and question the practices of church accounting.
AMERICA ONLINE *keyword* exchange→Home/Health Careers→Money Matters

Personal Finance Electronic Magazine A mailing list for people who have questions about a

variety of personal finance issues. No need to be intimidated; this mailing list isn't run by finance professionals, just frequented by people who want to discuss personal finance and share their real-life experience with one another. Topics include credit card usage and debt management, types of home mortgages, pensions and profit sharing questions, social security, Medicare and Medicaid questions, financing a college education, and building a secure retirement, among others.
EMAIL majordomo@shore.net ✍ *Type in message body:* subscribe persfin-digest
WEB http://www.tiac.net/users/ikrakow/subscribemsg

Real Life Parts of Real Life feel a bit like an extremely practical Oprah Winfrey show online. Average folks send in a description of their financial situation or problem, along with a picture of themselves. Then the audience (that's you) is invited to respond with feedback and advice via the message boards. Topics range from employment to relationships to investing. Everyman-oriented financial news, features on topics like family finances, links, advice for the individual investor—everything you need to make a messy life neat.
AMERICA ONLINE *keyword* real life

Your Money After the IRS and your landlord take their shares of your money, find out what to do with the rest of it. This introduction to the world of finance is designed to answer the most basic questions about credit, insurance, real estate, retirement planning, investments, education planning, and even those ubiquitous Internet scams. Each topic has its own message board for discussion and questions. There's also an FAQ and a growing collection of articles on personal finance written by the host, Richard A. Allridge, a certified financial planner.
AMERICA ONLINE *keyword* yourmoney

▼ Calculators

Financial Calculators These Web-based calculators, part of the home page of the financial services company Centura Banks, offer a quick and simple way to get an idea of what kind of personal, home, or auto loans you should apply for, what your monthly payments will be, and how much return you can expect from your savings over a given period.
WEB http://www.centura.com/formulas/whatif.html

The Personal Net Worth Program This service calculates your net worth by asking extensive questions about assets and liabilities, and then subtracting the latter from the former. In addition, it projects your future net worth, assuming a certain rate of growth. The service is free, unless you want a printed report mailed to you for $3.50.
COMPUSERVE *go* hom-16

▼ Indexes

Consumer World Money and Credit Page The *Consumer World* is a wide, wide world. You'll find thousands of links here, on a huge range of topics related to money and shopping. The Money and Credit page covers Investment, Insurance, Banking and Credit, and miscellaneous Money Matters. Some listings are flagged with a "Best Bet" tag.
WEB http://www.consumerworld.org/maps/../pages /money.htm

Personal Finance Web Sites This is one of the better sets of personal finance links online. Compiled by Ira Krakow and co-sponsored by MCI, it's comprehensive and intelligently organized. Choose from a wide range of categories, including College Planning, Investment, Job Listings, and Real Estate.
WEB http://www.tiac.net/users/ikrakow/pagerefs.html

Toss out the ol' shoebox of receipts and take your financial life to your desktop

COMPUTERS AND MONEY: They're a natural match. Computers are organized. They're good at remembering stuff, and they sure cost a lot of money. With personal finance programs, you can make your computer earn back some of its purchase price—earn its keep, so to speak. If you spend an hour or two a week inputting your home finances into one of these personal finance applications, you stand to save a lot of money over the long run: fewer finance charges, fewer bounced checks, fewer late bills, and a better return on your investments, just for starters. Which personal finance program is best? Consult the reviews below. And then let your computer worry about your money for a change.

The Best Personal

Kiplinger's Simply Money 2.0b

WEB http://www.cdtitles.com
COMPUSERVE *go* **simply**

Simply Money's recent history has been a bit tumultuous: This competitive, solid personal finance application was dropped by its home publisher, 4Home Productions, and sold to a discount CD-ROM publisher, CD Titles, which now sells it for a fraction of its former retail price. But don't let the low price tag fool you—Simply Money may be basic, no-frills software, but it's still a very functional package.

One thing Simply Money has going for it is name recognition: The Financial Advisor built into Simply Money was created by the editors of the *Kiplinger Letter*, a respected financial planning newsletter. You can consult the Advisor's wisdom on a particular decision or situation, and it will also volunteer advice if, in its humble opinion, you're getting yourself into trouble. Simply Money also has a nice selection of graphs and charts (though they lack the "drill-down" feature that lets you view the calculations that they represent).

Bring on the new Quicken
http://www.qfn.com

Finance Software

There are other areas in which the application doesn't compete quite as well. You can pay bills and track investments online (using CompuServe's market data), but there's no online banking. The interface is a little unusual: The many, many buttons can be either a help or a hindrance, depending on your tastes and temperament. The tax preparation tools are minimal, and the budgeting and check-writing features are merely average. But in terms of getting your money's worth—and isn't that what financial software is

THE GREAT MIGRATION

QI: I am interested in migrating from Managing Your Money for Windows, a program I have never been really satisfied with, to Quicken. Is Quicken capable of importing MYM files? I have far too much data stored to reenter everything by hand.

Q2: Quicken cannot read MYM files. I'd like to switch from the DOS version of MYM to Quicken 6, and am also seeking a conversion routine. I've heard (from the Quicken technical folks) that someone wrote a program that creates QIF files from MYM data files, but I haven't been able to find it. Any help would be much appreciated.

A: Go to the Unofficial Quicken WebPage (UQWP?) and under the Utilites section you should see where you can get a utility to convert MYM to Quicken."

—from comp.os.ms-Windows.apps.financial

about?—you could do a lot worse than Simply Money.

Managing Your Money

COMPUSERVE *go* meca
WEB http://www.mymnet.com/mym.htm

It's time to get to know the voice and "personality" of financial advisor Andrew Tobias very, very well. Tobias, author of *The Only Investment Guide You'll Ever Need*, is the good angel of Managing Your Money Plus, a personal finance software package that's particularly strong on financial planning and investment management features.

The first thing that distinguishes Managing Your Money Plus from its competitors is its user-friendly SmartDesk interface. Early versions of MYM had a reputation for being a powerful but challenging financial tool—investment wizards only, please. This time around they've come up with a new way of accessing the application's major functions: an emphatically non-threatening cartoon drawing of a little suburban-bourgeois study, with relatively intuitive clickable icons. The fountain pen takes you to the check-printing feature, for example.

MYM takes care of the functions you'd expect from any program in this genre: checkbook management, a comprehensive tax preparation utitility, investment tracking options, and so on. Its strongest features have to do with financial planning: its various utilities take care of insurance, IRAs, loans and mortgages, college, and more. Some lovely and intuitive graphing functions let you see the financial hell or heaven you may be plunging yourself into before you actually arrive there.

MYM is often ignored in the mighty struggle currently being waged between Microsoft Money and Quicken to be the supreme personal finance application, but it's running a very strong third, and it's improving all the time: It was recently purchased by a national consortium of banks, which should result in improved online banking features, and it has a close alliance with CompuServe, which provides users with securities information and special features for use with the CompuServe Visa Gold Card. Plus, it's one of the few major personal finance titles that runs on both Mac and PC, and hey, that counts for something, doesn't it?

Microsoft Money97

WEB http://www.microsoft.com/moneyzone
Quick! Word association test! Microsoft—did you think "memory-hog"? "Cumbersome"? "Slow"? If you've spent any time around Word 6.0, chances are you did. Well, think again. Microsoft Money is a different story: After Microsoft failed to buy out Intuit, makers of the massively comprehensive Quicken, Bill Gates's software leviathan decided to slim down its own product. Money97 is designed for speed and simplicity rather than frills.

What does that mean for consumers? First, that the program is easy to use. Without resorting to the cartoon-style interface of Managing Your Money Plus, Money97 manages to put together a system of screens that's wonderfully easy to get around in, relying on just three little icons for all your navigation needs: no toolbars, and few menus. You can pay bills electronically, track your portfolio, plan budgets, and prepare your taxes with admirable ease. The so-called "Wizards" of Money97 will talk you through any of its procedures that may be giving you pause, although, beyond a reg-

Who would have thought managing your money could be so easy?
http://www.cdtitles.com

QUICKEN BUGS

In Memorized Transaction List, one can't tell that a memorized transaction is a check if it's also a split.

Sometimes when I start Quicken it somehow forgets that I have the Warn before recording uncategorized transactions switch on and I have to go into Options and turn it on again.

The "balance" reported in the Account window (for investments) is estimated based on whatever price has the latest date, not on the price that was effective on or before the current date.

If you edit a scheduled transaction, and change the contents of the payee field so that it matches some memorized transaction payee, and then push the OK button, the amount of the scheduled transaction is silently updated to the value of the memorized transaction. QuickFill should only update all the transaction fields if you tab out of the payee field, and not if you press the OK button while still in the payee field.

—from the Unofficial Quicken for Windows Home Page

ular Tip of the Day, they don't offer much in the way of general financial wisdom. Another daily feature is the Chart of the Day, which starts each session off with a graphical rundown of a different aspect of your financial profile.

Microsoft Money pretty much invented electronic banking, and it still leads the pack in that particular field: You can get 24-hour access to your financial information, no matter what your bank is, plus constant stock price updates and online bill-paying. Money97 was the first personal finance application designed specifically for Windows 95, and it interfaces with that environment with maximum possible smoothness.

Quicken Deluxe

WEB http://www.qfn.com

You don't often see this much unanimity in the software community, but the critics agree when it comes

Gates uses it to pay his bills
http://www.microsoft.com/moneyzone

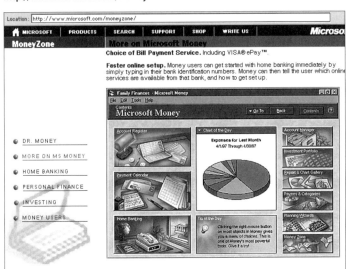

to Quicken. For full-service personal finance software, nothing can touch it. Those programming wizards over at Intuit have somehow managed to combine an unprecedented range and depth of features with an organizational scheme that allows you to navigate from one screen to another with ease.

Where to begin? Quicken presents your financial data in a nice variety of graphs and reports, and the Easy Answers feature allows you to generate customized reports that tell you exactly what you need to know (even if you don't necessarily want to hear it). Investment advice is provided by features like Quicken's amazing Mutual Fund Finder, which uses data and analysis from Morningstar. Full online banking, intelligent multimedia financial advice, a great tax preparation package (partly borrowed from TurboTax), online market data, and snappy check writing and budget planning features round out Quicken's suite of finance tools.

❝ You don't often see this much unanimity in the software community, but the critics agree when it comes to Quicken. ❞

Of course, Quicken's "more is more" programming philosophy tends to make the program something of a memory hog, so don't expect to be toggling back and forth between Quicken and Quake, unless you've got some serious RAM under the hood. Still, Quicken manages to be flexible: It runs on both Mac and PC, and it's not tied to the Windows 95 operating system. Who says you can't have it all?

FINANCIAL SOFTWARE Get Your Bucks in a Row

The Short List:	Kiplinger's Simply Money	Managing Your Money
What's in it for me?		
• Price	$20	$49.95
• Who should use this software?	People with basic financial management needs, but not much time to lavish on computing	People who are serious about their money, with a particular interest in investments
• How user-friendly is it?	Average	Average
• How adequate are the help functions?	Average	Average
Will someone hold my hand?		
• Where's the online customer support?	WEB http://www.cdtitles.com /support.htm	COMPUSERVE go meca
• Is it any good?	A little skimpy	More than adequate
• What about offline tech support?	(617) 642-1706	(203) 255-7562, M-F 9 a.m.-6 p.m. EST, exc. Wed. 10-6
How does it rate? (3 = great, 2 = adequate, 1 = not so great)		
• Household budgeting	1	1
• Portfolio management	2	2
• Financial planning	2	3
• Tax preparation	1	3
• Checkbook management	2	2
• Online banking	1	2
• Financial advice	3	3
Can my computer handle it?		
• How much space is the program going to take up on your hard drive?	6 MB	Mac: 7 MB PC: 14 MB
• What are the system requirements?	PC: • Windows 3.1 and higher • 386Mhz required • 4 MB RAM recommended	Mac: • 68030 microprocessor or higher • 8 MB RAM • System 7.0 or later • 2400 baud modem or higher • 2X CD-ROM Drive PC: • MPC 2 Multimedia PC • 486SX processor or better • 16-bit sound card • 2X CD-ROM drive • 6 MB RAM • Windows 3.1 or later

Microsoft Money97	Quicken Deluxe
$34.95	$59.95
People who are serious about their money, but don't want to make a full-time hobby out of it	People who are willing to invest a serious amount of time in managing their money
Wonderfully easy	Very
Excellent	Very
WEB http://www.microsoft.com/moneyzone	WEB http://www.intuit.com/quicken/technical-support/quicken/index.html.
Very thorough	It's adequate
U.S.: (206) 635-7131 Canada (905) 568-3503	Number varies for version and platform
3	3
2	3
3	3
2	3
3	3
3	3
1	3
11 MB	Mac: 24 MB free hard disk space PC: Windows 3.1: 27 MB Windows 95: 35 MB
PC: • 386DX or higher microprocessor; 486/50 or higher is recommended • Windows 95 operating system or Microsoft Windows NT workstation operating system version 3.51 or later. Online Services require TAPI and will not work with Windows NT 3.51, but will run on Windows NT 4.0 • 8 MB RAM on Windows 95; 12 MB RAM on Windows NT • VGA Graphics card or compatible video graphics adapter and monitor (Super VGA 256-color recommended) • 2400 or higher baud modem (14.4 recommended) to access the Microsoft MoneyZone.	Mac: • 68030 microprocessor • 8 MB RAM • System 7.0 or higher • 2400 baud or faster modem • 2X or faster CD-ROM drive PC: • IBM compatible 486 or higher PC • 8 MB RAM • Windows 3.1 or native 32 bit Windows 95 (both versions on same CD) • Hayes-compatible modem, min. 2400 baud or faster modem; 9600 baud recommended for Internet Services • MPC-compatible, double-speed CD-ROM drive, sound board & speakers

Online stores

ABACI's College Financial Aid Software We're normally suspicious of people trying to make a buck off naive newbies, but this guy has a daughter at Caltech, so he gets empathy points. Anyway, he's written a downloadable shareware program containing some financial aid worksheets and calculations, in a not-too-scary format. (The full version costs $39.50 and is for PCs only.)
WEB http://users.aol.com/abacifaw/faw.htm

atOnce Software Mail Order Store This America Online-based software retailer has a really great-looking site, with smart, easy-to-navigate product categories. The one mistake, though, is a pretty big one—the utter lack of separation between Mac and PC software. Mac gamers, for example, must weave through the numerous PC titles before coming across something suitable, instead of rifling quickly through a list of Mac-only titles. There's a decent selection of software to choose from, although atOnce could stand to diversify a little. If you'd like upgrades of MS

The household budget is a family affair
http://www.familysoftware.com

Word 6.0, for example, atOnce can help, but you won't find any WordPerfect products. The games categories cater to the well-seasoned player—titles are categorized according to distribution companies, giving customers one-click access to all the titles in stock by a given company.
AMERICA ONLINE *keyword* shop→Computer & Office needs

The Children's Software Company With software alternatives for children ranging from pre-schoolers to high schoolers, the Children's Software Company supports both PC and Mac users with discount titles. You'd be surprised how much kids' financial software is lurking in the Brain Teasers, Math, and Early Learning sections—everything from basic money-oriented math to market simulation games. There's also a review (effectively a promotional paragraph) for each product, a sample .GIF, pricing, and system requirements.
WEB http://www2.childsoft.com/childsoft

Educational Software Institute Many children today are computer users who shop at CompUSA at an age when yesterday's kids were still mastering the subtleties of Atari 2600 baseball. Apparently, if you want your children to get somewhere, they have to know computers. ESI has an online catalog filled with products designed to make the little rascals computer-savvy in today's competitive academic environment. Titles like First Money and Money Matters can get children started on basic money math and related concepts (remember, capitalism begins in the home). Teachers also can benefit from the instruction utilities on sale here.
WEB https://www.edsoft.com:443/

Egghead Software Well known as a successful retail chain, Egghead has now expanded its services to the Internet. The Personal/Home

section is your best bet for personal finance titles, although the Business section has a few as well. Members of the Cue Club (which originated through the mail order service) can save an additional 5 percent. Egghead also offers a cybersale to get rid of surplus items. Whether you're in search of the latest Java tool or looking to upgrade your word processor, this software store is a worthwhile visit. If you need a customer representative, this site can point you to the Egghead near you. Several software trials and demos are available free so you can try before you buy.
WEB http://www.egghead.com/

Where are the receipts from that plumbing work? You may not remember, but when the IRS comes calling, you may wish you did.

Family Software Center In the 1980s, parents' only recourse for aiding their children's studies was desperately hoping they'd tune in to PBS. With the arrival of interactive multimedia, children now have access to a wide variety of edutainment. At Family Software Center, visitors can cruise around the easy-to-shop catalog to call up the description, price, and system requirements of any titles that pique their interest. The center features an array of educational titles for kids, but there's plenty of personal finance software here as well, and at excellent prices.
WEB http://www.familysoftware.com

Home Record Keeping Software How much did you spend on your deck? When was the last time you painted your living room, and where

did you buy the paint? Where are the receipts from that plumbing work? You may not remember, but when the IRS comes calling, you may wish you did. If there's no proof of your home improvement spending, the IRS can disallow the improvements-making grand total subject to tax. This Home Record Keeping Software makes it easy to keep track of it all and avoid paying extra to Uncle Sam.
WEB http://www.homedrs.com/

Software Clearance Outlet Visiting SCO even feels like walking into an outlet store—almost no .GIFs adorn this Web site, so nagivation is easy and quick. The personal finance titles are pretty much split between the utilities and the business sections, although Mac titles are all grouped together in one leper-colony-like page. As for games, don't expect to find anything that's just hit the shelves to show up here—titles here are one to two years old.
WEB http://www.softwareoutlet.com

$Software Net With more than 20,000 business, financial, Internet utility, communications, and tax software, this Web site is certain to play better with the Wall Street crowd than the Barney generation. Not only are Windows and Macintosh supported, but so are DOS, OS/2 Warp, and Unix. One rare and interesting service found here is Electronic Delivery, which allows you to order and download certain programs to your computer rather than wait for snail mail. You'll be able to retrofit your desktop computer with anti-virus programs, memory managers, and diagnostic software, to name a few.
WEB http://software.net

Software Plus A rather cheesy but generally inexpensive site that carries an interesting hodgepodge of titles. Look in the utilities section for financial software offerings.
WEB http://www.lamere.net/softp/default.htm

THEY DIDN'T CALL IT HASSLEFREE

I've been using CheckFree with the CheckFree Manager for Windows software, ver. 2R2. Now I'd like to access CheckFree via Microsoft Money 97 software, but I cannot connect. I've tried to make initial test connections (one with no transactions to send and one with a test message to send). I'm getting the error message "Money could not complete the call because Online Services could not be found. If you cancelled a dialer for your Internet Service Provider, exit Money, restart, and try again. If not, run Online Services setup again."

I called Microsoft customer service, and they told me that before you start using CF with Money you have to call CF Customer Service so that they can make the necessary changes to your payee list. They said it's a piece of cake—it just requires a phone call. Don't bet on it! When I called Check-Free, they were completely confused by Money 5.0. From reading the newsgroups, CheckFree and Money, even when it does finally get "transfered," has nothing but problems. People can't get through, error messages keep popping up, and some kind of counter or something has to be constantly reset. Bottom line: Money 5.0 and CheckFree don't work. Of course, Quicken 6 won't help much either: their software can't talk to a modem unless it's on COM1! Nothing like the glory of technology, ain't it grand!

—from Microsoft Home Products Forum

▼ Product support

comp.os.ms-windows.apps.financial This high-traffic newsgroup is dedicated to questions about financial and tax software running under Microsoft Windows. The bulk of the discussion concerns Quicken, as well as the major tax and investment software, and it consists mostly of cries for help, well-informed answered, and lots of sympathy.
USENET comp.os.ms-windows.apps.financial

Intuit Intuit's forum on America Online offers FAQs, Intuit press releases, libraries with program updates, patches, and add-ons in several computer formats, and a message board where users can ask the Intuit staff questions about their products.
AMERICA ONLINE *keyword* intuit

Intuit Support Forum Intuit's CompuServe forum serves as one of the largest presences for Quicken on the Net, with support and information on all Intuit products. The libraries are filled with free updates, shareware, archives of message topics, and tech support FAQs. Most of the shareware in the libraries includes a few main functions: tax planning, incorporating downloaded quotes into Quicken, and converting Quicken files to and from other personal-finance software like Managing Your Money, Dollars & Sense, and Money. Intuit posts new product announcements, feature lists, and demos in the General Information section of the library. The message boards, divided by platform and program function, are also rich with information.
COMPUSERVE *go* intuit

MECA Forum What do I do if I damage my data? What's internal error No. 12? And how do I tell MYM (Managing Your Money) that I've paid off the mortgage? A huge number of people use MECA's Taxcut and MYM software packages—and many of them show up here with their questions.
COMPUSERVE *go* meca

Microsoft Excel Forum An active support forum for the popular spreadsheet program. From

how to average subtotals to how to work with passwords on files, this is an excellent resource for Excel users to troubleshoot and pick up tips. The libraries, including one for the Mac and one for the PC, carry a mix of functional and bizarre files: Baseball statistics or an amortization schedule, anyone?
COMPUSERVE *go* excel

Microsoft Home Products Forum This message board, part of the Microsoft Home Products Forum, is used by MS Money users to ask questions about all aspects of the program, from setup to updates. Come share the triumphs and the tragedies of one of the premier personal finance software titles.
COMPUSERVE *go* mshome

Microsoft Knowledge Base Most of the 18,000 documents here are excerpted from user manuals and help sheets produced by Microsoft. Warning: There's a lot of information here. Searching for "Excel" finds more than 1,000 articles. Changing the search to "Excel and export," narrows the choice to around 40 articles. Still, if you're fighting a no-holds-barred steel cage match with your personal finance software package, this could give you the edge you need.
AMERICA ONLINE *keyword* knowledge base

Simply Money This software package contains several useful budgeting, investment management, and organizational features. Its forum contains updates, demos, and documentation for the various versions of Simply Money. It's also a place where program users can post suggestions or complaints about the software.
AMERICA ONLINE *keyword* simply→Library→Simply Money
COMPUSERVE *go* simply

The Unofficial Quicken for Windows Web Page
Many of the Web's best sites are the product of individual passion. Andrew DeFaria's pas-

Does keeping track of your money make you want to scream?
http://www.cnet.com/Content/Reviews/Compare/Pfinance

sion just happens to be for a financial software product. DeFaria maintains this site devoted to all things Quicken because, as he puts it, "I like Quicken and use it myself. As such I would like to make it better." The site includes a sizable FAQ list and tips on hidden features that aren't mentioned in the user's manual. Quicken users all over the Internet have contributed to this mass of detailed information.
WEB http://quicken.sj-coop.net/Quicken.html

The World of Lotus A series of forums devoted to Lotus, including word processing, spreadsheet, technical, and German forums. The LDC Spreadsheet Forum is home to libraries and message boards devoted to advancing and troubleshooting use of Lotus 123.
COMPUSERVE *go* lotus

▼ Reviews

C|net Software Review: Personal Finance C|net's reviews are exercises in compare-and-contrast analysis. For their financial software section they chose five personal finance packages,

IS QUICKEN ACTUALLY A CULT?

RATTLESNAKE ANIMATION: Select About Quicken from the Help menu. Once the initial "splat" animation concludes, press the letter "r". This will cause a rattlesnake to scroll halfway across the screen, stop and hiss, and then scroll off the screen. Press Return to dismiss the About Quicken display.

CHISEL ANIMATION: Select About Quicken from the Help menu. Once the initial "splat" animation concludes, press the letter "p". The splat and chisel animation will be repeated. Note that if you have a sound card in your system, you will also get sound effects to accompany this animation. Press Return to dismiss the About Quicken display. The careful observer will note that the four available items from within About Quicken are triggered by the four letters R, S, V, P, which is an easy way to remember them. Any other key will dismiss the screen.

QUICKEN CREDITS SCREEN: Select About Quicken from the Help menu. Once the initial "splat" animation concludes, press the letter "s". This will cause a credits screen to appear, scrolling through the various individuals involved with the development of Quicken for Windows. Press RETURN to dismiss the About Quicken display.

—*from The Unofficial Quicken for Windows Web Page*

rently shopping around.
WEB http://www.cnet.com/Content/Reviews/Compare /Pfinance/index.html

ZD Net Software Reviews Looking for a searchable database of all the reviews and articles that have ever appeared in any of the group of magazines published by Ziff-Davis (*PC Magazine, Computer Shopper, Family PC,* and *Mac Week*)? Well, you've found it. This is an invaluable resource for anybody who's thinking about investing in some software: The reviews are always informed and opinionated, and they frequently provide shoppers with point-by-point comparisons of top products.
WEB http://www5.zdnet.com/findit/search.html

▼ Shareware libraries

Classifieds Software Library If you've just placed an ad on a classifed board and expect a flood of responses, you may want to pick up some software to manage the influx. Packed with shipping and tracking software, the library has an assortment of postal calculators, ZIP code databases, invoice generators, and address managers for Mac and PC owners.
AMERICA ONLINE *keyword* classifieds→Software Library

Info-Mac The Mac user looking for financial programs will find plenty here, in the form of applications that sound alarms when you're due for an appointment, help you develop a business proposal, calculate your profits (or losses), give you the area code for any street in America, and track your portfolio. Since the finance applications are interspersed with other applications, you may want to download the abstracts file to help you identify the programs of interest.
URL ftp://ftp.pht.com/pub/mac/info-mac/ • ftp://ftp .sunet.se/pub/mac/info-mac/app • ftp.funet.fi/pub /mac/info-mac/app

test-drove them, rated them from one to five in each of three categories (account creation and management; budget, tax, and investment planning; and electronic connections), and summed up with a recommendation, pro or con. The reviews are well-organized and readable, and should be useful if you're cur-

Info-Mac HyperArchive: Data Management Whenever you see a site with a default browser background, you know you're either dealing with a stripped-down, content-oriented operation, or with somebody who doesn't know much HTML. This site is emphatically the former. It's run by the MIT Computer Science Laboratory, and it's a huge archive of shareware programs. The Data Management section isn't strictly a financial section—it's got a few titles like Winehandler and Golfmeister—but mostly you'll find personal organizers and budget managers, along with short abstracts describing what they're for. It's all for Macs, and it's all for free.
WEB http://hyperarchive.lcs.mit.edu/HyperArchive /Abstracts/game/HyperArchive.html

Mac Applications Forum Like its PC counterpart, this forum contains Macintosh libraries for spreadsheets, accounting, databases, and general business and PIM applications. Looking for tax templates, 401(k) planners, investment managers, auto leasing calculators, or Excel calendars? Drop by.
COMPUSERVE *go* macapp

MacUser Software Central—Business and Productivity—Finance Mac users are famous for being fluffy and touchy-feely, but they'll be hyper-organized, hard-bitten accountants by the time they leave this site. Personal organizers, loan worksheets, budget crunchers, and ticket makers (yes, you can make your own tickets) are the order of the day. The site has a brief description of each application, the date it was posted, its size, and a rating: one to five mice, with five being the best.
WEB http://www.zdnet.com/macuser/software/browse _table1.html

PC Applications The software libraries are packed with business and financial applications for PCs. In the Productivity library,

there are sections for Address & Phone applications and Desktop & Time programs (there's even a Mayan calendar). The Databases library has sections filled with templates and add-ons for major PC database languages including Clipper, dBASE, and Paradox, as well as an entire section devoted to Windows PIMS & Databases. The Financial library seems endless, with sections devoted to Home Financial, Investment, Quicken Support, and Windows Financial. Still browsing for new programs? Head for the Spreadsheets and Word Processing libraries with templates and utilities. The forum's active message boards make this site even richer, providing a constant flow of questions, answers, and feedback on the applications.
AMERICA ONLINE *keyword* pc applications→Software Libraries

PC Applications Forum The business applications, personal accounting programs, and personal information managers will come in handy, and they're just a few of the titles available in this massive forum for PC appli-

---

Use your eyes to browse
http://www.zdnet.com/macuser/software/browse_table1.html

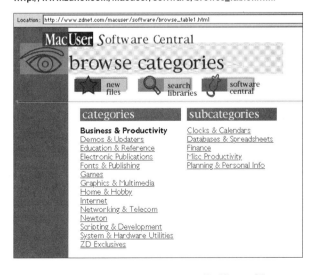

cations. Don't hesitate to poke around under "General Apps" and "Hobby/Home" if you don't find what you're looking for right away—there are grocery list programs in them thar hills. Turn to the message boards to ask for recommendations when choosing between two otherwise similar options.
COMPUSERVE *go* ibmapp

How can you be organized? Let us count the ways: Track your babysitters. Log your jogs. Inventory your house.

PC Software Libraries—Home Financial There's quite a load of code here: insurance, loan, and retirement calculators of all shapes and sizes, debt reducers, programs for printing checks, managing your investments, and find a mutual fund, tax preparation software, applications for graphing your home finances, and more. Each program comes with a description (a real description, which many shareware libraries lack) and instructions for downloading. You'll also find updates for some popular commercial applications, too, as well as product support files. All in all, it's an impressively thorough resource—unless you own a Mac.
AMERICA ONLINE *keyword* apps→Home Financial

PC World Software: Accounting & Finance Macs out of cyberspace! These applications are for DOS, Windows 3.x, and Windows 95 only. What you'll find here is a mixed bag: programs that analyze stock and mutual fund information, organize expense accounts and single-entry bookkeeping systems, and do your taxes. Each download comes with a terse one-sentence description, though other areas of the PC World site contain more in-depth reviews of current commercial software.
WEB http://www.pcworld.com/software/accounting_finance/

Personal Finance Software Forum This forum offers a generous selection of financial software, with hundreds of programs relating to accounting, career and job hunting, financial planning, home management, investment, loan calculation and amortization, organization, portfolio management, real estate, and taxes. America Online provides download assistance and reviews of especially popular financial programs. A software support section covers more than 50 companies whose wares range from market analyzers to personal organizers. Each company provides a corporate history and product list, and many have message boards for customers and technical FAQs.
AMERICA ONLINE *keyword* pf software

Productivity PC Software Library How can you be organized? Let us count the ways. Here you'll find free programs to organize food purchases and print out grocery lists (The Grocer), track your babysitters (Babysitter), log your jogs (The Runner's Log), and inventory your house (Organize Your Home).
AMERICA ONLINE *keyword* apps→Productivity

SimTel From bond calculators to loan managers, these sites carry a wide range of personal finance and investment software for the DOS user.
URL ftp://oak.oakland.edu/SimTel/msdos/finance
• ftp://ftp.funet.fi/pub/msdos/SimTel/finance

Virtual Shareware Library Carrying more than 60,000 shareware and freeware programs, this mammoth software repository (recently acquired by c|net) features an excellent search engine which allows you to search both file

names and file descriptions in up to six archives at a time. You can also narrow your search by platform and by release date. Descriptions of the titles are relatively terse, but if you know what you're looking for, you'll probably find it here.
WEB http://www.shareware.com • http://www.telstra .com.au/cgi-bin/shase

Windows One of the largest directories of software on the Net, this monstrosity is filled with finance and business applications for Windows users—you'll just have to sort through the hundreds of programs to find them.
URL ftp://wuarchive.wustl.edu/systems/ibmpc/win3/util • ftp://ftp.winsite.com/pub/pc/win3/util

Windows Forum As impressive a collection of Windows financial programs as you're likely to see, online or off. Head to the Applications library and get ready. There are sections for Excel, Paradox, MS Access, Ami Pro, and, hidden in the MORE folder, huge collections of software in the PIMS & Databases, Quattro, Quicken, Telecom, and Word for Windows sections. And you still haven't heard about the motherlode of financial software: the Financial section. Need programs to track your investments, calculate your child support payments, or invoice your clients? Of course you do, whether you realize it or not. They're here.
AMERICA ONLINE *keyword* win→Software Libraries→ Applications

Windows Shareware Forum If you're in the market for a Windows business or finance application, check out the library of personal information managers and the Business/Finance library for job hunting, check balancing, decision mapping, and stock tracking applications.
COMPUSERVE *go* winshare

Deck your desktop with lots of software
http://www.hotfiles.com/index.html

ZD Net Software Library—Personal Finance This is a marvelous resource: hundreds of shareware programs that do your taxes, organize your investments, plan your budget, and calculate your loans. Okay, they don't really do it for you, but they can save you a lot of time when you have to do it for yourself. Each program is listed along with the date it was posted and a rating by the editors of the Ziff-Davis magazines (*PC Magazine, Computer Shopper, Mac User,* and many more). There's also a charming tracking feature that lets you know how many other visitors have downloaded the same piece of software, just in case you want to do what the popular kids are doing.
WEB http://www.hotfiles.com/index.html

Zmac Download & Support Forum Big Brother is watching! You must enhance your productivity! And this area might just might help, with many intriguing little shareware programs for Macs. Time Trackers, Weather Trackers, AgendaMakers, even a Coffee Timer. All programs selected by the editors of *MacWeek* and *MacUser*.
COMPUSERVE *go* zmc:download

Chapter 3

Women & Money

Take charge of your personal finances because Prince Charming may never come; and even if he does, he'll want help with the house payments

THERE WAS A TIME when men learned about bulls and bears, and all a woman had to know about were men. A woman's financial prosperity was directly proportional to her ability to land a man with good prospects, and even if she happened to attend college, her goal was to graduate with a Mrs. degree. That was a long time ago, thankfully, in a galaxy that seems far, far away. Times have changed. Women comprise nearly half of the labor force today; more than half of all mothers are working moms. From Molly Dodd to Murphy Brown to Madonna, sisters are doing it for themselves. And if you want to find out more about how the the gender gap is closing in financial matters, go online, where resources for financially minded women abound.

Managing Money is

You've Come a Long Way, Baby —But Not Far Enough

How far have women come? Unfortunately, the news isn't all that good. Compared to men, women are still less involved in their family finances, less aware of their personal finances, and less prepared for financial upsets. The gender gap is supported by the simple—

and simply inconceivable—fact that women, on average, still earn only 60 to 80 percent of what men earn, even if they share the same occupation. Woman's Connection Online has lots of other disheartening statistics concerning **Economic Power for Women**; the 1995 United Nations Human Development report, for example, puts the United States behind 31 other nations when it comes to salary equity between men and women. Less income naturally leads to less savings, and less "disposable" income for investing. **Mary Hunt**, author of *The Financially Confident Woman*, encourages women to take more responsibility for their financial security. With nearly half of all marriages ending in divorce, it's increasingly likely that a married woman will find herself single again, and single living

Women's Work

means more financial pressure. One thing that women can do right away is save more; currently, single men save approximately 3 percent of their income, while single women are saving at only half that rate.

There is proof, however, that when women do get involved with finance, they enjoy a good deal of success. When it comes to investing, for example, they

CASH REGISTER

Economic Power for Women
WEB http://www.womenconnect.com /ca9075l.htm

Mary Hunt @ the Top After Scraping the Bottom
WEB http://www.wwork.com/Top /chpsk8.htm

Women & Money
WEB http://pathfinder.com/money /features/women/index.html

How Women Have Wised Up
WEB http://pathfinder.com/money /features/women/cov2.htm

Finances for Women
WEB http://www.moneyworld.co.uk /moneyworld/faqs/womfaq3.htm

Why Women Need to Take an Active Role
WEB http://www.workingwoman.com /articles/zwaddell.htm

Women's Money Challenges in the '90s
WEB http://www.fni.com/heritage /apr96/Almond.html

Financial Planning for Women: No More Ms-Takes
WEB http://www.uvol.com/woman /finance.html

Net Worth
http://cgi.pathfinder.com/cgi-bin /Money/r2.cgi

When net worth equals self-esteem
http://cgi.pathfinder.com/cgi-bin/Money/r2.cgi

often do better than men. A feature on **Women & Money** in *Money* magazine reports that the number of women who are playing the market and grabbing the financial reigns is "growing exponentially," and some of this may be due to distaff investment habits. While conventional wisdom holds that women invest more conservatively than men, new studies show that more and more women are making growth-oriented investments in stocks and equity mutual funds. The percentage of women and men who invest in stock funds are roughly equal, and both women and men allocate roughly equal amounts of their portfolios to equities. Women are just as successful as men when it comes to returns. If you check out *Money* Online, you'll find lots of evidence for **How Women Have Wised Up**. One study shows that women-only investment clubs tracked by the National Association of Investors (NAIC) earned 5.3 percent more than the men-only investment clubs on their average annual returns. It seems the fairer sex has the capacity to become the richer one.

Yes, Virginia, There is Such a Thing as Financial Planning for Women

All this talk of financial planning for women may have you a bit confused. Aren't women just men with cuter bodies? Does the world really need financial resources targeted specifically at female investors? The answer is yes, at least according to the FAQs at the Money-World guide on **Finances for Women**. Studies show that women approach the subject of money management differently than men. Between juggling family and work, women often don't devote as much time as they should to their own fiscal futures. Women also may have a lack of confidence when it comes to money matters. Married women often defer to their husbands when it comes to money management. Women may feel patronized by investment advisors or intimidated by the financial argot, which further prevents them from taking an active role in the planning process.

Working Woman magazine explains another reason **Why Women Need to Take an Active Role** in their financial lives. Women tend to get fewer retirement benefits, and smaller pensions than men—if they get any pension at all. Part of the reason for this is that a woman's working life is more likely to be interrupted by family responsibilities than a man's. If women generally outlive men by 5 to 7 years, some may find themselves under great financial strain in their mature years if they don't take an aggressive attitude while they're young.

Perhaps the most sobering of the **Women's Money Challenges in the '90s** is facing the fact that 90 percent of all American women will either stay single, become widowed, or get divorced. That means that at some time in their lives, 90 percent of women will find themselves solely responsible for their own financial decisions. Knowing how to gain control of the purse strings and keep them firmly in hand is an absolute necessity.

On the Net, you can find financial planners and advice specifically targeted toward women, such as **Financial Planning for Women: No More Ms-Takes**. The basic steps outlined here include defining your objectives, calculating your **Net Worth**, analyzing your cash flow, cutting back on needless spending, planning for retirement, reviewing your insurance needs, and investing. The bottom line, however, is that the prescription for a sound money management plan is the same regardless of gender. Start whipping your money into shape today, because your financial health is something you can't afford to ignore.

THINK ABOUT THIS

- Women live an average of seven years longer than men.
- 47 percent of all first marriages and 49 percent of all second marriages end in divorce.
- After divorce or separation, the average woman's income drops by 37 percent.
- Nine out of ten women will be responsible for managing the household finances at some point in their lives.
- Over 47 percent of wealthy Americans with assets of $500,000 or more are women.
- Even when men and women work in the same occupation, women earn between 60 percent and 80 percent of what men earn.
- 72 percent of adult women were employed in 1995 versus 29 percent in 1955.
- Single women save only 1.5 percent of their annual income, compared to 3.1 percent for single men.
- Women invest less than 14.6 percent of their non-real estate assets in equities, compared to 27.4 percent for single men.

—*from Mary Hunt @ the Top After Scraping the Bottom*

▼ Starting points

Cybergrrl Money Matters The conversational tone taken at Cybergrrl makes it seem as if it were only directed toward Gen Xers, but actually, this site is a good resource for every woman who is just starting to explore the financial jungle. This month, Money Matters covers choosing a stockbroker, pricing your business, and Q&A about IRAs with in-depth, incisive articles offering user-friendly advice. A glossary of basic financial terms, as well as links to other finance-minded Web pages is also available.
WEB http://www.cybergrrl.com/women/biz/money.html

MoneyWorld Guide—Finances for Women Who says the British are good for nothing except cheesy feet and Shepherd's pie? This extensive hypertext article addresses the specific financial concerns of women, and answers women's most frequently asked questions about financial planning, begining with "In which areas do women's financial affairs differ from those of men?" In providing answers, the article often branches out into Money-World's other comprehensive, gender-blind guides. Most of the advice is universal enough to apply to women in America, too.
WEB http://www.moneyworld.co.uk/moneyworld/faqs/womfaq3.htm

The New Realities: Working Women and Financial Protection Martha M. Harmon's contribution to the collection of financial articles for *Working Woman* magazine explores the changing economic landscape for working women. She states some inspiring stats—"Six million businesses are now owned by women, employing more people than all Fortune 500 companies. The majority of recent law school and college graduates are women,"—but warns against working women's potential complacency when it comes to personal finance.
WEB http://www.workingwoman.com/articles/zharmon.htm

Why Do You Need a Financial Plan? Cheryl Silling offers some insight into why so many of our financial plans fail to keep us afloat in stormy weather. The top six reasons behind financial failure? Procrastination, lack of a clear goal, insufficient understanding of what money can do to accomplish the goal, failure to take advantage of tax laws, unpreparedness for the unexpected, and Failure to Develop a Winning Financial Attitude.
WEB http://www.workingwoman.com/articles/zsilling.htm

Woman's Wire: Cash This is one of the best resources on the Net for women's money matters. The online magazine *Woman's Wire* has dedicated an entire section to "Cash" issues, with monthly features on such topics as women, divorce and money, how to get a small business loan, and joint checking accounts. Other rotating columns in the section include the advice column Ask Cash Flo, an investment guide

Is green your favorite color?
http://www.women.com/cash/

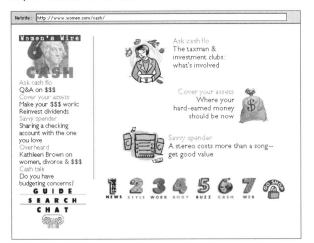

called Cover Your Assets, and Savvy Spender, which offers frugal tips and consumer advice.
COMPUSERVE *go* woman
WEB http://www.women.com/cash/

Women & Money Simply one of the best financial resources for women online. It's extensive, exhaustive, and up-to-date. Four supersections take you step-by-step through your finances, from waking up to financial responsibility to improving your already-successful investment portfolio. "How Women Have Wised Up About Money" offers an in-depth look into the historical and current trends in women's money management, and is chock full of both discouraging and inspiring stats and figures about women's current status in the economy. Check out the profiles of women who have played the market and won, and then get down to brass tacks with some targeted advice for getting a financial life. "Rev Up Your Portfolio" gives you 16 "smart choices" for hot stocks and bonds. There's even a form you can fill out to figure out your net worth, which will be sure to grow shortly after visiting this informative Web site.
WEB http://pathfinder.com/money/features/women/index.html

Women's Money Challenges in the '90s A financial advisor offers compelling reasons for the neccesity of understanding personal finance for women. The article outlines the foremost economic concerns that will face most women in their lifetime, including life expectancy, divorce, insurance, retirement, pensions, investing, and long-term care.
WEB http://www.fni.com/heritage/apr96/Almond.html

▼ **Articles & advice**

Be Sure You Get the Credit You Deserve This NestEgg article preaches to women, married or single, of the importance of obtaining, and maintaining, a good credit rating. If a woman is married, the risk of a divorce leaving her with no credit at all is one she can't afford to take, and if a joint account lists her as an "authorized user" as opposed to a "joint user," this will invariably be the case. The article encourages single women to start a credit history immediately, and warns them against credit-repair scams that seem like lifesavers when you're drowning in debt.
WEB http://nestegg.iddis.com/nestegg/may/05womfin.html

Cover Your Assets If you're looking for investment basics in easy-to-swallow articles, this is a nice little resource. The collected articles from this Women's Wire Cash column cover mutual funds, 401(k) plans, how marriage affects your taxes, budget plans, dividend investment advice, saving for your ultimate goal, and a word of caution about cautious investments.
WEB http://www.women.com/cash/cya/

Define your objectives.
Calculate your net worth.
Analyze your cash flow.
Plan for retirement.

Financial Planning for Women: No More Ms-Takes Barbara Curtis discusses the gender gap of financial security, and offers a strategy for women to seize control of their financial future. The steps? Define your objectives. Calculate your net worth. Analyze your cash flow. Start planning for retirement. Review your life and/or disability insurance. Be an investor, not a saver. What could be simpler?
WEB http://www.uvol.com/woman/finance.html

JOINT ACCOUNTS FOR COUPLES

Maintaining two separate accounts can waste money, especially at banks that charge service fees for accounts with balances under $1,000 to $5,000. Merging two accounts can raise your average balance, saving check-writing and other charges. It costs nothing to open a joint account or merge two separate accounts. If the two accounts are at the same bank, try to open a joint account and deposit both balances into it; otherwise the bank will pick one of the accounts (most likely, the man's) and deposit the other balance into it, thus wiping out your continued credit rating. If merging your checking accounts means your new balance is consistently more than a few thousand dollars, transfer some of it to a savings or money market account where it can earn interest. Some couples keep their finances separate in order to spare one spouse the consequences of the other partner's business losses or gambling debts, but the government and the IRS usually do not recognize these methods. Even couples who file separate tax returns can be liable for each other's filing errors.

—from More Savvy Spender

one-third of the income needed to retire comfortably."
WEB http://www.wwork.com/Top/chpsk8.htm

Merrill Lynch Investment Handbook Merrill Lynch Financial Services has put together a financial handbook made exclusively for women. Order your free guide at this site.
WEB http://www.plan.ml.com/products_services /womenguide.html

Money & Investing *Advancing Woman* magazine offers a short article meant to help woman jump-start their financial life. Brief advice for beginning investors is followed by a helpful list of financial resources, which are, for the most part, gender-blind. A booklist features Peter Lynch's *Learn to Earn*, and links directly to the Amazon online bookstore, where you can purchase it for yourself.
WEB http://www.advancingwomen.com/money.phtml

Money Matters Women Biz offers a series of articles on personal finance, covering investment topics such as mutual funds, retirement plans, and Social Security, as well as a couple of articles dealing with taxes. The site also asks for your editorial input, and showcases a number of offline money resources.
WEB http://www.frsa.com/womenbiz/money.html

More Savvy Spender The Savvy Spender column of Women's Wire gives you practical consumer advice. This is a small (but growing) collection of the Savvy Spender offerings from 1996. The articles cover buying a stereo, getting your first mortgage, hidden costs involved in buying a car, and the decision to open a joint bank account with your spouse.
WEB http://www.women.com/cash/savvyspender

Women and Family Finances: A Survival Strategy
It's not a romantic notion, but marriage, says Elizabeth Moss, should start with a financial

Mary Hunt @ the Top After Scraping the Bottom
Mary Hunt, founder and editor of *Cheapskate Monthly*, shares the story of a woman who was "scared straight" after falling into credit hell. This encouraging, but chilling story shows how easy it is to be trapped by credit-card debt, and how you can overcome it. It also offers a number of stats on the state of women's finances including the startling estimation that "Given their traditional savings and investing patterns, women who are retiring in the next 20 years will have less than

plan. The threat of divorce, or even, God forbid, death of a spouse is a very real one, and the woman who has been dependent on her husband up until that point will find herself on shaky ground. The article discusses the economic consequences of divorce for women, and gives out some enlightening information on the "myth" of alimony. Offline resources and a short bibliography are also listed.

WEB http://nestegg.iddis.com/nestegg/feb/women.html

Women's Web Magazine While *Women's Web Magazine* does offer it's own section on business, you'll want to browse through the entire magazine to find money management advice and discussion of financial issues; they lurk in features such as the January cover story on Entrepenurial Trailblazers. You'll often find specific advice for women consumers in the Living section.

WEB http://www.womenswebmagazine.com/

▼ Calculator

Your Net Worth *Money* magazine's net worth calculator makes organizing your finances easy. Those just starting out in the real world won't find much use for this worksheet, but those women with mortgages, real furniture, pensions and other assets and debts will find it a godsend.

WEB http://cgi.pathfinder.com/cgi-bin/Money/r2.cgi

▼ Retirement

Retirement is Coming! Laura Bell gives you the low-down on retirement and what you can do right now to ensure that your future is secure. It offers targeted advice on retirement planning, offline resources that will help you build your portfolio, basic info on IRAs, and a final word on personal responsibility. In other words, you can't count on the government to take you through your golden years. You have to do it yourself.

WEB http://www.advancingwomen.com/retire.phtml

Women's Finances: Retirement Shortfalls Hit Women Hardest This article encourages women in their 30s and 40s to jump start or rev up their retirement planning. Experts say you will need 70 to 80 percent of your pre-retirement income in order to retire comfortably. Women often have smaller pension plans than men, and time taken off from work to raise children often takes a substantial bite from their company-sponsored retirement plans, so Peter Maloney warns women that they can't depend on their workplace to provide for them. Several model financial situations are studied in detail, and pointed advice is given for each situation.

WEB http://nestegg.iddis.com/nestegg/articles /ret_l.html

▼ Survey says...

Clinique Survey Clinique wants to know what your economic concerns are, and how you are dealing with your finances. Take the survey, and compare your answers with the results the magazine has already collected. Visiting expert Ann B. Diamond offers targeted advice on how you can start managing your money now.

WEB http://www.clinique.com/app/nph-surv05.cgi

Women Settle for Less Money This short but provocative article reveals the results of a sociological experiment performed at the University of Guelph. The study showed that women have a "lower sense of income entitlement" than men, and are more likely to ask for and expect less money for services rendered than men do.

WEB http://www.uoguelph.ca/atguelph/96-04-03 /serge.html

Chapter 4
Banking Online

Do your banking online and never stand in line again!

NOTHING QUITE MATCHES the frustration of waiting in line for two hours at an ATM during lunchtime, then trying to figure out your transaction history while a hundred hungry customers stand behind you tapping their feet, clucking their tongues, and making death threats under their breath. Well, thanks to the wonders of modern technology, these and other frustrating, time-consuming tasks can be avoided through online banking. All you need is a PC, a modem, a checking account, and, depending on what kind of transactions you want to complete, some inexpensive personal finance software.

Banking On the Future

If you've been online lately, you've noticed that every bank in the universe has a Web site. Up until around 1994, most of these sites were simply advertisements. The really accomplished banks had home pages that offered information on all their services and products, and a precious few even had some interactive features such as mortgage calculators and ATM branch locators. But according to the IT Online News Service, **Internet and online banking are set to change the face of banking forever**. By the end of 1996, more than 100

IN THIS CHAPTER

▶ **Update account info on the Net**   ▶ **Pay your bills online**
▶ **Transfer funds by modem**   ▶ **Download digital money**

banks and credit unions had launched home banking programs across the country and around the world, and a handful of banks were scheduled to go completely virtual, with no offline branches in existence. Home banking sounds revolutionary. But what is it?

Well, it's not just one thing. Home banking is one of those catch-all phrases that can designate any number of services, but most banks offer two types of programs: Web banking and PC banking.

Web banking enables you to access all your account information over the Internet, including your checking account and credit card statements, your transaction history, and ATM and debit card charges. You also have the ability to transfer funds between accounts, which can be accessed either through the bank's home page, or a dial-up account. Most banks charge a monthly fee for this service, but some banks give you free, unlimited access.

PC banking works with personal finance software. It downloads your bank information into such programs as Quicken, Microsoft Money, Money Managing, and BankNow for AOL, so you can manage your money in a variety of ways. Options include paying bills online, budgeting, getting tax help, and investment planning. Many banks give you your choice of free software when you sign up for PC banking, and almost all of them charge a monthly fee for this service. Unfortunately, most of the software, apart from

CASH REGISTER

"Internet and online banking set to change the face of banking forever"
WEB http://www.itweb.co.za/opinions /0496robo.htm

Online Banking Via the Internet
WEB http://banctechnologies.clever .net/docs/net.htm

Off the Record—Internet Commerce & Banking
WEB http://www.mediapool.com/off therecord/banking.html

Online Banking
WEB http://new.popsci.com/content /computers/features/onlinebanking /ob.l.html

The Complete Guide to Online Banking
WEB http://www.cnet.com/Content /Features/Dlife/Banking/

American Home Financial Services Survey
WEB http://etrg.findsvp.com/financial /highlights.html

Quicken, is IBM-compatible only, so Mac users are often left in the dust when it comes to these more complex, and very enticing, services.

Home banking not only benefits the customer, but also helps smaller banks survive in an increasingly competitive industry. BankTechnologie's **Online Banking Via the Internet** tells us that since 1978, when "Congress deregulated interest rates and opened up the industry's business to anyone with a computer," banks have been struggling for survival. And now banks are slowly coming to the realization that the option of home banking is an issue when consumers choose their bank, and they may even be in danger of losing customers to virtual banks. According to **Off the Record** the war between the banks and technology companies has already begun. But even among the cyber-savvy banks, competition is fiercer than ever. As offline branches become less and less essential, consumers will be able to choose their bank based solely on the quality and value of the services; location won't be a consideration. In other words, when it comes to home banking, every bank has a branch as close as your computer.

But the technology hasn't quite forced offline banks out of existence—yet. Although ATMs have made teller-free transactions commonplace, there are still a number of transactions that need human contact—certifying checks, replacing ATM cards, and reporting credit card fraud, to name just a few. Hence, the reality of online banking doesn't quite match the theory.

Even online transactions are complicated things. Although bill paying costs less online (no envelopes or postage), and takes less than half the time, the dream of being able to send your rent check to your

When it comes to your cash, safety first
http://www.mediapool.com/offtherecord/banking.html

landlord at 11:59 the night that it's due, is still a dream. The reality is that most vendors, not to mention individuals, are not set up to receive electronic payments. According to PopSci's comprehensive article on **Online Banking**, over 95 percent of "electronic" payments are made with paper checks. This is how it works: You instruct your software to send an online payment, this command prompts your modem to call a network of computers that records the info and, once a day, transmits all the transactions from all over the country to a forms printing company. The forms printing company prints out the checks and their mailer forms, sorts by destination, and ships by U.S. mail to a local airport for a regular old U.S. Post Office trip to the payee. This process takes several days, and if you are sending checks locally, it may even cost you time to do it electronically. Updating your account takes a chunk of time as well. When the check is cashed or deposited, it slowly winds its way back, again through the regular mail, through several financial clearinghouses to your bank, where the check is marked cleared.

Online banking also allows for automatic regular payment; according to c|net's **Complete Guide to Online Banking**, one of the most important services to look for is the ability to pay off mortgages, loans, and utilities. But if your finances aren't that stable, and your budget, payments, or collectors change from month to month, you may decide that paying electronically isn't the best way to go.

None of this means, however, that online banking isn't a huge convenience. Informational services—account information, money management programs—are practically problem-free online, and certainly a benefit to anyone who lacks the patience and mathematical abil-

Are "electronic" payments a misnomer?
http://new.popsci.com/content/computers
/features/onlinebanking/ob.l.html

ity to keep on top of their finances. If you choose your online bank wisely, costly transaction histories can be a thing of the past; you can pull up graphs that tell you how much of your paycheck goes toward clothing; you can figure out how many years it will take you to pay off that impulsive pillar candle binge at Pottery Barn; and those pesky ATM charges won't ever sneak up on you again. And most simply, but most importantly, you will always know how much money you have—account information is updated once a day.

❝ Is home banking really a quick fix, or is it just another hyped-up piece of Net technology that is actually more complicated than its real-life counterpart? ❞

So is home banking really a quick fix? Or is it just another hyped-up piece of Net technology that is actually more complicated and dangerous than its real-life counterpart? Well, almost everyone agrees that the future of the industry is bright. According to a 1996 **American Home Financial Services Survey**, 9.2 million households (27 percent of PC households or 10 percent of U.S. households) now use online services and/or the Internet for various financial services. As with most technologies, increased use means increased demand for convenience, and increased demand for convenience means increased supply. If the banks, the vendors, and the consumers all climb aboard the online banking bandwagon, online banking may finally turn the corner from minor inconvenience to major convenience.

Get with the online banking program
http://www.cnet.com/Content/Features/Dlife/Banking/

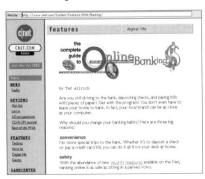

▼ Banks

Advance Bank There are two virtual banking services available to PC users at Australia's Advance Bank. The first is a basic online banking service that lets you monitor your accounts and allows you to transfer funds, and the second is a bill-paying program that lets you pay bills with certain merchants, or others you nominate. You can apply for either service online, and all your questions are answered with an FAQ, a security feature, and a demo. Other features at this home site include pages on Home Loans, Managed Investment, Business Banking, and Economic News.

WEB http://www.advance.com.au/

Atlanta Internet Bank Atlanta Internet Bank does one thing, and it does it well—virtual banking at a high 7 percent (6.18 percent APY) NetVantage Money Market Rate. The reason they can offer such a great rate? This bank only exists online. Bill paying services and online checking are also available. The only problem? Atlanta Internet Bank has plenty of strings: "Introductory rate on Net-Vantage Money Market through Dec. 31, 1996 of 7 percent—6.18 percent annual percentage yield (APY)—for the first 120 days. After that time the interest rate will be based on the current money market rate, which is 5.5 percent as of Nov. 11, 1996. Maximum deposits up to $100,000. You must maintain a $2,500 daily balance to receive rate. If your daily balance is $2,499.99 or less, the interest paid drops to 3 percent with an APY of 3.05 percent. Only personal accounts are eligible. Fees could reduce earnings. Interest rates subject to change at bank's discretion." If you're still interested, despite the fine print, you can view a demo and then sign up for the service online.

WEB http://www.atlantabank.com

Bank of America Every month, the Money Page releases a Top Ten list of the best banking sites on the Net. And every month, Bank of America is listed at the top. *PC Computing* magazine also ranks it first in online banking. So what separates this service from the rest? HomeBanking, Bank of America's PC banking program, is compatible with a variety of software packages, including Managing Your Money, Quicken, Microsoft Money, and most ordinary spreadsheets. More than 50,000 merchants accept Bank of America's virtual payment system. The system can be accessed through the Web, through America Online, or through Managing Your Money, and users an access and integrate up to 50 different Bank of America accounts. For a flat, $6.50 fee, Bank of America offers unlimited access to the service, unlimited bill payments, and unlimited pay-by-phone service. The home page furnishes extensive info on HomeBanking, including an enormous FAQ which answers all of your security questions. But the best reason for choosing this PC banking service over the others is this—Bank of America is running a contest for HomeBanking participants, and

---

Will the next customer please step up to the browser window?
http://www.advance.com.au/

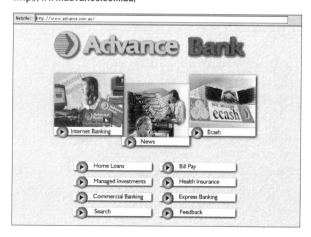

the prizes are spectacular. "A Free Month's Mortgage or Rent Payment, up to $5,000! Full Payment of Your Credit Card Balance, up to $2,500! Three Months of Auto Loan Payments, up to $2,500! Or a $50 Credis for Your Internet Service Provider!" Check out the online demo, and then sign up for the service on the site.

AMERICA ONLINE *keyword* bofa
WEB http://www.BankAmerica.com • http://www.bofa.com

Any bank that offers a Shockwave version of its Web page has got to have a hot service, right?

BankNet Electronic Banking Service The British companies MarketNet and Secure Trust Bank plc have joined forces to offer you an online banking service that acts as a Secure Trust current account with plenty of additional features—no transaction charges even if overdrawn, interest on credit balances, check book, guarantee card, and cash card. The service offers live Web access to account info, the ability to write electronic checks, and more. You can sign up for the service and download the software on-site. The home page also offers details on interest rates and bank charges, a list of foreign transactions available, an FAQ, and links to other virtual banking sites. And you don't have to be a U.K. resident to open an account with this British bank.

WEB http://sest.mkn.co.uk/help/bank/info

Baybank Online Baybank recently merged with Bank of Boston to become BankBoston, and the new home page for the Boston bank is impressive and user friendly. You can sign up for their PC banking service—Homelink—on this home page. What does Homelink allow you to do? Well, the program is available for Macs and PCs, and lets online account holders pay bills or make payments, transfer funds between accounts (including Baybank credit accounts), review account activity, interface with Quicken to manage their finances, and check interest rates on CDs and money market accounts. An online demonstration of Homelink is available on the site, and Bank-Boston also addresses security concerns by explaining the entire encryption and safety system that protects banked monies.

WEB http://www.baybank.com

Britton & Koontz Electronic Banking Center Don't judge a bank by its cover. The graphically unimpressive Britton & Koontz Electronic Banking Center is one of the most interactive banking sites online. The bank offers some of the most extensive services to its account holders, including account info and balances, stop payment orders, personal preferences, fund transfers, money wiring and more. Virtual services available to everyone include opening an account, applying for a credit card, mortgage prequalification, customer service, personal loan application, and access to CD, loan, and mortgage rates. The site also offers a loan and mortgage calendar, and an investment calculator.

WEB http://www.bkbank.com/

Capital Bank Louisiana's Capital Bank has a no-nonsense Web site offering brief overviews of all their services. Get info on loans and mortgages, checking and savings accounts, and IRAs, as well as commercial banking services, and deposit account rate. Web users even get a special offer on a low-rate CD. Caplink, the bank's virtual service, lets you view account information, transfer funds, order checks and pay bills from the comfort of

your home, or download the software directly from the site.
WEB http://www.capbank.com/

 Chase Bank Any bank that offers a Shockwave version of its Web page has got to have a hot online banking service, right? Right. Deep within this enormous, cyber-savvy site, within the Day In/Day Out sub-sub-section of the Your Money at Chase sub-section, is the Online Banking section, which claims that Chase's virtual money management programs will make banking fun again (was it ever fun?). Chase offers PC owners a choice of Microsoft Money or Quicken for Windows; there are applications for both software packages online. In addition to the dozens of info pages on the banks services and products, the home page includes ATM and branch locators and loan request forms.
WEB http://www.chase.com

Commerce Bank Offline, Commerce Bank services Metro Philadelphia, South Jersey, and the Jersey Shore, but online they service the entire U.S. An illustrated guide shows you how easy it is to get account information, pay bills, and manage your money with the best financial software on the market. The rest of the site contains a branch locator, commerce news, and details on personal, business, and investment banking services. Be sure to check out the bank's Community Service feature, which showcases its commitment to local charities and organizations. And if you open an account with Commerce online, you'll receive a free Motorola Cellular Phone and your choice of a $10 credit or free checks.
WEB http://www2.yesbank.com/commerce/

Deposit Guaranty Bank DGB has an especially comprehensive home page, with areas devoted to breaking DGB news, personal

banking, business banking, student banking, and high-tech banking. You can even customize the site for easy access to the pages that interest you most. Personal services include the GuarantyConnect ScreenPhone, which offers many of the PC banking features through a specially designed "superphone"; GuarantyConnect PC Banking, which includes all the usual transactions and account monitoring services; and a Guaranty-Connect program that manages all your personal finances from home banking to retirement planning. You can enroll for the PC services online, and a demo is available for the lower-end program. The software is IBM-compatible only.
WEB http://www.dgb.com/

First Chicago First Chicago has a friendly, fun site, with sections for Personal Finance, Corporate Finance Services, and Small Business Finance. Personal Financial services include features on Insurance, credit cards, banking and investment, a student center, and even a trivia game. Bank a la Modem allows First Chicago customers to use Quicken, Microsoft Money, and BankNOW on America Online

Home banking is the Bank of America way
http://www.BankAmerica.com

to bank from home. All the info on the program is available on the home page, and you can apply for the service online. Some software is available for Macs, but most runs on Windows only.

AMERICA ONLINE *keyword* first chicago
WEB http://www.fcnbd.com/per/fcb/fcmenu.html

First Union This slick site offers an abundance of information on First Union's various personal and business banking services. Incredibly detailed overviews take you step by step through basic services such as checking and savings accounts, loans and mortgages, investing, and credit. And then there are the advanced services like CAP accounts, retirement services, VISA Cash, Insurance, and Estate Planning. Many of these services are available online. Go into the Access Account section to choose from basic cyberbanking, Retirement Services, and WebInvision. Cyberbanking, which carries an undisclosed monthly fee, includes account inquiry, funds transfer, and online bill paying. Retirement Services gives you account balances, financial projections, maturity dates, lets you update withholding elections and distribution frequency, and much more. WebInvision allows

you to view account information and book transfers, stop payments, and make credit inquiries.
WEB http://www.firstunion.com/

Fleet Fleet Bank has 950 branches throughout the northeastern United States, and they've just opened up an international branch—online. This comprehensive site offers a company bio, a weekly economics newsletter, and of course information on all the bank's services and products, including business banking and personal banking services. Many of Fleet's services that could be handled on their Web page—such as loan and credit card applications—are still only available by phone, but there is an entire section devoted to Fleet PC Banking with Managing Your Money. Their virtual banking services cover income tax management, financial planning, and investment, as well as traditional bill paying and account review tools. While a demo is not available at this time, instructive graphics and detailed description of the program are offered. Strangely enough, you must apply for the software over the phone.
WEB http://www.fleet.com/

Home Savings of America Cool design and easy navigation make the Home Savings of American home page a treat to browse. Whether you're interested in business or personal banking, loans, investments or PC banking, you'll find tons of info relayed in a conversational tone, and interactive features that make banking easier. The PC banking program works with Quicken and Microsoft Money, and you can sign up for access online. The services are somewhat limited—account access and bill payment only—but depending on what kind of account you open with the bank, there are all sorts of special savings available.
WEB http://www.homesavings.com/

You're the missing piece to this banking puzzle
http://www.huntington.com/

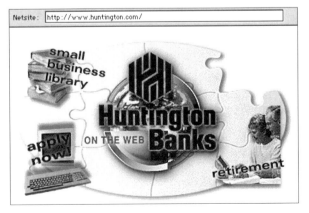

Huntington Banks Huntington Web bank is a full service virtual bank that allows you to view all your accounts and transactions, pay bills, generate account activity reports, and transfer your accounts to personal finance software programs—all online. The service is just $5.95 per month, and you can apply online. Huntington offers an exhaustive FAQ on its site, including an entire section on security, and you can even see a demo of the service before you sign up. Other features on the bank's home page include an organizational profile, retirement and credit card sections, even net worth and retirement planning calculators.
WEB http://www.huntington.com/

Mellon Bank Mellon Bank has a strong presence online, with many services available over the Web. Full-service PC banking is available, with free software for either Mac or Windows, the programs let you check your account balances, transfer money between eligible accounts, review bank or credit card records, pay bills, order checks, and receive stock and mutual fund price quotes. You can fill out an application form online. Other online services available through the Web site include mortgage and loan calculators, a branch locator, online credit card applications, and even an online resume generator—Mellon was recently recognized as one of the best places to work by *Computerworld* magazine. The home page offers extensive overviews of all personal and business banking services, as well as associated investment services.
WEB http://www.mellon.com/

NationsBank What's at NationsBank? A step-by-step virtual tour of its online services, which include access to all NationsBank accounts (checking, savings, money markets, and credit cards), as well as the ability to transfer funds between

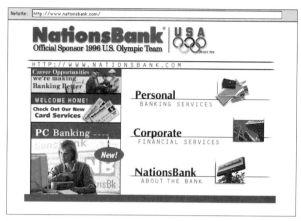

Can you bank from wherever you are?
http://www.nationsbank.com

accounts, pay bills online, and track transactions. You can also manage your finances by categorizing expenses, paying bills online, and utilizing tools that help you plan for mortgage financing and retirement. With a checking account, you receive free PC banking service, and free Managing Your Money software. Bill paying costs $5.95 per month, and is waived for the first two months. Unfortunately, online banking with NationsBank is available in less than a dozen states, so check the availability map before you're sold.
WEB http://www.nationsbank.com

Salem Five Cents Savings Bank If you don't know the first thing about online banking, this is not the site for you. Salem doesn't go into too much detail about its dial-up virtual banking—it simply gives you an overview of the services it provides, including account monitoring, money transfers, virtual loan services, and a virtual money market account. A demo is available, and applications are taken by phone. The rest of the cyber-savvy site offers online finance calculators, and even a real estate listings section with classifieds in the New England area.
WEB http://www.salemfive.com/index.html

Signet Bank Whether you're interested in commercial, personal or virtual banking, in employment info or money for college, Signet's slick site has what you're looking for. When it comes to virtual banking, Signet offers you two options—Web banking, which takes place over the Net, and PC banking, which interacts with personal finance software enabling you to do all your banking from home. Comprehensive info on the PC service is available on-site, including an FAQ and a feature on online security, and you can receive information on the Web banking service through email.
WEB http://www.signet.com/

Smith Barney Financial Management Account
Smith Barney encourages you to use your Financial Management Account as your checking account, citing stats that say FMA money funds get higher yields than the interest earned on bank checking accounts. As an added incentive, the bank offers an FMA one

service that works with Quicken and Microsoft Money to help you balance your checkbook, pay your bills, organize your financial statements, and track expenses. A short overview of the services, with illustrations, is available here.
WEB http://www.smithbarney.com/

Toronto-Dominion Bank Toronto-Dominion has a full-service Web site with sections devoted to business and personal banking, buying a home and mortgages, economic reports and articles, stock quotes, and financial planning. TD Access, the virtual banking service of Toronto-Dominion Bank, doesn't just offer personal banking, it also offers services for business banking and investment banking, so that all your finances can be organized and accessed online. All you need is an IBM-compatible 368 PC, Microsoft Windows, and a modem, and you can pay bills, transfer money, view your banking and credit accounts, as well as obtaining quotes and submitting equity, option and mutual fund orders. Read up on every aspect of online service, and download a preview of the program before you subscribe.
WEB http://www.tdbank.ca

U.S. Bank Free online banking is no longer a distant dream. It's here, at U.S. Bank, where all you need is Net access, a current browser, and a U.S. Bank ATM card to get a variety of online services at no charge. You can view account information, including transactions for the past eight weeks; transfer money between U.S. accounts; keep track of, and pay off, your credit cards; and contact service representatives directly. If you want to juice up your PC banking, the service works with all the best financial software (take your choice for free). The slick home page offers tons of online features such as loan worksheets, guidebooks to

Coffee and your account balance, to go!
http://www.signet.com/

Netsite: http://www.signet.com/

personal finance, and financial aid links, and gives comprehensive coverage of services from trust services to small business banking.
WEB http://www.usbank.com/

Wells Fargo Bank Basic online banking at Wells Fargo is free, and offers checking, savings, credit card account management, fund transfers, and the ability to integrate your account activity with personal finance software. For $5 a month, you can add a full-service bill-paying feature. The home page has detailed info on every aspect of the service, including a complete demo and online application. The site also provides coverage of small business and international trading, offering features such as economic reports and employment opportunities. And just in case all this talk of money is making you feel like you'd like to spend some, there's even a virtual mall.
WEB http://wellsfargo.com/

Wilber Bank Wilber Online Banking can be accessed by touch-tone phone, screen phone, modem, or Internet, and offers all of the usual services: account information, the ability to transfer funds between Wilber accounts, and the ability to pay bills online. It also has some more exclusive features that are only available here. You don't need to change your current bank in order to use the services—with Inter-Bank Transfer, you can connect to your existing checking account and move funds from bank to bank. You can also make deposits and withdrawals from non-Wilber Bank ATMs with no charge. Bill-paying and PC banking software can be downloaded from the home page at no cost. The page contains a section on security, and is one of the most forthright sites when it comes to showing exactly how much you'll end up paying for each individual online service.
WEB http://www.wilberbank.com/

▼ Bill-paying software

CheckFree CheckFree allows unconditional online bill payment, "any amount—to anyone—any bank, anywhere, any time." For the cost of start-up software and monthly charges, CheckFree designs a home electronic-payment system for you. Just enter the necessary information (amounts, accounts) and dial your local access number. Four business days later, CheckFree pays off your creditors. Because it accesses the Federal Reserve system, CheckFree can be used with any bank, and it includes elaborate security measures to ensure that your financial information isn't filched from the phone lines. The program is compatible with many popular finance software packages, including Managing Your Money, Quicken, and Microsoft Money. CheckFree software is available for Mac, DOS, and Windows platforms. CompuServe members can download a demo or order the software online, and Internet users can download the full version of the software.
COMPUSERVE *go* checkfree
WEB http://www.checkfree.com

Too bad you can't be BillFree
http://www.checkfree.com

Imagine sending your nephew's birthday money straight to his laptop

Banking online enables your computer and modem to do practically everything except spit out crisp twenties. But what if you didn't need cold, hard cash? Enter the world of digital money, where virtual currency can flow straight from your bank account to your desktop to any online merchant in cyberspace. Sure, you can purchase goods and services with a credit card, but prohibitive processing costs put a minimum on the amount you can charge. Digital cash schemes promise to enable consumers to conduct monetary transactions

Digital Money

involving low sums—as low as a fraction of a cent—as well as transfer funds to just about anyone with Internet access. Right now, the world of digital money falls into two categories: digital currency, such as **DigiCash** and **NetCash**, and digital payment systems, such as **CyberCash** and **First Virtual**. Digital currency, which promises anonymity and flexibility, attempts to emulate the function of cash in the real world. Digital payment systems provide secure and sometimes anonymous ways to pay for items online using credit cards, debit cards, and electronic checks and coins. Of course, there are technological hurdles to overcome. Double-spending is one of them: If cash is digital and you keep it on your desktop, what's to stop you from copying the money file over and over? Dozens of cryptographers and microentrepreneurs have been working on that problem, and others just like it. But nothing will replace the uniquely satisfying sensation of having a pocket full of crisp twenties.

CASH REGISTER

DigiCash
WEB http://www.digicash.com/

NetCash
WEB http://gost.isi.edu/info/netcash

CyberCash
WEB http://www.cybercash.com

First Virtual
WEB http://www.fv.com

▼ Digital currency

DigiCash This ecurrency company was founded by David Chaum, who pioneered the concept of digital money. Ecash, or CyberBucks as it's known in the beta test version, is DigiCash's software-only form of electronic cash. No credit cards are required in this scheme, but thus far, the Mark Twain Bank in Saint Louis is the only bank that will open accounts from which users can withdraw ecash. Users must first deposit money there in a non–interest-bearing account and then conduct transactions using the ecash software, which displays a status window showing how much cash is in your account and little icons for basic functions. Transactions can be made for purchases costing as little as one cent. When you want to make a purchase, use the icon buttons to withdraw money from your account. Digital "coins" are sent to you via encrypted email, which you then unencrypt and store on your hard drive to spend with merchants as you please. While the system affords anonymity, if your hard disk crashes, you could lose your money.
WEB http://www.digicash.com/

Millicent Digital's contribution to the micro-economy. Purchases can be made for items costing as little as one cent. Wired magazine called the concept "fake money akin to Geoffrey Bucks at Toys 'R' Us." Purchases can be made for items costing as little as one cent. Unfortunately, the system affords users no anonymity, and merchants could potentially make off with the user's money.
WEB http://www.research.digital.com/SRC/millicent/

NetBill Electronic Commerce Carnegie Mellon's project, which has undergone only limited testing. Purchases can be made for items costing as little as five cents.
WEB http://www.ini.cmu.edu/netbill

NetCash Facilitates anonymous payments made over open networks, developed by the GOST (Global Operating Systems Technology) Group, who are actually a bunch of faculty and students from the Information Sciences Institute of the University of Southern California. These are the folks responsible for Kerberos, the computer network security system. They are also working on NetCheque, which supports electronic payments by check in real time or by email. Apparently, the GOST group hasn't been working very hard lately: You can't yet buy anything with Net-Cash, and the only thing you can buy with NetCheque is a pay-per-view recipe for "Spicy, Cheap, and Unhealthy Cooking."
WEB http://gost.isi.edu/info/netcash

▼ Digital payment systems

CyberCash "A CyberCash Wallet is like an armored car for your credit cards. It is password protected and only you know the code." Consumers can download the free CyberCash Wallet software and just type in their credit card number. The "wallet" provides "indus-

---

Nanobucks won't be an alien concept
http://www.research.digital.com/SRC/millicent/

Cold, hard (disk) cash
http://www.cybercash.com

trial-strength" security and can "contain" credit cards, ATM cards, or debit cards, all of which you can use to purchase stuff online. In late 1996, electronic coin and check services will be available (you can sign up now to become a beta tester). Once the wallet is active, shop your heart out, and when you want to make a purchase, click on the Cyber-Cash icon, select a credit card from your wallet, and hit the "pay" button. Although the system does not provide anonymity, consumers are protected by the usual dispute and limited liability rules that apply to credit card purchase. So far, CyberCash has garnered the attention of about 700,000 users.
WEB http://www.cybercash.com

First Virtual With ordinary email, the First Virtual Payment System promises a secure online transaction method by issuing a VirtualPIN that users submit to merchants instead of their credit card number. To activate a First Virtual Account, users must complete an application and register their credit card number. They are then assigned a VirtualPIN, which acts as a kind of alias for the user's credit card number. First Virtual confirms every use of that PIN by email; the user can reply with "yes" to confirm (and authorize First Virtual to charge the user's credit card), "no" to cancel, or "fraud" to immediately and permanently cancel the VirtualPIN if the user believes it has been stolen. The actual credit card transaction is conducted offline. The system provides anonymity, but it relies on email confirmations, and everyone knows how easy it is to hack email. First Virtual seems to think its "fraud" option is enough to allay consumer fears. Currently, there are about 150,000 VirtualPIN holders.
WEB http://www.fv.com

▼ Commerce resources

Digital Cash and Monetary Freedom A discussion of the differences between true digital cash, paper cash, and "mere encrypted credit card schemes." Outlines the key elements necessary to private digital cash schemes, which (in case you were wondering) include security, anonymity, portability, durability, divisibility, acceptibility, simplicity, and other such sterling qualities.
WEB http://info.isoc.org/HMP/PAPER/I36/abst.html

How is digital cash possible? Are there different kinds? And what is the double-spending problem?

Digital Cash Mini-FAQ For newbies trying to get up to speed, this little FAQ answers the questions: How is digital cash possible? Are there different kinds of digital cash, and what is the double-spending problem? Jim Miller origi-

nally wrote this piece of change for a journalist who was writing about electronic commerce. You'll find it thankfully free of jargony, technical terms.
WEB http://ganges.cs.tcd.ie/mepeirce/Project/Mlists/minifaq.html

Electronic Frontier Foundation Privacy/Online Commerce Archives The advocacy group's collection of articles on secure transactions. Includes articles on DigiCash and double spending.
WEB http://www.eff.org/pub/Privacy/Digital_money

Electronic Payment Schemes With its "three-layered model" for comparing payment schemes ("Policy, Data flow, and Mechanism"), this paper is a bit on the verbose side, but its listing of resources is extensive, and it's nice to know that someone out there is theorizing about all this stuff.
WEB http://www.w3.org/pub/WWW/Payments/roadmap.html

Network Payment Mechanisms and Digital Cash Links to articles, resources, and mailing lists. The section on payment mechanisms designed for the Internet lists links to dozens of methods that have been tried, are still trying, or have just plain stopped trying.
WEB http://ganges.cs.tcd.ie/mepeirce/project.html

Scaleable, Secure Cash Payment for WWW Resources with the PayMe Protocol Set The most secure payment scheme for the Internet is one in which the money being spent cannot be linked with its owner. PayMe is just such a system, combining the best features of Ecash and NetCash to achieve the safest in online payment protocol. The paper presented at this Web site explains the theoretical PayMe system in detail.
WEB http://www.w3.org/pub/Conferences/WWW4/Papers/228

EASY MONEY

Q: How is digital cash possible?

A: Public-key cryptography and digital signatures (both blind and non-blind signatures) make digital cash possible. It would take too long to go into detail how public-key cryptography and digital signatures work. But the basic gist is that banks and customers would have public-key encryption keys. Public-key encryption keys come in pairs. A private key known only to the owner, and a public key, made available to everyone. Whatever the private key encrypts, the public key can decrypt, and vice versa. Banks and customers use their keys to encrypt (for security) and sign (for identification) blocks of digital data that represent money orders. A bank "signs" money orders using its private key and customers and merchants verify the signed money orders using the bank's widely published public key. Customers sign deposits and withdraws using their private key and the bank uses the customer's public key to verify the signed withdraws and deposits.

Q: Are there different kinds of digital cash?

A: Yes. In general, there are two distinct types of digital cash: identified digital cash and anonymous digital cash. Identified digital cash contains information revealing the identity of the person who originally withdrew the money from the bank. Also, in much the same manner as credit cards, identified digital cash enables the bank to track the money as it moves through the economy. Anonymous digital cash works just like real paper cash. Once it is withdrawn from an account, it can be spent without leaving a transaction trail. You create anonymous digital cash by using numbered bank accounts and blind signatures.

—*from Digital Cash Mini-FAQ*

YOUR CREDIT HISTORY: It's the repository for some of your deepest, darkest secrets, but what do you really know about it? Have you ever even seen it? Before you sign up for one more instantly approved department store credit card just to get a 10-percent discount, consider this: Your decision to apply for another piece of plastic may lower your credit rating. Think you'll get low-risk rates for car insurance just because you've never gotten a parking ticket? Well, you might have—if you hadn't let your Visa bill roll over for three months back in 1993. Welcome to the murky and frustrating world of consumer credit reporting. But don't start wringing

In the school of life, your credit history is your report card. Here's how to get straight A's

Don't Know Much About

your hands just yet. An hour or two spent online can get you the information you need to get oriented and on the road to good credit.

The first thing every consumer should know about credit reporting, and one of the only things that everybody agrees on, is that companies offering to repair your credit are a waste of your money. There are hundreds of these companies online, and by and large you should ignore them: The services they provide are either fraudulent or something a consumer can already get for free. The government pamphlet **Credit Repair: Self-Help May Be Best** explains the basics. But what if you really need help resolving personal and credit problems? Call a legitimate non-profit organization like the **Consumer Credit Counseling Service**. What you'll find at these sites, though, is that only time and good behavior can repair damaged credit completely.

What should you do if you don't know what your credit rating is? Well, that's an easy one—request a credit report on yourself. There are dozens of companies that claim to know all about your credit, but there

CASH REGISTER

Credit Repair: Self-Help May Be Best
WEB http://www.ftc.gov/bcp/conline
/pubs/credit/repair.htm

The Consumer Credit Counseling Service
WEB http://www.powersource.com
/cccs/

Equifax
WEB http://www.equifax.com
/consumer/index.html

Experian
WEB http://www.experian.com

Your Credit History?

are only three that really matter: **Equifax**, **Experian** (formerly known as TRW), and TransUnion. These are the only agencies that potential landlords, car dealerships, and credit card companies call to check your credit standing. If you have been denied credit, you are legally entitled to a free copy of your report; otherwise, a fee ranging from $8 to $15 will apply. Experian waives the fee, offering every American one free copy per year regardless of whether or not credit has been denied. And there's even a special bargain for online

CASH REGISTER

Microsoft Network
WEB http://www.msn.com

Sample Credit Report
WEB http://www.experian.com/is
/sample.html

Victims of Consumer Reporting
WEB http://pages.prodigy.com/ID/vcr
/vcr.html

Scoring for Credit
WEB http://www.ftc.gov/bcp/conline
/pubs/credit/scoring.htm

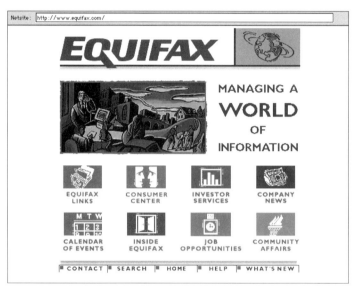

If you can't get credit, Equifax will tell you why
http://www.equifax.com/consumer/index.html

users—members of the **Microsoft Network** can fill out a request for a credit report from Equifax online. The rest of the online and offline world has to use the regular U.S. mail.

So that's how to get your credit report. But besides the history of missed payments and collections, what's in a typical credit report? ID information like name, address, date of birth, marital status, and Social Security number (race, sex, and religious affiliation is not included). Employment data like your present position, length of time at that job, and previous jobs. Public record information like civil suits and judgments, tax liens, and bankruptcy records, or any other legal proceedings that have financial consequence; criminal and non-financial records are not included. And finally, any inquiry information—in other words, a listing of all credit grantors who have requested a copy of your credit file within the last two years. Experian has a **Sample Credit Report** online.

Not everybody is happy about the power that credit reporting firms have over consumers. For example, if most credit firms currently use a 1 to 1,000 scale to calculate consumer credit—the number represents the chance of default by that particular consumer—and banks and other companies often base their decisions on these ratings, even though it's widely considered to

❝ Consumers are legally entitled to know which factors caused their credit rejection. ❞

have little practical meaning. Since consumers are legally entitled to know which factors caused their credit rejection—and since consumer copies of the report rarely include this reductive risk rating—rating systems have become a vexed legal issue. Many civil liberties activists have opposed this rating policy, including the group **Victims of Consumer Reporting**. More information on the credit scoring process is available from the Federal Trade Commission's pamphlet **Scoring for Credit**.

Only time and good behavior can repair bad credit
http://www.powersource.com/cccs/

Location: http://www.powersource.com/cccs/counsel/default.html

Counseling Services

Financial problems can happen to anyone, regardless of income. Those problems can range from minor budgeting difficulties to major concerns that threaten bankruptcy. They may stem from a sudden loss of income, unexpected expenses or uncontrolled spending. Unfortunately, financial difficulties frequently aggravate existing problems and create new ones. People experiencing money troubles are sometimes surprised by how rapidly the situation affects their job performance and personal relationships.

▼ Advice & information

Are You Credit Ready? OK, so it's all just a PR front for American Express. Who cares? It's a great introduction for those who are duffers in the big bad world of credit—and when it comes down to it, most of us are. Are You Credit Ready? is clearly pitched toward the college crowd, but anybody could learn something from the credit glossary—just what is "affinity credit," anyway? There's also an introduction to credit, a guide to credit choices everybody has to make (which credit union is right for you?), and a readable article on how to avoid credit trouble.
WEB http://www.americanexpress.com/student/moneypit/credit/credit.html

Associated Credit Bureaus: Consumer Credit Information What's in a credit report? How accurate is the information? How quickly can mistakes be fixed? Can anyone really repair my credit? The trade association for the consumer credit reporting industry answers many of the most frequently asked consumer questions.

Take courses for credit at the Amex University
http://www.americanexpress.com/student/moneypit/credit/credit.html

Return to the ACB home page to learn about recent changes to the Fair Credit Reporting Act which clarify consumer rights, including the right to challenge the accuracy of any information.
WEB http://www.acb-credit.com/q&a.htm

Cheapskate Monthly The *Cheapskate Monthly* site is essentially an ad for the non-free print publication of the same name, but a visit here might yield some free advice. Mary Hunt, former debtor, passes on tips and financial wisdom for the debt-ridden. You can drool over the horror stories, rejoice over Mary's success story, and, most importantly, view an online sample copy of the magazine itself, a subscription to which costs $16 a year and features dollar-stretching tips, as well as tea-and-sympathy encouragement. The page also tries to sell you books from a line of self-help titles, but take a page from Mary's own book and decline.
WEB http://www.cheapsk8.com

Commercial Transactions Law Cornell Law School has put together a comprehensive outline of major areas in the laws governing commercial transactions—that is, buying stuff—completed with a great set of hypertext links. These laws have everything to do with your credit: There are separate sections for laws dealing with Bankruptcy, Creditor/Debtor issues, and Consumer Credit. Dry it may be, but if you want to find out exactly where you stand on a particular point, this is the place to go.
WEB http://www.law.cornell.edu/topics/topic2.html #commercial transactions

Consumer Education Publications: Consumer Credit This group of Federal Trade Commission pamphlets outlines everything the educated consumer could possibly want to know about self-help techniques for credit repair

and potential credit repair scams: This is solid information, straight from the source. There are 25 brochures online, covering issues from privacy rights to warnings about gold and platinum cards, from general introductions ("Building a Better Credit Record") to more specific analyses ("Women and Credit Histories," "Secured Credit Card Marketing Scams").
WEB http://www.ftc.gov/bcp/conline/pubs/credit/credit.htm

The Consumer Law Page Informational Brochures An independent law firm put together this collection of useful brochures on a whole range of credit-related issues; the brochures are mostly authored by the Federal Trade Commission. "How to Dispute Credit Report Errors" is notable among them—it lets you know what to do when you're refused a loan because someone with your name racked up a giant credit-card bill and fled to the Maldives. Other topics include "Credit and Divorce," "Credit and Older Americans," and "Using Plastic: A Young Adult's Guide to Credit Cards."
WEB http://consumerlawpage.com/brochure/index.html #credit

Consumer World: Credit and Banking Links As directory pages go, Consumer World errs on the side of completeness: Everything's here but the kitchen sink. From Abandoned Bank Accounts to Visa, if it's even remotely connected to credit or banking—we're talking two or three associative leaps here—Consumer World has a link to it. Plus, it flags sites that are new or especially useful. Consumer World also has pages and pages of other resources, including shopping, consumer advocacy, insurance links, and an ATM locator.
WEB http://www.consumerworld.org/pages/money.htm #ban

Credit Crossroads Credit Crossroads is a good example of what's good and bad about the Internet: There's a huge amount of credit information here, but it's not that well-organized, and one can't quite be sure how reliable it is, because it's covered by numerous disclaimers. But why be suspicious? After all, nobody's making money off it. What you will find here is lists, FAQs, free advice, government pamphlets, and Usenet posts relating to all aspects of credit and debt. Poke around—you're bound to learn something.
WEB http://amdream.com/credit/cr_index.htm

Make sense of all those offers that arrive in the mail each day for "pre-approved credit."

Credit FAQ This comprehensive FAQ is garnered from the newsgroup misc.consumers, and covers topics ranging from the differences among various credit cards to understanding credit reports. The FAQ also contains concise instructions for obtaining and revamping your credit report, battling billing errors, and making sure your cards are working for you and not solely for the credit company. For straight, well organized, old-fashioned, heart warming honesty in a field dominated by oily scam artists, you can't beat the FAQ.
URL ftp://rtfm.mit.edu/pub/usenet-by-group/misc.answers/consumer-credit-faq

Credit Libraries You'll find Federal Trade Commission publications addressing issues such as how to get a credit history, repair bad credit, combat false credit reports, and avoid credit scams. The files Credit Card Blocking and Credit Repair Scams help you make

CREDIT MYTH-APPREHENSIONS

1. *Credit bureaus are empowered with some kind of governmental authority.* No, they are not. In fact, they have no authority at all. They are stores, just like any other store, like a hardware store or a clothing store.

2. *Credit bureaus own the information on your credit report.* No, they do not. But you don't own it either. It is owned by the individual merchant who put it there. They also have the power to change it.

3. *Credit bureaus are required to keep derogatory items on your credit report for seven years, or if it is a bankruptcy, for ten years.* Just the opposite is true. Credit bureaus are required by law to automatically remove all derogatory information older than seven years, or in the case of a bankruptcy, older than ten years. In fact, there is no requirement in law that credit bureaus report anything on you at all.

4. *Bankruptcies are impossible to get removed from your credit report.* Bankruptcies come off just like any other derogatory information that is incorrectly reported, obsolete, erroneous, misleading, incomplete, properly challenged, or that cannot be verified.

5. *Information on your credit report cannot be changed.* Of course it can be changed. Remember who owns that information? In fact, the Fair Credit Reporting Acts, both Federal and State, REQUIRE that it be changed or removed if it is not accurate or cannot be verified.

—from American Credit Counseling

sense of all those offers that arrive in the mail each day for "pre-approved credit." Also watch out for those "fix bad credit—remove bankruptcy" offers which seem like dreams come true to those with damaged credit. If you have been wrongly denied credit, learn how to fight back by reading How to Dispute Credit Report Errors, which describes what you need to do to fix it and who to contact for help. Citizens' rights under the Fair Credit Reporting Act, Equality in Lending and Truth in Lending Acts are clearly explained. The file Women and Credit Histories offers useful tips for fiancées, wives, divorcées, and widows on how to get and keep a credit record of their own.
COMPUSERVE *go* conforum→Libraries→Banking & Credit

Credit Scoring—The Impact on Mortgage Loans
The name says it all, doesn't it? This informative article is a quick primer on ways in which the process by which mortgage loans are evaluated and approved is changing—it's becoming much more dependent on the potential borrower's credit rating, the same way car loans already are. C. M. Corky Watts breaks down the situation for you, in refreshingly clear language.
WEB http://www.webspace.com/~watts/score.html

Fair Credit Billing Act: Facts for Consumers
Congress passed the Fair Credit Billing Act (FCBA) in 1975 to help consumers resolve disputes with creditors and to ensure fair handling of credit accounts. Basically, it protects you and your credit rating in the event that something crops up on a bill that you think shouldn't be there, like a purchase made on a stolen credit card. This neat, concise little document fills you in on what rights the FCBA gives you, and how you can exercise them.
WEB http://www.webcom.com/~lewrose/brochures/fcba.html

FAQ About Credit Experian, one of the major credit reporting companies, maintains this page, which provides answers to questions like, "How are credit granting decisions made?" and "How does divorce affect a person's credit?" There's also a clear, concise explanation of the Fair Credit Reporting Act of 1971, which states that you can access someone's personal credit history only if you have a legitimate business need, and that you must also have the consent of the individual whose credit report you're requesting. The full text of the act is here as well.
WEB http://www.experian.com/is/isdiv.html

Managing Credit and Debt You'll find quite a bit of advice and information here, mostly in the form of brief, informative articles. The focus is on credit cards—which ones to get, how to use them safely, why debit cards can be more useful—but you'll also find significant resources on other topics, like bankruptcy and credit repair. These resources are all part of the MoneyWhiz area, which also offers weekly chats (including one on credit and debt), plus columns and Q&A articles. Oh, and they also have cheesy cartoons.
AMERICA ONLINE *keyword* moneywhiz→Finance Center→ Managing Credit and Debt

▼ Credit counseling

American Consumer Credit Counseling, Inc.
ACCC is a non-profit organization that offers confidential debt counseling and education. Its site is a well-meaning but extremely introductory resource for information about credit-related issues ("Did you know that: Almost anything can be purchased with credit, including college tuition, dental expenses, even groceries?" Unless you live under a rock, you probably did.) A brief newsletter appears here regularly.
WEB http://www.consumercredit.com/

In debt? Give yourself credit for getting help
http://members.aol.com/DebtRelief/index.html

American Credit Counseling It's not abundantly clear who or what American Credit Counseling actually is, but they'll assemble a credit report on you if you fill out their online form and give them your credit card number. While it's probably a better idea to get this kind of information straight from one of the major credit monitoring agencies, ACC has quite a few useful resources on its site, including ten myths about credit and an FAQ.
WEB http://www.firstconsumer.com/

Bankruptcy Alternatives, Debtor's Options According to Mory Brenner, Attorney at Law, many attorneys automatically put their debtor clients into bankruptcy without looking at all the available options. Out of the goodness of his heart, Brenner has put together a set of FAQs with information about workouts and other options for those who owe. He's also got a set of links to other credit counseling sites.
WEB http://apocalypse.berkshire.net/~mkb/

Center for Debt Management Family Debt Arbitration and Counseling Services, Inc. is the friendly organization behind this page of resources: The name of its game is debt counseling, creditor negotiations and debt management services for individuals

and families who are over-extended and/or contemplating bankruptcy. The FDACS site on the Web is a kind of online encyclopedia of credit and debt information: The highlights are a comprehensive library (literally, a library) of pamphlets, plus centers for debt counseling and debt management.
WEB http://members.aol.com/DebtRelief/index.html

Consumer Credit Counseling Service The Consumer Credit Counseling Service (CCCS) is a free program that does what it says: It helps people deal with their debt problems. The CCCS is not a government agency, it's a non-profit community action organization, run by responsible citizens like yourself. This site, which is maintained by a local branch of the CCCS in Houston, is wonderfully helpful and comprehensive, including question-and-answer columns by expert debt counselors, and a thorough listing of links and offline CCCS resources. Topics include Credit Bureaus and Credit Reports, Dealing with Creditors, Credit Rejection, Choosing a Credit Card, and more. For help with debt online, start here.
WEB http://www.powersource.com/cccs/

Getting out of debt shouldn't put you deeper in the hole
http://www.cccsdc.org/index.html

Consumer Credit Counseling Service of Washington, D.C. A number of local chapters of CCCS maintain useful informational Web pages, but only this one has dancing pyramids with eyes on it. It's also got quite a few credit management resources. There's an interactive fitness quiz, a "personal inventory" page that helps you evaluate your budget and your net worth, and a copy of the CCCS Credit Guide, which makes good—if slightly dry—reading. The Budgeting in Six Easy Steps section includes a handy expense sheet that you can print out.
WEB http://www.cccsdc.org/index.html

Debt Counselors of America The Debt Counselors of America offer to retrieve your credit records from major rating agencies and review them with you for $50. Nowhere on the site do they inform you that the credit agencies are legally required to let you review your credit history once a year at little or no cost—a DCA spokesman said they inform callers of this fact. This makes DCA's collection of tips on recovering from debt seem like a little less than the straight dope. The site does have a page of testimonials from people who say they've been helped by DCA's services.
WEB http://www.dca.org

Debtor's Anonymous Mailing List Share your experiences and your support with other people who are struggling with debt. Warning: "D.A. is run by recovering debtors, and as such suffers from many of the same problems as its members. Be patient when dealing with them."
EMAIL majordomo@toto.com ✍ *Type in message body:* subscribe solvency

Getting Out of Debt "The largest dangers facing the credit user are overuse and misuse." This and other obvious-but-true nuggets of credit wisdom are featured on this page of credit advice, aimed particularly at people who have trouble with credit card abuse. Sponsored by the BankCard Holders of America, it describes strategies for managing and eradicating credit card debt, and it explains some of the techniques, programs, and other resources the BHA offers its members.

WEB http://www.epn.com/bha/out-debt.htm

National Credit Counseling Services
NCCS is a national non-profit organization that dispenses advice and counseling to people who are having trouble with credit and debt. It can also take on the management of your debts for you, distributing payments to creditors and generally setting things in good order. The Web is a natural tool for groups like NCCS, and this site makes excellent use of the its potential. You can take a confidential credit evaluation quiz here, and read articles on a range of credit-related topics, like bankruptcy, credit cards, and IRS audits.

WEB http://www.nccs.org/Welcome.html

Recovery Forum—Compulsive Debt "Eligible for credit on my own for the first time in my life... I get all panicky whenever I use any of it... of course I have good reason to... I'm pretty well maxed out now for Christmas..." Sound familiar? You might find friends here, at this supportive message area for people who have real trouble dealing with debt. The message board is not affiliated with Debtors Anonymous, although many people here go to DA meetings.

COMPUSERVE *go* recovery→Browse Messages→ Compulsive Debt

United Debt Counseling, Inc. UDC is a not-for-profit Inc., dedicated to rescuing people from debt without resorting to overly drastic measures: "While other companies will want to cut up your credit cards, we understand that credit is a part of our lives and we all need to

WHEN GOOD SPOUSES HAVE BAD CREDIT

Dear Susan,
My domestic partner declared bankruptcy under Chapter 7 approximately four years ago. How will this affect our ability to obtain a mortgage for a home in the next few months? My credit is good, but my income alone won't qualify for a mortgage.
—Prospective Homebuyer

Dear Prospective,
Creditors are most interested in the last 24 months of a person's pay history. Since your partner's bankruptcy occurred four years ago, it shouldn't affect your ability to obtain a mortgage although the interest rate may be higher. He/she should be prepared to explain the circumstances of the bankruptcy. Don't forget that the lender must take into consideration any liens, judgments, debt ratios, previous foreclosures and employment history. Also, be prepared for a down payment which will vary according to the lending program you use. If there are Community Homebuyer Programs in your area, plan to attend one to obtain valuable home-buying information. Best wishes.
—Susan

—from Consumer Credit Counseling Service

obtain and use it wisely." In other words, you may be addicted, but that doesn't necessarily mean you have to go cold turkey. It's hard to trust anybody who offers to help you to "SAVE $ NOW," but UDC has some sound advice on its page.

WEB http://www.800web.com/udc/

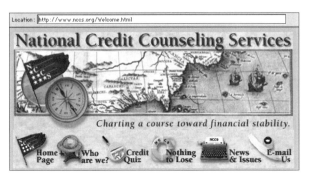

Discover the world of solid credit
http://www.nccs.org/Welcome.html

Credit repair

Banking and Credit Library Here you'll find a grab-bag of documents and shareware for helping you handle any number of different credit issues. For those who are not adverse to using the credit laws to their own advantage, a user has uploaded "Ten Steps to Improving Your Credit." This is trench warfare strategy for those with bad credit histories. For example: "Since credit rating companies have only 30 days to verify a bad risk incident, keep questioning them until they miss the deadline."
COMPUSERVE *go* conforum→Libraries→Banking & Credit Libraries Ten Steps to Improving Your Credit

Bankruptcy is a Ten-Year Mistake This brief but forceful diatribe outlines some good reasons why even if things look black, filing for bankruptcy may not be your best option. The page also links to a service called Attorneyfind, which can provide you with a list reputable lawyers who handle cases dealing with credit and debt.
WEB http://www.attorneyfind.com/bankruptcy.html

Clean Up Your Credit Report Yourself A California branch of the Consumer Credit Counseling Service maintains this simple but hard-hitting list of steps you can take to get control over your credit report and clean it up. Steps like "Contact your creditors" and "Document everything" seem a little obvious, but they're undeniably good sense. Most of the advice is tailored to specific predicaments: "what to do if information should have 'aged off'"; "what to do if someone is using your ID to obtain credit"; "what to do if you have duplicate information"; and so on.
WEB http://www.cccsebay.org/cleanup.html

Credit Repair Scams This page is a vital tool if you're looking for help with your credit on the Web. The first thing you'll notice when looking into credit agencies online is how stridently everybody promises to cure what ails you; learn to know what's possible and what's obviously fraudulent. This page is part of a larger site called the Advertising Law Page, which includes hundreds of useful brochures, including titles on obtaining business credit and choosing a credit card that's right for you.
WEB http://www.webcom.com/~lewrose/brochures /creditrepair.html

This is trench warfare strategy for those with bad credit histories.

Electronic Credit Repair Kit Many caveats and legal disclaimers accompany what is actually a refreshingly excellent product in a field where scams abound. It was created by Michael Kielsky, "not a lawyer," who collects $30 a pop if you decide to write to him for a hard copy—though you can view it on the Web for free. The repair kit itself is just a no-nonsense batch of good sense, made up of simply presented information about credit and credit agencies, designed to arm the average debtor against his or her natural foe. You'll also find useful items like effective sample letters to credit agencies, and links to legal and credit wisdom.

WEB http://www.primenet.com/~kielsky/credit.htm

Managing Your Debts A fellow named Richard Rogers created this extensive debt-management guide completely free of charge. It's a practical text-only booklet on getting your finances in order, beginning with a mini-glossary of credit card terms, moving through the process of developing a debt-reduction plan, and finishing with recommendations of where else to go for help. Considering that Rogers pulled this guide together himself, free of charge, it's an impressive and useful resource. Also included are some sobering statistics: "The number of people seeking debt counseling help are at their highest levels since the early 1970s. The average person has about eight credit cards with outstanding balances of $20,000 or more."

WEB http://members.gnn.com/rrogers/finance /ccdebt.htm

Victims of Credit Reporting Everyone's heard a credit report horror story—the responsible person mistaken for someone with an abysmal credit history, the computer glitch that changed a mortgage refinancing to a bankruptcy, and so on. These poor unfortunates have a defender in Victims of Credit Reporting, or VCR. VCR is an international advocacy group that opposes the entire credit reporting industry, as well as the Federal Trade Commission.

WEB http://pages.prodigy.com/ID/vcr/vcr.html

Your Money—Your Credit History Jane Bryant Quinn, one of the most sensible, easy-to-understand personal finance columnists in the magazine world, wrote this article for *Good Housekeeping* magazine. It outlines what's in a credit report, who can see it (including

CREDIT CARD TERMS TO KNOW

PERIODIC RATE: The periodic rate, sometimes called the monthly interest rate, is the interest rate you are charged each month. The periodic rate is calculate by dividing the Annual Percentage Rate (APR) by 12 since there are 12 months in a year. Accuracy is important. Always carry out the periodic rate to at least 5 decimal places.

Example: 17.9% divided by 12 = 1.491667%
Convert to decimal: (divided by 100) = 0.014916

The periodic rate is converted from a percentage to a decimal so it can be used in calculations

MONTHLY FINANCE CHARGE: This is the amount of interest that accumulates on the outstanding balance during the billing month. Basically it is the fee you pay for the privilege of borrowing money . The Monthly Finance Charge is calculated by multiplying the Periodic Rate by the outstanding balance.

Example: 0.0149167 X $2,500 = $37.29
This would be the Monthly Finance Charge for the first month. It changes each month depending on the outstanding balance.

MONTHLY PAYMENT PERCENTAGE: This is how credit card issuers figure the Minimum Monthly Payment for each statement. This information can be found in the "Cardholders Agreement", which you get when you receive your cards or if there is a change in policy. It is also included as part of the fine print on each months bill. Typically this percentage ranges from 1/25th to 1/60th of the outstanding balance.

—*from Managing Your Debts*

insurers and potential employers), and what constitutes a bad report. Quinn helpfully lists times when you should request a copy of your credit report—such as when you're separating from a spouse, after you've canceled credit cards, and after you've successfully disputed a charge. Naturally, you should request a copy of your report if you've been turned down for any type of credit. Under those circumstances, the credit report is always free. (Otherwise, there may be a small fee, even if you go through the three major bureaus.)
WEB http://homearts.com/gh/betterw/03bwjqfl.htm

▼ Credit companies

Credit Management Information & Support Though it's primarily an information resource for people in the credit business, this site can be useful for consumers who are interested in the larger context in which their own credit report is but one tiny data-point. The most interesting feature here is Creditworthy News, an email newsletter that covers credit-related business news both in the U.S. and abroad.
WEB http://www.creditworthy.com/

Credit Union National Association What's a credit union? It's a kind of cooperative bank owned

and controlled by the people who use its services. More than 70 million Americans are members of credit unions. The Credit Union National Association provides background on the history of credit unions, what they can do for you, and how to find one in your neighborhood. For an extra thrill, download some vintage footage (and sounds) from the national credit union archives.
WEB http://www.cuna.org

Equifax One of the big three credit reporting agencies, along with Experian and Trans-Union. Some companies claim to be able to give you the lowdown on your reputation as a debtor, but if somebody's seriously considering taking a risk on you, they'll call one of these three. Equifax's helpful online consumer center includes a section titled "How You Can Get a Copy of Your Credit Report." While the typical procedure involves either snail mail or a phone call, Equifax also offers Microsoft Network members the option of requesting their credit reports online.
WEB http://www.equifax.com/

Experian Experian (formerly TRW, Inc.), one of the big three credit-reporting outfits, processes 43 million pieces of credit-related data every day, and some of that data is yours. Experian is the only credit-reporting company that will send you your credit report free of charge once a year, although for confidentiality reasons they won't do it by email—snail mail only. The Experian Web site features a helpful FAQ, which includes a sample credit report.
WEB http://www.experian.com

Fair, Isaac Consumer Credit Information The developer of the most commonly-used scoring models for personal credit ratings has provided this interesting guide to a procedure that determines the fates of millions of people

The path to obtaining your credit profile
http://www.equifax.com/

and their money. While it's true that scoring systems such as this one make instant credit approval possible, the consumer's inability to find out exactly what his or her assigned number is, or which factors were taken into account to obtain that number, remains one of the biggest bones of contention among civil liberties activists.

WEB http://www.fairisaac.com/consumer/consumer.html

▼ Credit cards

The Credit Card Network If you're interested in getting a new credit card, and you're serious about finding the one that's right for you, the Credit Card Network may be for you. It can also help you if you're having trouble dealing with the credit cards you already have. It can also give you shareware for managing your credit card bills, and link you to sites where you can apply for cards online. Get the picture? This site pulls together an amazing variety of resources from all over the Internet.

WEB http://www.creditnet.com/

12 Credit Card Secrets Banks Don't Want You to Know If you're looking for something to get mad about, this list, maintained by the Massachusetts Executive Office of Consumer Affairs and Business Regulation, should be enough to make your blood boil. Interest backdating, double fees on cash advances, two-cycle billing, misleading monthly minimums—it's a hall of shame featuring all the deceitful, misleading, mealy-mouthed, two-faced strategies banks have for milking millions out of their credit card customers. If you learn one thing from this site, it's that banks are not your friends. Elsewhere on this site you'll find resources relating to consumer rights in Massachusetts, as well as other informational brochures like "How to Get a Copy of Your Credit Report."

WEB http://www.consumer.com/consumer/CREDITC.html

CREDIT CARD SECRETS

I. INTEREST BACKDATING. Most card issuers charge interest from the day a charge is posted to your account if you don't pay in full monthly. But, some charge interest from the date of purchase, days before they have even paid the store on your behalf! REMEDY: Find another card issuer, or always pay your bill in full by the due date.

2. TWO-CYCLE BILLING. Issuers which use this method of calculating interest, charge two months worth of interest for the first month you failed to pay off your total balance in full. This issue arises only when you switch from paying in full to carrying a balance from month to month. REMEDY: Switch issuers or always pay your balance in full.

3. THE RIGHT TO SET OFF. If you have money on deposit at a bank, and also have your credit card there, you may have signed an agreement when you opened the deposit account which permits the bank to take those funds if you become delinquent on your credit card. REMEDY: Bank at separate institutions, or avoid delinquencies.

4. FEES ARE NEGOTIABLE. You may be paying up to $50 a year or more as an annual fee on your credit card. You may also be subject to finance charges of over I8 percent. REMEDY: If you are a good customer, the bank may be willing to drop the annual fee, and reduce the interest rate—you only have to ask! Otherwise, you can switch issuers to a lower-priced card.

—*from 12 Credit Card Secrets Banks Don't Want You to Know*

Tightwads online have tips to help you keep your expenses down and your chin up

D O YOU SAVE foil wrappers? Reuse sandwich bags? Smash soap scraps together to get a longer-lasting bath bar? If you can admit to any of these habits or are struck by the genius of their frugality, you are not alone. There's a community of misers on the Net—one of the last places on earth where information is free (or at least the cost of your monthly service provider). Maximize your penny-pinching skills on the Internet by following these simple suggestions guaranteed to save you $500 in the first month.

Proud to be a

Tight-wadding

"What is it?" and "Does it hurt?" are probably your first two questions. Tight-wadding has emerged as a culturally acceptable phenomenon, due in part to the generous efforts of Amy Dacyczyn, author and creator of *The Tightwad Gazette* book series and newsletter. Several years ago, Dacyczyn spearheaded a movement to cut costs in her own family when saving to buy a house. Her ideas were so successful, she decided to pass the wisdom on by publishing a monthly newsletter. Amy's philosophy on saving money is basically that it's a round-the-clock job. She insists the only way to save money is to ask yourself the question "Do I really need this?" before every purchase. Even before buying a soda on the street, she suggests considering if spending the money now is more satisfying than the greater goal, especially when you've got perfectly good sodas at home. As of December 1996, however, Amy's newsletter will be defunct, forcing devoted fans to reminisce on unofficial fan pages about leftovers for lunch and the joys of library books. But don't despair, there will always be tightwads out there—check out **Tight-Wadding with Doris O'Connell** and **Julie's Frugal Tips**.

Penny Pincher

Talk to Your Neighbors

Get comfortable swapping, trading, and bartering—information, that is. Scan newsgroups for tips and secrets from someone who's already been there. Expecting a new baby? Want to know the low-down on diapers? Hear the latest on the cloth vs. plastic debate from budget-savvy parents at **misc.consumers.frugal-living**. Personal Web pages can sometimes be the most useful resource for stretching your dollar. **The Pennypincher**, created by a crafty housewife and mother is a cost-cutter's dream. The site offers everything from

CASH REGISTER

The Unofficial Tightwad Gazette Fan Club Home Page
WEB http://users.aol.com/maryfou/tightwad.html

Tight-Wadding with Doris O'Connell
WEB http://pages.prodigy.com/Tightwadding-frugal-living

Julie's Frugal Tips
WEB http://www.brightok.net/~neilmayo/

USENET misc.consumers.frugal-living

The Pennypincher
WEB http://home.sprynet.com/sprynet/Thrifty

Virtual Flea Market
WEB http://www.HUB.ofthe.NET/~zachd/fleal.htm

Ian's Fabulous Free Archives
WEB http://www.fabfreebies.com/

Totally Free Stuff!
WEB http://adhere.on.ca/free

FORGET THE DRAMAMINE

Wow. I've felt guilty for a long time for reading so many great tips, but hardly ever having one to post. Here's one you can try if you get motion sickness. (I was told this originally came from Dear Abby.) I tried it on a plane and felt nary a twinge—I wish I'd met the woman who told it to me on the boat ride TO the island, instead of on the way back after I was already doped up with dramamine. That would have been the true test. However, I usually feel a least a little nauseated on planes, and like I said—nothing. Cover your navel with scotch tape. That's it! I don't know how this works, and I'd love to hear the theories. Test it out—tell me how it goes!

P.S. I also don't know how it would work with outies.

—*from misc.consumers .frugal-living*

Ian's not only frugal, he's free
http://www.fabfreebies.com/

household tips, such as recipes for making your own window cleaner to business advice, such as getting the most out of tax returns.

The Free Things in Life are Best

Never, ever turn down something that's free. The Net is filled with sites that offer free stuff. What's the catch? Sometimes your name and address are added to a list for "People Who Want Superfluous Mail Sent to Their House." And sometimes, it's just free. At **Ian's Fabulous Freebies Archive** you can peruse virtual aisles of goodies for just the right free item. Or go to **Totally Free Stuff!** for a list of freebies, which is updated daily.

If it goes against your grain to get something for absolutely nothing, online tag sales such as the **Virtual Flea Market** can be great places for finding bargains. If you don't mind used merchandise or are looking for vintage pieces, hunt them down online. A bonus: You'll never have trouble finding a parking space again.

▼ Starting points

The Bag Lady's Cart Full of Abe Pinching Links Got a penchant for pinching a penny? Well, drop into the Bag Lady's virtual cart for more budget links than you can shake a coupon book at! She's compiled a list of literally hundreds of sites in different frugal categories including bartering, free stuff, and recycling. She also has a special area of links dedicated to weddings on a budget.
WEB http://www.angelfire.com/ia/baglady

The Cheapskate Monthly Mary Hunt had a terrible problem with overspending—maxing out dozens of credit cards and bouncing checks at the bank her husband managed—but she overcame all that, and now she publishes *The Cheapskate Monthly*. At the Cheapskate site, you'll be able to read her success and horror stories, preview a copy of the newsletter, and of course, subscribe to the newsletter or buy Hunt's books. By the way, "cheapskate" need not have negative connotations. It is defined here as "one who saves consistently, gives generously, and never spends more than he or she has."
WEB http://www.cheapsk8.com

The Dollar Stretcher Easy-to-use, honest, and well-organized, the Dollar Stretcher is a great column that penny pinchers worldwide should read. Written by Floridian Gary Foreman, the site covers many aspects of family finance, including auto-theft prevention. The archive displays a variety of topics from making your own natural cosmetics to planning kids' birthday parties on a small tab. You can sign up for a free subscription via email to The Dollar Stretcher. This site has won a number of Net awards, and it's no surprise, since the information supplied here is so universally practical.
WEB http://www.stretcher.com/dollar

MAKE YOUR OWN PLAYDOUGH

KOOL-AID PLAYDOUGH RECIPE:
2 1/2 cups flour, 2 Tablespoons oil, 2 cups boiling water, 1/2 cup salt, 2 packs of unsweetened Kool-aid (same flavor)
Mix all ingredients together. Your choice of Kool-aid will give the color and the smell. Must be boiling water or the consistency won't be correct.

REGULAR PLAYDOUGH:
4 cups flour, 1/4 cup powdered Tempera, 1/4 cup salt, 1 1/2 cups water, 1 Tablespoon oil
Mix together flour, powdered paint and salt. Mix water and oil. Gradually stir water and oil mixture into flour mixture. Knead the mixture as you add the liquid. Add more water if too stiff, more flour if too sticky. Let the children help with measuring and mixing. (You can add color by adding it to the cold water before mixing it with the flour.

ALUM PLAYDOUGH:
2 cups flour, 1 cup salt, 2 Tablespoons alum, 1 cup water, 2 tablespoons oil, liquid food coloring
Pour dry ingredients into a large pan. Stir together to mix well. Stir oil and food coloring into the water. Pour liquid into the dry ingredients while mixing, squeezing, and kneading the dough. If too sticky, add more flour. Keeps best in a covered container in refrigerator.

—from 25 Frugal Tips for Families

Frugal Corner If you're online and interested in saving money, you should definitely have a bookmark for Frugal Corner and visit it often. It's the Web site for misc.consumers.frugal-living and was inspired by the *Tightwad Gazette*. The main goal here is "to minimize

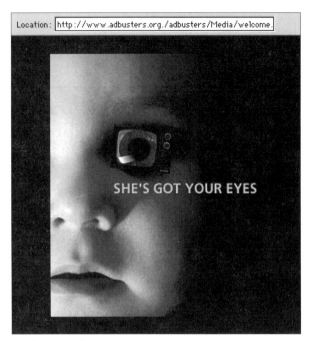

Location: http://www.adbusters.org./adbusters/Media/welcome.

SHE'S GOT YOUR EYES

...and your nose for money
http://www.adbusters.org./adbusters/main.html

your spending of money and consumption of products in ways that allow you to be happy and not feel deprived." Divided into several sections, including frugal living and consumer resources, mailing lists, and newsgroups, the Frugal Corner is a key site for those trying to live life on a shoestring budget.
WEB http://www.best.com/~piner/frugal.html

Frugal Living Book List Part of Tightwadmama's homesteading page, this is a compilation list of dozens of books and articles on maintaining a frugal lifestyle. Consider it a budget bibliography, but take a tip from the tightwads themselves and don't buy the books—borrow them from the library!
WEB http://pages.prodigy.com/ASCD29A/books.htm

Frugal Living Resources @ IGC EcoNet's Frugal Living Resources page mostly features the ubiquitous links to other Web sites, including

important information on how to live a more conservative lifestyle. The Frugal Living Tip File consists of posts from the misc.consumers.frugal-living newsgroup. Specific advice ranges from suggestions on battling dry skin ("Try bathing instead of showering. Put oil in the water. I use inexpensive Sav-On drugstore oil. Don't spring for expensive brands; they're all basically mineral oil.") to opinions on cordless tools ("Avoid them. They are sold to those who know no better.").
WEB http://www.igc.apc.org/frugal

Kathy's Cyber Page Kathy's site is a simple one that's most useful for her supportive attitude. She's assembled a page of links to her favorite Web sites which include a number of freebie pages. There's also a guide for developing a frugal/tightwad debt-free lifestyle that she created based on her own experiences.
WEB http://pages.prodigy.com/frugal-tightwad-debtfree

misc.consumers.frugal-living "Can you lengthen the life of men's underwear by line drying instead of putting the underwear in the dryer?" If you've ever had a question about the art of saving money, here's the place to ask it. You'll find suggestions regarding ants, cats, toys, cars, weddings, and just about anything else a consumer is interested in. A number of posters engage in an activity called "dumpster diving," where they pick up other people's trash—either from households or stores—and use it. (Dumpster diving is also a technique used by private detectives, so if anyone asks, you can always say you're on a case.) Hints abound, including ways to salvage leftover mashed potatoes.
USENET misc.consumers.frugal-living

The Unofficial Tightwad Gazette Fan Club Home Page Fans celebrating Amy Dacyczyn's now-defunct newsletter for saving money have gathered on the Web to share tips and success

stories. The site's creator, who was able to secure a house deposit by using Tightwad tips, lists some of her favorites, including "Get your books from the library," "Change to a vegetarian or semi-vegetarian diet," and "Don't go to first-run movies at prime time."
WEB http://users.aol.com/maryfou/tightwad.html

▼ Tight-wadding tips

Battern Family Tightwadding Tight-wadding, according to the Battern family is "an art form. It is a way of life. It is saving money." Read some of the Batterns' tips, and you're sure to pick up some innovative ideas. Ever heard of TVP? It's a texturized vegetable protein that serves as a cost-efficient replacement for meat. The Batterns have also included a number of links to cost-efficient cooking sites. Now that's supercalifrugalistic.
WEB http://www.arc.net/Users/batfam/tightwad.htm

Bet you didn't know that you can refresh faded black clothing by adding coffee grounds to your rinse cycle!

Frugal Living Although this bulletin board is part of Dialog at Parentsplace.Com, it's not just for those with little tykes running around the den. All frugal ideas, questions, and tips are welcomed at this friendly bulletin board. Recipes for toffee, suggestions for toy purchasing, and gift ideas were recently shared.
WEB http://www.parentsplace.com:8000/dialog/get/frugal.html

Frugal Living Online Go with the F.L.O.! Formerly Leah's Odds and Ends, this Web site focuses on frugality with ideas on crafts and gift-giving. There's a great section devoted to alternative cleansers and laundry tips; bet you didn't know that you can refresh faded black clothing by adding coffee grounds to your rinse cycle!
WEB http://wwwl.kingston.net/~goju/leah

Frugal Tip of the Week Want a simple way to be a bit more frugal? Visit this site to pick up Julie's tips of the week, most of which are submitted by fellow netsurfers who have their own little ways of cutting back costs. Check out the previous tips for an extensive list of ways to hold on to your cash.
WEB http://www.brightok.net/~neilmayo • http://sooner.brightok.net/~neilmayo

The Frugal Gazette Here's a newsletter dedicated to life, liberty, and the pursuit of frugality. The site is effectively an ad trying to sell subscriptions—can you blame them for trying to make a buck?—but you can glean a number of sample recommendations for free. Reduce the interest on your credit card. Dress your child for less than $100 a year. Save 50 percent on over-the-counter medicines. If you like what you see, request a free sample of *The Frugal Gazette* (a year's subscription will cost you about $16).
WEB http://www.frugalgazette.com

The Pennypincher Nikki is a Seattle housewife with three sons who all drive used cars. Her helpful Web page includes hints on everything from gift-giving to automobiles. She even talks about the benefits of a digital piano over a baby grand! There's also kitchen advice and recipes, as well as Nikki's favorite inspirational quotes.
WEB http://home.sprynet.com/sprynet/Thrifty

 Tight-Wadding with Doris O'Connell
Doris O'Connell is also known as Tightwadmama, and it's really no

MIX CAREFULLY

If you decide to make your own cleaners, use and store them safely. While the ingredients in home-made cleaners are safer, they are not all nontoxic. Remember these guidelines: Be careful mixing chemicals. Some chemicals, such as chlorine bleach and ammonia, produce a toxic gas when mixed together. Do not mix more than a month's supply at a time. The chemicals may lose their effectiveness. Mix solutions in a well-ventilated area. Store all cleaning solutions out of reach of children. Store solutions in unused, store-bought containers. Use permanent storage containers that will be put in a permanent location. Never put them in old food containers. Chemicals may interact with residue from the original contents or the container may be mistaken for a food or beverage. Label containers carefully. This is especially important if other people in your home clean or have access to the cleaners.

—from Household Cleaning Products

surprise. She explains that "Modern Tightwads are not scrooge-like characters. We are living frugally and cutting expenses in areas that are not important to us in our variableexpenses, so that we have the $'s for the things that are important to us." Her frugal living site is more extensive than the rest; it covers the usual household and credit topics, but also includes information on paying for college and investing. There's even a budget seminar that you can download! Save even more by subscribing to Doris's Tightwad/Frugal electronic newsletter. It's free!
WEB http://pages.prodigy.com/Tightwadding-frugal -living

Tips for Frugal Living Stretch that dollar bill! This no-frills site delivers on its promise: to share tips for frugal living. There are only a handful of suggestions, but the site's creator promises frequent additions. A sample: "Try generic. Many times, generic is just as good as name brand, but you don't pay for fancy labeling or advertising." If you simply must have your White Cloud toilet paper or your Kellogg's Special K, then you may at least want to consider "[adding] up the cost of drinking tea or pop when dining out" to make you more conscious of spending.
WEB http://sooner.brightok.net/~trader/frugal.htm

Tips to Save Money This is a simple list of helpful suggestions and resources for those trying to hold on to some of their hard-earned money. For example, "Save your fresh milk for drinking; use powdered milk for baking and cooking."
WEB http://www.spots.ab.ca/~ics/sav.html

25 Frugal Ideas for Families Compiled by Stephanie Brown from various resources, including other areas of Parentsplace.com, this handy list covers a number of ways any family can save money. The list is comprised mostly of make-it-yourself tips (playdough, baby wipes) and general suggestions (quit smoking, breastfeed).
WEB http://www.parentsplace.com/readroom/articles /frugal.html

▼ Household hints

CTW: Household Hints Sponsored by the *Sesame Street* portion of the Children's Television Workshop Web site, this helpful spot features several articles for parents trying to keep their expenses down. Cutting corners by mail-order shopping, environmental protection in the home (reuse, reduce, recycle!), and hand-me-down clothing are some of the topics addressed in an easy-to-understand manner.
WEB http://www.ctw.org/TOPICS/ti0l03.htm

Do It YourSelf HQ If you fancy yourself a Tim Allen type, this site is calling you home. Money-saving ideas and online resources for home improvement, maintenance and repair are collected all in one place, which is probably more than you can say for your tools. You can search for category-specific information, browse at the bookstore, or check in at the new products page.
WEB http://pwp.usa.pipeline.com/~sivprob

Household Cleaning Products Dr. Frances C. Graham, an extension housing specialist at Mississippi State University, has written a guide to all the types of cleaners you use in your home. For example, alkalies "are soluble salts that are effective in removing dirt without excessive rubbing." There's lots of useful information here, including the fact that laundry detergents can be used for housecleaning. "Detergents loosen dirt, and if complex soluble phosphates (called 'builders') are added to a detergent, they will remove oily dirt. If a builder is added, the cleaning product is marked 'heavy duty' or 'all-purpose.'" Check out the guides to making your own household cleaning products, including oven cleaner.
WEB http://www.ces.msstate.edu/pubs/isl436.htm

sci.electronics.repair FAQ You'll be shocked by all the resources available for fixing home electronics. At the FAQ for the sci.electronics.repair newsgroup, you can find information on repairing CD players, CD-ROM drives, mircowave ovens, and even lawn mowers. So, if you're going to do it yourself and save on repair costs, visit this site. Then read the safety precautions, or you might really get shocked!
WEB http://www.paranoia.com/~filipg/HTML/REPAIR

Stain Removal Guide You may need to buy such basic supplies as acetone, amyl acetate (banana oil), crystal salt, rust remover, turpen-

---

MAKING THE MOST OF KIDS' CLOTHES

- Buy unisex garments.
- Avoid items that clearly indicate gender.
- Keep clothes clean.
- Prevent food stains by making sure that small children wear bibs during meals. Treat soiled items with presoak stain remover or detergent before throwing them into the hamper.
- Don't let children play outside in dress clothes.
- Make repairs right away.
- As soon as you notice rips, holes, or loose buttons, set aside time to fix them.
- Vary your child's wardrobe.
- Items that are worn too often wear out sooner. To ensure equal usage, periodically move clothes from the bottom of your child's drawer to the top.

—*from CTW: Household Hints*

---

tine, and white vinegar to perform some of the techniques suggested here, but at least you won't have to throw your favorite shirt into the trash. Save money (and your wardrobe) by checking in at this site the next time you've spilled milk, or any one of dozens of substances, on your precious threads.
WEB http://www.ces.msstate.edu/pubs/publ400.htm

▼ Buying cheap

Deals of the Day A plain-paper copier for $211? A digital thermometer for just $5.99? Have these retailers gone mad? No, it's just another day of bargains courtesy of IMALL. If you don't want to be tempted by the regularly priced merchandise available at the IMALL, subscribe to the Deals of the Day mailing list and get the skinny by email.

EMAIL majordomo@imall.com ✍ *Type in message body:* subscribe deals-of-the-day
WEB http://www.imall.com/dotd/dotd.shtml

The Internet Flea Market It calls itself the greatest little market on the Internet, and even if it's not the best, it's certainly the most active. Based in the United Kingdom, the Internet Flea Market has several sections, where you can find classified posts from people around the world selling all types of items. There are many topics to choose from, and for example, when you enter the market stalls, you can choose ads by country or by dozens of categories, including books, fashion, and toys.
WEB http://www.compulink.co.uk/~internetfleamarket/

Internet Resale Directory If you're ever looking for information on a flea market in Mobile, Ala., this is the place to find it. The Internet Resale Directory lists flea markets, thrift stores, antique vendors, consignment shops, and liquidators all across the country. There are even some listings for Australia, Canada, the United Kingdom, and the West Indies. But there's more than just listings available at the Internet Resale Directory. You can also find dozens of links to money-saving Web

Low prices for those with high tastes
http://www.pricesmart.com/PSINDEX.HTM

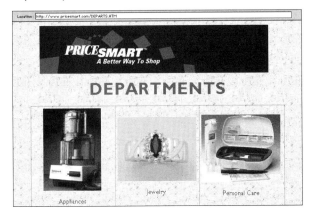

sites and a classifieds section.
WEB http://www.secondhand.com/index.html

Lee's Flea Market Guide Hardly a comprehensive listing of all the flea markets in the United States, but a good start nonetheless. If you're traveling, or looking for different bargain markets where you live, it might be worthwhile to check this site first. If a favorite market that you know of is not listed, go ahead and add it to the site's database. There's also some wholesale information available, as well as a group of links to more flea market, bargain, and wholesale sites online.
WEB http://www.bargain-mall.com/fleas.htm

PriceSmart Organized by the Ralph's Supermarket chain, PriceSmart is a handy, shop-at-home tool with discount prices. Choose from their selection of housewares, appliances, jewelry, cameras, watches, and more. Are there many other places you can get a set of four Mikasa lead crystal goblets with gold trim for less than $20? PriceSmart is a must-see for frugal shoppers with finer tastes.
WEB http://www.pricesmart.com/PSINDEX.HTM

Rummaging Through Northern California Run by the same person behind the Internet Resale Directory and frequently updated, Rummaging Though Northern California lives up to its promise of helping bargain hunters in the San Francisco Bay Area. But it also has information for frugal types worldwide; the library of previous articles covers topics ranging from how to save money with charity donations to how to successfully buy and sell at yard sales. If you are a Californian, don't miss Shoptalk, an extensive, bimonthly column about the latest news and stores for bargain shopping.
WEB http://www.sonic.net/~rtnc/

The Shopping Wizard What's bright and yellow and can help save you lots of money? It's The

Shopping Wizard, a monthly publication about bargains, rebates, coupons, and other cash-retaining offers. If you don't want to subscribe, you can still get lots of information from the Web site. There are many different areas here, including Shopper's Alert, a list of in-store promotions; Bartering Corner, a place to trade your extra coupons and rebate forms; and Baby Connection, for new parents and parents-to-be.
WEB http://pages.prodigy.com/shoppingwizard /home.htm

Student Market If you're a student, or just someone who loves to read textbooks but doesn't like to pay the exorbitant prices, a trip to Student Market is in your immediate future. After you complete a simple (and free) registration process, you can browse, search, or post your own listing for used academic textbooks at discount prices. Unfortunately, this site isn't very active, but when word gets out, it will be.
WEB http://www.studentmkt.com

▼ Buying less

Adbusters Culture Jammers Headquarters This somewhat radical zine seeks to pop the culture of ads that have created the "Northern American pig—bloated with excess." Ever find yourself in limbo between "Just Say No" and "Just Do It"? Free your mind. Learn about the evils of ads and inform yourself about alternative ways to live. The message: Don't allow advertising, media, big corporations and socially accepted perceptions of what is "in" rule your life. Ask yourself, "Are you a citizen or a consumer?"
WEB http://www.adbusters.org./adbusters/main.html

alt.consumers.experiences Consumers unite online in order to discuss ways on how to save money. At this newsgroup, you'll find posted

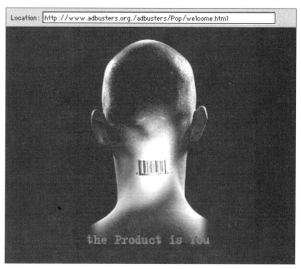

Location: http://www.adbusters.org./adbusters/Pop/welcome.html

the Product is You

Does Madison Avenue have you by the scruff of your neck?
http://www.adbusters.org./adbusters/main.html

suggestions regarding how to cut the cost of living expenses. Fellow subscribers share secrets on how to avoid getting duped by mutual fund magazines, gyms, stores, and all types of consumer goods. Others warn against the marketing tactics used by companies in order to sell off unnecessary and junky things.
USENET alt.consumers.experiences

Ben's Progressive CounterCulture Pages The "you are what you buy, so buy our cool stuff" motto is the most obvious ploy marketers use to get brainless consumers to purchase their goods. But you are not what you buy, say the authors of this site, which encourages consumers to begin exercising their rights of economic democracy. Get instructions on how to successfully boycott goods, celebrate Buy Nothing day, and take part in the ongoing debate about ethical consumerism online. Plus, get the real deal on McDonald's ethical standing and judge for yourself whether you'll have another Big Mac in this lifetime.
WEB http://www.envirolink.org/homepp/leamy /ethical.html

Have a Big Mac Attack of conscience
http://www.envirolink.org/homepp/leamy/ethical.html

Junk Mail FAQ Frequently asked questions on how to get rid of unwanted and unsolicited junk mail. Follow the simple steps on how to reduce the influx of junk mail (write the direct-mail marketing companies and tell them to take your name off the list) and prevent the spread of your name and personal information online.
WEB http://www.cis.ohio-state.edu/hypertext/faq /usenet/privacy/junk-mail/faq.html

Never Enough? Anticonsumerism Campaign Did you know that the U.S. alone, with only 6 percent of the world's population, consumes 30 percent of its resources? If you didn't, the Never Enough? Anticonsumerism campaign will clue you in. The campaign's online brochure provides a critical look at consumerism, poverty, and the planet. The endless cycle of buying is so deeply entrenched in our society that it is impossible for an individual living in the U.S. to stop buying completely. Hang up your mall sneakers, hand in your credit card, and you're well on your way to living lightly, according to these advocates of anti-consumerism.
WEB http://envirolink.org/issues/enough/index.html

Overcoming Consumerism Do you suffer from the learned behavior of consumerism? If you're like most Americans, you do. This site may help you break free from the cycle of spend and waste. Discover the many ways you'll benefit by overcoming consumerism, then look over the suggestions for taking action—you don't necessarily have to go dumpster-diving. For the radical anti-consumer, there are suggestions on how to get aggressive.
WEB http://www.hooked.net/users/verdant/index.htm

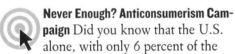

▼ Coupons

alt.coupons Though unfortunately subject to lots of spamming, especially those annoying "get rich quick" scams, alt.coupons is a good place to check for special offers online. Posters here are mostly those looking to trade coupons, so this may be the place to be if you don't have time to surf all of the coupon traders' sites.
USENET alt.coupons

Benetta's Refunding Resource Benetta Johnson could be considered one of the more obsessive frugal shoppers in cyberspace, bless her soul. She's listed all of her coupons and rebate forms on her home page, and they're all available for trading. Also, she's compiled a list of manufacturer's Web sites, and information on rebates, including an extensive dictionary of rebate codes to be used when they're posted online for trades. There are also some freebies and great deals listed.
WEB http://members.tripod.com/~Bennetta/homepage 3.htm

Ca$h In Tired of coupon hide-and-seek? Well, this could be just the product for you. Ca$h In is software for organizing your coupons so you can shop in an orderly, money-saving manner. Best of all, you can download it for

free at this Web site. You can also check out a helpful list of savings tips for shoppers.
WEB http://www.savesyou.com/index.html

Doug Creighton's Refund/Coupon Web Site Be prepared to cover your eyes when you arrive at Doug Creighton's helpful refund site, because he uses the most insidious HTML tag ever created. If you can stand the eyesore, you'll be able to get a list of refund publications, send email to Sandy Gebo, "the coupon queen," and follow links to a number of frugality sites online, including The Dollar Stretcher.
WEB http://members.tripod.com/~Doug_Creighton /index.html

National Brand Coupons This is the old fashioned way of keeping on top of your budget. Make a list of necessities, things you know you always purchase, then order coupons for those items from this online brochure. National Brand coupons guarantee that the coupons you purchase can be used anywhere in the country, not only in a particular district. For only $3 you get coupons worth $100 in savings. If you spend a little, you'll save a lot.
WEB http://www.azlink.com/~coupons/index.html

RebateNet RebateNet is under serious construction, but already you can tell what a worthwhile and helpful service it will be for people trying to keep their shopping expenses down. For now, you can participate in the rebate, coupon, and sweepstakes exchanges, where people post news and information about the latest savings options they've found. Gatorade, tobacco, yogurt, and thousands of other product offers are discussed; there's truly something for everyone. You'll also find information on catalogs, special discounts, UPC code trades, and the occasional free merchandise offer.
WEB http://www.rebate.com/

The Stevens Network Coupon Connection With so many different coupon offerings online, it can be difficult to decide which one to order from. At this coupon connection, you can peruse a brochure before you send in your order. You decide if the coupons they are offering are worth your money before laying out the cash you're so desperately trying to save. Read the testimonials from people who took a chance and saved serious cash.
WEB http://pwl.netcom.com/~lifenet/coupon.html

▼ Eating cheap

Jolly Time Pop Corn Madonna survived her salad days by eating popcorn. You can, too. Feed your brain while you're at it with facts, answers to some of the most frequently asked questions, and different recipes for this inexpensive snack. Online users who register with Jolly Time will receive coupons that will save them money on their next popcorn purchase.
WEB http://www.jollytime.com/

Kitchen Science Who would have ever thought to put a citrus fruit in the microwave before squeezing? According to one tightwad tip submitted to

Pay now, get cash back later
http://www.rebate.com/

Welcome To RebateNet!

Get the juice on squeezing fruit and pinching pennies
http://www.bizcom.com/kitchenscience/

this site, it makes the fruit easier on your hand, and you get a lot more juice out of it! The real geniuses of kitchen science are the pennypinchers whose tips are collected here. If you have your own helpful hints, don't hesitate to speak up.
WEB http://www.bizcom.com/kitchenscience/

rec.food.recipes Recipes for everything from Caesar salad dressing to low-fat oatcakes. If it's not here, it's probably not on the Net. No visit to these newsgroups would be complete without checking Amy Gale's fantastic recipe archive, which is organized by category, including breads, seafood, salads, cookies, cakes, and chocolate. Saving money never tasted so good.
USENET rec.food.recipes
Archive: **URL** ftp://ftp.neosoft.com/pub/rec.food .recipes/
Archive: **WEB** http://www.vuw.ac.nz/who/Amy.Gale /recipe-archive.html
FAQ: **WEB** http://www.vuw.ac.nz/who/Amy.Gale /cooking-faq

USDA Guide to Home Canning Home canning is "a safe and economical to preserve quality

food at home." If you are looking to pinch a penny without denying your family the nutritional value it needs, canning is the perfect solution. At this page, you'll find all the necessary information and instructions that will guide you through the process. Fact sheets, guidelines, directions and updates will help you through the slicing, dicing, fermenting and pickling that is waiting for you in the kitchen.
WEB http://www.agen.ufl.edu/~foodsaf/canhome.html

▼ Free stuff

alt.consumers.free-stuff Attenion frugal shoppers! Here's something better than cheap; it's free. You'll want to visit this newsgroup, which dwells with near-obsessive fervor on the practical aspects of no-cost acquisition. What companies are running giveaway initiatives? What companies pretend to offer free services but load up on invisible charges? What are the best toys you can get from cereal these days? And does the Internet itself qualify as "free stuff"?
USENET alt.consumers.free-stuff

Fat Cat Cafe One of the best free stuff and contests site, and definitely the cutest. An adorable orange cat leads you through various categories of free stuff: coupons, food, clothes, mousepads, and so on. Some of these offers are just transitory promotions, most of them are still valid, and all of them are at least a little bit tempting. What do you have to lose? In most cases, just some demographic information about yourself. If you feel the need to communicate with other bargain hunters, feel free to join in the Fat Cat Chat.
WEB http://www.fatcatcafe.com/freecont.htm

 Free-n-Cool It's free. It's cool. It's Free-n-Cool, the best place on the Web to find out about free stuff. The

organization behind it is impeccable, and it's definitely worth the time to check on a daily basis. You can find out about general free stuff like stationery or chocolate covered potato chips, win stuff, participate in Web marketing surveys that pay, or just visit some cool sites that Free-n-Cool's creator suggests. You can even search the site. The genius behind free and cool is its structure, especially the "What's New" page, which is an update of all new items, contests, and promotions changed on a daily basis. You can also browse by offer type, age or geographic restrictions, and expiration date. There are also links to other free stuff sites, but you may not need them after spending some time at Free-n-Cool.
WEB http://www.free-n-cool.com

Free Stuff Look in the dictionary under "bad Web copy" and you might find the phrase "!Amazing **FREE STUFF** The craze that every Internet insider is talking about." Except for this one lapse in taste, this page (which forms part of the Internet Shopping Directory) is nicely designed, and well-organized to boot. It includes a special section listing of free stuff available from the government. Watch out for the annoying MIDI theme and the many blinking NEW signs.
WEB http://www.isdirectory.com/free_stuff.htm

Free Stuff This site doesn't try to overwhelm you with sheer numbers, but the free offers are impressive. It's simply organized into categories including food and drink, health and beauty, computer-related, pet items, magazines, and miscellaneous.
WEB http://www.dezines.com/free

Free Stuff There's not much offered at this page, but since the information comes from the Debt Counselors of America, you know it's bound to be helpful. You'll find computer programs to assist you with financial situations, information to help you get out of debt, and best of all, a free "Debt Sucks" bumper sticker—you only have to send in a SASE.
WEB http://www.dca.org/free.htm

The Free Stuff Continuum There are more than 200 free samples listed at this site, and that's just the beginning: CDs, posters, 800-numbers, sweepstakes, the works. Adam, who organizes this site, has used a simple, easy-to-use design, that makes this one of the best free stuff sites. But, it doesn't seem to be updated as often as some of the others, so you may want to check their offers first.
WEB http://www.owlnet.com/adam/free.html

FreeShop Online It's a win-win situation. For companies, free stuff means good advertising; for consumers, free stuff means free stuff. The FreeShop Online is the middleman. It acts as a clearinghouse for promotional items and services from companies all over the world. Examples? Free trial issues of magazines like *Today's Woodworker*. Free books from the Detective Book Club. Free demo software for teachers. The stuff is never that amazing, but frugal minds will like to visit.
AMERICA ONLINE *keyword* freeshop

FreeWeb FreeWeb has a little more variety than a lot of other free stuff pages, since it handles free offers both online and offline. Some of them include free Internet access, free faxes, and free classified ads. The FreeWeb creators have added a free magazines section, where you can get a few sample issues of a number of computer mags.
WEB http://freeweb.com/freeweb/index.html

Ian's Fabulous Freebies Archive Ian categorizes his free stuff into neat little groups from free audio stuff to free gifts to free videos. And he provides links not just to free stuff, but to

sweepstakes, contests, and other fun ways to spend time, and not money.
WEB http://www.fabfreebies.com

Next to Nothing Interested in picking up some super-grow dinosaurs? Or, how about a two-day sample of Metamucil? Julie Pederson's Next to Nothing site is a haven for free and almost free offers that range from bibles to sex guides. Her site is updated late on Friday nights, and there's an archive of the previous weeks' offers available at all times. When you've finished ordering all your goodies from here, check out the extensive list of links to other free stuff sites.
WEB http://www.winternet.com/~julie/ntnl.html

What do Mohandas Gandhi, Confucius, Ben Franklin, Mark Twain, Leo Tolstoy, and Henry Thoreau have in common? They are all role models for light living.

Totally Free Stuff!! This could be your one-stop shop for all the free stuff you could really ever want. CD-ROMs, posters, mouse pads, pet food, condoms, software, stickers—the usual (free) suspects. Each listing links to the page that's making the offer. The site's creator adds new freebies every day, so set a bookmark and you won't miss out on any gratis goodies.
WEB http://adhere.on.ca/free/

Volition Volition is very into its name: Everything here is Volition this, Volition that. It's more of a discount site than an absolutely free stuff site, but they've got a lot of variety, and

most of it is free. There's a free digital post-card service, a whole lot of free contests, a bookstore with tips on how to get free stuff, and some pretty good links. And the Volition to Eat Well section which features links to about a dozen food and recipe sites.
WEB http://www.volition.com

▼ Simple living

Living Lightly What do Mohandas Gandhi, Confucius, Ben Franklin, Mark Twain, Leo Tolstoy, and Henry Thoreau have in common? They are all role models for light living. Each of these men contributed to the philosophy of living one's life away from unlimited and wasteful consumption. As this site explains, a higher standard of living does not guarantee a more fulfilling life. If you find yourself caught up in a vortex of senseless consumerism, stop by for a reality check.
WEB http://www.scn.org/earth/lightly/vslinks.htm

The Simple Living Journal You can be a billionaire—in your heart. This journal advocates the simple life, which is also less expensive. Instead of spending your day trying to figure out how to aggregate more money, take voluntary steps toward a simpler way of living. Thoreau was in the "simple living" state of mind when he built a house at Walden Pond. Learn how to become rich by structuring your life and following your dreams.
WEB http://www.simpleliving.com/

The Simple Living Network Home Page Looking to lead an earth-friendly and less consumptive lifestyle? Learn to tread lightly on your planet. This site's got everything you need, including links to natural products and services, newsletters, books, and plenty of simple-living tips.
WEB http://www.slnet.com/

PART 2

Make Money

NOW YOUR FINANCES are in perfect order. You pay all your bills on time, and your credit card debt is just a memory. Every week (or at least every month), you sit down at your computer and dutifully type in your expenditures using one of the personal finance software packages we've recommended. You've even managed to save money. But it still seems like you're a long way from the total financial freedom you desire. The solution is to increase your income. In this part, we've outlined three ways for you to make more money: One, post your resume online and land the job of your dreams. Two, start a business on your own—doing it from home is all the rage. And three? Win the lottery!

Chapter 7
Getting a Job

Land Your Perfect Job Online

SIMPLESTEPS

You can pound the pavement without wearing shoes. Just get online and sell yourself

I **Figure out what kind of job you want.** Take a personality or self-assessment exam. The well-known **Myers-Briggs Personality Test** may only be administered by a licensed practitioner (read: It will cost you money), but there are several free alternative tests you can take online, such as **The Keirsey Temperament Sorter** and those offered at the **Job Analysis & Personality Research** site for finding the color of your parachute. You can also peruse job descriptions, earnings projections, and career advice at the **Occupational Outlook Handbook** and **Exploring Occupations** sites. If you're looking for career suggestions, *Money* magazine lists its annual **Top Jobs** chart on the Web.

2 **Create your resume.** First, collect your thoughts—and relevant information about your past job experiences—with a little help from the articles at **JobSource**. Then, **Resume Formats: Which One Works?** will help you decide what kind of resume is best suited to you. AboutWork's **Resume 123** will let you experiment with both chronological and functional resumes so you can decide which you like best. And when effective word choice means the difference between employment and unemployment, *CareerMag* comes to the rescue with an article on **Key Word Resumes**. Remember: Print resumes rely heavily on verbs, but electronic resumes depend on nouns (Employers search on positions, skills, etc.).

JobSource
WEB http://www.jobsource.com/index
.html

Resume Formats: Which One Works?
WEB http://www.espan.com/docs
/resform.html

AboutWork's Resume 123
WEB http://www.aboutwork.com
/resume/

Key Word Resumes
WEB http://www.careermag.com
/careermag/newsarts/resume/1046
.html

An alternative to the Myers-Briggs Personality Test
http://harvey.psyc.vt.edu/

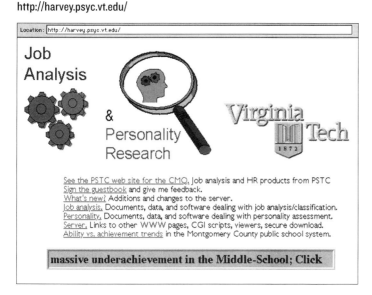

Location: http://harvey.psyc.vt.edu/

Job Analysis & Personality Research

Virginia Tech 1872

See the PSTC web site for the CMQ. Job analysis and HR products from PSTC
Sign the guestbook and give me feedback.
What's new? Additions and changes to the server.
Job analysis. Documents, data, and software dealing with job analysis/classification.
Personality. Documents, data, and software dealing with personality assessment.
Server. Links to other WWW pages, CGI scripts, viewers, secure download.
Ability vs. achievement trends in the Montgomery County public school system.

massive underachievement in the Middle-School; Click

Location: http://www.ajb.dni.us/

Welcome To America's Job Bank

With more than 250,000 jobs in the database, surely you'll find one right for you
http://www.ajb.dni.us/

Elements of Style
WEB http://www.columbia.edu/acis
/bartleby/strunk/

Hypertext Webster Interface
WEB http://c.gp.cs.cmu.edu:5103
/prog/webster

Style FAQ
WEB http://www.rt66.com/~telp
/sfindex.htm

Finally, don't send out a resume with a mistake. Proofread it with the help of online resources such as **Elements of Style**, the **Hypertext Webster Interface**, and the **Style FAQ**. Once you've created a hard copy of your resume, it's time to start thinking electronically. We spell out the steps to creating an online resume in the next feature.

3 **Master the art of the cover letter.** Once you've created the perfect resume, the way to make it stand out in an employer's "in" box (electronic or otherwise) is to wow him or her with your cover letter. CareerCity's **Cover Letters** section offers advice for creating the perfect cover letter for any situation.

Cover Letters
WEB http://www.careercity.com/edge
/getinter/getinter.htm#Cover Letters

4 **Network.** Some things never change: In the online job hunt, as in the traditional employment search, it's all about who you know. So make the Net work for you by networking with those in your industry. Professional mailing lists and online forums will let you rub elbows virtually with the leaders in your line of work. If you're interested in a new media job, don't miss **YPN's Top Ten Sites for Jobs in the Valley and the Alley**.

5 **Search the national classifieds.** Start with the national listings at **America's Job Bank**, which boasts more than 250,000 listings, or the **Best Jobs in the USA Today** database. Register at **CareerPath.com** and search the help wanted sections of six major dailies across the U.S. The newsgroups **misc.jobs.misc** and **misc.jobs.offered** may be cluttered, but they list thousands of jobs a week, particularly computer-related positions.

6 **Look locally.** Newspapers on the Web often have a searchable classified section. Some have even built mini-career advice centers around their job listings. Editor & Publisher's list of **Online Newspapers** allows you to link to newspapers in every state—look for your local paper or search for one in the city of your dreams. YPN also offers an enormous database of other online **employment classifieds by state** and **occupation**.

7 **Email your resume to the human resource departments of companies.** More and more companies are now accepting resumes electronically. In fact, big companies often have email addresses for job listings on their Web sites or for accepting resumes. (Hint: Don't send your resume to a company's webmaster, email him for the appropriate address or check a list of company addresses, like **Hoover's Job Register**.)

8 **Post your electronic resume to a job board.** Thousands of job seekers upload information for review by potential

YPN's Top Ten Sites for Jobs in the Valley and the Alley
WEB http://www.ypn.com/mm-bin /genobject/article/newl9960925

America's Job Bank
WEB http://www.ajb.dni.us/

Best Jobs in the USA Today
WEB http://www.bestjobsusa.com

CareerPath.com
WEB http://www.careerpath.com/

USENET misc.jobs.misc

USENET misc.jobs.offered

Online Newspapers
WEB http://www.mediainfo.com /ephome/npaper/nphtm/e-papers /e-papers.us.html

YPN: Classifieds by State
WEB http://www.ypn.com/topics /880.html

YPN: Classifieds by Occupation
WEB http://www.ypn.com/topics /88l.html

Hoover's Job Register
WEB http://www.ypn.com/topic/ll89 .html

Monster Board
WEB http://www.monster.com

Online Career Center
WEB http://www.occ.com/occ
/HowToEnterResumes.html

A+ On-line Resumes
WEB http://ol-resume.com

Internet Resume Services
WEB http://home.earthlink.net/~irs

Ten Common Interviewing Mistakes and How to Avoid Them
WEB http://www.cweb.com/dimensions
/Career_Dimensions4.html#Interview

Face to Face Interview Preparation
WEB http://www.careermag.com
/careermag/newsarts/interview
ing/1003.html

Job Hunting Tips from a Corporate Headhunter
WEB http://www.cja-careers.com
/getjob.html

employers. Before you drop yours off, however, carefully consider each board's instructions. **Monster Board**, for example, encourages job-seekers to use the site's fill-in-the-blank forms which then generate a resume. Other sites, like **Online Career Center**, accept pre-formatted resumes. Unlike many of the big job boards that rely on employers to visit the sites and search for potential employees, **A+ On-line Resumes** and **Internet Resume Services** will email your resume directly to possible employers—for a fee.

9 **Prepare for the interview.** Once you've landed an interview, it's time to sell yourself to your prospective employer offline and face-to-face. Career Dimensions will clue you in on **Ten Common Interviewing Mistakes and How to Avoid Them** (Mistake #1: Winging It), while *Career Magazine* will assist with **Face to Face Interview Preparation**. Pick up **Job Hunting Tips from a Corporate Headhunter** and learn how to answer interview questions effectively and how to master the two-minute response. At the end of an interview, you will often be asked if you have any questions. Seek out advice from the Univer-

Don't count on your employer's insobriety to get you through the interview
http://www.kaplan.com/career/hotseat/

sity of Massachusett's School of Management on **Questions You Should Ask at Your Job Interview**. (Do ask questions that indicate you've done some research on the company. Don't ask about vacations.) Once you've created your Q&A list, test your interviewing technique in a **Virtual Interview** from the Student Center. Then, wind down with Kaplan's lighthearted **HotSeat** game—choose the best answer and you move closer to a regular paycheck and benefits.

Nothing will make you look better in an interview—except perhaps the proper **Dress** recommended by Career City—than knowing a little something about the company you want to work for. You can inexpensively and quickly research company history, revenue figures, recent changes in management, the company's competitors, and timely news stories. Start by checking a company's Web site for information. (You can search **InfoSeek** to see if the company you want to work for has a Web site. In addition, the Insider's Investor Relations page allows you to search for public companies with a Net presence.) Company profile databases such as *Career Magazine*'s **Employer Profiles** and **Hoover's Online** company profiles are perhaps your best bets for company info. Hoover's offers in-depth information on more than 2,600 public and private companies to its members for $9.95 a month. For recent stories in the online business press, visit sites like **Barron's Online**, **Fortune**, or **Worth**.

IO **Send a thank-you letter.** It's best to send a thank-you letter immediately following your interview. The Student Center will remind you, **Don't Forget to Say "Thanks,"** and has online tips on how to do it, complete with sample letters. Remember, sending a letter won't guarantee that you'll get the job, but it certainly couldn't hurt.

Questions You Should Ask at Your Job Interview
WEB http://esther.som.umass.edu/som/resource/place/P0572.html

Virtual Interview
WEB http://www.studentcenter.com/brief/virtual/virtual.htm

Kaplan: HotSeat
WEB http://www.kaplan.com/career/hotseat/

Dress
WEB http://www.careercity.com/edge/getjob/getjob.htm#Dress

InfoSeek
WEB http://www.infoseek.com

Quicken: Insider's Investor Relations
http://networth.galt.com/www/home/equity/irr/

Employer Profiles
WEB http://www.careermag.com/careermag/employers/index.html

Hoover's Online
WEB http://www.hoovers.com/

Barron's Online
WEB http://www.barrons.com

Fortune
WEB http://pathfinder.com/fortune/index.html

Worth
WEB http://www.enews.com/magazines/worth/

Don't Forget to Say "Thanks"
WEB http://www.studentcenter.com/brief/thank/thank.htm

Create an Electronic Resume

SIMPLESTEPS

WHO NEEDS PAPER? INTERNET ACCESS AND A FEW CHOICE WORDS WILL GO A LONG WAY

1 Collect your thoughts—and your experiences. Before you try to get it all down on paper, take stock of your strengths and goals. **JobSource**'s articles can help you evaluate your talents and come up with a plan to sell yourself to potential employers.

JobSource
WEB http://www.jobsource.com

YPN's resumes page
WEB http://www.ypn.com/topic/883 .html

Monster Board
WEB http://www.monster.com/jobseek /resumeon/resumehows2.html

How to Write an Electronic Resume
WEB http://www.occ.com/occ/JLK /HowToEResume.html

2 Determine how you'll distribute your resume. Will you get noticed traditionally (by mail), electronically (via email, the Web), or both? **YPN's resumes page** points out the differences between the paper resume and the online resume. The excerpts from **How to Write an Electronic Resume** by Joyce Lain Kennedy, are also helpful.

3 Choose a style for your resume. Will you organize your resume functionally or chronologically? **Resume Formats: Which One Works?** describes the most common formats and the merits of each. At About Work's **Resume 123**, you can experiment: Just fill in the fields, submit the informa-

The field is wide open
http://www.jobsource.com

tion, and the site will generate a chronological or functional resume. You can then print the finished product. The USC Career Center's advice on **Organizing Your Resume**, on the other hand, walks you through the standard resume categories and provides a list of questions to ask yourself once you've written a rough draft.

4 **Choose your words carefully.** In a traditional resume, verbs are important, and there are online sources to help you pick the perfect ones. JobWeb has a list of **Action Words for Resume Writing** and Ball State University's Career Services has a list of **Power Words for Your Resume**, reminding job-seekers to use phrases like "advanced to" rather than "promoted to" and "earned" rather than "was given." Since online databases, such as **Resume City**, allow employers to search by criteria like title, skills, or location, electronic resumes will benefit from the right nouns. *CareerMag*'s article on **Key Word Resumes** shows you how to pepper your resume with effective nouns to aid an employers' searches.

Resume Formats: Which One Works?
WEB http://www.espan.com/docs/resform.html

Resume 123
WEB http://www.aboutwork.com/resume/

Organizing Your Resume
WEB http://www.usc.edu/dept/cdc/resume.htm#Organize

Action Words for Resume Writing
WEB http://www.jobweb.org/catapult/guenov/action.html

Power Words for Your Resume
WEB http://www.bsu.edu/careers/verbs.html

Resume City
WEB http://beast.monster.com/recruit/rescity/smplsrch.htm

Key Word Resumes
WEB http://ww.careermag.com/careermag/newsarts/resume/1046.html

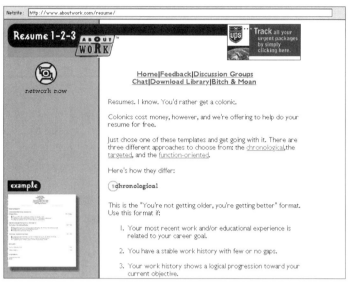

It's easier than getting a colonic
http://www.aboutwork.com/resume/

5 **Proof it.** Online style and grammar guides can help you decide between a comma and a semicolon. Among the best are William Strunk, Jr.'s classic, **Elements of Style**, and Purdue University's **OWL Handouts**. You can also refer to the **Style FAQ**, sponsored by the Copyediting-l mailing list. Of course, don't forget to spellcheck. And then, just to be sure, double-check with the **Hypertext Webster Interface**. If you're going with a traditional resume, don't forget to include your email address below your phone number, as well as the URL for your home page, if you have one. Don't trust yourself to catch the typos? You can pay an expert to look over your resume; **Editorial Services Online** is a good place to find copyeditors-for-hire.

6 **Get feedback.** If you're willing to pay, **AAA Professional Resume Service** will analyze your finished product (**Resume Helper** will provide a very brief initial critique at no charge). But there's plenty of free feedback on the Net, too. Whether you want to work in a **museum**, a **lab**, or at an **architecture firm**, you can get helpful hints from a newsgroup or mailing list related to your career interests. Keep your posts specific, avoid looking too self-serving, and you'll probably find that other people in the field have some great advice about what works on an area.

Resume Helper
WEB http://rampages.onramp.net /~resumes/critique.html#In Depth

USENET bit.listserv.museum-l

USENET sci.research.careers

USENET alt.architecture

7 Prepare your resume for emailing. You'll need two versions of the same resume: a formatted resume with attractive fonts and layout that you can attach to your email message and an ASCII resume (no fonts, no tabs, no special characters) that you can paste into the message body of your email message. Why both? The formatted version is certainly the more attractive option (assuming you use standard fonts that the employer will have). In fact, the formatted version is probably the same one you're printing out and handing out to potential employers, but many companies (even the most wired companies) won't bother to convert an attached file. They'll just skip you. Therefore, it's always a good idea to include an ASCII version of your resume. There are three main rules to follow in order to ensure readability

" Many companies (even the most wired companies) won't bother to convert an attached file. "

of an ASCII resume on every monitor: Use a fixed width font (this is how most people read their email); hard-wrap your lines, i.e., put a paragraph return, after every 40 to 60 characters (it will make lines break where you want them to); and use spaces, not tabs (tabs look different on different computers). Also, don't use special characters such as smart quotes, bullets, or em dashes; they'll appear as odd combinations of let-

Location: http://www.infi.net/~resume/

Is something wrong with your resume? Find out—for a fee
http://www.infi.net/~resume/

ters. It's strongly recommended that you email your resume to yourself before emailing it anywhere else: That way, you'll get to see your life on screen just as an employer would see it—and you can make sure that there aren't any formatting mistakes.

8 **Email your resume to the human resource departments of companies.** More and more companies are now accepting resumes electronically. In fact, big companies often have specific email address for resumes. (Hint: Don't send your resume to a company's webmaster, email him for the appropriate address or check a list of company addresses, like **Hoover's Job Register**.)

Hoover's Job Register
WEB http://www.ypn.com/topic/1189
.html

9 **Post your electronic resume to a jobs board.** **Monster Board** and the **Online Career Center** are just two of many resume banks on the Net. Before you drop yours off, however, carefully review each board's instructions. Some resume boards (like Monster Board) actually provide job-seekers with a fill-in-the-blank form, which then generates a resume especially for its database; be ready to abandon your own resume and adjust to a different system if necessary. Other sites, like **Online Career Center**, will allow you to email employers your own resume, but you'll need to make sure you follow the instructions.

Monster Board
WEB http://www.monster.com

Online Career Center
WEB http://www.occ.com

❝ Go straight to an online resume service to transform your experience into a Web page. ❞

IO Put your resume on the Web.
Not ready for HTML coding? Go straight to an online resume service to transform your experience into a Web page that prospective employers can visit. IGuide's **Resume Maker** offers a choice of three formats, asks you to submit the pertinent personal information, and converts it into a resume you can either print from your browser or include on your home page. YPN's **Resume-O-Matic** requests your career information and then turns it into a Web page. Resume-O-Matic will keep a copy of your resume on the Web for a year, for free.

Resume Maker
WEB http://www.iguide.com/work
_mny/resume/rmaker.htm

Resume-O-Matic
WEB http://www.ypn.com/jobs
/resumes/

Batteries included
http://www.ypn.com/jobs/resumes/

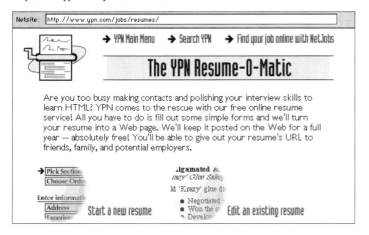

Netsite: http://www.ypn.com/jobs/resumes/

→ YPN Main Menu   → Search YPN   → Find your job online with Net.Jobs

The YPN Resume-O-Matic

Are you too busy making contacts and polishing your interview skills to learn HTML? YPN comes to the rescue with our free online resume service! All you have to do is fill out some simple forms and we'll turn your resume into a Web page. We'll keep it posted on the Web for a full year -- absolutely free! You'll be able to give out your resume's URL to friends, family, and potential employers.

→ Pick Section
  Choose Order
Enter information
  Address
  Experience   Start a new resume   Edit an existing resume

Toss your credentials up online and let the bosses fight over you

Ten Best Places to Post

RESUME BANKS USED TO BE A "what have you got to lose" proposition; they required little effort but were unlikely to return many results. That's changed. Today, they are one of the most proven ways to land a job. They are efficient and easy to use, and in the last several months they've begun to deliver in the way that the medium has always promised.

For the job seeker, resume banks are often free or charge nominal fees, and they're not just passive places to post your resume. The best resume banks help you craft an effective resume, send your resume directly to relevant employers, or post your resume to a network of online databases and newsgroups. They also offer candidates the opportunity to list their resumes in several categories (you don't have to limit yourself with a single objective statement) and to block current employers from finding them. Perhaps more significantly, resume banks are attractive to employers, who are turning to them for the same reasons that they turn to recruiters. Since resume banks are generally much cheaper than recruiters, employers are using them not only to find management but also entry level employees. In short, you'd be a fool not to list your credentials with a few resume banks. Which few? Although there are now hundreds of resume banks on the Web, some have emerged as the clear leaders. We've chosen, in no particular order, the top places to post your resume. Here are our picks for the ten best:

▶ **Monster Board Resume Services** This accommodating monster has assembled a collection of job-hunting resources that will take the bite out of looking for a job. The main attraction of the page is its job database, and with more than 48,000 job listings, it's a job force to be reckoned with. The Monster Board maintains a resume bank called Resume City. Follow the simple steps for developing your online resume, then sit back as your personal contact information is dispatched to a sophisticated database. When an employer's search for skills and experience matches your qualifications, the employer can then purchase your name and contact

Your Resume Online

information from Monster Board. Tips and FAQs make posting to the Monster Board a relatively stress-free experience.

Things that go bump on the Net
http://www.monster.com

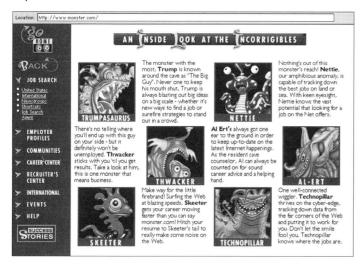

A life saver for job seekers
http:www.jobsource.com/resume/index.html

Price: Free
WEB http://www.monster.com

▸ **JobSource Resume Generator** This is one of the best places to go if you don't have an offline resume, or if you feel your text resume is not as well organized or Web-friendly as you would like. JobSource doesn't ask for your ASCII resume; it simply offers you a series of online forms that help you to outline information pertinent to potential employers, and then creates a marketable resume from scratch. The service is free, but there is no resume security provision, which means that current employers can check to see if you're thinking about taking flight. Still, JobSource is an up-and-coming service in the online employment market; its cleanly formatted resumes are perfect for the keyword searches that Net-savvy employers use to line up interviews.

Price: Free
WEB http://www.jobsource.com/resume/index.html

▸ **E-Span Job Search** To say that this free service is no-frills is an understatement. The E-Span resume form, which requires registration, has only three fields—email address, name, and body of resume. However, there are a couple of compelling reasons to post your resume at E-Span. It allows HTML formatting, which means that those who have worked in the online industry can link to sites as illustrations. But the best reason to use E-Span is that it sends your resume to other popular Internet employment sites. Each time E-Span posts your resume to another site, your chances of attracting an employer increase exponentially. Although the site does not specify which databases it posts to, any publicity is good publicity. And E-Span is a great way to get your resume on the Usenet newsgroups—the service will automatically post it for you.

If your resume is already pretty solid, and you need a quick, totally painless way of reaching potential employers, E-Span is the service for you.
Price: Free
WEB http://www.espan.com/js/js.html

❝ If your resume is already pretty solid, and you need a quick, totally painless way of reaching potential employers, E-Span is the service for you. ❞

▶ **Job Center Resume Services** The tag line says it all: "Finding a job has never been easier." For a modest subscription fee, Job Center will work with you until you land the position you want. After either completing an online form (cut and paste information from your existing resume) or emailing your resume, your cyberCV will be posted. Then, a Job Center representative will phone you with advice for sprucing it up. After completing the online resume process, you should begin receiving email containing comprehensive listings from companies with openings matching your qualifications and interests. Job Center provides simple instructions for updating your posted resume on the service and also posts your resume to all appropriate newsgroups.
Price: $20 for six months
WEB http://www.jobcenter.com/jol/resume.htm

▶ **Internet Resume Services** You'll have to pay a hefty fee for Internet Resume Services, but with that money you're buying a guarantee. The company posts your resume on its site as well as to appropriate newsgroups, sends it to National Job Banks employers, and promises to dispatch your resume to a minimum of 150

All the job tools you need are down at OCC
http://www.occ.com

job openings over a period of six weeks. To start the process, you must send a copy of your resume (hard copy or IBM-compatible diskette) by snail mail or an ASCII version by email along with a list of job titles or categories you are qualified for and your preferred geographic areas of relocation. Within days, you should begin receiving phone calls from potential employers. *Price:* One-time fee of $85
WEB http://home.earthlink.net/~irs

▶ **Online Career Center** This well-designed site is a not-for-profit cooperative that provides career counseling and a growing database of about 8,000 jobs and resumes. Thousands of private and public institutions list their job openings with the Online Career Center. The openings range from trading-room support on Wall Street to emergency room nurses in Ohio to marketing executives in Zurich. In addition to the large number of entry-level positions for the Net-savvy college crowd, the OCC lists opportunities for experienced professionals. You can submit your resume to OCC for free in one of several ways: Email it in ASCII format, submit it in HTML (following OCC's specified outline for doing so), pay "Hyper Resumes" to create a resume in HTML for you, or send them your dead-tree version. Register to use Career Manager, and your resume will be on one of the most dynamic, well-known career centers on the Net till the end of time. In addition, you can edit, delete, deactivate, or reactivate your resume at any time. The OCC also offers articles on employment-related topics such as choosing a career or understanding what to expect from professional career advisors. You can even access a calendar of local offline career fairs and professional conventions.
Price: Free
WEB http://www.occ.com

▶ **A+ On-line Resumes** The company charges $40 for a three-month membership fee, but claims that the price is a bargain. Why? Because A+ "actively markets and promotes this site to ensure that the human resource and business community know that they can easily locate qualified job seekers in their area through our services. Furthermore, your resume will be registered with the most popular search engines using your name, job type, and 'resume' as keywords." The service's user-friendly resume form takes only minutes to complete, but for now there are too few resumes to attract the number of employers and recruiters that would make A+ worth the money.
Price: $40 for three months
WEB http://ol-resume.com

" This resume builder offers a two-page form which lets you summarize your job-seeking qualifications. "

▶ **America's Job Bank Resume Builder** So, you want to have an easy-to-read resume full of the phrases employers love to read ("self-starter," "proficient in QuarkXPress," "HTML programming skills"). But you also want your resume to furnish more details that may mean the difference between a call-back and the slush pile. What to do? Visit America's Job Bank, where you can have your cake and eat it, too. This resume builder offers a two-page form which lets you summarize your job-seeking qualifications and criteria (position preferred, willingness to relocate , etc.). Job Bank then provides a field in which you can enter your entire print resume, or even a little essay, so that interested employers can get a more in-depth view of your background.
Price: Free
WEB http://db.jobbankusa.com/leapfrog.cgi?task=create _resume_stepl

▶ **Career Mosaic Resume Services** This user-friendly resume builder doesn't just instruct you to paste your ASCII resume into a form field and then throw you to the wolves. This service offers guidelines on building a Web-friendly resume, and even furnishes samples to show you how it should be done. Then it throws you to the wolves. There is no such thing as employee security here, so if you want to make absolutely sure that your boss doesn't know you're planning to jump ship, this isn't the place for you. Still, this resume creation and posting site does have one distinct advantage over other similar services—it's part of Career Mosaic, one of the most comprehensive and popular career centers online.
Price: Free
WEB http://www.careermosaic.com/cm/cm39.html

▶ **Intellimatch Power Resume** With a name like Power Resume, it's got to be good, right? Intellimatch offers an exhaustive, and rather exhausting online resume service free of charge. The site warns that it will take you at least a half an hour to complete the process, and the estimate is a fair one. This resume builder not only lets you display the full text of your ASCII resume, but also highlights quick-reference criteria for potential employers including a summary of your objectives, a detailed skills profile, educational achievements, information on your availability and work status, and even an overview of your employment preferences. There are two levels of security available for the Power Resume—The Standard Plan allows you to block your current employer from seeing your resume, and lets employers contact you directly. The Gold Plan not only sets up a block, but requires that Intellimatch contact you before releasing information to potential employers.
Price: Free
WEB http://www.intellimatch.com/watson30.html

The wolves are hungry for fresh meat
http://www.careermosaic.com/cm/cm39.html

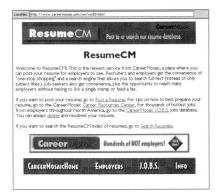

▼ On the prowl

America Online: Career Center's Help Wanted Ads
With sporadic job opportunities that run from coast to coast, job-seekers who peruse these classifieds had better have no qualms about relocating. General searches will produce nationwide matches, while sorting by state produces a much smaller regional yield. The best thing about Career Center is its neat search engine, but the entries are relatively sparse.
AMERICA ONLINE *keyword* career center

America Online: Employment Board You can come to the Board for three main reasons: to find a job, to advertise a position, and to get help with job hunting. Well posted with diverse classified ads, AOL's Employment Board is at once expansive and yet underwhelming. This is due to the fact that job categories, (divided into types ranging from Salaried Jobs: Education to Salaried Jobs: Trade/Industrial) can hit a high of 266 posts and a low of 23 posts, depending on where you look.
AMERICA ONLINE *keyword* jobs

America's Job Bank With links to the Employment Services of all 50 states, this board offers a job database of close to 250,000 listings. There is no cost either to the job seekers or employers who utilize this service (America's Job Bank is funded through the Unemployment Insurance taxes paid by employers). Those looking for work can choose to browse the listings under the Military Specialty, Job Code, or Federal Opportunities sections; or they can execute a self-directed search by choosing from a detailed menu of job criteria (industry, title, location). America's Job Bank also maintains links to the job boards of about 100 companies from ADEPT, Inc. to Zeitech, Inc.
WEB http://www.ajb.dni.us/

biz.jobs.offered The basic title doesn't do justice to the vast employment bounty that is biz.jobs.offered—thousands of openings in just about every state in the Union are posted here, especially openings for network developers, programmers, engineers, technical writers, and clinical applications specialists. There's so much job action that professional recruiters often post here hoping to pick up business. Post your own job listing, look for a job, and get into the fray.
USENET biz.jobs.offered

The Classifieds How large would a newspaper classifieds section be if it contained thousands of detailed descriptions of jobs in more than 25 fields? Too heavy to carry with you on the subway in the morning! But thanks to The Classifieds on America Online, you don't need to worry about managing a mountain of paper. The listings are neatly organized by job field. Of course, the Computers section contains the most listings, but even a less wired occupation like mechanic has close to 100 ads. So stand back *New York Times*, *Chicago Tribune*, and *Los Angeles Times*, The Classifieds is here and bigger than all of you put together!

A familiar site for the unemployed
America Online *keyword* career center

Help Wanted Ads

- About Help Wanted Ads
- How To Search Help Wanted-USA
- How To Search The E-SPAN Datal
- How To Post Ads Online
- Additional Help Wanted Ads
- Search Help Wanted-USA Databas
- Search E-Span Database
- Help Wanted Ads Library

Search Help Wanted-USA   Federal Jobs Library   How To Post Ads

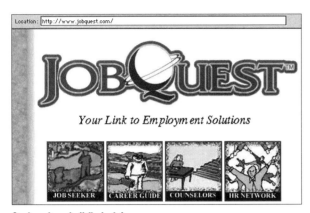

Seek and ye shall find a job
http://www.jobquest.com/

AMERICA ONLINE *keyword* classifieds→Business & Jobs→Professional Salaried Jobs

Cool Jobs If you laugh in the face of convention and you march to the beat of a different (cooler) drummer, you may just meet your future profession by surfing at Cool Jobs. Indeed, why make quick money programming C++ when you can rake in five times that as a Jeopardy contestant? Job contacts for Cirque du Soleil, Carnival Cruise Lines, congressional intern positions, and other opportunities straying off the beaten path are bountiful at this frosty page. The sensible-minded will scoff, but the best of them have dreamed of being Dallas Cowboy Cheerleaders at one time or another. Right, boys?
WEB http://www.cooljobs.com

E-Span on Compuserve This job service is the backbone of CompuServe's employment area. Feel free to peruse to the classified ads; vistors don't pay any fees. Searches are very specific yet easy to use, narrowing down searches to city. Unfortunately, like many similar services, finding enough relevant posts to make the search even worth your while is a challenge.
COMPUSERVE *go* jobs

Help Wanted USA California hospital seeks transplant specialists. Small Wisconsin company seeks accountants. Brooklyn school department seeks teacher to work with AIDS children. This database claims more than 4,000 job listings each week, collected by private consultants nationwide, and while there aren't always jobs listed in Arkansas (sorry, Bill), larger states are usually well represented. Broader in appeal than the job newsgroups, this database offers a good selection of computer-related jobs, along with large numbers of medical, social service, and business positions. Search the database by specific terms (obstetrics RN) or by general terms (sales and marketing). Updated every Wednesday.
AMERICA ONLINE *keyword* help wanted

The Internet Job Locator This Internet employment service piggybacks several search engines from major services such as the Monster Board, Federal Jobs Database, and Best Jobs in the *USA Today* and other non-job specific resources like AltaVista and DejaNews. Feel free to test them all out. While such varied options are nice to comtemplate, the lack of centralization and focus, and the resemblance to a crippled Yahoo! is a little disheartening. Among the more promising search engines is Monster Board, though it would make more sense to simply go directly there instead.
WEB http://www.joblocator.com/jobs/

Jobquest Thousands of jobs posted by hundreds of employers nationwide can be at your disposal, for a nominal fee. There are also additional products and services to help you navigate the rough, murky waters of seeking employment. Job Browser Pro is a program that can access all Dictionaries of Occupational Titles, while the Job Search report is intended to help you tailor your resume for specific jobs. For those of you who get queasy

at the thought of spending money in order to make money, you'll probably want to take advantage of Jobquest's free advice area. Access Jobquest's Career Guide, a starter kit of sorts to help you decide career moves, where to look, and how to prepare.
WEB http://www.jobquest.com/

▼ Resume banks

Career Shop First there were banks. Then there were eye banks and organ banks. The '70s brought us sperm banks and today, we have resume banks. The placid reds and blues that grace this resume bank are a nice touch that will make you feel oh-so-Zen for all of about five minutes, reminding you to keep calm and focused when looking for your dream job. As for content, Career Shop's services are similar to other job/resume database companies: You can have your resume displayed or search job listings at no cost. Employers, on the other hand, pay a monthly fee to run searches on the database and to post ads. If you're not satisfied with merely having your online resume, do a little self-promoting by opting for a personal attractive color banner, however narcissism comes at a cost. Monthly charges apply.
WEB http://www.careershop.com/

Careersite Job searching at Careersite is as easy as pie. You fill out basic information such as occupation, industry, location, and benefits and enter it. You can even set it to meet specific criteria, by filling out a special criteria field, though the mind boggles at how that's incorporated into the search function. The occasional glitches in the search result (system administrator jobs appeared while searching "publishing") may result from such liberal search options, so here's a word of advice: Keep it basic!
WEB http://www.careersite.com/

▼ Business directories

BigBook Although it's been harmlessly designed to be used as a directory of businesses which brings customers and companies together, BigBook can be used for much more malevolent ends. Well, not really. Job seekers who want to search for companies directly can use this page, which operates like a business yellow pages online. The catch is that they don't charge at all for their listings, which may make for a large and comprehensive database.
WEB http://www.bigbook.com/

BizWeb In spite of an uninspiring design, BizWeb appears to have been better thought out than many of its peers. Inquiries are not performed via nebulous searches with clumsy search parameters but rather by category. Your searches are hierarchical and easy to follow if you have the patience. One really thoughtful feature is its entry total, which currently stands at over 9,000. A seasoned job-hunter scouring the Net can use numbers like that to determine his interest. If you can't find a job here then you're not looking hard enough.
WEB http://www.bizweb.com/

Yahoo!: Business and Economy: Companies When it comes to company listings, it would be hard to surpass this online juggernaut; its comprehensive categories and links are absolutely enormous. With at least several hundred company listings in all categories—several easily break three thousand—a search of this magnitude should not be feared, it should be embraced. If you're looking for the Web page of a major company, it'll almost certainly be represented here. Yahoo! is the first and probably the best place to look for these types of searches.
WEB http://www.yahoo.com/text/Business_and _Economy/Companies/

Are you ready for the most challenging and lucrative career move of your life? These days, home is where the office is

S O YOU NEED TO MAKE a living. But you want to be your own boss, and you don't want to leave your house. You're not alone. Working at home has been one of this decade's hottest trends—more than 43 million people either run a business or telecommute from home. Who are these people? Victims of downsizing. Mothers who want to spend more time with their children. Minority employees who have headaches from hitting the glass ceiling. And, of course, those with an uncrushable entrepreneurial spirit. If you're ready to invest in your own potential, check out the online resources for

Do Try This at Home

SOHOs—small office/home office, that is. You can get just about all the information you'll ever need to make a living without having to sit through another interview. Your entrepreneur friends on the Web have been there, done that, and are willing to help you out (and only some of them will want your money).

The Proper Tools

If building a business is like building a house, you'll need the proper tools to do the job. Thank the Net for

CASH REGISTER

CCH Business Owner's Toolkit
WEB http://www.toolkit.cch.com/

How to Prepare a Business Plan that Guarantees Big Profits
WEB http://www.webcom.com/
seaquest/sbrc/busplan.html

Federal Acquisition Jumpstation
WEB http://procure.msfc.nasa.gov
/fedproc/home.html

the **CCH Business Owner's Toolkit**, which has the full text of the *SOHO Guidebook*, covering everything from determining whether you should start your own business (are you willing to sacrifice? are you organized? do you have good interpersonal skills? are you optimistic?) to managing your business finances once you do. The Business Tools section has downloadable samples of business documents (letters, contracts, policies), financial spreadsheet templates, and checklists. You can use them as they are or customize them to suit your business.

The Game Plan

Any entrepreneur will tell you that your SOHO will be a no-go unless you've mapped out the specifics in a business plan. It's this stage in the game when you decide the nature of your enterprise, determine your strengths and weaknesses, and access your financial situation. Having one will not only keep you focused on your main goals and create a formula for success, it will also cast a solid impression on any potential financiers you may be courting. So what should it look like and how can you create your own? The Small Business Resource Center has an answer with its article on **How to Prepare a Business Plan that Guarantees Big Profits**. You won't need an M.B.A. to understand the concepts involved in a business plan as they are outlined here, from the title page to the statement of purpose to the projected profit/loss, and operating figures.

CASH REGISTER

Federal Web Resources
WEB http://www.nbn.com/people/rjb/cbloch.html

Small Business Administration Home Page
WEB http://www.sbaonline.sba.gov

SBA Online's Women's Business Ownership
URL gopher://www.sbaonline.sba.gov/II/Business-Development/Womens-Business-Ownership
WEB http://www.sbaonline.sba.gov/womeninbusiness/

How the Experts Raise Capital
WEB http://www.hoaa.com/capitall.htm

Ways To Kick Start Your Cash Flow
WEB http://www.ecn.net.au/~murray/5ways$$.html

Can SOHO Entrepreneurs Really Compete with Big Corporations on the Web?
WEB http://www.wilsonweb.com/articles/compete.htm

Web Marketing Information Center
WEB http://www.wilsonweb.com/webmarket/

Business@Home
WEB http://www.gohome.com/

SOHO America
WEB http://work.soho.org/SOHO/

They wrote the book on SOHOs
http://www.toolkit.cch.com/

Cash in a Flash

Whether your company is still in the womb, crawling on all fours, or off and running, it will always need capital to live long and prosper. Sinking investments into your baby isn't as difficult as it sounds, particularly when it comes to government assistance—if you know where to look. In fact, if you qualify for some of the government's SOHO-specific programs, the subsequent financial boost could really give your company some legs. First check out the **Federal Acquisition Jumpstation**, a government hubsite which can route you into common SOHO destinations, such as the Patent and Trademark, Acquisitions, and Commerce offices. But the numerous pages devoted to grant and contract information are more likely to catch your eye. In addition, you'll be linked to government-related programs like the home pages of the Small Business Administration and the Minority Business Development Agency. The official-sounding **Federal Web Resources** is not a government-sponsored site but it does feature links to federal procurements for SOHOs.

> **Whether your company is still in the womb, crawling on all fours, or off and running, it will always need capital to live long and prosper.**

Many small business owners will tell you that the government would rather give big corporations tax breaks and subsidies than help out the little guys who really need it. Perhaps. But even so, SOHO owners haven't been completely left in the lurch. **The Small Business Administration**'s home page is an excellent resource which features an array of assistance programs, educational workshops, and disaster relief programs to help keep you competitive. Another great resource for start-ups here is the small business FAQ. The "31 Most Asked Business Questions" will answer the important money questions shadowing all entrepreneurs, like how much money you need to get started and how to get a loan. Women entreprenuers should take a look at **SBA Online's Women's Business Ownership** for facts and figures on women business owners as a group, information regarding the Women's Prequalification Loan Program, and an invaluable list of women's business ownership representatives from every state.

Read the article on **How the Experts Raise Capital** by A. David Silver at SOHO Central. It offers insights into the cunning minds of lenders and offers suggestions on how to "sell them a credit," or, in layman's terms, convince them your biz will float. A less elaborate Web site is **Ways To Kick Start Your Cash Flow**, which features some key tips for retailers to inject cash rapidly for short-term investment.

Hanging Out a Shingle on the Web

The Internet is perhaps the least expensive and most efficient way for SOHOs to globally market their goods and services. But **Can SOHO Entrepreneurs Really Compete with Big Corporations on the Web?** An encouraging article from the Web Marketing Today archive answers in the affirmative, and explains the advantages that small businesses have over large corporations on the Internet. While large companies can afford banner advertising on high-traffic Web sites and constantly updated content on their own sites, they're often slower to act on marketing trends and more conservative in their approach. SOHOs, on the other hand, can exploit niche markets, experiment with new approaches, get

FRANCHISE FOLLIES

I would like some feedback on franchises. Can you really make money or are you making other people's money?

Franchises are for unimaginative sheep. People buy into them believing that with a name and program they cannot fail. Any business, whether it's your own or a franchise is marketing, marketing, marketing. And of course, lots of hard *smart* work. And BTW, if you come up with your own creative idea and are thinking of franchising it remember this: There are plenty of idiots out there with money who could mess up a wet dream and they could become a franchisee. When they fail, they're going to come after you and blame you for their failure. Offhand, that's what contracts are for. The responsibilities of each party should be clearly laid out.

—from misc.entrepreneurs .moderated

Not just another day at work
http://www.gohome.com/

lower rates on Web site production, offer more personalized service to attract customers, and survive on a lower profit margin than big corporations. And SOHOs can be just as visible on the Internet, especially considering that every company is only going to be listed once on the search engines. For more specific advice, visit the **Web Marketing Information Center**, which links to hundreds of articles about marketing on the Internet, from designing a Web site for your business to how to conduct secure electronic transactions.

Lifestyles of the Rich and Home-Bound

Those who work at home have a different set of concerns from those who work on Madison Avenue. How should you dress when you're working at home? Is there such a thing as a "power robe"? How do you keep yourself in work mode when the television is in the next room, just waiting to be turned on? What if your 2-year-old spills orange juice all over your keyboard? Should you fire her? For advice on dealing with family relationships and humorous anecdotes written by the work-at-home crowd, visit **Business@Home**, an ezine that will help SOHO owners with living, not just

> **❝ Is there such a thing as a 'power robe'? How do you keep yourself in work mode when the television is in the next room, just waiting to be turned on? ❞**

making a living. For more practical assistance, the non-profit membership organization **SOHO America** has news and reference resources, as well as benefits such as discounts to travel, delivery, and supply services you're likely to use.

▼ Starting points

CyberPreneur's Guide to the Internet An excellent compilation of mailing lists, newsgroups, gopher, and Web resources for "cyberpreneurs." The descriptions, evaluations, updates and pricing for entries are extremely useful for business people to sort out the resources appropriate for their situation, as well as seek a community of peers in cyberspace.
URL gopher://una.hh.lib.umich.edu/00/inetdirsstacks /cyberpren%3aschwilk

Entrepreneur's Small Business Square Although many netsurfers cringe at the thought of paying commercial service fees, sometimes the investment really pays off. "Thorough" is the best way to describe this whirlwind of resources. The Entrepreneur's Small Business Square is an eclectic medley of market and finance data, trademark and patent info, federal resources, and business news magazines. There's something for entrepreneurs in all phases of the game, from the start-up to the established. However, before you turn your frown upside down, keep in a mind that a few of the databases here level additional charges in addition to CompuServe's monthly fees.
COMPUSERVE *go* bizsquare

Idea Cafe: The Small Business Channel Chat rooms, bulletin boards, news, and features by and for entrepreneurs. The tone and flavor of discussion here are more in the sensitive, Ben & Jerry style.
WEB http://www.IdeaCafe.com

 Inc. Online The Net offspring of *Inc.* magazine is one of the best friends of small businesses in cyberspace—if you're looking to jump-start your startup, look no further. Unlike many sites that offer a little help and a lot of hype, *Inc.* Online is a site of real substance. Topic-threaded bulletin boards, interactive worksheets written by experts, and a database of 4,000 articles from *Inc.*, among other features, will make this one of the most useful and attractive sites on the Web for the small-business owner. Note that many of Inc. Online's features, such as *Zinc*, a sassy little ezine for young entrepreneurs, don't appear in the print version.
WEB http://www.inc.com

Palo Alto's Business Essentials This business software company features some notable resources which can be used for free. The Business Essentials Library has short articles on the planning phases of creating a business. With answers to neophyte questions like "What is a business plan?" and "Why plan?," even Vinny Barbarino wouldn't be intimidated. Palo Alto has also added a free, searchable database of more than 13,000 financing sources for small businesses at the Library.
WEB http://pasware.com/

 Small Business Forum "How much risk are you willing to shoulder? There are four kinds of risk in owning a

This baby can help your fledgling venture
http://www.inc.com

small business: personal, career, psychological, and financial. Some businesses are more risky than others: Restaurants are high risk, service businesses (usually) low risk..." This sound bit of advice is but one footnote in AOL's extensive walk-through for aspiring business owners. Covering everything from conventional mom-and-pop stores to online cash cows, this service for entrepreneurs is hands down the best and most informative resource for those who are just starting out. What kind of computer setup will you need? Why incorporate? Do you really need a Web site? AOL's Small Business Forum will hold your hand through start-up to success.
AMERICA ONLINE *keyword* small business

Small Business Resource Center Access free advice and business acumen derived from the experiences of a Web entrepreneur. You're likely to find yourself caught up in his spirited do-it-yourself sensibility as you read his compilation of practical, no-nonsense approaches to creating a viable business. Of course, if you're particlularly gung-ho, you can purchase the instructional books and tapes that the webmaster feels can give you a competitive edge. Simultaneously free, engaging, and

---

And are you master of your domain?
http://www.frsa.com/womenbiz/

useful, SBRC is definitely worth at least five minutes of your time.
WEB http://www.webcom.com/seaquest/sbrc/welcome.html

The Small Business Advisor It is unlikely that you'll find a more helpful free site than this one. If you own a small business or you're thinking about starting one, The Small Business Advisor should be first on your itinerary. Packed onto this Web site are management and organizational tips, articles, software reviews, and links to a slew of business-related newsgroups. Read up on "Money Saving Tips for Your Business," "Ten Marketing Mistakes to Avoid," and other savvy advice articles to help you avoid the pitfalls of small business. In addition, you can opt for counseling by Informational International, the parent company of this home page, which assists companies in doing business with the U.S. government.
WEB http://www.isquare.com/fhome19.htm

SmartBiz: Doing Business on the Internet A good resource for those interested in conducting Web ops. If you're not interested in buying any of the books, tapes, videos, and other entrepreneurial aids, let your eyes linger around the compilation of cyberpreneurship features. You'll find such gems as a professional perspective on online business opportunities, marketing dos and don'ts for Net-based business owners, and an article on privacy issues. Plus, email newsletters and HTML resource pages will instruct the intrepid businessperson braving the World Wide Web on how to hold one's own.
WEB http://www.smartbiz.com/sbs/dobiz.htm

SOHO Central The Web headquarters of the Home Office Associates of America, this company offers its networking services to enhance your home business, but its anemic

home page may induce mild skepticism of its success rate. However, the efforts at providing content are solid, most notably those under the Hot Info for Home Business section, which includes a "Step-by-Step Guide to Working with Your Lawmakers" and "How the Experts Raise Capital."
WEB http://www.hoaa.com

WomenBiz If you're a female entrepreneur, WomenBiz will help you make your private business ambitions a reality. Start at Biz Tips for a test on your franchise inclinations, then find out what key points to hit in your business plan. Afterward, head to the Web resources for start-ups. Finally, feel free to jump into the fray at the Women Biz Discussion Board, where you'll find lots of entrepreneurs seeking business consultation, offering their services, and dropping helpful hints.
WEB http://www.frsa.com/womenbiz/

▼ Advice

The ABCs of the Web "Get a good server: When you put your Web site on a server, you are trusting the people who manage that server to make sure your page is accessible on the Internet. Get recommendations." This handsome site passionately hails the Internet as the next communications revolution in a short treatise on the medium. Placing it on par with television, the author briefly outlines her belief in its massive potential as a lucrative hub for businesses. If you're already well-aware of the power of the Web, head straight to the "ABCs of Marketing on the Web," which offers five lessons in the creation, marketing, budgeting, and management of a Web site.
WEB http://www.rbloch.com/

alt.business.misc While originally devised to promote the discussion of miscellaneous busi-

DO YOU BELIEVE IN ANGELS?

Q: Can anyone tell me if it is realistic to look for an angel-type venture capitalist to help seed a start-up company? Our field would be the Internet, a definite growth and 'prestige' industry, but is it realistic? It stinks having a great idea but absolutely zero cash to put it into action.

A: If your product or idea is good enough, it is possible to find financing from "angels" or others willing to make direct equity investments in seed companies. The problem is gaining access to these investors. There is a growing network of angels, but it will take a recommendation for you to present your business to them. These angels can provide the $100,000 to $500,000 in seed capital that more traditional venture capitalists are currently shying away from. I have access to a number of these "angels" so I will give one bit of advice which will help you: People will be much more likely to invest if you truly devote a significant amount of your time and, in a sense, money.

—from Inc. Online's Zinc bulletin boards

ness topics, much of the dialogue is way off course. In fact, the spam from this newsgroup is best met by focused readers with iron stomachs. There's an obscene amount of get rich-quick-without-leaving-your-house schemes, although occasionally a decent thread on business-related subjects will worm its way in. And as for the good news? No one seems to be hawking Ab Rollers in the group.
USENET alt.business.misc

alt.make.money.fast If you've ever concocted a get-rich-quick scheme or thought seriously

DO I KNOW YOU?

Every day we learn something new, however it is the day that you can actually see that new thing in action that you truly learn. Years ago, I read that using a photo of yourself is a good marketing technique. Sort of a putting a face to the offer type of premise. In the past, I have tested this technique and found the results to be mixed. Never understanding how anyone could use this item to extract the Big results... Until now... For several issues of a magazine called *Sparetime*, one of the members to this group has been writing articles regarding a specific topic "New Releases." Each month or so I would look at her picture and read the article. This months issue had an extra in it. Placed near the back, nestled in next to the World's Greatest Business and the Bronze Babyshoe Franchise was a small display ad containing the same photo that I had been looking at for months. It virtually leaped out of this sea of advertisments and screamed "You know who I am and I always have some snippet of useful info..." Instead of just turning the page, I had to stop and read the message. She basically got me! The picture did it, the headline was irrelevant and nothing about this ad was spectacular except the familiar face.

—from misc.entrepreneurs.moderated

about making one work, this may be the place for you. From telemarketing to Herbalife to O. J. Simpson T-shirts to NuSkin, this newsgroup preaches the gospel of lining your pockets without lifting a finger. Half consumer-warning forum, half celebration of the easy strike, it's a schizophrenic place where the hum of fast money is always in the air.
USENET alt.make.money.fast

biz.marketplace.discussion Lounging in this newsgroup from night to night is like having conversations in stereo with Don Lapre and Tom Vu. Like those infomercial kingpins, the residents of this newsgroup have more tapes, more books, more schemes, and more advice to sell than any infomercial ever did. However, this alarming exercise of free speech-meets-capitalism may just be the charge that jumpstarts your career ambitions. With topics ranging from, "Earn $5,000+ at home!" to "Family Bakery for Sale," you'll find just about everything imaginable turning up in this way station.
USENET biz.marketplace.discussion

The Critical Link "Danger—entrepreneurship could land you in divorce court! Before going forward with any entrepreneurial venture, strengthen your relationship with some outside counseling, or you may find yourself in divorce court before your business dreams are realized." The entrepreneurial couple, an important issue overlooked by most SOHO sites, is directly addressed at The Critical Link. With Tony Robbins-meets-John Bradshaw sensibility, the Critical Link helps you navigate the emotional waters of the partner/spouse relationship while keeping both unions afloat. Learn "the 10 most common mistakes made by unhappy entrepreneurial couples" and discover if your relationship is ready to tackle a business.
WEB http://www.ltbn.com/azriela/

Janet Ruhl's Computer Consultant's Resource Page While the main attraction at Janet Ruhl's page is, not surprisingly, Janet Ruhl's books, she does post business-related information to make the surfing worth your while. For starters, aspiring computer consultants can check out the extensive "Real Consulting Rates" chart, which delineates the booty that consultants are pulling in based on a regional survey. Should you join a firm? Should you opt for royalties when designing custom programs? Janet's got insights on these and other career moves for industry people, not to mention a few books to sell. Good advice for newbies from a veteran in the business.

WEB http://ourworld.compuserve.com/homepages /JanetRuhl/

misc.entrepreneurs You would think that this newsgroup would be a two-for-the-price-of-one deal, as a site for entrepreneurs to discuss their marketing and expansion strategies and as a place for them to practice those strategies. Sadly, it is all too similar to its other business-related Usenet brethren; refrains of "Have I got a deal for you" and its (ever more creatively disguised) variations comprise the majority of the discussion.

USENET misc.entrepreneurs

misc.entrepreneurs.moderated One of the best forums for sincere entrepreneurs looking to ask some questions, post some answers, or make a few contacts. The number of posts are somewhat low in comparison to other business-related newsgroups, but that's what you get when the newsgroup moderator weeds out all the spam found in this group's Usenet counterparts. With the field clear of pyramid schemes and fast-buck promises, the denizens chat about franchise viability, the shotgun clause for partnership agreements, and trademark questions. The sincerity and productivity among this tight group is certainly refreshing; perhaps the best of the bunch.

USENET misc.entrepreneurs.moderated

PHK CPA: Your Home Business This small business consultant's Web site has spun off a page offering biz tips for SOHOs. As befits his profession, the knowledge dropped is tax-related, with tidbits hitting all the major and minor concerns regarding W-2s, IRA withdrawals, the IRS, spousal deductions, write-

offs, etc. Because every kernel of thought here is encapsulated, bulleted, and individually shrink-wrapped, you won't find anything addressed in great depth, although the webmaster raises some tax situations many SOHO owners may want to consider.

WEB http://www.discribe.ca/yourhbiz/yourhbiz.htm

Ways To Kick Start Your Cash Flow Is it enough to advertise "30 percent off all stock"? Not according to this site, which advises making the headline "more compelling and benefits/results orientated. The key to this is to dramatically illustrate the incredible price-to-value relationship and make it very compelling." Read up on other business basics, such as how to make a quick sale, how to lock down cash in advance, and how to double your profits.

WEB http://www.ecn.net.au/~murray/5ways$$.html

Every kernel of thought here is encapsulated, bulleted, and individually shrink-wrapped.

Working-From-Home Forum This CompuServe forum caters to people who don't have to go very far to bring home the bacon. Whether you're a freelance writer or a medical transcriptionist, you'll find some advice to help you do your at-home job better. In addition to the populist message boards, the Library is full of downloadable articles such as "115 Ways to Make Money with a Computer," "Home Office Space Alternatives," and "Kidproofing the Computer," organized under two dozen broad topics, from accounting to telecommuting.

COMPUSERVE *go* work

As Seen on TV

The Web has the potential to be as popular as television. But when commercial TV debuted in the 1940s, a lot of marketing people thought it was a mere fad. Yet there were others who could envision the phenomenal impact it would have have in the years ahead. Indeed, the hypertext medium of the web is in its infancy, and many marketers and communicators are finding new ways to implement effective promotional programs. So why use the Web? How can it be an effective marketing tool? Here's a few reasons...

Interactivity: Using various techniques, including forms visitors fill out at your site—you can build a dialog with prospects and customers, find out information about them and use this information for later follow up marketing efforts.

Reasonable Cost: You can start a simple Web site for as little as $500 or so (even less if you do all the work yourself), then expand the site as you need to. Once it's created, updating your site can be done very quickly and inexpensively.

A Good Selling Medium: You can sell directly from the Web via credit card. Though some feel sending credit card data over the Internet is not particularly secure, it's as safe as giving your charge number over the telephone, which people do all the time. And there are various "pay-per-access" payment processes being tested.

A Good Promotional Medium: When people can't come to your store, you can still tell your customers about new product lines and special sales. You can provide publicity for your organization or even run a contest. There's really no limit to what you can do."

—from *The ABCs of the Web*

▼ Franchises

Franchise Opportunity SuperStore Located within the online Branch Mall, this company operates like a matchmaking service between franchises and prospective buyers. At no cost to you, the SuperStore will match your interests with appropriate franchises, and send you brochures, publications, and other information. Simply fill out a form relaying your interests, your investment range, your launch window, etc. and the SupersStore will customize a search for you. What's in it for them? Nothing yet. But if a love connection is made eventually, it wants a cut of the franchise fee.
WEB http://branch.com/franchise/franchise.htm

FranNet If you can't come up with your own idea for a business, you can always buy someone else's. At FranNet, you can begin your long journey along the road to franchise wisdom by learning about the history of franchising, determining if franchising suits you, and discovering how you can purchase one. This package of information is brought to you by a franchise-consulting firm and includes a list of companies that offer these opportunities.
WEB http://www.frannet.com

▼ Government resources

Consumer Information Catalog—Small Business Do you remember how as a small child you sent away for those consumer catalogs from Boulder, Colo., just because they were free and you loved getting mail addressed to you? Now the government agency that gives you free and low-priced pamphlets offers much of these items online. Find "Basic Facts About Registering a Trademark," "Starting a Business," "Guide to Business Credit for Women, Minorities, and Small Businesses," and more from this page at no charge.
WEB http://www.pueblo.gsa.gov/smbuss.htm

Federal Acquisition Jumpstation While the name of this page sounds like deep-space sci-fi jargon from *Babylon 5*, this jumpstation is very much rooted in the reality of private businesses. With a jumble of links concerning multiple business applications, the small business owner can glean some invaluable URLs pointing toward procurements and business opportunities from several government agencies, grant and contract information pages, and organizations like the SBA and the Minority Business Development Agency.
WEB http://procure.msfc.nasa.gov/fedproc/home.html

Federal Web Resources A decent site with information and links concerning buying and selling with the Feds electronically. Special emphasis is placed on the Electronic Commerce through Electronic Data Interchange, which streamlines the process of exchanging documents between private businesses and the government.
WEB http://www.nbn.com/people/rjb/cbloch.html

SBA: Small Business Administration Home Page If your small business is feeling the financial crunch, you don't have to tackle all the pressures and uncertainties of entrepreneurship alone. The federal and state governments offer plenty of assistance, subsidies, and educational workshops, but you have to know where to look. The SBA home page is an excellent starting point. Covering everything from disaster relief to business counseling programs, the SBA even has its resources listed by state. The "31 Most Asked Business Questions" will help aspiring entrepreneurs who are wary of getting in over their heads learn how to ask the right questions (How much money do I need to get started? What do I have to do to get a loan?). The SBA is a must-see for SOHO-owners who need to cushion what's bound to be a bumpy ride.
WEB http://www.sbaonline.sba.gov/

SBAonline: Womens Business Ownership "Women employ 11 million workers, more than the Fortune 500 worldwide. It is projected that by the year 2000 women will own 40 percent of all businesses." The SBA page covers woman-owned small businesses and is equipped with statistics, facts, a list of women's business ownership representatives (sorted by state), and information regarding the Women's Pre-qualification Loan Program. Also note the gopher resources directory, which features programs for training and counseling, government procurement, and the Demonstration Project.
URL gopher://www.sbaonline.sba.gov/11/Business-Development/Womens-Business-Ownership
WEB http://www.sbaonline.sba.gov/womeninbusiness/

You don't have to tackle all the pressures and uncertainties of entrepreneurship alone.

Small Business Innovation Research Program (SBIR) According to this Web page, certain federal agencies, including the EPA, NASA, and NSF, are required to allocate part of their R&D budgets for small business competitions. The SBIR, or Small Business Innovative Research project, is a competition that offers hundreds of thousands of dollars to small companies that can develop technological solutions to problems relating to the commercialization of the private sector. If your company deals with advanced-technologies problem solving, perhaps you can benefit from a federal research commission. This Web site will give you the ABCs of the SBIR, with news on the project and sample proposals submitted by other companies. Uncle

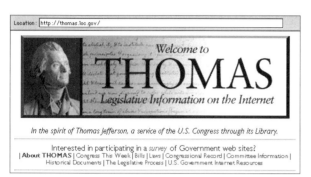

Location: http://thomas.loc.gov/

Welcome to THOMAS
Legislative Information on the Internet

In the spirit of Thomas Jefferson, a service of the U.S. Congress through its Library.

Interested in participating in a *survey* of Government web sites?
| About THOMAS | Congress This Week | Bills | Laws | Congressional Record | Committee Information |
Historical Documents | The Legislative Process | U.S. Government Internet Resources

Don't doubt the resources at THOMAS
http://thomas.loc.gov/

Sam's money is waiting for a savvy business mind to come along and take it.
WEB http://www.dsu.edu:8000/ • http://www.sbaonline.sba.gov/sbir/sbir.html

THOMAS: Legislative Information on the Internet
While Congress might seem to some like a private party behind closed doors, certain Web sites sponsored by the government do wonders to pull average citizens into the loop. THOMAS, for example, is a legislative search engine that allows you to sort out relevant topics that have received recent congressional consideration. You can check the All Bill Summary & Status Info page as well as the Floor Actions Only and Detailed Legislative History pages. If a bill to provide tax relief for small businesses, protect jobs, create opportunities, and increase the take-home pay of workers was bounced around the floor of Congress like jai a lai, shouldn't you know about it? You can get it from THOMAS.
WEB http://thomas.loc.gov/

U.S. House of Representatives: Committee on Small Business So you've started your own business and you don't want to step on any federal toes. Where do you go? To the source, of course! In this podiatric analogy, the foot in question would be our esteemed congressional committee from the House of Representatives, and the aforementioned extremities would be the laws they pass. Ordinary citizens like you would be privy to SOHO-related legislation that most people won't otherwise hear about, such as updates on government programs or revisions on current laws. Within the same legal stew, you'll also find current committee wranglings over bills with congressional contact names and numbers of the supporters, info on committee members, and an explanation of rules, jurisdiction, and agenda. So if "a bill to amend the Internal Revenue Code of 1986 to allow a family-owned business exclusion from the gross estate subject to estate tax" has your brain doing cartwheels, you can get the contact number for Senator Dorgan at this Web site.
WEB http://www.house.gov/smbiz/

U.S. Patent and Trademark Office "For over 200 years, the basic role of the Patent and Trademark Office (PTO) has remained the same: To promote the progress of science and the useful arts by securing for limited times to authors and inventors the exclusive right to their respective writings and discoveries." So begins the introduction to the PTO site. It's this respect for intellectual property that the office feels has jumpstarted America's well-known industriousness and ingenuity. The aspiring inventor/entrepreneur can learn the parameters of the patent process and obtain the proper forms. Who knows, you could be the next Thomas Edison or, better yet, the next Dave Thomas.
WEB http://www.uspto.gov/

U.S. Senate Committee on Small Business Implemented to inform citizens of small business legislation, this government-sponsored page manages to be magnificently succint. "Women's Business Training Centers Act of 1996," "The National Small Business Regula-

tory Relief Act of 1996," and other bills that are currently receiving congressional attention are listed here with minimum fuss and maximum clarity. A click on any law will produce a menu furnishing the full text, co-sponsor, floor statements, summaries, section-by-section analysis, legislative status, purpose, and press releases relating to it. With this site serving the public, you won't need to be Matlock to know the score.
WEB http://www.senate.gov/~sbc/bills.html

▼ Books

The Entrepreneur's Bookstore The books offered here cover numerous money-making models for the small and home business owner, including Internet business paradigms. The prices are low and the scope is wide. You'll find titles relating to such respectable businesses as carpet cleaning, resume writing, bartending, franchise, and mail order, just to name a few.
WEB http://kwicsys.com/books/

Entrepreneur's Wave An online bookstore with a selection that canvasses the marketing, financial, and legal concerns of both online and offline entrepreneurs. While there's no actual content on the Web site, the business insights from these books can be reaped for a price, and you can order directly from the Web site.
WEB http://www.en-wave.com/

Nicholas Direct While the connection isn't immediate, Ted Nicholas conjures up that uncanny separated-at-birth resemblance to the *Love Boat*'s smarmy Doc, a.k.a. Bernie Kopel. However, with titles like *Wipe Out Personal Tax* and *Publish Your Own Book*, this Doc wants to heal your financial wounds with his series of how-to books. One of his other titles—*How to Form Your Own Corpo-*

ration Without A Lawyer For Under $75—is a standout, and, according to the author, has sold more than a million copies. Shoppers may wonder if "under $75" includes the book's $19.95 cover price.
WEB http://nicholas-direct.com/

▼ Software

Mac Business/Home Office Software Libraries
There are several resources for financial software here: The Application library is loaded with programs to manage your mortgage, schedule your day, and log addresses and phone numbers, as well as one called Pogo Your Logo that will transform your company logo into a bouncing screen saver. The Spreadsheets, Templates/Misc. Files, and Business Utilities libraries are also filled with Mac programs that will make the administrative duties of working at home proceed a bit more efficiently.
AMERICA ONLINE *keyword* mbs→Software Libraries

"Using a photo of yourself is a good marketing technique"
http://nicholas-direct.com/

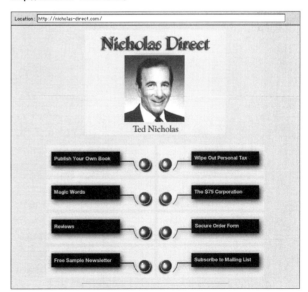

Small Business Software Library Part of Microsoft's Small Business Center, this software library contains dozens of Macintosh and IBM programs designed to help small-business owners start and operate their companies.

AMERICA ONLINE *keyword* small business→Software Library

If you have any kind of a home office set-up, you'll probably find something useful here.

ZD Net Business Forum Libraries This isn't really the place to be if you're just looking to coordinate your kids' allowances, but if you have any kind of a home office set-up, you'll probably find something useful here. The Business Forum software library has an impressive range of general finance applications, from payroll to inventory to addressbook software. In the Professional library, you'll find programs for home day care providers, motel and inn owners, firefighters, and bicycle dealers, to name but a few. Resume-writing software is located here, as well.

COMPUSERVE *go* pbs→Business Forum→Browse Libraries

▼ Organizations

National Minority Business Council The NMBC is an umbrella organization that includes hundreds of small businesses located in the U.S. and around the world. It offers programs and advocacy and networking support to its members, for a price. Members are privy to the NMBC's business referral service, international trade programs, corporate education program, and other services that foster busi-

ness relationships and promote training. The Web site, however, suffers from a broken link or two.

WEB http://www.panix.com/~nmbc

Small Business Advancement National Center According to the SBANC, which hints at some vague affiliation with the University of Central Arkansas, the organization's purpose is "to provide small businesses, entrepreneurs, educators, economic development officers, government, associations, and small business counselors with the necessary resources to further their business and economic efforts and goals." This includes seminars held at the university that targets new and established businesses in an effort to improve their marketing strategies. However, the Web site of SBANC already has a wealth of information that SOHO owners can take advantage for free. Get briefed on legislative action summaries, marketing strategy theses, and government loan program instructions. Peruse the entries from the Journal of Small Business Strategy, which publishes applied research on topics related to entrepreneurship and business operations. There's even finance-related software regarding profit-and-loss statements, business loans, and cash flow. If you're interested in government assistance, the Web site supports several databases to help you find it.

WEB http://www.sbaer.uca.edu/

Small Business Foundation of America This independent research and educational nonprofit claims to sponsor unbiased research on small business and its influence on the nation. It also provides "technical assistance that will help ensure the growth and success of this vital segment of the U.S. business community." You can obtain summaries of its findings in reports such as "Twenty Years of Job Creation Research: What Have We Learned?,"

"Is the Independent Entrepreneur A Valuable Organizational Form?," and "Does Superfund Create Barriers to Capital for Small Business?". Expect to pay from $10 to $20 for full disclosure.
WEB http://www.miep.org/sbfa

▼ Indexes

Business Resources on the Web: Small Business A great links site. You'll find numerous URLs on starting up, financing, administrating, business journals, franchising, and conducting international operations. In addition, there are several government links on safety, trademarks, and development. For cyberpreneurs, try the a handful of links distinctly geared towards doing business on the Web.
WEB http://www.idbsu.edu/carol/smallbus.htm

CyberPreneur Its slogan is "Where the World Connects," which won't sound quite so boastful once you've seen CyberPreneur. The multiple set of links here ranges from business opportunities to private and government resources for the small business owner. There are also financial, real estate, and business classified ads to let you know what's on the auctioning block. Because this Web site tries to do so much, it will probably require a little patience on your part to separate the wheat from the chaff.
WEB http://www.cyberpreneur.com/

Small and Home Based Business Links Dozens of links to SOHO pages, neatly sorted into "filing cabinets." Pick a category, such as reference, franchises, opportunity, news, marketing, or services, and meander through the offerings from business newsgroups to marketing services to specialty book sellers. Given the service-oriented nature of the site, you'll find price tags dangling from most items—but you know, sometimes you have to

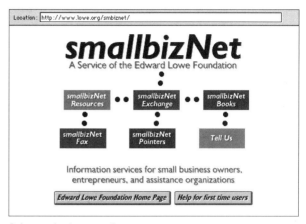

A thousand pointers to sites
http://www.lowe.org/smbiznet/

spend money to make money.
WEB http://www.ro.com/small_business/homebased.html

SmallbizNet This service of the Edward Lowe Foundation provides a number of online resources for entrepreneurs. There's a lot of information available here, but most of the resources cost $2 to access, by download or fax. Includes a searchable database of more than 5,000 articles related to small businesses, from legal issues to record-keeping to taxes. Also available is a giant list of pointers to other sources of similar information, both on and off the Net.
WEB http://www.lowe.org/smbiznet/

SOHO So Far You may want to avoid all the product endorsements that pepper this home page and head straight for the meat. The key informational source here is the Small Business Resource Center, which is actually a links page that takes you to several SOHO stops on the Web. Find everything from organizational tools to legislation updates, all divided under clearly labeled categories such as Government Info, Online Magazines and News, and Yellow Pages and Directories.
WEB http://www.sohosofar.com

They call it the stupid tax, but you could be laughing all the way to the bank

YOU'VE GOT A JOB. You've got a deck of credit cards. You've even got your mattress lined with cash. But you're still looking for supplementary income. Do you play the lotto on the side? The lottery—the oft-played, seldom-won, high-stakes game of chance—has been jokingly referred to as a tax on the stupid. But even though you know you have a slightly better chance of winning a Nobel Prize than winning the lottery, do you sometimes find yourself dashing off to the local convenience store whenever the Lotto announces another $10 million jackpot? If so, you'll definitely want to take your

Hey, You Never Know

lotto fever onto the Internet. From cyberlotteries to random number generators, you can prime yourself for lottery success just by clicking around the Web.

Unless you're a diehard lottery player with a memory like an elephant's, you're probably confused by the multitude of games at your local bodega—Daily, Pick 4, Keno, and seasonal specialties like Shamrock Bucks and Santa's Little Windfall. If the games intrigue you, drop in on **Lottery News on the Web**, which explains game play of the lotteries of several major Eastern states, and also gives the pros and cons (e.g. large pay-off, high tax rate) of each. **LottoWin** drops numerical and statistical science on its Tips & Hints Page, although cutting through this math lesson is like reading Stephen Hawking's *A Brief History of Time*. If you're feeling really lucky, take your chances with the myriad of lottery software being hawked online at sites such as **Entertainment-On-Line**. Their marketers claim they choose "good" numbers, crunch statistics, chart trends, all using the power of mathematics to give you the scientific edge. Be careful, though. Lottery numbers are drawn randomly, and the longer you forget that, the greater the chance that you'll end up joining in the chorus of bilked hopefuls on **rec.gambling.lottery**. And for those of you who love the unpredictability of

---

Be a power player—if you're feeling lucky
http://www.eol.com/

CASH REGISTER

Lottery News on the Web
WEB http://www.lotterynews.com/index.html

LottoWin
WEB http://www.bluequetzal.com/LottoWin/lth.htm

Entertainment-On-Line
WEB http://www.eol.com/

USENET rec.gambling.lottery

Mr. Lotto
WEB http://q2000.com.au/Mr_Lotto/Amer_text.htm

InterLotto
WEB http://www.interlotto.com/

Cyberlottery
WEB http://www.hol.nl/~cyberlot/

American Lotto Exchange
WEB http://www.netsurf.net/lotto/index.html

International Lottery in Liechtenstein
WEB http://cyber.nis.za/lotto.htm

Publisher's Clearing House Company
WEB http://www.pch.com/

Face it: You are probably not already a winner
http://www.pch.com

You gotta pay to win
http://www.lotterynews.com/index.html

life, **Mr. Lotto** is a free number generator that will produce six random selections with the click of a button.

After you've picked your numbers and bought your ticket, the next step, naturally, is to get the results. Check **InterLotto**, the unofficial scoreboard for the lottery scene online. This exceptional Web site tracks lottery games in 38 states, posting the latest results, the drawing schedules, and the booty, all at no charge.

Keep in mind that your chances to play and win don't have to be limited by mere geography. "Lottery brokers" will represent you in foreign games for weekly or monthly fees. The **Cyberlottery** Web site carries several from Europe while **American Lotto Exchange** canvasses games from Canada. There's also a cyberlottery operated by the **International Lottery in Liechtenstein**. Also known as Interlotto, the service carries games with payoffs of over $1 million. To ensure legitimacy, it's audited by Coopers & Lybrand (plus, it fields a professional, sharp-looking home page).

Finally, let's not forget the only lottery-style game with personality. Ed McMahon's personality, that is. The erstwhile talk show sidekick and former spokesperson for **Publisher's Clearing House Sweepstakes** has practically become synonymous with the ubiquitous mail-subscription lottery game. Now, the Publisher's Clearing House Company has moved online with its sweepstakes, eliminating the cumbersome snail mail process for Internet-advantaged folk and, incidentally, eliminating Ed as well. From its home page you can try for its $10 million giveaway just by filling out its Web form—every day, if you'd like. And that doesn't even begin to cover the wonderful magazine discounts...

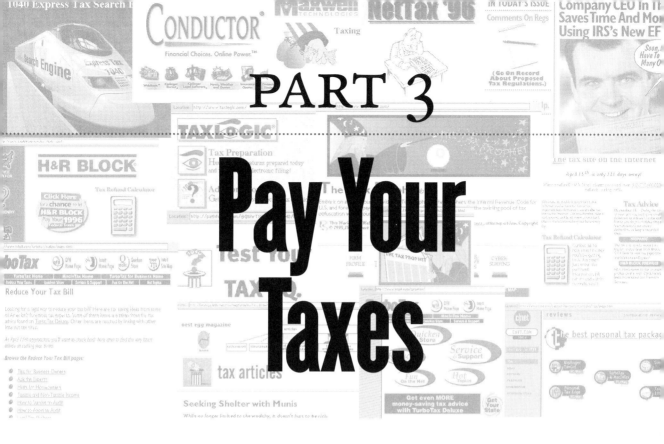

PART 3
Pay Your Taxes

YOU'VE ACHIEVED YOUR GOAL of making more money. But now you realize that the more money you make, the more taxes you'll have to pay. Instead of deciding to make less money, you should use the Internet to minimize your taxes. In this part, we'll show you step-by-step how to prepare your tax returns using the most user-friendly software on the market. We'll help you file your taxes online so you'll get your refund fast—without sacrificing any trees. And we'll point you toward the best sources of free tax advice on the Web. You'll never have to hire an accountant again!

How to File Your Taxes

SIMPLESTEPS

You haven't got time for the pain—or the paper. You need the right Web connections

D O YOU EVER PLAY that game where you wonder which celebrities are brushing their teeth at the same time as you? Mick Jagger might have just finished brushing his teeth before you started brushing yours. Michelle Pfeiffer might be brushing hers right now.

If that seems a bit frivolous, imagine which celebrities are filing their tax returns as you're filing yours. Tax returns are the one things that no one, no matter how famous, can avoid. Try to dodge them, and you'll be a different kind of celebrity. But tax returns are also a legendary headache, full of duplicate forms and ink-stained worksheets. Many people hire accountants to complete their returns. But in the new world, many are using the Internet. With the IRS online, and plenty of

The Tax Prophet wil help you profit from taxes
http://www.taxprophet.com

Location: http://www.taxprophet.com/pubs/pubs.html

additional help available for the resourceful taxpayer, the Net is an accountant, a tax counselor, and a post office all rolled into one.

I **Get motivated.** You don't really need to get motivated to do your taxes. You need to do them, whether you're motivated or not. Unconvinced? Visit **The Internal Revenue Service Web Site**, a huge and valuable resource with daily tax news updates. You don't see this kind of aggressive, proactive behavior from government agencies who are merely recommending action. After you visit the IRS, stop by **TaxWeb**, a consumer-oriented tax resource that covers the basic tax filing process in easy-to-understand language. And then visit other valuable starting points—Web sites like **Maxwell Labs' Taxing Times** and

The Internal Revenue Service Web Site
WEB http://www.irs.ustreas.gov/

TaxWeb
WEB http://www.taxweb.com/

Maxwell Labs' Taxing Times
WEB http://www.scubed.com/tax/tax.html

The IRS never seemed so friendly
http://www.irs.ustreas.gov/

Location: http://www.irs.ustreas.gov/prod/cover.html

IN TODAY'S ISSUE

Comments On Regs

(Go On Record About Proposed Tax Regulations.)

Comments & Help.

Forms And Publications.

Company CEO In Thrifty Saves Time And Money By Using IRS's New EFTPS.

Soon, I Won't Have To Write So Many Of These!

The Tax Prophet, commercial service forums like CompuServe's **Tax Connection** and AOL's **Tax Forum**, and even the online homes of commercial tax preparation giants like **H&R Block**. Notice how all of these colorful, perky sites attempt to make taxes seem fun, almost like a party—and everyone's invited. So come on and join the fun. If that—and the fear of incarceration—doesn't work, another way to motivate yourself is with the promise of a reward; use the Net to figure out how much money is coming your way from the IRS. With **H&R Block's Refund Estimator**, you can enter your filing status and some basic income information, click on "Calculate My Refund!" and then attack your taxes with a renewed fervor in anticipation of a hefty refund. **Net-Tax '96** will also calculate your refund (or remittance due), as well as provide a tutorial of sorts by emulating an actual 1040 and providing hyperlinks to IRS explanations of key terms found on it.

If you're still feeling exhausted by the prospect of tax season, think about investing in one of the popular tax preparation software packages. We recommend **TurboTax/MacInTax**, **Kiplinger TaxCut**, or **Personal Tax Edge** (see reviews that follow). All three have online sites that offer tax help and software troubleshooting. And if you absolutely can't work up the requisite energy, at least get official permission to have no energy. Get that permission from **Filing Extensions**. Now take a deep breath and relax. You'll have until October to tense up again.

2 **Collect the proper forms.** Gone are the days of waiting in line at the post office to photocopy forms with names that sound like distant stars. Now you can simply go online and download your forms instantly.

The Tax Prophet
WEB http://www.taxprophet.com

Tax Connection
COMPUSERVE *go* tax

Tax Forum
AMERICA ONLINE *keyword* tax

H&R Block
WEB http://www.handrblock.com/tax/index.html

H&R Block's Refund Estimator
WEB http://165.121.1.171/tax/office/estimator.html

Net-Tax '96
WEB http://www.vni.net/~nettax

TurboTax
WEB http://www.intuit.com/turbotax/

Kiplinger TaxCut
WEB http://www.conductor.com

Personal Tax Edge
WEB http://www.parsonstech.com/software/ptefinal.html

Filing Extensions
WEB http://www.taxweb.com/extend.html

First, find out what tax forms you'll need. Most tax-payers need their 1040, their W2, and their 1099s, as well as receipts for all major purchases and itemizable expenses. Any computer user will want to look into the possibility of the 1040PC, which does away with the physical formatting of the 1040 form and strips it down to its basic data. And any computer user with tax preparation software has his or her forms already electronically encoded; all the top software packages include IRS-approved forms you can print out in 1040PC or regular format.

But what if you're a netsurfer without tax preparation software, who wants a wide variety of forms? Well, then, go on the Web, where you can have your forms for free. First stop: the IRS. **Tax Forms and Publications** serves as a clearinghouse for all IRS documents, from the classic 1040s (Schedules A through R) to the pro-crastinator's Form 8736 (Application for an Automatic Extension). If the IRS is busy—it will be busier as April approaches—try **FedWorld Tax Forms**, which offers a complete library of IRS forms and publications. Though not as user-friendly as the IRS site, it's just as current (updated every morning).

Note that the majority of the forms available online are encoded in PDF, a document-reading format developed by Adobe. You'll need the PDF decoder **Adobe Acrobat** to read the forms if you're downloading them from the Web. Luckily, the program is available for free.

3 **Prepare your return.** So you have the requisite motivation. You have the nec-essary forms. Now, all you have to do is fill out your return. Again, those with tax preparation software have it easy—all the major packages have

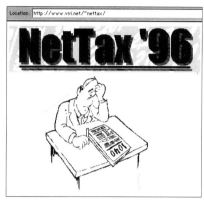

Lessen the tax on your brain as well as on your income
http://www.vni.net/~nettax

Tax Forms and Publications
WEB http://www.irs.ustreas.gov/basic
/forms_pubs/index.html

FedWorld Tax Forms
URL ftp://ftp.fedworld.gov/pub/irs-pdf
/irs-pdf.htm

Adobe Acrobat
WEB http://www.adobe.com/Acrobat
/readstep.html

Don't let the IRS push your buttons
http://www.handrblock.com/tax/index.html

pre-programmed guided tours, or at least a Q&A that helps you minimize your payments.

Otherwise, you'll want to lessen your tax burden through some research of your own. In the next chapter, we've reviewed the best free tax advice sites online, as well as dozens of subject-specific resources that will help you have a happy tax day with many happy returns. At the very least, try not to make any of the **25 Most Common Tax Preparation Errors**. And if you have any additional questions, try **1-800-TAX-LAWS**.

Once you've decided how you're going to play your return—itemize expenses or take a straight deduction? declare yourself self-employed or not?—all you need to do is fill out the forms. Tax preparation software packages let you type the numbers directly into a linked set of forms, and they even alert you when numbers don't accord with numbers you've entered elsewhere in your return. Otherwise, you're on your own.

But not totally on your own. The Net is home to dozens of businesses that are basically online accoun-

25 Most Common Tax Preparation Errors
WEB http://www.ey.com/us/tax/25error.htm

1-800-TAX-LAWS
WEB http://www.5010geary.com

tancy firms. They'll take your return, prepare it, and try to do your taxes so that you save the maximum amount of money. The **TaxWizard**, a husband-and-wife CPA team who sometimes hang around at the **misc .taxes** newsgroup, will take care of your 1040 for $80. If you need other forms prepared for your return, you can order them à la carte. An interactive Tax Organizer lets you input your financial data online by secure Web browser. When complete, your prepared returns are mailed back with enough copies for you, the feds, and the state agency. **Net-Tax** also lets you enter your tax information at its site. Transmit the data and your return will be prepared and mailed back within 48 hours for a fee of $59 (payable by credit card). Neither of these services offers electronic filing, so you'll have to file yourself by snail mail in both cases. Still, you may be willing to pay the $50 to $80 to have your return handled by confident professionals.

4 **Get them to the Feds on time.**
Now comes the big step—filing your return. If your tax situation is simple enough to use a 1040EZ, doing your taxes can be as easy as picking up the phone. Millions of lucky, single folks without dependents will receive a **TeleFile** package with their 1040EZ, and they can file by phone in about ten minutes. To use TeleFile, you must be filing a 1040EZ, must be filing from the same residence as the previous year, and must have a touch-tone phone.

Even if you don't qualify for TeleFile, you may still be able to take advantage of electronic filing. If you are one of the millions of taxpayers looking for money back from Uncle Sam, you can submit your return through the wires, and expect that your refund check will be on its way to you in a matter of days.

TaxWizard
WEB http://www.taxwizard.com

USENET misc.taxes

Net-Tax
WEB http://rampages.onramp.net /~daywag/taxintro.htm

TeleFile
WEB http://www.irs.ustreas.gov /basic/elec_svs/telefile.html

Again, tax software users have it easy. Most of the major software packages have their own built-in electronic filing hotlines; if you want to avail yourself of these services, follow the instructions in your software. Otherwise, be on the lookout for electronic filing services that have set up shop online. Many are also preparation services. **TaxLogic**, for example, both files and prepares, with preparation charges starting at $75 fee for the basic 1040 (with unlimited W2s and 1099s). If you use TaxLogic to prepare, electronic filing is free and you can get your refund in as little as 10 days. TaxLogic also offers a tax advice service, free if you're filing, $5 per question if you're not. Most of the electronic filing services, from **Electronic Filing Service** to **GFN's Electronic Tax Filing**, charge a moderate fee for handling the electronic paperwork, somewhere in the neighborhood of $50. Still, it's hard to argue with the convenience—no stamps, no danger of lost mail, and a licensed filing and preparing company attesting to the fact that your return was submitted in plenty of time. At present, electronic filing is still somewhat experimental, but each year the IRS expands its pilot programs considerably, and before long electronic filing may be the rule rather than the exception.

5 **After the storm.** So, it's April 16. You've sent off the return, and now you're collapsed on your bed in a heap, with crumpled scraps of paper on one side and half-eaten Oreos on the other. Don't implode. Get back on the Net and begin your post-filing responsibilities. Check on the status of your return with **So... Where's My Refund?** And then fight back those nightmares of being audited with **Criminal and Civil Tax Violations Discussion Group**. You'll feel better, stronger, faster... and more prepared for next year's tax season.

TaxLogic
WEB http://www.taxlogic.com
AMERICA ONLINE *keyword* TaxLogic

Electronic Filing Service
WEB http://www.efs.com/

GFN's Electronic Tax Filing
WEB http://efiling.com/

So... Where's My Refund?
WEB http://www.taxweb.com/refund.html

Criminal and Civil Tax Violations Discussion Group
WEB http://205.177.50.2/crimel.htm

The logical solution to online filing
http://www.taxlogic.com

The Best Tax Preparation Software

▶ **Kiplinger TaxCut** Multimedia enhances this tax preparation software, which can handle most moderately complex returns. You can enter data by importing it from personal finance software, type directly onto the forms onscreen, or go through a step-by-step interview process, which inputs the numbers where they belong automatically. The Shoebox feature simplifies data entry for those who don't use high-tech personal finance software. The Audit Buster and Deduction Sleuth will point out missing data or additional deductions you may have overlooked, and additional advice is available from the TaxCuts feature, which draws from the vast storehouse of knowledge that can only result from H&R Block and the Kiplinger's publishing financial empire, which jointly contribute to this product.
List Price: $29.95
PC or Mac: Both
Downloadable from the Web site: Yes
State forms: State supplements cost $24.95 (the Windows version has 23 states, but the Mac version has only Calif. and N.Y.)
1040PC Forms: Yes
Electronic filing: $9.95
Headstart version: Yes
WEB http://www.conductor.com

▶ **Personal Tax Edge** If your tax situation is fairly basic, this might be a good bargain software choice. You can import financial data from Quicken, Managing Your Money, Microsoft Money, or any other software program using the TXF (tax exchange format). The other methods of data entry include answering interview questions or filling in figures directly onto the tax forms onscreen. The software includes an audit feature that will inform you if you've made the sort of mistake

A well-engineered tax strategy
http://www.conductor.com/

Turbocharge your tax return
http://www.intuit.com/turbot

with which the IRS might take issue.
List Price: $19
PC or Mac: Both
Downloadable from the Web site: Yes
State forms: $19; all states with income tax available
1040PC Forms: No
Electronic filing: $15 (mail diskette, send file via modem, or through AOL or CompuServe)
Headstart version: No
WEB http://www.parsonstech.com/software/ptefinal.html

▶ **TurboTax Online** Imagine having a tax advisor right inside your home computer. That's how this best-selling tax software product is often described and, judging from the market share it garners year after year, most people like keeping a tax consultant at their disposal. When it comes to making taxes less of a chore, Intuit's TurboTax (and its Mac sibling MacInTax) reigns supreme. Even complex returns can be handled easily (those filing K-1 partnership and self-employed Schedule C forms get special attention in the latest version). You can import data from a personal finance program and then complete the interview in either long or short form or input numbers directly onscreen. Tons of advice is available with the program (the deluxe CD-ROM contains whole books and videos), as well as audit features and tax-minimizing tips.
List Price: $49.95
PC or Mac: Both
Downloadable from the Web site: Yes
State forms: $24.95; available for all 43 states with income tax
1040PC Forms: Yes
Electronic filing: Yes (for a small fee?)
Headstart version: No
WEB http://www.intuit.com/turbot

▼ Starting points

CompuServe Tax Connection A menu linking to all of CompuServe's tax resources, including H&R Block tips, support forums for tax software, and an electronic filing service.
COMPUSERVE *go* taxes

The Department of the Treasury: Internal Revenue Service If only the IRS made the tax process as easy to navigate as this Web site. Stop by the Information Highway outpost of the country's most hated government agency if you want tax forms, instructions, information about where to file, IRS telephone numbers, Adobe Acrobat Readers, and more. The site links to the IRS-UTL Library on FedWorld, which is packed with fact sheets and articles about taxation and IRS services.
WEB http://www.irs.ustreas.gov/

State Tax Information Serves as a gateway to government information for the 43 tax-happy states in the Union; income tax information is easily retrievable from state-by-state menus.
WEB http://www.loc.gov/global/state/stategov.html

Tax Forum America Online's tax forum unites some of the biggest players in the tax world—government agencies like the Internal Revenue Service, software companies like Intuit, financial analysts like Kiplinger, accounting firms like Ernst & Young, and professional organizations like the National Association of Enrolled Agents— and delivers enough tax information and advice to stun an ox. With a news feed dedicated to tax-related articles, an archive of tax shareware, and a full complement of tax forms, this is the main center for tax information on AOL. The Tax Forum even offers taxpayers a wealth of more general personal finance software, from budget planners and

mortgage calculators to utilities like Adobe Acrobat Readers, which enable the viewing and printing of tax forms in .PDF format. During tax season, the forum includes a link to a service that lets taxpayers file their taxes electronically.
AMERICA ONLINE *keyword* tax

Taxing Times Taxing Times is the premier source for tax resources online. Created by Maxwell Labs, a leading developer of defense technology, the site carries more than 750 official federal and state tax forms in different formats, including TIFF, PostScript, and .PDF. Any graphics program (e.g., Photoshop, GraphicConverter) will handle the TIFF format, and any PostScript laser printer will handle PostScript formats, but you must download the Adobe Acrobat Reader to view and read .PDF files. Without the ability to download files, you can order forms and instructions by email. In addition, you can order the tax preparation software MacInTax/TurboTax; download the U.S. Tax Code; and link to the misc.taxes newsgroup, tax software FTP sites, and the

Take the bullet train to tax heaven
http://www.ezone.com/taxman

Location: http://www.scubed.com/tax/tax.html

Taxing Times 1997

MacInTax $
$ TurboTax

Keep Uncle Sam's hands out of your pockets
http://www.scubed.com/tax/tax.html

archives of *The Tax Digest* newsletter.
WEB http://www.scubed.com/tax/tax.html

TaxSites Like everything else, taxes attract both casual fans and obsessed fanatics, and only someone truly obsessed with taxes could have created this site. Need to look up the California tax code or get an overview of tax law in Estonia? Afraid of missing really important changes to the federal tax laws? Curious whether you can deduct gourmet coffee as a work-related expense (productivity drops precipitously without that morning pick-me-up)? Interested in downloading a shareware tax program to help you get organized? TaxSites does a great job of linking to and listing most tax-related resources on the Internet. While the organization of the resources isn't always clear, there's a search function to help you navigate. It also maintains summaries and reviews of tax software for professionals (TurboTax for the Average Joe isn't covered, but the ProSeries version of the program is) and articles and FAQs on taxation written by the Web site creator. And then there's the Authoritative References section. Webmaster Frank McNeil, a regular participant on the misc.taxes newsgroup, has

gathered hundreds of tax-related links ranging from sections of the U.S. tax code to IRS rulings to the Income Tax Treaty between the People's Republic of Hungary and the United States.
WEB http://www.best.com:80/%7Eftmexpat/html/taxsites.html

TaxWeb A consumer-oriented tax resource that covers the basic tax filing process in easy-to-understand language. Find out how to get tax forms, where to file, what to do if you can't file on time, and other taxing solutions.
WEB http://www.taxweb.com/

1040 Express Tax Search Engine Everyone knows that a space-age, zippy-fast vehicle makes almost anything fun—even paying taxes. Well, at least this fetch program makes the annual headache a little less painful. The search engine, the creation of a California law firm, gleefully pops up online sources for federal tax forms, the Tax Code, online tax preparers, and other unfortunate necessities. And an email link promises a swift response for those searching for out-of-date and otherwise obscure tax forms.
WEB http://www.ezone.com/taxman

▼ Forms

FedWorld Tax Forms The FedWorld Information Network's download site for the complete library of IRS forms and publications. Though not as user-friendly as the IRS site, it's just as current (updated every morning).
URL ftp://ftp.fedworld.gov/pub/irs-pdf/irs-pdf.htm

IRS Tax Forms and Publications IRS forms and publications available in PDF, PCL, PostScript, or SGML Text formats. Every tax form you could possible need, from the classic 1040s (Schedules A through R) to the procrastinator's Form 8736 Application for an

Automatic Extension are downloadable here.
WEB http://www.irs.ustreas.gov/basic/forms_pubs
/index.html

Nest Egg IRS Tax Information Center The IRS
isn't the only game in town when it comes to
downloadable tax forms. *Nest Egg* magazine
carries (in .PDF format) the same tax forms,
instructions, and publications as the IRS Web
site. While it's not as frequently updated as
the IRS site, it is much better designed and
includes descriptions of each file.
WEB http://nestegg.iddis.com/irs/irsdown.html

▼ Refund calculators

H&R Block's Refund Estimator Enter your filing
status (single, married, etc.), the number of
dependents you have, whether you want the
standard or itemized deduction, the amount
you've paid in federal taxes (from your W2),
and your gross income. Click on "Calculate
My Refund!" and either gasp in horror at how
much you owe or attack your taxes with a
renewed fervor in anticipation of a hefty
refund.
WEB http://165.121.1.171/tax/office/estimator.html

Net-Tax '96 A free tax tool that walks you
through a stripped-down version of the basic
1040 and calculates your refund. If you don't
understand the meaning of terms as they
appear on the form ("Filing status? What's
that?"), hyperlinks will connect you directly
to an explanation straight from IRS. After the
tutorial, link to the official IRS site, download
the forms and do your taxes for real.
WEB http://www.vni.net/~nettax

▼ Software

**C|net Comparative Reviews—Personal Tax Pack-
ages** C|net specializes in reviews that compare
the performance of a group of software pack-

ages all designed to do the same thing. In this
case they ran five popular tax applications—
programs that help you choose your tax
forms, organize your papers, interface with
your accountant, crunch your numbers, and
file electronically—through two contrasting
tax configurations, one simple and one more
complex. This format works well: It provides
a clear evaluation of the various packages.
WEB http://www.cnet.com/Content/Reviews/Compare
/Tax/

You'll either gasp in horror at how much you owe or anticipate a hefty refund.

Individual Income Tax Preparation Software If
information about individual income tax
preparation software is what you're after,
you'll find a wealth of it here: titles, prices,
manufacturers, ratings, the whole shebang.
The reviews are written by freelancers, rather
than by a staff who can be held accountable,
but then again, you can be sure that they're
untainted by any untoward corporate biases.
WEB http://www.best.com/hGET/~ftmexpat/html
/taxprep.html

Software can cushion the blow of doing your taxes
http://www.cnet.com/Content/Reviews/Compare/Tax/

Is your tax I.Q. as high as 1040?
http://165.121.1.171/tax/office/index.html

Simply Tax The simplest way to get through the chore of filing your taxes—short of hiring an accountant—is to use tax preparation software. This forum offers updates, demos, and docs for Simply Tax, as well as comments from program users and manufacturers.
COMPUSERVE *go* simply

Tax Software Uncluttered by forms and tax advice, this library is devoted exclusively to programs to prepare or estimate your taxes.
AMERICA ONLINE *keyword* tax→Tax Software

The future is upon us. At least it is upon those who are single, have no dependents, and are qualified to file a 1040EZ.

Taxes While America Online has several libraries with tax-related programs and resources, this one offers the widest selection. As tax season hits full swing, look for the library to fill with tax calculators, programs to complete state taxes, tax tutorials and strategy guides, and umpteen federal tax-preparation programs. Since America Online rarely cleans out its libraries, programs from past tax seasons are also available.
AMERICA ONLINE *keyword* pcapplications→Browse the Software Libraries→Financial→Taxes

▼ Online preparers

H&R Block Filing Service America's largest firm dealing with the preparation of federal, state, and local income tax returns, offers a wide range of tax services on CompuServe, including preparation.
COMPUSERVE *go* hrb
WEB http://165.121.1.171/tax/office/index.html

1-800-TAX-LAWS Gather your tax information, sit down at the computer, fill out a Web page prompting you for financial information, click the "Yes, File My Taxes Now!" button to send your data, and then wait for a professionally prepared return to show up in your mailbox. For 1-800-TAX-LAWS, the Internet is merely the most efficient way to communicate with its clients; you may also speak by telephone with a tax practitioner or be referred to a local accountant who's a member of the 1-800-TAX-LAWS network. Prices for a basic return run from $75 to $200; "additional forms or additional information would be billed accordingly." The Web site also describes the tax services provided by members of the 1-800-TAX-LAWS network and lists contact information to help you find an offline tax preparer in your area.
WEB http://www.5010geary.com/index.htm

▼ File-by-phone

TeleFile The future is upon us. At least it is upon those who are single, have no dependents, and are qualified to file a 1040EZ. The lives of those lucky few have just gotten even easier. If you receive the special TeleFile tax package with your 1040EZ, you'll be able to phone in the details of your tax return and have it filed electronically—automatically! As long as you keep your financial life simple (stay unmarried and childless), you may never have to touch a paper tax form again.

WEB http://www.irs.ustreas.gov/basic/elec_svs /telefile.html

▼ Tax fun

Tax Trivia People in China paid their taxes with large sheets of pressed tea. Jivara tribesmen paid with shrunken heads. And scientists believe that there may be civilizations on other planets where taxes are paid simply by opening the eyes very, very wide. These and other fascinating facts about death's unavoidable partner are available as part of H&R Block's online tax service on CompuServe.

COMPUSERVE *go* hrb

Test Your Tax I.Q. Last year *Money* magazine asked 500 people a set of 15 tax questions by telephone. None of them answered all 15 correctly, and most answered at least six incorrectly. If you're curious to see if you could have done better, the questions are online here in hypertext format. Click the answer you think is correct and, if it is, there will be a brief explanation of the implications of this tax fact. If not, you'll hear about it.

WEB http://pathfinder.com/Money/features/taxquiz _0295/taxquiz.html

▼ Indexes

The Insider: Taxes A directory of tax sites on the Web broken down into federal taxes, state taxes, Canadian taxes, and British taxes.

WEB http://networth.galt.com/www/home/insider/tax .htm

Taxation Without Relaxation

I received a letter from the collections department of the IRS that they had not received a 1989 tax return from me. The notice said that I had failed to respond to prior attempts. The problem is that this is the first notice I ever received about it! I never heard from Under reporter, just from collections. This seems odd to me, and I think that the IRS has made a mistake. Unfortunately I do not have a copy of my return from '89, but I am almost certain I received refund that year. I AM positive that I filed.

This whole thing makes me very angry because what I fear will happen is that, since late filing precludes itemization, I will have to re-file, and I will owe interest and penalties for that year. It seems to me that there is SOMEONE in the IRS who has a record of having sent me out a refund check in 1990.

Isn't there anything else I can do? Why wasn't I contacted sooner? This all could have been straightened out years ago. And, do I have the right to request proof from the IRS that they have attempted to contact me about this matter before this time?

I know I have a lot of questions, but I am very frustrated. My refund for this year is being held up over this nonsense, and there is a chance, now, that I won't get it at all. I feel like the department of the treasury already rapes me every week, without having to contend with this nonsense. Something has to be done about this IRS system. It is oppressive!

—*from America Online tax*

Time to do your taxes again? On the Internet, every day is April 15th

THE TAX MAN COMETH and the tax man taketh away. There are those of us who actually considered voting for Dole because of his proposed flat tax. But the nation decided that there's more to life than taxes (although nothing is more certain except death), and so the paying goes on. But with this handy stash of free tax advice online, you'll never need to hire an accountant—or bother your CPA uncle—again.

The Best Free Tax

Just the FAQs

▶ **misc.taxes FAQ** This FAQ doesn't stop at answering common tax questions—"I've received an old chair and $3,000 as an inheritance. Are they taxable?" It also lays out the protocol for participating in the misc.taxes newsgroup, explains how to contact and receive information from the IRS, and provides a list of other Web sites containing tax-related information.
WEB http://www.cis.ohio-state.edu/hypertext/faq/usenet/taxes-faq/

▶ **IRS FAQ** Odds are that you are not unique. Sorry, but it's true. The questions you have about your taxes ("How can I check on the status of my refund?" "Can

I ask to make installment payments on the amount I owe?" "Can I get the earned income credit?") have probably been asked and answered thousands of times. And if you can't celebrate your own uniqueness, you might as well benefit from the experience of others. Here's a document with answers to dozens of common questions asked of the IRS by taxpayers.

URL ftp://ftp.fedworld.gov/pub/irs-utl/irisfaq.txt

COMPUSERVE *go* usnforum→Libraries *Search by filename:* irs.faq

Advice Online

It's in the Mail—Email, That Is

▶ **FedTax-L** "Help! I've just sold my two-family home (owner-occupied in half), and I am not completely up on the tax ramifications. Here's the story..." Let's skip to the end of this story—Charles is curious whether capital gain taxes are due on the income half of the property, and, if so, how he should file them. One post later, someone was asking if being out of the country on the tax due date was a reasonable excuse for filing late. FedTax-L offers a forum where subscribers can participate in practical as well as theoretical discussions of federal taxation and get answers to their questions. Members are often taxpayers concerned about what they owe, but there are also many

H&R online is a chip off the ol' Block
http://165.121.1.171/tax/tip/

CASUALTY LOSSES

Q. My home was recently destroyed by a flood. How will this affect my income tax return?

A. When property is damaged or destroyed due to a flood, the loss is called a casualty. Damage caused by other events such as earthquakes, tornadoes, storms, fires, vandalism, and automobile accidents may also qualify as casualties. The amount of your casualty loss is either your adjusted basis in the property (generally measured by your cost or investment in the property) immediately before the casualty or its decline in fair market value (generally measured by the cost of repairs) as a result of the casualty, whichever is smaller. The loss is reduced by any insurance or other reimbursements you receive. In the case of personal-use property, such as your home, the amount of the loss you can deduct on your tax return is further reduced by $100 per casualty and by 10 percent of your adjusted gross income.

—from H&R Block Tax Tips

accountants and attorneys on the list speculating on the interpretation and application of tax law. Issues of the *FedTax* digest are also posted to the newsgroup misc.taxes.
EMAIL listserv@niord.shsu.edu
URL ftp://Niord.SHSU.edu/fedtax-l/ • gopher://Niord.SHSU.edu:70/lftp%3ANiord.SHSU

▶ **misc.taxes** Who knew there was so much to say about taxes? From heated debates over the verity of tax facts (true or false: 95 percent of all Americans don't really have to pay taxes) to huge, ongoing discussions about the right to protest taxes (more than 300 posts in a week) to questions about tax software (is TaxWare as good for tax professionals as TurboTax?), this newsgroup is incredibly active year-round. Tax questions flood the group daily, and there are more than enough accountants, lawyers, and tax preparers online here to offer informed answers for most questions. It's the kind of place where William can drop by to ask about the appropriateness of an employment tax deduction: "I'm starting a new job soon. This job has a much stricter dress code, so I will have to spend some cash on more formal clothing. Is this money tax deductible in any way?" And it's the kind of place where William can expect an answer the same day: "Only if you must wear them as a condition of your employment and they are not suitable for everyday wear."
WEB http://www.kentlaw.edu/cgi-bin/ldn_news/-T+misc.taxes

Take It From the Pros

▶ **H&R Block Tax Tips** The famous tax preparation company has prepared a long and useful list of tax tips for individuals in many different situations. How do you handle jury duty pay? Child care costs? A change in marital status? A property donation? You'll also find

long and helpful checklists intended for people in many different tax situations.
WEB http://I65.I2I.I.I7I/tax/tip/

The Ernst & Young Tax Guide An excellent online resource, this forum carries the full text of the huge *Ernst & Young Tax Guide*. Each chapter is broken down into a separate folder (e.g., "Chapter 3: Personal Exemptions and Dependents"), and the entire book is searchable. In addition, the Tax Hints section features, among other information, a tax calendar, lists of changes in tax laws, and tips on avoiding common errors and overlooking deductions.
WEB http://www.ey.com/us/tax/eyustax.htm
AMERICA ONLINE *go* tax guide

▶ **J.K. Lasser's *Your Income Tax*** One of the most popular tax guides is being sold online, but it's also giving away a significant amount of tax advice for free. The Web site offers, in the form of FAQs, information from the tax guide on many issues, including home owner-ship, children, investments, self-employment, travel, retirement, and property. If your question wasn't cov-ered in the FAQs, check out the Tax Alert Hotline sec-tion, which includes more than 50 fact sheets that J.K. Lasser representatives use to answer tax questions on their telephone hotline.
WEB http://www.mcp.com/bookstore/jklasser/jklhome.html

▶ **Reduce Your Tax Bill** The makers of the popular tax software TurboTax have posted a series of pages con-taining tax-saving tips, some of which you'll also find in the TurboTax Deluxe version. Topics include tips for business owners, hints for homeowner, how to sur-vive an audit—and how to avoid one. One of the site's articles states: "Fear of the Internal Revenue Service is justified. According to a study commissioned by the

Everyone's tax bill could stand to lose weight
http://www.intuit.com/turbotax/reduce/index
.html

COMPUTER DEDUCTIONS

You may use a home computer for your work. The fact that you consider it a necessary business tool is not sufficient to get you a deduction for depreciation or first-year expensing. Tax deductions for using a home computer are generally not available to employees because they can't show that the computer is required for the job. Merely getting a letter from your employer stating that the computer is needed for your position won't get you a deduction. To date, the IRS has not provided any example of a computer-job requirement that would support the deduction. However, if you can show that your home computer is indeed required for your job, claim the deduction for unreimbursed expenses on Form 2106, but be prepared for a possible IRS disallowance. The computer must be used more than 50 percent of the time for your job to qualify for first-year expensing or accelerated depreciation. Otherwise, only straight-line depreciation may be used. Rules are relaxed for the self-employed. The point is to show that you use it in a regular business office.

—from J.K. Lasser's Your Income Tax

Federal Administrative Conference, the Internal Revenue Service has been found to be 'whimsical, inconsistent, unpredictable, and highly personal' in dealing with those caught in its machinery." To avoid an audit, the advice boils down to this: "Never cheat on your income taxes. If you do, never anger anyone who might know about."
WEB http://www.intuit.com/turbotax/reduce/index.html

▶ **The Tax Prophet** Tax attorney Robert L. Sommers, dubbed the Tax Prophet, is the wizard for whom this site is named. Sommers' Web site features several articles that he's written about taxes for the average taxpayer (e.g., "IRS Audit? Have No Fear"). It also provides information for foreign taxpayers and "quizzes" to help taxpayers determine their residency and employment status. Despite impressive multimedia decorations, this is a rather unfocused site, with one important exception—the monthly Hot Tax Topics column, which skillfully digests a broad range of tax issues, from legal rulings (can law firms deduct the cost of litigation?) to legislative developments (what exactly is the flat tax proposal?). Still haven't had your fill of taxes? Consult the Prophet's links to other tax-related sites.
WEB http://www.taxprophet.com/

▶ **Ask the CPAs** Open year-round, this forum collects the wisdom of thousands of accountants and dispenses it on a broad range of accounting topics, from forensic accounting to S-corporation issues. But Ask the CPAs comes to life in the winter, when America goes into its annual tax frenzy. So if you're not sure which software to use to generate W-2s and 1099s, or which forms to file if you gave piano lessons in your home last year, calm down and come over.
COMPUSERVE *go* accounting→Messages and Libraries→Ask the CPAs

▶ **Information USA—Taxes** Where's your refund? What do you do if you get an overdue tax bill from the IRS? What are the advantages of filing electronically? How can you get in on the IRS's sale of confiscated jewelry? Matthew Lesko, the author of this large database of government information and contacts, answers these and dozens of other questions in a series of informative and entertaining articles. Organized around subjects like "Learning Loopholes," "Avoiding Audits," "Making Money from the IRS," and "Getting Free Tax Preparation Help," the site offers detailed instructions for taxpayers on how to handle the IRS and the tax process.
COMPUSERVE *go* ius-5494

🙶 Where's your refund? What do you do if you get an overdue tax bill from the IRS? How can you get in on the IRS's sale of confiscated jewelry? 🙷

▶ **TaxLogic Message Boards** If you don't have a CPA in the family, this message board is the next best thing. Post questions on any of four topics—individual tax; business tax; estates, gifts, and trusts; and "the IRS and You"—and the TaxLogic experts will post an answer as soon as possible. Each topic has dozens of folders to organize information even further. On the individual tax message board, questions on IRAs, investments and capital gains, and electronic filing are particularly hot topics, with hundreds of posts logged into each folder.
AMERICA ONLINE *keyword* taxlogic→Message Boards

The wonderful wizard of Tax
http://www.taxprophet.com/

AND DON'T FORGET TO SIGN YOUR RETURN

1. Most importantly, check your math.
2. Double-check that your Social Security number has been correctly written on the return.
3. Include your Social Security number on each page of the return so that, if a page is misplaced by the IRS, it can be reattached.
4. Check that you've claimed all of your dependents, such as elderly parents who may not live with you.
5. Include on the return the Social Security numbers for all dependents who are 1 year old and over.
6. If you received a state tax refund, make sure you have not included too much of your refund in your income. State tax refunds may not be taxable if you did not get a tax benefit from deducting them. If, for example, you used the standard deduction in the year in which the taxes were paid, you do not have to include the refund in income this year.
7. Recheck your basis in the shares you sold this year, particularly shares of a mutual fund. Income and capital gains dividends that were automatically reinvested in the fund over the years increase your basis in the mutual fund and thus reduce a gain or increase a loss that you have to report.
8. If you have large deductions or other items that are specially treated, check to see if you are subject to the alternative minimum tax.
9. Fill out Form 8606, Nondeductible IRA Contributions, for your contributions to an IRA, even if you don't claim any deduction for the contribution.
10. Claim the additional standard deductions if you are blind or 65 years of age or older.

—from Twenty-Five Most Common Tax Preparation Errors

▼ Basics

50 Ways to Cut Your Taxes Paul Simon never wrote a song about it, but if did, these excerpts from the book Kiplinger's Cut Your Taxes could serve as the lyrics. You'll find dozens of tips on minimizing your tax burden. Did you know that if your spouse died last year, you can still file a joint return? Or if you own shares in a mutual fund that invests in foreign securities, you may qualify for a foreign tax credit? Now you know.
WEB http://www.conductor.com/lalas/taxcut /taxadvice.htm

Filing Requirements, Filing Status, and Exemptions
Do you know who you are? It's a question a therapist might ask. It's a question a parent might ask. It's also a question an accountant filling out your tax forms might ask. But in tax lingo, it's called filing status. This section of H&R Block's tax information covers such taxing topics as what forms to use, whether or not to claim older children as dependents, and extensions for members of the military.
COMPUSERVE *go* hrb→Filing Requirements, Filing Status, and Exemptions

Twenty-Five Most Common Tax Preparation Errors The 25 most common errors have inspired Ernst & Young to create a document with the most incredibly obvious suggestions for taxpayers. To wit: "Check your math."
AMERICA ONLINE *keyword* tax guide→Tax Hints→How to Avoid 25 Common Errors
WEB http://www.ey.com/us/tax/25error.htm

What to Do If You've Made a Mistake On Tax Forms
Don't spend sleepless nights worried about the food in federal prison. If you have income you forgot to declare on your return, take a deep breath and read about the IRS's provi-

sions for dealing with mistakes on tax returns.
COMPUSERVE *go* infousa→Libraries *Search by filename:*
taxerr.txt

▼ Business taxes

The Art of Paying Taxes on Home Office Furnishing
An article about deductions for home office
furnishings.
AMERICA ONLINE *keyword* work→Libraries *Search by*
filename: furnis.tax

Bankruptcy Tax To stay on top of developments
relating to taxation and bankruptcy, subscribe
to this list. The moderator, a staff member of
the Tax Analysts, posts summaries of relevant
legislation, court rulings, and changes in the
tax industry. Not much discussion.
EMAIL bankruptcy.group@tax.com ✎ *Type in message*
body: subscribe
Archive: **WEB** http://205.177.50.2/bkrpt.htm

Business Tax Information Many taxpayers want
to know what they can deduct if they use
their home for business, whether as a sole
proprietor they need an employer identification number, and whether they have to pay
estimated taxes. In fact, so many taxpayers
want answers to these questions that the IRS
has created a brief FAQ addressing them.
TELNET telnet://fedworld.gov2/go irisbtiFrequently
Asked Tax Questions • telnet://fedworld.gov /go irisbti
URL ftp://ftp.fedworld.gov/pub/irs-utl/btifaq.txt

Business Taxes Your accountant is saying one
thing. The IRS seems to be saying something
very different. And your brother-in-law insists
that you're a chump. When it comes to taxes,
business can be very confusing. Maybe you
need a better perspective. The Business Taxes
message board offers just that. Post a business
tax question or scenario, and other AOL
members will offer advice. Throughout the
year, business owners and tax preparers stop

by to ask about deducting car expenses,
depreciating equipment, filing as a partnership or corporation, doing state taxes, figuring
out self-employment taxes, and more.
AMERICA ONLINE *keyword* naea→Business Taxes

Buying Equipment Now Can Net Tax Gains An article from the November/December issue of
Home-Based Business News that covers the
tax advantages of buying equipment.
COMPUSERVE *go* work→Libraries *Search by file name:*
taxes

Employment Tax Are there any changes in the
final IRS regulations on liability of third parties for withholding taxes? Are law clerks and
home improvement salespeople employees for
purposes of employment taxes? What's the
status of Revenue Procedure 82-20? The
mailing list reports on employment tax issues
like these and solicits subscriber feedback.
EMAIL employment.group@tax.com ✎ *Type in message*
body: subscribe
Archive: **WEB** http://205.177.50.2/employl.htm

IRS Guidelines for Independent Contractor and
Employee Status Is the woman who works in
your home three days a week required to follow instructions about when, where, and how
she works? If so, she meets one IRS criterion
for the status of employee. Or does this
woman accomplish certain ends, but follow
her own instructions? Then she might be an
independent contractor. This is a list of IRS
guidelines for determining whether an
employee should be classified as an employee
or an independent contractor.
WEB http://www.primenet.com/~laig/proserve/bulletin
/bu0001.htm

Tax Tips Newsletter for New Businesses The IRS
publishes a monthly newsletter for the new
business owner with tax tips on topics ranging from deducting travel expenses to rectify-

ing mistakes with the IRS. The newsletter is free and may be mailed through the postal service to the business owner or downloaded from the Net (in .PDF format).

TELNET telnet://fedworld.gov→2→/go irisbti→Tax Tips Newsletter for New Businesses
URL ftp://fwux.fedworld.gov/pub/irs-utl/irs-utl .htmBTITTNB

▼ Deductions

50 of the Most Easily Overlooked Deductions Did you spend money on an alcohol or drug treatment program? A cellular telephone for business? Prescriptive birth control pills? If so, you can claim them as deductions. This site carries fairly detailed descriptions of 50 deductions taxpayers often forget to claim. The information was compiled by Ernst & Young. An abbreviated version, with page references to the *Ernst & Young Tax Guide 1997*, can be found on the Web.
AMERICA ONLINE *keyword* tax guide→Tax Hints→50 of the Most Easily Overlooked Deductions
WEB http://www.wiley.com/ey/50.html

Gone are the days of deducting after-work cocktails and mid-week junkets to Vegas as business expenses.

How to Claim Casualty Losses This article outlines the nuances of deductions based on property loss due to earthquakes, floods, tornadoes, storms, fires, accidents, and vandalism.
COMPUSERVE *go* hrb→Deductions & Credits→How to Claim Casualty Losses

Numerous Medical Deductions Overlooked It's been a bad year. You broke your leg, strained your back, and had a voluntary tonsilectomy to prevent your recurring strep throat. According to the folks at H&R Block, many people don't know the full extent to which they can deduct medical-related expenses. Read about some of them here.
COMPUSERVE *go* hrb→Deductions & Credits→Numerous Medical Deductions Overlooked

Substantiating Business Travel and Entertainment Gone are the days of deducting after-work cocktails and mid-week junkets to Vegas as business expenses. At this Web page, the Checkers, Simon & Rosner accounting firm provides a concise breakdown of what you must prove for travel and entertainment expenses to count as valid tax deductions. Remember, keep those receipts!
WEB http://www.checkers-llp.com/biztravl.htm

Tax Deductions for Charitable Solicitations Whenever you're feeling generous, consider donating money to charity. It's the gift that gives back by taking away from your tax burden. This document explains the difference between tax exempt and tax deductible organizations (make sure you give to the right one), lists the various categories they fall under (charitable, religious, educational, etc.), and provides tips on deducting your contributions. A list of additional IRS publications is also included.
WEB http://www.bosbbb.org/lit/0050.htm

Ten Little Known Tax Deductions If you make a legally enforceable loan to someone who later won't pay up, then the debt can be deducted from your tax return. Read about cutting your losses through the tax system, and other issues to do with deductions, in this article.
WEB http://victorvalley.com/health%26law/hlaw-mar /tax.htm

▼ Domestic

Dependency Exemption for Divorced Parents
Learn about the impact of divorce and child custody on tax exemption status.
COMPUSERVE *go* hrb→Filing Requirements, Status, and Exemptions→Dependency Exemptions for Divorced Parents

Earned Income Tax Credit FAQ The FAQ outlines the criteria for getting an Earned Income Tax Credit (available to lower income taxpayers) and the procedures for getting it.
URL ftp://ftp.fedworld.gov/pub/irs-utl/itieic.inf

How to Claim Dependent Care Credit Make the most out of child care expenses on your tax return.
AMERICA ONLINE *keyword* hrb→Deductions & Credits→ How to Claim Dependent Care Credit

Nannygate Reconsidered: Do You Really Owe Taxes On Your Baby-Sitter? This explanation of Section 530 of the Revenue Act of 1978 describes how a household worker should be classified—either as an employee or as an independent contractor.
WEB http://www.taxprophet.com/nanny_ar.html

Unwed but not Unwise "Unmarried couples usually do much better than their married counterparts on their federal income taxes." Tax attorney Robert Sommers addresses tax issues for unmarried couples who own a residence together.
WEB http://www.taxprophet.com/pubs/unwed_tm.html

▼ Estate taxes

Estates, Trusts, Gifts Not everyone is lucky enough to have a trust fund, inherit or own a large estate, or be given a sizable gift. And those who do should be happy, right? Not always. The reality of and confusion over

DEATH AND TAXES

The institution of marriage may be sacred, but not when it comes to our nation's income tax laws. Unmarried couples usually do much better than their married counterparts on their federal income taxes. But what the tax man giveth in life, he taketh away at death: Unmarried couples could pay dearly when it comes to estate taxes.

Consider the following example: John and Sally, who are unmarried, purchased a home 20 years ago as joint tenants for $50,000 and paid off the mortgage in full 10 years ago. Neither has retained any records relating to their purchase. Assume when John dies the home is appraised at $1 million and it comprises his total estate. The home's entire value will be included in John's estate for federal estate tax purposes, unless Sally can prove her actual contributions to its purchase. Because Sally retained no records, John's estate will include the entire value of their home. Consequently there will be a federal tax of approximately $153,000 and a tax lien will attach to the home. Since Sally now owns the home as the surviving joint tenant, she becomes personally liable for the full amount of the estate tax. What a penalty—one that could easily have been avoided. Upon death, the decedent's estate may be taxed by the federal government, for the "privilege" of passing property to the decedent's beneficiaries.

—from Unwed But Not Unwise

taxes can bring doom and gloom even to such seemingly fortunate events. You can work through some of the confusion on this message board. Ask whether an estate valued at less than $650,000, set up as a trust, and passed on to children is taxed. Ask whether money from a trust used to pay last year's taxes can be deducted from your income. Ask

whether an educational trust you set up for your infant son that currently includes under $1,000 must be claimed as income on your tax form. Ask about taxes owed on large gifts that you gave. Ask and you will usually get replies from others who've worked through similar tax questions.
AMERICA ONLINE *keyword* naea→Estates, Trusts, Gifts

Planning is Key to Estate Taxes A two-part article on estate tax planning, with sections on wills, revocable living trusts, joint tenancy, community property, planning for minors, and more.
WEB http://www.taxprophet.com/pubs/plan_tm.html

▼ Real estate

Real Estate Discussion Group Keep track of what decisions Congress, the courts, and the IRS are making that affect real estate-related taxes. The moderator reports on these developments, and subscribers can comment.
EMAIL realestate.group@tax.com ✎ *Type in message body:* subscribe
Archive: **WEB** http://205.177.50.2/realesl.htm

Real Estate Taxes A large message board with folders for discussions on mortgage interest deduction, tax-deferred exchanges of real

estate, capital gains, tax liens, property taxes, and other real estate tax topics.
AMERICA ONLINE *keyword* real estate→Real Estate Message Boards→Message Boards→Taxes

Your Home as a Tax Shelter Besides sheltering you, your home can also shelter your money. Learn how to deduct 100 percent of your mortgage payments on your taxes.
COMPUSERVE *go* hrb→Deductions & Credits→Your Home as a Tax Shelter

▼ Tax shelters

Seeking Shelter with Munis An overview and explanation of how municipal bonds can provide a tax shelter for investors.
WEB http://nestegg.iddis.com/nestegg/articles/tax_8.html

The Tax Haven Gambit Adam Starchild offers his tips on tax havens for investors and international entrepreneurs. According to Starchild, there are ways to save up to 40 percent on your taxes through wisely constructed havens.
AMERICA ONLINE *keyword* invforum→Libraries *Search by filename:* gambit.zip

▼ Getting audited

How to Deal with IRS Demands Get through an audit with grace and style by using the tips from this article, which discusses the audit process and a taxpayer's rights during an audit.
WEB http://www.taxprophet.com/pubs/audit2_tm.html

How to Survive a Tax Audit Written by a former IRS agent, this tutorial explains the audit-selection process and offers tips on how to handle the IRS during the dreaded ordeal. Hint: Try not to make them angry.
AMERICA ONLINE *keyword* pcsoftware→File Search— Over 60,000 Files *Search by filename:* irsaudit.zip

---

This tax shelter is no hat trick
http://nestegg.iddis.com/nestegg/articles/tax_10.html

Seeking Shelter with Munis
While no longer limited to the wealthy, it doesn't hurt to be rich.

IRS Audit? Have No Fear Robert L. Sommers, the Taxman at Tax Logic, outlines IRS collection procedures and tells you how to sue any IRS employee who recklessly disregards them in their dealings with you.
WEB http://www.taxprophet.com/pubs/audit_tm.html

The Naked Truth About Tax Audits Subtitled "How to Fight the IRS Without Losing Your Shirt," this article examines who gets audited, what to expect from the IRS, and where to get help.
WEB http://nestegg.iddis.com/nestegg/articles/tax_10.html

What You Need to Know If You Fear an IRS Audit Assuage your fears of an audit by mailing away for in-house IRS audit manuals (the ones they use to teach their people how to do it!). This article lists all available titles, their prices, and where to get them. Read all the manuals and you'll know as much about your audit as the auditor.
COMPUSERVE go infousa→Libraries Search by filename: audit.txt

▼ News

Legislative and Policy Issues Tax Discussion What's happening in the world of tax legislation this week? This newsletter reports on court, IRS, and congressional developments related to tax legislation and tax policy. The moderator posts the news and subscribers may send in their comments.
EMAIL legpolicy.group@tax.com ✍ Type in message body: subscribe
Archive: **WEB** http://205.177.50.2/legis.htm

The 1996 Tax Changes In 1996, Congress approved three new pieces of legislation that may affect your taxes this year. Deloitte and Touche has provided this comprehensive overview summarizing the changes on individuals and businesses, including pension

DON'T PANIC

What should you do if you receive a notice of delinquent taxes from the IRS? First, don't panic. Remember you have rights, and take things one step at a time. First, assume you are right, and the IRS is wrong. Read your notice carefully. Which tax year(s) are involved? What information is the government requesting? If you used a tax preparer, contact him or her. If your tax preparer is unresponsive or you feel your preparer is covering up his or her mistake, immediately get a second opinion. Review the interest charge: It is estimated the IRS miscalculates interest charges 25 percent of the time. Determine whether interest is based on the correct year; then, check the amount. Calculate a rough estimate of interest at 1 percent per month. If you owe interest on $1,000 for two years, the notice should state approximately $240 in interest. The IRS cannot normally negotiate interest due. Check the penalties: Often, an IRS computer generates penalties that can be abated in full. A negligence penalty, for instance, does not automatically apply if the taxpayer is wrong—the taxpayer must be negligent. Unlike interest, penalties are negotiable, so always try to get penalty charges excused. Put everything in writing: Avoid negotiating over the telephone, but if you do, immediately write a letter confirming your conversation. Keep copies of all your correspondence, and don't throw it away. As your case progresses, invariably the IRS will ask you for all copies of previous correspondence. Don't pay until you are certain the IRS is correct: Once you pay an erroneous statement, it is difficult to get a refund. As long as the IRS wants money from you, your bargaining position is stronger. But once you determine taxes are owed, and that the interest is calculated correctly—and if you cannot reduce or eliminate the penalties—then send in a check. Keep copies.

—from How to Deal with IRS Demands

simplifications and new allowable IRA withdrawals for certain medical expenses.
WEB http://www.dtonline.com/tnv/taxchanges/cover.htm

Tax News Archives of press releases and news briefs about tax issues from several tax organizations, including the IRS, Tax Management Inc., and the National Association of Enrolled Agents.
AMERICA ONLINE *keyword* tax→Tax News

Tax Notes Newswire Updated three times a day, the Web site features brief reports on tax news worldwide. Not surprisingly, U.S. policy and legislation dominates the coverage. It's not the sexiest of presentations but we are talking about taxes, after all. The Tax Analysts organization, which sponsors the news wire, also publishes a series of databases and publications that are widely used among tax professionals.
WEB http://205.177.50.2/news.htm • http://www.tax.org /news.htm

▼ Laws

Browse the Federal Tax Code "Welcome to the Federal Tax Code." It is being progressively turned into hypertext to make it more accessible and manipulable as you browse from Chapter 1 on normal taxes and surtaxes to Chapter 98 on the trust fund code.
WEB http://www.tns.lcs.mit.edu/uscode/

Changes in the Tax Law A brief overview of tax changes affecting your family and business.
AMERICA ONLINE *keyword* tax guide→Tax Hints→ Changes in the Tax Law

Criminal and Civil Tax Violations Discussion Group Taxpayers, no matter how nice they are, often try to defraud the IRS. And the IRS, no matter how bureaucratic, still tries to catch them. This moderated list carries summaries,

reports, and court case synopses relating to how the IRS combats fraud.
EMAIL criminal.group@tax.com ✍*Type in message body:* subscribe
Archive: **WEB** http://205.177.50.2/crime1.htm

Legi-Slate This database of legislation chronicles the passage of every tax bill proposed in Congress. The site is updated daily and carries archives that date back to the 103rd Congress. The site lets taxpayers follow legislation, read drafts of proposed bills, see roll call votes, access Federal Register documents as well as specific bills and resolutions, and research *Washington Post*, *National Journal*, and *Congressional Quarterly Weekly Report* articles. The service offers two levels of access—one to the public and the other to paid subscribers. See "About the LEGI-SLATE Gopher Service" for a description of what the public and the subscription services offer.
URL gopher://gopher.legislate.com/

Tax Legislation Updates A summary of last year's tax law changes, reports about proposed tax legislation, and a link to Thomas, a site sponsored by the U.S. Congress that carries the full text of proposed legislation in both the 103rd and 104th Congresses. If you want to stay on top of changes in tax law, or even proposed changes, check here regularly.
WEB http://taxwizard.com/taxwizard/updates/home .html

▼ Calendars

Tax Calendar April 15 isn't the only date you need to remember when it comes to staying in the good graces of the tax man. The IRS publishes quarterly tax calendars. Check for them in these libraries.
TELNET telnet://fedworld.gov→2→guest→/go IRISMTI
URL ftp://fwux.fedworld.gov/pub/irs-utl/irs-utl.htm

PART 4

Invest Your Money

SO YOU'VE PAID YOUR TAXES and you actually had fun. You even have plenty of savings left over, but it's just sitting in your bank account and you have no idea what to do with it. The answer? Start investing. Money, you see, is like a child. You have to send it out into the world to play with other money so that it can develop, grow, and multiply. We'll teach you everything you need to know, beginning with the bulls and the bears. Practice what you learn by playing simulated stock games, and when you're ready for real risk, go for an online discount broker. And don't forget to do your homework. Whether your investment strategy involves mutual funds, stocks, or IPOs, all the best investment research and advice you need is available online.

Everything you need to know you can learn on the Internet. It's as easy as A-B-C

WHEN IT COMES TO MONEY, you're a dummy. Watching cable news with the stock ticker running across the bottom of the screen makes you dizzy. You don't know an IPO from an IRA or an LBO from your elbow. Even the thought of touching a dollar bill makes your palms sweat. You know you need help, but you have high finance anxiety. One way to dip your toe into the big investing pool is to become familiar with the financial argot. At times, it may seem like learning another language, a devilishly confusing one in which familiar-sounding words never

Financially Speaking

mean what you think they mean. But if you bookmark the glossaries in this section and refer to them again and again, soon you'll be speaking the language of the street—Wall Street, that is. Before consulting the glossaries, however, take this brief pretest, which can help you assess your financial vocabulary level.

▶ **Talk like a trader**

▶ **Increase your financial vocabulary**

▶ **Master basic investing principles**

▶ **Play market simulations**

Financial Vocabulary Quiz

Match the word with the definition:

1. Stock

    A. the thing you make soup out of—comes in chicken and beef flavors

    B. an investment vehicle that gives you a right to the company's profits

    C. an ownership interest in a company, also known as "shares" in a company

> ❝ **Stock: the thing you make soup out of—comes in chicken and beef flavors.** ❞

2. Bond

    A. the emotional connection you feel with another person

    B. an investment vehicle that gives you a share in a company's profits

    C. an IOU issued by a company, government, or institution to finance a certain aspect of its operation

3. Gap

    A. a clothing store

    B. the difference in price of a stock between any two points in time

    C. a void on a stock price chart caused by the stock opening and subsequently trading at prices away from the prior day's close

4. Bull

A. a scary animal with horns

B. the stock market when all stock prices are going down

C. a person who believes the market will go up

5. Bear spread

A. what you see when a bear bends over

B. the amount of time between two bear markets

C. a spread in which a decline in the price of the underlying stock will theoretically increase the value of the spread

6. Head & shoulders

A. a dandruff shampoo

B. a bull market between two bear markets

C. a chart formation in which a stock price reaches a peak and declines; rises above its former peak, and again declines and rises (but not to the second peak); and then declines again

7. Scalp

A. what you use the Head & Shoulders on

B. any illegal trading activity

C. to trade for small gains

8. Pink sheets

A. another word for pink slips—the official notice that you are given when you are fired

B. the receipt for purchasing a stock or bond

C. the lists of over-the-counter stocks and the brokers who make a market in them, published daily by the National Quotation Bureau

9. Macaulay duration

A. the number of years between *Home Alone* sequels

But she didn't say, "Simon Says"
http://www.simonsays.com/titles
/0684812134/index.html

Location: http://www.simonsays.com/titles/0684812134/index.html

Get a Financial
LIFE
BY BETH KOBLINER
Personal Finance In Your Twenties and Thirties

B. the quantified impact of inflation on stock prices

C. the weighted-average term to maturity of the cash flows from the bond, where the weights are the present value of the cash flow divided by the price

𝟔𝟔 Andrew's Pitchfork: a label applied to something to distinguish it from Ann's Hoe. 𝟗𝟗

10. Andrew's pitchfork

A. a label applied to something to distinguish it from Ann's Hoe

B. three bull markets separated by two bear markets

C. a trendline study that consist of three parallel lines drawn from three points on your charts

Scoring: The correct response in all cases is "c."

- If you answered anything but "c" for questions 1 and 2, go to the Introductory Glossaries.
- If you answered 1 and 2 correctly, but made a mistake on any of questions 3 through 8, go to the Intermediate Glossaries.
- If you answered 1 through 8 correctly, but were stumped on 8 and 10, head straight to the Advanced Glossaries.
- If you scored 100 percent, then you don't need to read this. Relax while the rest of us catch up.

Introductory Glossaries

To refresh your memory about basic terms such as principal, return, yield, and inflation, check out the **Get a Financial Life Glossary of Financial Terms**. This double handful of money words was penned by the woman who wrote the bestselling book on personal finance for

Wall Street City is paved with gold
http://www.wallstreetcity.com/glossary.htp

CASH REGISTER

Get a Financial Life: Glossary of Financial Terms
WEB http://www.simonsays.com
/titles/0684812134/index.html

Investorama's Glossary
WEB http://www.investorama.com
/gloss.shtml

Fidelity's Investment Glossary
WEB http://personal.fidelity.com
/funds/glossary.html

Vanguard Glossary
WEB http://www.vanguard.com/educ
/glos.html

Research Magazine Online's InvestorNet Glossary
WEB http://www.researchmag.com
/investor/glossary.htm

CNBC's Investing Terminology
WEB http://www.cnbc.com
/tickerguide/termin.html

Stock Option
WEB http://www.cnbc.com
/tickerguide/termin.html#stop

twenty- and thirtysomethings. There's also a brief exegesis on the difference between an IRA and a 401(k) here. For completeness and simplicity, **Investorama's Glossary** is a site worth bookmarking, especially if you're trying to invest in common stocks without the help of a broker. The list contains more than 200 words and phrases for the individual investor. Find out about no-load and low-load funds here, but be patient—this site is a slow load. Once you're ready to find out the meanings of aggressive, conservative, and other basic personal investing terms, **Fidelity's Investment Glossary** provides concise, easy-to-understand explanations. **Vanguard**, another popular mutual fund company, has a basic glossary, though its prose is somewhat dry (market risk is summed up as "the possibility that stock or bond prices will fluctuate").

Intermediate Glossaries

If you want just enough terminology to impress your broker when you talk to her on the phone, try **Research Magazine Online's InvestorNet**, which has a concise list of basic trading terms—ask, bid, proxy, prospectus—with clear, brief definitions as provided by the SEC. **CNBC's Investing Terminology** has plain-language definitions that you may have forgotten since economics class in college. (In a bull market, stock prices are rising. In a bear market, they are falling. Got it?) Still, they'll instantly remind you of cramming for finals, and the way youth made everything seem simple. A "call option," for example, is defined concisely as a "stock option giving the holder the right to buy shares at a given price," while a "put option" is defined as a "stock option giving the holder the right to sell shares at a given price." What could be simpler (assuming you've already learned the definition of **Stock Option**, of course)? If you don't know what "IPO" stands for, Olde Discount Brokerage's **Abbreviations of Investments Terms** will enlighten you. Olde's **Definitions of Investment Terms**, on the other hand, is a weird mix of the basic, the lyrical, and the arcane. You'll find a deadpan definition for "taxes" alongside such dubious traderspeak as "big board" (a.k.a. the New York Stock Exchange). Some of the more obscure terms sound alternately like bodily functions ("accreted interest"), mathematical constants ("cusip number"), and Elizabethan prose ("debenture"). Olde deserves a bookmark, if only for its eccentric charm. The **American Association of Individual Investors Glossary** delivers a mix of basic and more complicated terms and describes the difference between a Treasury bill, a Treasury bond, and a Treasury note in a prose style that is strictly textbook.

Once you have a firm handle on the basics, you may want to keep the **WashingtonPost.com's Business Glossary** at hand to help you stay on top of the tougher concepts. Its database contains more than 1,250 business and financial terms compiled from various sources. You can search by word, browse by chunks of the alphabet, or download the hefty 158K Master Glossary

CASH REGISTER

Abbreviations of Investments Terms
WEB http://www.oldediscount.com
/term/abbnet.htm

Definitions of Investment Terms
WEB http://www.oldediscount.com
/term/dictnet.htm

American Association of Individual Investors Glossary
WEB http://www.aaii.org/glossary
.html

WashingtonPost.com's Business Glossary
WEB http://www.washingtonpost.com
/wp-srv/business/longterm
/glossary/glossary.htm

Vanguard shows you the ropes
http://www.vanguard.com/educ/glos.html

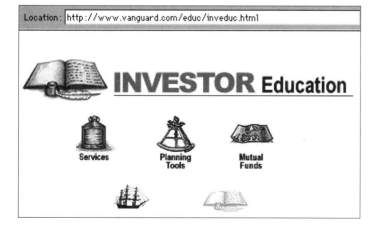

CASH REGISTER

Wall Street City's Glossary
WEB http://www.wallstreetcity.com
/glossary.htp

**American Commodity Research
Technical Trading Terms**
WEB http://www.wsdinc.com/pgs_idx
/w_indi.shtml

**Campbell Harvey's Futures and
Options Glossary**
WEB http://www.duke.edu/~charvey
/Classes/glossary/g_index.htm

Glossary of Futures Terminology
WEB http://www.cbot.com/cbotglos
.htm

If you're new to investing, Olde will help you
http://www.oldediscount.com/term/dictnet
.htm

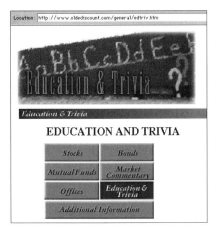

Index, print it out, and read from it at bedtime. Definitions are hyperlinked, so if you don't understand all the words in a definition, you can instantly click on the confusing word to link to its meaning.

Advanced Glossaries

Now that your feet are wet, why not dive in? **Wall Street City's Glossary** contains dozens of sophisticated financial terms, each defined in 25 words or less. Unfortunately, brevity prevails at the expense of clarity. A "put-to-call time premium," for example, is defined rather obliquely as "a ratio of the time premiums for put and calls for a given option." If you're feeling as if your head's barely above water, take a look at the lexicon prepared by **American Commodity Research**, whose Web site has a slick and comprehensive list of dozens of highly technical trading terms. If you're still hungry for more, visit **Campbell Harvey's Futures and Options Glossary**, where you can click on any letter of the alphabet and open a Pandora's box of financial terms, such as "homogeneous expectations assumption" and "two-fund separation theorem." This stuff's strictly academic, but what do you expect from a Duke University business school professor? He speaks a language so advanced, he doesn't even bother to define such "simple" concepts as "mutual fund". If you want to be a master of the financial universe (or just look like one), check out the Chicago Board of Trade's **Glossary of Futures Terminology**, which is excerpted from CBOT's Commodity Trading Manual. Its spare interpretations of arbitrage, charting, and hedging will help you talk the talk, even if you can't walk the walk. You may even surprise yourself with what you already know—amazingly, the hog/corn ratio really does have something to do with pigs and what they eat.

▼ Starting points

Investorama Investorama is a surprisingly stylish site put together by Douglas Gerlach, a private investor and financial journalist. He gives short descriptions of many of the 2,163 links he lists, which is an improvement over most investment hubsites. Investorama covers most of the major topics—taxes, technical analysis, real estate—and it also includes a stock pick of the week, an advice column, and Gerlach's feature articles, which describe stock-selection techniques and offer plenty of examples. Check out the section on investment mailing lists; they can often be hard to track down on your own.
WEB http://www.investorama.com/

InvestorGuide If numbers impress you—and they should if you're interested in investing—you'll be happy to learn that this massive site contains more than 4,000 links. Naturally, you'll get tons of pointers to information on stocks, bonds, quotes, market summaries, and personal finance. You'll also find clear and concise basic educational resources, such as "Advice on Taking Advice" and "Ten Principles of Investing and Personal Finance." But the great service here is the *InvestorGuide Weekly* newsletter, which you can read at the site or have delivered free by email. It has the scoop on major happenings that may affect the way you invest, keeping a close eye on electronic commerce and Internet-related companies. You can also keep abreast of new investment sites as they go up and link directly to the best articles at the major magazines online (e.g. *Worth, Money*), without having to visit them individually. Finally, don't miss the fully hyperlinked guide to "Investing in Internet Companies."
WEB http://www.investorguide.com

Max's Investment World In his online investment world, Max is a balding, red-headed cartoon, but in reality, Max is short for Maxine, a three-legged cat. Maxine, in case you're wondering, belongs to a friend of Howard Isenstein, a former finance reporter and one of the masterminds behind this Web site, along with Xiaou Wang, an NYU economics Ph.D. candidate. Confused? Don't worry. This is as complicated as things get at Max's Investment World, where you'll find plain-language advice on "the best ways to divvy up you investment dough" (i.e., portfolio structuring), savvy stock selections, and market commentary. Stock picks follow a contrarian investing style ("That means we look for good companies that are temporarily cheap").
WEB http://maxinvest.com/

Microsoft Investor Microsoft's new interface for individual investors hits all the bases with a Portfolio Manager to monitor your investments, Company News to fill you in on business happenings, Historical Charts to help you analyze stock performance, and a Market Summary so you can check market activity in seconds flat. A Quote Lookup for the latest stock prices and an Online Trading department for 24-hour trading give this hubsite the practical functionality it needs to make it worth your bookmark. Charles Schwab is currently the only online broker available through the Investor site, but if we know our favorite corporate monolith like we think we do, more companies will jump on the Microsoft bandwagon soon.
WEB http://investor.msn.com

The Motley Fool What's at the famous Motley Fool? Friendly, down-to-earth investment advice delivered with a bad case of Dadaist hiccups. For instance, in this forum "foolish" is the greatest honorific for an insight or moneymaking stock trade. The hard-working

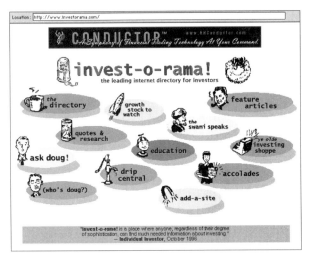

Play the investing game and double your money
http://www.investorama.com/

staff, which includes a former writer from Louis Rukeyser's *Wall Street Week*, has created what some consider to be the finest online corrective to the macho mumbo jumbo that characterizes most stock-tip services. One highlight of the Web site is the Fool's School, site of a small library of background reading for new investors; and on the AOL Motley Fool message board area, no question goes unanswered, no matter how foolish. Then, there's the Fool Portfolio, a fully managed, real-money online portfolio. Unlike most show portfolios, "intentions to buy, sell, or sell short a stock are announced the night before doing so." This makes it possible to follow right along with your own investments, rather than learn at the end of the day that you missed getting in on a rally or out of a crash.
AMERICA ONLINE *keyword* fool
WEB http://www.fool.com

PCFN Both personal investors and high fliers from "The Street" will feel welcome at this investment site. Its easy-to-use interface offers quick stock-ticker look-ups from the front page, and in-depth analysis from its commodious interior. Even better, PCFN puts you in direct contact with the burgeoning world of online trading. You can get execution reports within 60 seconds, practice your puts, and exercise options with ease. All this speed-of-light Net trading is backed up by a hefty dose of information, including real-time stock quotes, Reuters Business/Company News, Zacks Earnings Forecasts, and Standard & Poor's MARKETSCOPE@home. Elsewhere this information could cost you dearly—here it's free.
WEB http://www.pcfn.com

Wall Street City This investing supersite will help ease you down the yellow brick road to the Emerald City of financial prosperity. Read market commentary updated twice a day, get current stock price and market index quotes, search for hot stocks or the highest-yielding mutal funds, and keep track of industry group performance. You can even create your own stock ticker, so you can watch the prices of only those stocks you're personally invested in. Premium services, which cost as little as $9.95 a month, include more in-depth coverage and access.
WEB http://www.wallstreetcity.com

▼ Crash courses

EduStock's The Stock Market "The center of our Nation's economy does not rest at Fort Knox with its millions of dollars worth of gold, or even the Treasury that prints the money that you use. At the center of the United States economy is Wall Street." So begins the rather ponderous (but not entirely inaccurate) tutorial on the stock market at this educational Web site for the young and old alike. Take a walk through the history of the New York Stock Exchange from its inception to current market trends, or choose only those topics you'd like to learn about (there's one thing you could never do in school). Then learn how to pick a stock and try your newfound skill with the EduStock Simulation, which uses "real-time" (20 minutes delayed) stock data.

WEB http://tqd.advanced.org/3088/stockmarket /introductionnf.html

Investing Basics If you're starting from square one of the Rubik's cube known as investing, the American Association of Investors have a great framework approach to get you off and running. You'll learn about the all-important principle of risk and return, and discover how to determine how much risk you can stand to achieve your desired return. You'll find out how to build an investment plan from scratch, especially if you're young and don't have scratch, and you'll also learn how to tailor your strategy as the years go by without feeling pins and needles. Even seasoned investors might gain insight from the section on "Picking Stocks: Techniques that Stand the Test of Time." And if the articles contain any unfamiliar terms ("market-price-to-book-value ratio" springs to mind), the site also provides a handy glossary.

WEB http://www.aaii.org/basics/invbasics.html

▽ Q&A

The Investment FAQ When you're dealing with financial resources, it's sometimes difficult to know whose advice to trust—everyone's out to make a buck , and damn anyone who happens to get in the way. This FAQ, compiled by Christopher Lott and designed to "improve the signal-to-noise ratio" on misc.invest, serves as an unbiased introduction to personal investing, including sections on analysis, stocks, bonds, stock exchanges, software, trading, taxes, and even market regulation (i.e. "How to Survive a Bankrupt Broker").

WEB http://www.cs.umd.edu/users/cml/invest-faq

ONE-LINE WISDOM

1. Hang up on cold calls. While it is theoretically possible that someone is going to offer you the opportunity of a lifetime, it is more likely that it is some sort of scam. Even if it is legitimate, the caller cannot know your financial position, goals, risk tolerance, or any other parameters which should be considered when selecting investments. If you can't bear the thought of hanging up, ask for material to be sent by mail.

2. If it sounds too good to be true, it probably is [too good to be true]. Also stated as "There ain't no such thing as a free lunch." Remember, every investment opportunity competes with every other investment opportunity. If one seems wildly better than the others, there are probably hidden risks or you don't understand something.

3. If your only tool is a hammer, every problem looks like a nail. Someone (possibly a financial planner) with a very limited selection of products will naturally try to jam you into those which s/he sells. These may be less suitable than other products not carried.

—from The Investment FAQ

misc.invest.misc "We are seeking $50,000 at 15 percent for one year." "Hollywood movie investment!" Plaintive appeals for unsecured loans and dubious investment opportunities promising returns of 200 percent abound on this newsgroup, but amid the dross, there are a few nuggets of valuable information and genuine discussion of investment topics. If you happen to come across the message titled, "Wall Street Analyst for sale," don't begin fantasizing about what to do with a stockbroker slave. It refers to software. Pity.

USENET misc.invest.misc

Online stock simulations let you play for fun and imaginary profit

MAYBE YOU'VE SEEN **Warren Buffett** on TV, looking somewhat shy and reclusive, but also looking like a man who has made more than $15 billion for himself—and countless billions for his investors—by playing the market better than any other man alive. Maybe you've thought to yourself, "Sure, Buffett only started with an investment of $300,000, and sure he was ahead of the curve on American Express, Coca-Cola, Wells Fargo, Cap Cities, and the *Washington Post*, but what's he got that I ain't got? Why couldn't I make investment choices that are just as smart as ol' Warren?"

Playing the Market

Well, you can try. With the Net's investment games, you can put your money where your mind is, and try to parlay an initial investment into untold riches, simply by making smart stock picks. Convinced that Apple is going to rebound? Pessimistic about the future of tech stocks like **Yahoo!** and **Netscape**? Let your gut instincts guide your decisions, then step back to see if your gut instincts are more profitable than the gut instincts of others. What are the best virtual stock-picking games online? Here are the ones you should invest your time in:

Primarily intended for use as an educational simulation, **Stock-Trak** follows the rules of classic market simulation games—players get $100,000 and strict instructions to strike it rich. The Web site includes an

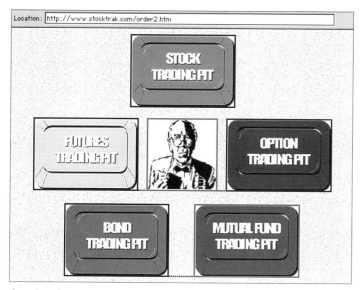

Location: http://www.stocktrak.com/order2.htm

STOCK TRADING PIT

FUTURES TRADING PIT

OPTION TRADING PIT

BOND TRADING PIT

MUTUAL FUND TRADING PIT

Jump into the money pit
http://www.stocktrak.com

CASH REGISTER

Warren Buffett
WEB http://www.cyberuniverse.com
/investor/buff.html

Yahoo!
WEB http://www.yahoo.com

Netscape
WEB http://www.netscape.com

Stock-Trak
WEB http://www.stocktrak.com

E*Trade Electronic Stock Game
WEB http://www.etrade.com/html
/visitor_center/game.htm

nVESTOR
WEB http://www2.investorsleague
.com/investorsleague/

The Boston.com Stock Portfolo
WEB http://www.boston.com
/business/quote/bizport.htm

Avid Trading
WEB http://avidinfo.com/contest.htm

explanation of the game, a list of the Stock-Trak company's management services (portfolio reports, etc.), and a pricing structure for professors. The Web also has free versions of the $100,000-per-investor market scenario, including the **E*Trade Electronic Stock Game** and The League of American Investors' **nVESTOR.**

The *Boston Globe* has designed a new twist on the traditional stock-picking game. On July 1 of last year, the *Globe* invested $100,025 of virtual cash in stocks based on the recommendations of users. It then turned over the management of the portfolio to **Boston.com** visitors, who can send in recommendations about what to do with the portfolio that month. (Note: If you intend to buy and sell real stock based on what Boston.com is doing, be careful; the portfolio value had dropped to $96,267.375 last time we checked.) Then there are the more idiosyncratic investment related competitions, like those at **Avid Trading**, which challenges would-be investors and investment counselors to predict various

CASH REGISTER

Profits Warning
WEB http://www.team17.com/TGR
/profits

Play-Stockmarket Game
WEB http://www.vero.com/play
-stockmarket

The Rogue Market
WEB http://roguemarket.com

Web Market Game
WEB http://www.webmarketgame.com

Robban's Home Page
WEB http://www.robtex.com/robban
/r.htm

The Town of Dodgeville
WEB http://www.geocities.com
/CapitolHill/1798/

market factors—for example, which stock will be the biggest gainer of the coming week, which stock will be the biggest loser, and how high or low the Dow Jones Industrials will rise and fall.

While these competitions and simulations are good for the ego, any investor knows that the only real reason to pick stocks is for profit. As a result, you may want to try your hand at the investment games that incorporate a real-world profit motive. The British-based **Profits Warning** costs £25 in real money for £100,000 in imaginary money and a chance to increase your poundage with wise investments. First prize for each three-month game is a BMW328si or £25,000 in real cash. The **Play-Stockmarket Game** is a 1/100th scale stock-trading game; players buy their shares at penny-to-the-dollar prices and then profit or lose on that same reduced scale. One catch: The company will admit only players who spend $50 or $100 in real money,

Nothing ventured, it's just a game
http://www2.investorsleague.com/investorsleague/

Location: http://www.vero.com/play-stockmarket/

The Play-Stockmarket Game

PLAY THE STOCKMARKET FOR PENNIES A SHARE

...AS A GAME

This Is a game to be played for fun, diversion, to learn more about the Stockmarket, to challenge one's stock-picking ability or that of others, be they friends, co-workers, or other groups, such as classes In corporate finance at other colleges, or brokers In other brokerage firms.

It's not how much money you win or lose, it's how you play the game
http://www.vero.com/play-stockmarket

and while that means $5,000 or $10,000 in Playshare stocks, it's still a large initial outlay. In addition, Play-Stockmarket charges a $5 management fee.

❝ The Rogue Market lets you trade in cultural events. How are your Ted Turner shares these days? ❞

Not all the market simulations online are financial. **The Rogue Market** lets you trade in cultural events. How are your Ted Turner shares these days? Network buyouts precipitate downturn. How about Madonna? New maternal softness triggers gains. And could anyone, even Warren Buffett, have foreseen how quickly Divine Brown stock would go down? There's even the **Web Market** game, which trades stocks for Web pages and calculates their value based on the number of hits they receive. Available stocks include **Robban's Home Page** and **The Town of Dodgeville**. And remember—simply by going to look at your prospective purchase, you'll increase its value.

Why buy the Dow when you can get better advice for free?

YOU SORELY NEED some investment advice, but you certainly don't want it from every Joe Schmo with a modem on the **misc.invest** newsgroup. If you like your advice free, authoritative (i.e., straight from the "experts"), and quick (i.e., without all the investment newsletter ads and solicitations from companies seeking investors), you'll have to be selective on the Internet. Here are our picks for investment columns that more than meet our top two criteria: well-written and quick to read.

Top Investment Gurus

Ask Doug Every couple of weeks, Doug Gerlach, the individual investor behind the huge **Invest-O-Rama** Web site, answers questions on how investors can use the Internet. Email him yours. Whether you're interested in investment simulations, insurance company ratings, or information on technology stocks, Gerlach's column is an excellent place to find the investment resources you need on the Net. Past columns are archived.

Glassman on Wall Street James Glassman, an investment columnist for the *Washington Post*, writes two weekly columns: not only Glassman on Wall Street, but also another quick-tip format called The Inside Scoop.

Readers can search an archive of Glassman's columns (1995 to present) by topic; Glassman also fields questions from *Post* readers online and joins investment discussions on the *Post*'s message boards.

Peter Lynch The well-known stock picker, author, and vice-chairman of Fidelity Management and Research is a frequent columnist for *Worth* magazine. Peter Lynch's current column is usually featured on the magazine's front page, but archives of past columns are also online. Investors can ask Peter Lynch questions directly or post messages for him on the *Worth* discussion boards.

Investing Foolishly Robert Sheard, one of the Foolish faithful, writes two columns for the highly successful Motley Fool Web site. Sheard's daily column, Investing For Growth, focuses on mid- to large-cap growth stocks. Every week, he posts a list of recommended stocks for investors who are just starting to build a growth portfolio; the column monitors changes in those stocks. The second column, The Dow Approach, focuses on high-yield Dow Industrial stocks. It includes a list of the ten highest-yielding DJIA stocks and a daily monitor of the stocks' progress.

Net Gains Every Monday, John Waggoner explains the mutual funds market to Net readers and answers their questions in his exclusive online column for the *USA Today* Web site. The column is available all week. The

CASH REGISTER

USENET misc.invest

Ask Doug
WEB http://www.investorama.com/askdoug.shtml

Invest-O-Rama
WEB http://www.investorama.com/

Glassman on Wall Street
WEB http://www.washingtonpost.com/wp-srv/business/glassman.htm

Peter Lynch
WEB http://www.worth.com/articles/PL0.html

Investing Foolishly
WEB http://fool.web.aol.com/invstng/if_mn.htm

Net Gains
WEB http://www.usatoday.com/money/waggon/colwagl.htm

John Waggoner
WEB http://www.usatoday.com/news/comment/colwag.htm

Money Talks
WEB http://www.talks.com

Barron's Online
WEB http://www.barrons.com

USA Today Web site also publishes the **John Waggoner** print column on mutuals.

> ❝ The names of the columns? Shaking the Money Tree, More Power to You, The Buck Starts Here, The Emporium, Portfolio. The topics of the columns? Varied, but never less than interesting. ❞

Money Talks Six regular columnists write about investment for the individual investor in this magazine sponsored by the PR Newswire. The names of the columns? Shaking the Money Tree, More Power to You, The Buck Starts Here, The Emporium, Portfolio, and Matador. The topics of the columns? Varied, but never less than interesting.

Barron's Online *Barron's*, one of the nation's leading investment newspapers, touts six weekly columns on mutual funds and investing for the online investor. While subscription to *Barron's* is required, it's also free.

Barron's is a fertile world of investment advice
http://www.barrons.com

Netsite: http://www.barrons.com/

December 9, 1996
COVER STORY

Danger?

GREENSPAN'S REMARKS DEFLATE THE DOW. A LOOK AT WHAT'S MAKING THE MARKET SO NERVOUS.

BARRON'S Online ℠

Market Surveillance for the Financial Elite

THERE'S NOTHING AMERICANS love more—indeed, there's nothing more American—than stories about ordinary people who become filthy rich on the strength of their own intelligence. And that's why Americans love stories about investment clubs. In recent years, the press has lionized the Beardstown Ladies, a group of women from a small Illinois town whose investment savvy turned modest initial investments into huge nest eggs, and the Klondike Club, a group of 17 investors in Buffalo, Wyo. that enjoyed a three-fold gain in 1996. The 30,000-plus investment clubs in the country make for great copy for financial reporters; witness the dozens of articles online about the phenomenon, including **Investment Clubs Take a Long View**. Some reports even suggest that profitable investment clubs are the rule rather than the exception—a recent study indicates that more than 70 percent of clubs post better profits than profession-

Would you want to join an investment club that would have you as a member?

Members Only

ally managed funds. From coast to coast, investment clubs are touching off a populist revolution in financial management.

And part of that revolution is occurring online. The Net is the perfect place for investment clubs—in fact, you could argue that the entire Internet is an investment club, a way for investors to come together and trade their stock tips and caveats. Certainly, the giant Internet newsgroups, like **misc.invest.stocks**, are little more than informal investment clubs. On an average

Up the Dow staircase
http://www.better-investing.org/clubs
/thirteen.html

Location: http://www.better-investing.org/clubs/thirteen.html

Suggested Steps For Starting An Investment Club

CASH REGISTER

Investment Clubs Take a Long View
WEB http://cnnfn.com/mybusiness
/9606/20/yobiz_sm_investors

USENET misc.invest.stocks

USENET misc.invest.financial-Plan

Investment Clubs on the Net
WEB http://www.computerland.net
/~missouri/investment_club.htm

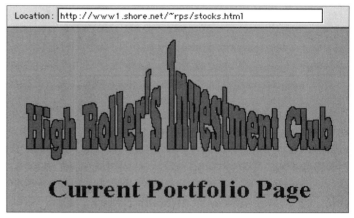

Location: http://www1.shore.net/~rps/stocks.html

In many ways, investing is like gambling
http://wwwl.shore.net/~rps/hiroll.html

day on the newsgroup, Mark might argue that Janus International is a significantly undervalued stock that deserves consideration as a prime pick, while Joel might lament that an entire class of microbrew stocks are valued on the performance of a single company. But in some important respects, newsgroups work against what investment clubs are supposed to accomplish. In fact, large unmoderated forums violate some of the central precepts of successful investment clubs —modest membership numbers, common goals, and obligatory participation. Even newsgroups with sharper charters, like **misc.invest.financial-Plan**, are subject to the same risks. When it comes to thinking of the online world as a giant investment club, investors should narrow their sights somewhat, and think about turning to Web-based clubs.

How do you find those clubs? Visit one of the indexes of online investment clubs—**Investment Clubs on the Net** is the best of them, with a list of dozens of clubs updated regularly. Unfortunately, the problem with online investment clubs is similar to that with online investment newsletters—there are so many of them that netsurfers can easily begin to feel swamped by options, none of which seem qualitatively superior. **The Aviano Investment Club Home Page**, for example, lists the stock picks of this Italian investment club, along with a number of more general links (to financial news, to companies, even to other investment clubs). But how easy is it to assess whether Aviano's expertise is superior to that of the **High Roller's Investment Club** of Cape Ann, Mass., or the **Investment Club**, which promises "profitable stock picks by Richard Vicars"? Most online investment clubs furnish charts and tables to help visitors learn how their picks stack up against professional managers and benchmarks. The **Haas Investment Club** at the University of California, Berkeley's School of Business, for example, has been consistently outperformed by the Willshire 5000, but still has posted a 10 percent gain since March 1996. Nationally famous investment clubs have been known to pop up as well; The Klondike Investment Club has appeared on CompuServe's **Money Magazine Forum**.

When you're playing the investing game, go long
http://cnnfn.com/mybusiness/9606/20/yobiz_sm_investors

Not all of the investment clubs online are echoes of offline clubs. There are a number of investment clubs that exist only in cyberspace, letting geographically distant netsurfers join and spend real money making real stock picks. The **Financially Rewarding On-Line Investment Club**, also known as FROLIC, maintains a site with instructions on how to join, as well as a sum-

> **" Maybe you don't want to visit any of the clubs online. Maybe you don't want to listen to the experts. Maybe you want to start your own club. "**

mary of the club's current portfolio. **The National On-line Investment Club** has closed its membership at a dozen, but conducts most of its business over the Web. And then there are those clubs that forge community in more than one way, like the **Chuma Investment Club**, whose members met on a mailing list devoted to African-American issues. The best way to pick an investment club, ultimately, is to know your own needs—are you looking to invest small sums of money

It's hard to measure up to the Wilshire index
http://haas.berkeley.edu/~whsbic/index.html

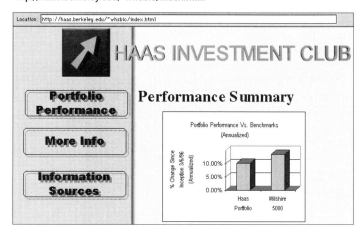

Don't judge a club by its home page
http://www.cris.com/~rjvicars/index.shtml

CASH REGISTER

NAIC-National Association of Investors Corporation
WEB http://www.better-investing.org

NAIC & Investment Clubs
WEB http://www.better-investing.org /clubs/clubs.html

Suggested Steps For Starting An Investment Club
WEB http://www.better-investing.org /clubs/thirteen.html

Family Investment Clubs
WEB http://www.better-investing.org /clubs/famclubs.html

So You Want to Start An Investment Club
WEB http://www.users.interport.net /~gerlach/club.html

and turn a modest profit quickly, or would you prefer to make a large contribution and see it increase in value steadily over the next decade or so? Choosing a club is considerably simpler once you have clarified your investment objectives.

But maybe you don't want to visit any of the clubs online. Maybe you don't want to listen to the experts. Maybe you want to start your own club. There are still plenty of resources online, mostly in the form of hints and tips for founding your own club. **The NAIC-National Association of Investors Corporation** is the headquarters online. The NAIC has a special section on **NAIC & Investment Clubs**, which include articles that range from **Suggested Steps For Starting An Investment Club** to **Family Investment Clubs**. And investment guru Douglas Gerlach also publishes an online tip sheet entitled **So You Want to Start An Investment Club**. In the end, the cardinal rule for investment clubs is the same as for professional financial managers—don't lose money.

▼ Directories

HandiLinks to Investment Newsletters Follow the smiley face for annotation on (and links to) dozens of online investment newsletters. Unfortunately, some of the HandiLinks are significantly out of date.
WEB http://www.ahandyguide.com/catl/i/i56.htm

INVESTools Newsletters INVESTools is the home to several newsletters, including *The Turnaround Letter*, *The Staton Institute Advisory*, and *Richard C. Young's Intelligence Report*. The service sorts by topic, and also offers pricing information, a digest, and even a tie-in with Hulbert Financial Newsletter Reviews, which serves as the Siskel and Ebert of the offline financial newsletter industry.
WEB http://www.investools.com/cgi-bin/f/4

n-Print A commercial mall for investment newsletters that offers each publication space for a basic informational listing (contact name, frequency of issues, and subscription information), a description of the topics covered, and a sample issue for downloading. At the present, there are only a half-dozen

Find the best newsletter in the haystack
http://www.margin.com

You can enter a single symbol or up to seven multiple symbols each separated by a space. You also can set up a personal portfolio.

newsletters which have chosen to list with n-Print.
WEB http://n-print.com/

Newsletter Network With hundreds of investment newsletters on the Web, how do you even begin to choose? Well, you can browse the Web on your own, or look at the selection we've culled. If neither of those options interests you, you can visit the Newsletter Network, a service established to help investors wade through the swamp of financial advice publications online. The library serves as a headquarters for dozens of newsletters, containing pricing and subscription information along with free sample issues. If you want to download current issues of publications like *The Capital Growth Letter*, *Braddock's Solid Value Report*, *Daily Technical Market Comment*, and *Martin Pring's Weekly Update*, you'll need an account with the Newsletter Network.
WEB http://www.margin.com

▼ Forums

Decision Point Daily analysis on 150 stocks, weekly charts on a variety of stocks, popular proprietary market indicators, and ample regular market commentary. To those uninitiated into the finer points of financial analysis, the reports of moderator Carl Swenlin might have a maze-like quality. Hang in there, though, and soon you'll be talking about apparent and actual bottoms forming on the "Short-Term Volume Oscillator." Decision Point comes to life with a busy message-based forum (fundamentalists and techies trading I-told-you-so's), a real-time chat conference area, and a mid-size library of charts and other data. Who knows, you might even enjoy Carl's right-wing political postscripts.
AMERICA ONLINE *keyword* dp

Wall Street SOS Forum In addition to Wall Street SOS and Wall Street SOS Options Alert, SOS Forum includes a variety of other publications and recommendations that follow the ROC (Return On Capital) method of common stock evaluation and the market timing system known as the Bull/Bear Index. In addition to an archive of the Bull/ Bear Index, the forum contains the daily SOS Top Stocks List, SOS Top Funds List, and the SOS Weekly Market Commentary, which concentrates on the weekly performance and prophecies of Jeremy Gentry's market models. Investors who want to bite back can do so on The Wall St. SOS Board, which hosts investment chat on topics such as NAIC—Investment Clubs, Stocks, and Mutual Funds.

AMERICA ONLINE *keyword* SOS

▼ Recommendations

Hulbert Financial Digest Tracking the world of financial newsletters isn't an easy job, but somebody's got to do it. And that somebody is Mark Hulbert, who publishes a financial digest that assesses the performance of hundreds of stock-picking newsletters. Hulbert's site offers a year's subscription to his service, which not only includes the digest, but also a newsletter directory and long-term performance ratings

WEB http://cybersurfing.com/hfd/hfd.html

Investment Newsletters "Of the hundreds of investment newsletters," says the introduction to this list, "few outperform the market. Here is a sampling of letters we deem worthy of your own due diligence, if you are inclined toward incorporating this approach in the asset allocation of your portfolio." What does that mean in layman's terms? That most newsletters offer advice that's the equivalent of a coin flip, and that if

LET THE BLUE CHIPS FALL WHERE THEY MAY

You know, they say you can learn a lot by talking with your elders. My parents and their generation have lived through the Great Depression and World War II. Some pretty amazing and tough times. They have seen it all. When I try to elicit from them the best investment strategies and greatest success stories, it always comes back to one thing—investing in Blue Chip stocks. I hear stories about how nominal or moderate investments in stocks such as Exxon and AT&T have grown to very large sums in the course of 20 to 30 years. But I don't believe that all Blue Chip and Blue-Chip-type stocks are created equal. To be able to identify a good Blue Chip investment, you need to find out where a company has been—has it been successful and is it a leader? But more importantly, you need to know where a company is going. There are Fortune 500 companies like Motorola, which are really going places. And then there are Fortune 500 companies that are going nowhere fast. This is where Investment Insights can help you most. In Issue One, I outlined my Choice Portfolio of Blue Chip and Blue-Chip-type stocks. In this issue, I will tell you which of these stocks are the best of the best. You might be surprised by what you hear.

—from Investment Insights

you want to know which ones can call the flip at a better than 50 percent clip, come here. Recommended newsletters are divided into categories like General, Speculative, Conservative, Mutuals, and so on—general newsletters getting the nod include *Investment Quality Trends, Investors Intelligence, InvesTech,*

Systems & Forecasts, and *MPT Review.*
WEB http://www.investec.com/newslet.html

On Choosing a Financial Newsletter
Financial newsletter analyst Mark Hulbert wrote this short article, which gives investors tips on picking a good newsletter. Hulbert's three criteria: performance, risk, and the amount of time it takes to follow the recommendations of a particular "expert." This is excellent, no-nonsense advice for those who feel lost in the welter of financial advice newsletters.
WEB http://pawws.secapl.com/Mfis_phtml/nl06.shtml

▼ Selected newsletters

Colloquium A newsletter published by the Manhattan investment banking firm of Wertheim Schroder & Co. Tailored to the needs of professional investment managers, it nonetheless can be a good source of useful tips for individual investors. On the site, *Colloquium* includes a sample issue (from September 1994), along with additional materials. Registration is required.
WEB http://www.hydra.com/ws/colloquium.html

Day Traders Online Day Traders offers advice and recommendations for short-term

---

Tune in for the investment forecast
http://Wall-Street-News.com/forecasts

---

investors. New visitors are welcome to a free two-week trial. After that, they'll have to pay the $15 monthly fees, which give you access to the nightly newsletter and Web chat rooms.
WEB http://www.daytraders.com

Growth Stock Gazette This newsletter is dedicated to finding fast-growing stocks for rapid appreciation of initial investments. Download the current issue for only $29 (payable by major credit card), and get an additional issue at no additional cost.
WEB http://home.navisoft.com/gsg/

Investext Investment Reports Information on earnings, stock value, management changes, business climate changes, competition, and new products. The service permits detailed searches of the database of more than 320,000 investment reports, and offers weekly market commentary and historical portfolios.
COMPUSERVE *go* investext

Investment Insights A quarterly newsletter that focuses on high-growth and secure stocks, as well as mutual funds, *Investment Insights* is available for $35 yearly. The newsletter is not currently online, but interested investors can view a sample issue.
WEB http://www.investin.com

Market Advantage Promising competitive research recommendations, Traders Edge offers a trial subscription for $20. What's here? Sample portfolios, equity recommendations, and more, including a Wall Street Forum where subscribers can share their experiences picking stocks.
WEB http://www.tradersedge.com

Profit Letter Not every investor wants low-cost securities. But if you're one of those who do, then you'll want to consider subscribing to the Profit Letter, which special-

izes in low-cost stocks.
WEB http://www.stockgroup.com/profit

Stock Sector Analysis Newsletter Extremely technical, this newsletter takes $26 of your money each year and returns what are either can't-miss stock tips based on high-end number crunching or columns of numbers with no particular significance. Pray for the former.
WEB http://ourworld.compuserve.com/homepages/ssan

Thomas Nelson's Weekly Market Overview
Although Thomas Nelson is in Germany, his free newsletter is on the Internet, which means it reaches the world. Nelson collects world market statistics and U.S. market statistics, and publishes his findings, along with market commentary, weekly.
WEB http://Olis.North.DE/~tnelson/wmo.html

Turnaround Letter Some stocks are winners from the start. Others are perennial losers. And still others are losers with the potential to suddenly emerge as profitable investments. That's what the Turnaround Letter looks for. Read a sample issue or get a trial subscription for $39.
WEB http://www.turnarounds.com/tl.html

U.S. and World Early Warnings Report Weather trends can affect commodities, and then they can affect companies, and eventually they can affect stock prices. In other words, a low-pressure system over Jakarta can spell doom for your bank account. A little melodramatic? Perhaps. But the Early Warning Report knows that we're all in this together, and that's why this newsletter tracks global trends with an eye toward their domestic effects. Subscription prices are often offered on the cheap as part of special deals.
WEB http://www.subscriptions.com/beacon/

Wall Street News The *Wall Street News* keeps its ear to the ground of the world's most

MARKET ADVICE

This doesn't mean that all investment newsletters beat the market, needless to say. As is also true of mutual funds and professional money managers, most of them don't. But we all are better off for their trying, since in the process we discover those promising new strategies that otherwise would have gone unnoticed. "Investment letters are the guerrilla troops of the financial world," writes *Forbes* senior editor Peter Brimelow in his classic work on the investment letter industry, *Wall Street Gurus*). "By following them, and halting if they terminate in a smoking crater, you can see what techniques work."

—*from On Choosing a Financial Newsletter*

important financial thoroughfare, scanning the newsletters published by financial experts and then issuing up-to-the-minute recommendations for stock purchases and sales.
WEB http://Wall-Street-News.com/forecasts/

Wall Street Traders This newsletter, which is delivered using the now-antiquated technology of the fax machine, screens more than 750 issues each day and recommends six for purchase.
WEB http://www.wstraders.com/

Zack's Investment Research Zack's runs a company and industry research service, but its investment newsletter has a fairly specific approach, summarizing the buy/sell recommendations and earnings per share (EPS) estimates of more than 3,500 Wall Street analysts and processing them to yield red-light or green-light recommendations on individual companies and industries. Subscriptions to reports are available for $14.95 per month.
WEB http://www.investools.com/cgi-bin/Library/zacks.pl

T RACKING A PORTFOLIO used to require vigilant monitoring of the stock pages in the newspaper, a separate portfolio management system (note pad, software program, etc.), and a broker to help you buy, sell, and make investment decisions. To get stock quotes, you had to wait for the newspaper or the evening news. Maybe you called your broker if you had a feeling something was happening, but you couldn't exactly stay on the phone all day. Now, you don't have to wait for the newspaper to arrive; you can find a quote for a stock or mutual fund in seconds-and for free. Online services delivering

No more squinting at the newspaper's ink-smudged stock pages

Portfolio Tracking Online

quotes on a 15-to-20 minute delayed basis are now quite common on the Net (soon, kids pages will probably start popping up with them).

But don't give up on newspapers just yet. The online versions of some of the nation's biggest papers are letting investors set up easy-to-manage personal portfolios online. Investors can then drop by the newspaper as often as they like (bookmark your portfolio page!) to check on how well individual stocks are doing or on the valuation of the entire portfolio as of 15 minutes ago. Many newspapers are also linking the portfolio area to company profiles, business news, and market summaries.

Online, newspapers are making the process of tracking stocks and calculating the value of portfolios easy, personal, and private. You don't need a magnifying glass either.

▶ **The New York Times Personal Portfolio/The Los Angeles Times Personal Portfolio** In conjunction with Quote.com, the *New York Times* and the *Los Angeles Times* let you track up to seven stocks and mutual funds. You can quickly retrieve current quotes for each issue in your portfolio, but you can't yet calculate the value of a portfolio. The big advantage? You can easily access your portfolio from any of these sites.

▶ **WashingtonPost.com Personal Portfolio** Track a portfolio of up to ten stocks and funds. Click on Current Price for a detailed quote summary for each issue (last quote, year high, year low, volume, etc.) or Calculate Value to figure out how much profit you've made. The Main Stocks Page links to market news, company profiles, investment columns, AP market stories, and a ticker symbol lookup feature.

▶ **Personal Journal Portfolio** The *Wall Street Journal* will keep track of up to 30 stocks and mutual funds, providing composite prices for each issue and a calculation of the total portfolio whenever you link to the

CASH REGISTER

The New York Times Personal Portfolio
WEB http://www.nytimes.com/partners /quote/index.cgi?portfolio.html

The Los Angeles Times Personal Portfolio
WEB http://fast.quote.com/fq/latimes /quote

WashingtonPost.com Personal Portfolio
WEB http://www.washingtonpost.com /wp-srv/business/longterm/stocks /porthelp.htm

Personal Journal Portfolio
WEB http://interactive6.wsj.com /portfolio-bin/PortfolioDisplay.cgi

Investor's Edge Portfolio
WEB http://www.irnet.com/pages /gatelogin.stm

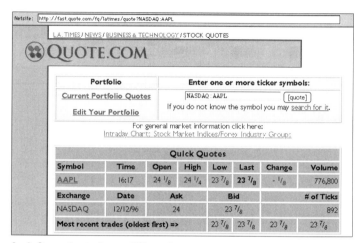

Apple Computing took a small bite today
http://fast.quote.com/fq/latimes/quote

page. Setting up your portfolio is incredibly simple. Just enter the names or symbols for each issue along with the number of shares in the blanks provided, and click Update Portfolio. Considering making changes? The *WSJ* provides easy access to market information, including full-text searches of the paper, Briefing Books for stocks, and a separate quote search. The portfolio follows the same pricing structure as the rest of the journal-it costs money, except for Microsoft Explorer users.

▶ **Investor's Edge Portfolio** The Gate (the online home of the *San Francisco Chronicle* and the *San Francisco Examiner*) has teamed up with InvestorsEdge to offer registered members (no fee) the ability to create and monitor a personal portfolio of 15 stocks. Design and navigation are not as friendly as the other personal portfolio services, but the site offers additional functionality. Investors can download data to Quicken, calculate the value of the entire portfolio, and view individual quotes. They can also take advantage of other free premiums offered by InvestorsEdge for a limited time to attract paid subscribers.

What goes up doesn't necessarily come down
http://www.washingtonpost.com/wp-srv
/business/longterm/stocks/porthelp.htm

▼ Company research

Avenue Company Profiles Avenue sells online company profiles of more than 25,000 businesses. From this page, you can pick up an order form and get samples of the reports. If you were interested, for example, in working for Birkenstock Footprint Sandal, Inc., you could receive a report listing the top executives, the estimated yearly sales of their products, and recent company news. Here's a sure way of getting your Paris, Milano, or Arizona in the door.
WEB http://www.avetech.com/avenue/home.html

Barron's Online Business Dossiers You'll have to register for the online version of Dow Jones and Company's weekly business magazine, but once you do, you'll have access to a wealth of company information. Enter a ticker symbol (or search in the Company Index) to see some basic information—a brief company description and where the company's stock trades. You'll also get a choice of financial performance overviews that include a Tradeline Performance Snapshot, an Annual Fundamental Snapshot, a Quarterly Fundamental Snapshot, and a Total Return & Industry Comparison Snapshot. In addition to this data—which is often rendered in easy-to-read graphs—*Barron's* helpfully reprints the 20 most recent news articles relating to the company. If there's a problem with *Barron's* offerings, it doesn't lie in the data, which is unimpeachable, but rather in the breadth of coverage—only a few hundred companies are covered here, which means that the service is likely to be passed over in favor of those company directories with thousands of entries.
WEB http://www.barrons.com/dossier/index.html

Companies Online Co-sponsored by Dun and Bradstreet and the Lycos search engine, Companies Online gives you the best for less—specifically, basic information on 60,000 companies at the unbeatable price of absolutely nothing. Search by name or criteria, and get a thumbnail sketch that includes basic information on industrial classification, ownership structure, and even online address. Then register for more comprehensive information, including annual earnings, number of employees, corporate parents, and more.
WEB http://www.CompaniesOnline.com

Company Analyzer Provides U.S. stock prices on 15-minute delay, as well as a detailed profile of each company selected, including price and volume history, dividend history, bond and option issues, financial statements, management discussion, officers, and salaries. The service also furnishes CUSIP numbers (Committee on Uniform Securities Identification Procedures), which are useful for other corporate databases.
COMPUSERVE *go* analyzer

Company Research Know your key competitors and your stock picks inside and out with the help of these company news updates, in-

---

D&B boasts a database of more than 10 million companies
http://www.dbisna.com/

When you want to pick up every last piece of dirt
http://hoovweb.hoovers.com

depth spotlight features on specific companies, and company profiles that list the intimate details of hundreds of companies (from basic overviews to the names of their mailroom personnel). Free access to earnings estimates and historical data are available from FirstCall—great for anticipating what an earnings report might do to a stock's price.
AMERICA ONLINE *keyword* company research

Dun & Bradstreet Along with Hoover's, Dun & Bradstreet is one of the premier suppliers of information about companies in the world. Long a staple of CompuServe's business research package, D&B is now on the Web with a fairly comprehensive service that lets visitors search from a database of more than 10 million companies worldwide. While there is no charge for searching, you'll have to shell out $20 for each comprehensive Business Background Report.
WEB http://www.dbisna.com/

Hoover's Business Profiles Suck up the dirt on your investment picks by searching Hoover's Handbook's detailed profiles of nearly 2,000 of the largest and fastest-growing public and private companies in the U.S. and the world. Profiles are exhaustive, with info that includes

assets, sales figures, number of employees, CEO and CFO salaries, and company products. They also feature long and gossipy descriptions of company history and culture. Get the location of a company's office, its future goals and ongoing programs, and its recent stock prices, plus phone, address, and fax information. The exhaustive resources at Hoover's Business Profiles will help you get to know the market one company at a time. Note: A Web subscription isn't free, though AOL and CompuServe members have special access.
AMERICA ONLINE *keyword* hoover
COMPUSERVE *go* hoover
WEB http://www.hoovers.com

▼ Company research

Hoover's Business Rankings Rankings are fun. Which company's the richest? Which is the most environmentally conscious? Which has the best record when it comes to gay employees? What are the 25 largest brokerage houses and the 10 oldest companies in America? Get the answers to these and other ranking questions with Hoover's—number one in business rankings.
AMERICA ONLINE *keyword* rankings
WEB http://www.hoovers.com/lists.html

I/B/E/S Earnings Reports If you want earnings forecasts, you want I/B/E/S, and specifically the company's Earnings Surprise Report. For $2.50 per report, I/B/E/S will furnish actual and expected earnings per share information on all companies that have reported results in the past day. I/B/E/S also offers the Daily Consensus Earnings Reports service—also $2.50 per report. Daily Consensus Earnings data includes average price and earnings, and high and low estimates for the current fiscal year, the next fiscal year, the current quarter, and the next quarter. If none of these reports meet your needs, I/B/E/S will be happy to turn its research professionals loose on custom reports—but you'll have to pay for the pleasure. All in all, I/B/E/S has information on more than 16,000 stocks from 47 different countries.

WEB http://networth.galt.com/www/home/equity/ibes/home.html

Market Guide Market Guide has earned the ultimate online distinction—a link from Hoover's Company Capsules section—and for good reason. With basic information on more than 8,300 publicly traded companies, this is one of the best sources of company data online. The free Company Snapshot Reports—which are summoned instantly as soon as the netsurfer (that's you) enters the company's ticker symbol—include earnings ratios and other statistics such as market capitalization, dividends, and earnings per share. Market Guide also offers more comprehensive reports such as the Earnings Estimate Report, which runs $2.50 per company.

WEB http://www.marketguide.com

PR Newswire: Company News On Call As the name implies, PR Newswire is a wire service that distributes press releases from public and private companies to the news media. Companies often make major announcements and release their earnings reports through PR Newswire and/or Business Wire, a competing service. PR Newswire's Web site lets you look up press releases filed by company name.

WEB http://www.prnewswire.com/cnoc.html

S&P Online For a fee, this service distills the recent business histories of more than 5,000 companies to bring you essential information, including recent market activity, dividend information, product line summaries, and earnings estimates. Get the skinny on a com-

pany before an interview, or browse for a company that might be hiring.

COMPUSERVE *go* s&p

Wall Street Journal Briefing Books For investors who want company information, the highlights of the *Wall Street Journal*'s site are the Journal's Briefing Books. What are Briefing Books? Comprehensive corporate profiles on over 9,000 major U.S. and global companies that include background information, stock performance charts and data, additional company news, press releases, and a financial overview section with quarterly and annual information revenues, net income, and earnings per share. You can subscribe to the *Wall Street Journal* for $49 a year ($29 if you subscribe to the print version).

WEB http://www.wsj.com

Which companies are socially responsible and which ones belong in the Three Mile Island category?

Wet Feet Press Which companies are socially responsible and which ones belong in the Three Mile Island category? Which consulting companies offer the most reliable growth trajectories and which ones have softball teams? Wouldn't it be a shame if you invested in the wrong company because you didn't have a handle on stock refunds or profit strategies? Get the jump on the next guy. Though it's geared primarily toward job applicants, Wet Feet Press will help you get the scoop on hundreds of American companies no matter if you're an interviewee or an investor.

WEB http://www.wetfeet.com

Market Guide Investment Center

Welcome to the Market Guide Investment Center, a comprehensive web site designed to provide you with a wealth of investment and financial information, including research reports on over 8,300 publicly traded companies. If you are an experienced or professional investor, you can find all the information you need to make informed investment decisions. If you are new to investing you can learn how to become a better investor by using the tools of the professional investor.

Also home to dead presidents
http://www.marketguide.com

▼ Directories

BIZ*FILE A huge online Yellow Pages that indexes more than 10 million businesses in the United States and Canada. Search by company name, geographical location, telephone number, or type of business. More detailed reports disclosing juicy tidbits are available for an additional fee.
COMPUSERVE *go* bizfile

The Insider: Public Companies Access more than 800 company home pages and press releases from the Insider. Indexed alphabetically and equipped with a sturdy search engine, this site is indispensable if you want to begin researching companies by looking at how they present themselves online. And even if you don't, you may want to check it out.
WEB http://networth.galt.com/www/home/equity/irr

JobTrak Company Profiles Though it's geared toward job seekers rather than investors, Job-Trak's directory of major companies is valuable both for the short summaries of corporate philosophy and history and for the links to the companies' home pages.
WEB http://www.jobtrak.com/profiles/

Thomas Register of North American Manufacturers Remember the scene in Henry James' *The Ambassadors,* in which Lambert Strether won't tell Maria Gostrey the flagship product of the Massachusetts company that has sent him to Paris in search of Chad Newsome? Today, Strether wouldn't stand a chance: All Maria would have to do is to run a search in this database of North American companies, products, and services.
COMPUSERVE *go* thomas

▼ Industry research

clari.biz.industry* To check on the latest media merger or the latest coal mine opening in West Virginia, consult this family of newsgroups, which lists developments in a variety of fields ranging from agriculture to aviation to manufacturing to mining. Divided by industry, these newgroups are repositories for news stories from major wire services. Fee based.
USENET clari.biz.industry*

Hoover's Industry Profiles Facts and figures on nearly 200 U.S. industries ranging from construction to health care to transportation. The comprehensive list includes 30 service and 150 manufacturing industries. Filled with projections, trend analysis, and statistics from American companies (supplies, expenditures, employee numbers), the reports are long and detailed. If you want a quick but smart rundown of issues and challenges facing an industry for your market analysis, these reports spell those out well. All in all, one of the finest company research sites around.
AMERICA ONLINE *keyword* industry profiles

Industry Outlook From aerospace to publishing to wood products, Industry Outlook will always give you the most up-to-date information about manufacturing businesses in the

U.S., from statistics on American employment to the working environments of particular industries.

WEB http://www.jobtrak.com/jobsearch_docs/indoutlk.html

▼ International companies

Access Information Company Profiles For a $5 fee, get basic information on any company publicly traded in India. Reports include name and address of the company, name of the chief executive, business profile, bankers, location of the company's plants, details on installed capacity, and more. Access Information also publishes reports on Indian industries.

WEB http://www.infoindia.com/access/services.html#CP

Australian/New Zealand Company Library Directory and financial information on almost 100,000 private and public companies in Australia and New Zealand. Drawing on such financial databases as Dun & Bradstreet's Australian and New Zealand listings and full-text news archives like Global Textline, the library permits searches by company name, geographic location, industry code, or keyword.

COMPUSERVE *go* anzcompany

Canadian Stockwatch A real-time news release database that includes information on all publicly traded Canadian companies. All told, Canadian Stockwatch contains more than half a million news releases.

WEB http://www.canada-stockwatch.com/

D&B International Company Profiles Dun & Bradstreet's European and Asia/Pacific databases, plus financial information on hundreds of thousands of African and Indian companies.

COMPUSERVE *go* dbintl

German Company Library Directory and financial information on roughly 50,000 German companies.

COMPUSERVE *go* gerlib

Investor Relations Asia Want to check in on the activity of the First Philippine Holding Company? Or maybe you're thinking of dumping some cash into Hong Kong but unwilling to move before you see at least an interim report from the Kwong Sang Hong International Limited. Well, with the Investor Relations Asia database, your informational prayers have been answered. Enter the desired company's ticker symbol or browse a list divided by country. The database contains hundreds of publicly traded Asian companies.

WEB http://irasia.com/listco/index.htm

Want to check in on the activity of the First Philippine Holding Company?

Lexisvision Company Information Link to home pages for Swedish companies listed on the Stockholm Stock Exchange (SSXE), and get basic information about those companies.

WEB http://www.lexivision.se/company/eng/

UK Company Research Center Directory and financial information on millions of U.K. companies, with gateways to databases such as Dun & Bradstreet's European Market Identifiers, the ICC British Company Directory, Jordan's Registered Companies, and Kompass UK. The service also accesses such financial databases as Extel Cards, Financial Times Analysis Reports, and Infocheck UK. Search by company name, geographic location, number of employees, or keyword.

COMPUSERVE *go* couk

Chapter 15

Basic Trading

You don't have to bet the farm to realize big gains

N THE FINANCIAL WORLD, getting wired is all about getting an edge. When they talk about the Net, investors talk about newsletters, investment clubs, discussion forums, 15-minute-delayed quotes, and portfolio management tools. The advantage is clear: more information, faster information, and more convenient information delivery. But information is not the bottom line—cost is. And the Net's giving investors a competitive advantage in this regard as well. Brokerage houses doing business online—and there are several, ranging from the promi-

Run With the Bulls

nent to the experimental—often offer steep discounts to investors using their online trading services. In other words, online trading is cheaper. But cheaper than what?

Let's start from the beginning. The services at most online brokerage firms are comparable to those offered by trade-by-telephone offline discount brokerages. They usually don't provide much investment advice and are limited in the type of "extra" services they offer (e.g., no trading on IPOs), but interested investors can buy and sell for low, cut-rate commission fees. Full-service offline brokerages, on the other hand, charge much higher commission fees, but offer personal investment counseling and a full range of investment services.

If saving money is your goal and you're sold on the steeper discounts, you'll need to register with an online brokerage firm. All of them require you to submit an application (or a signed contract) by mail. The minimum balance, which varies from $0 (PCFN) to $10,000 (ebroker), is then mailed in to the brokerage. This is the money you'll use when trading. Typically

Without Having a Cow

you'll have to wait up to two weeks for the broker's trading go-ahead, although PCFN lets some investors begin trading instantly. Once you've placed a trade, you have three days to make sure you get the full balance in your account; if you expect to make some big trades, keep a higher balance.

That's the trading procedure. But what about the selection procedure. In other words, what should you look for when shopping for an online broker? Minimum balances, commission rates, and additional services (real-time quotes, credit card deals, etc.). If you already use an offline broker, check to see if the ser-

Web trading should be this easy
http://www.schwab.com

CASH REGISTER

Charles Schwab
WEB http://www.schwab.com

eSchwab
WEB http://www.eschwab.com/

ebroker
WEB http://www.ebroker.com

E*Trade
WEB http://www.etrade.com

Lombard
WEB http://www.lombard.com/Help
/fees.html

National Discount Brokers
WEB http://www.pawws.com/Broker
/Ndb

The Net Investor
WEB http://www.pawws.com/Broker
/How

PC Financial Network
WEB http://www.pcfn.com/

vice offers online trading discounts; you may be able to immediately access your current account online. Otherwise, consider these popular online brokerages:

Summaries of Online Brokerages

▶ **Charles Schwab** Schwab lets customers trade both stocks and mutual funds on the Web. All the investor needs to do is open an account; then log in from any computer to check account status, access real-time quotes (not the 15-minute-delayed variety), and place an order. Charles Schwab also runs a new service known as **eSchwab**, which offers lower commission rates ($29.95 for up to 1,000 shares and 3 cents a share for trades over 1,000 shares) and portfolio management capabilities. Schwab requires Windows software.
Commission: 10 percent lower than Schwab's standard scheduled commission rates for stocks, options, mutual funds and fixed income. Requires a $39 per trade minimum.
Minimum Deposit: $5,000
Additional Services: Real-time quotes. Don't expect to find much guidance at this site—you're pretty much on your own.

▶ **ebroker** Here's its pitch: For $12 you can trade any number of shares of common or preferred stock. You can also trade option contracts with a minimum commission rate of $35. Not bad, not bad at all. The no-frills ebroker service is an Internet-only entity, but it's making quite a name for itself in investment circles. All account application forms are online and the straightforward FAQ sums up the company's services quite nicely. The drawback? A large minimum deposit is required.
Commission: $12 for any number of shares of common or preferred stock.

Minimum Deposit: $10,000
Additional Services: Don't hold your breath. You can, however, buy real-time quotes for $30 per month.

❝ Investors can access their accounts through the Web, telephone, or a direct-dial modem connection. ❞

▶ **E*Trade** E*Trade claims that its founders were the first to introduce electronic brokerage services to the individual investor. Investors can access their accounts through the Web, telephone, or a direct-dial modem connection to E*Trade. Visitors to the E*Trade Web site can play a stock game and get 20-minute delayed quotes.
Commission: $14.95 for any size market order; or $19.95 for OTC and other listed orders; options trades carry a minimum $29 commission rate.
Minimum Deposit: $1,000 for cash accounts or $2,000 for margin accounts.
Additional Services: Unlimited real-time quotes; charts and real-time news; checking.

▶ **Lombard** Not the prettiest site in cyberspace, Lombard Brokerage Inc. nonetheless delivers all the right services. Investors can trade stocks, options, mutual funds, and bonds, and take advantage of the site's many portfolio management services.
Commission: $14.95 for market orders, and $19.95 for limit orders on listed stocks. Trades over 5,000 shares are charged at a rate of 1 cent per share for the entire order. The commission for OTC stocks is $14.95 for market orders and $19.95 for limit orders. Stocks under $1 are charged at their standard rates.
Minimum Deposit: $500
Additional Services: Real-time quotes, intraday charts, and portfolio and trade information.

Don't get a big head when you get rich
http://www.ebroker.com

$12 Trades!

▶ **National Discount Brokers** National Discount Brokers is one of PAWWS Financial Network's affiliate brokers. (PAWWS is a huge investment site which brings together a wide range of investment services—some free, some not.) Just how cheap is NDB? Its Web site features a commission calculator that lets you figure out how much you'd pay for a specific stock trade at competitive online trading houses like Lombard and PC Financial Network compared to what you'd pay at NDB. Investors can also register for additional services such as investment reports and a free asset management account.

Commission: $20 for NASDAQ or OTC trades; $25 for any listed trades (add $3 postage/handling fee for listed trades); $35 for options plus $2.50 per contract; $50 flat fee for bonds.

Minimum Deposit: $5,000 in cash or securities

Additional Services: Relies on the PAWWS site to provide investors the additional services they need.

" Just how cheap is NDB? Its Web site features a calculator that lets you figure out how much you'd pay for a stock trade at competitive online trading houses. "

▶ **The Net Investor** Another one of PAWWS Financial Network's affiliate brokers, The Net Investor received Barron's highest rating for ease of use, range of offerings, and overall service. This site lets you trade stocks, options, mutual funds, and bonds online. It also offers investors deep discounts and the Why We're Better page compares Net Investor's online trading options to Lombard, E*Trade, and Schwab. And if you fax your application and wire funds, The Net Investor will expedite opening an account.

Commission: $29 plus a 1.5 cents per share on the

first 3,000 shares, 1.5 cents thereafter.
Minimum Deposit: $5,000 ($2,000 for IRA)
Additional Services: Information from market
sources such as Morningstar, Telescan, Hoover, and
DTN; free historical price graphs of 4,600 stocks; free
real-time quotes to frequent traders; portfolio reporting; and free checking; a VISA debit card; and choice
of Money Market Funds.

▶ **PC Financial Network** If you were picking an online
broker by the site's design, the PC Financial Network
would definitely get your business. But it's more than
just a pretty face. PCFN received the highest ratings
for online trading capabilities in a *Worth* magazine
survey of investors, and it offers trading via three
major online networks: the Internet, Prodigy, and
America Online. Investors can trade a full range of
securities, including listed stocks, OTC stocks,
mutual funds, options, bonds, CDs, and more. The
service also offers its investors access to other trading
services, from real-time quotes to market news information. Vistors get plenty of freebies, too, including
stock reports, quotes, and the ability to set up model
portfolios.
Commission: PCFN offers a 70 percent discount on
commissions as compared to a full commission broker;
the pricing structure is complicated but requires a $40
minimum charge on stocks trading over $1.
Minimum Deposit: None required. PCFN can automatically approve investors for up to $15,000 in online
trading. Cash or securities to cover the trades must be
received within three business days.
Additional Services: Real-time quotes, investment
news and research, interactive model portfolios, investment screening and selection tools, and customized
portfolio alerts.

No minimum required for maximum gains
http://www.pcfn.com/

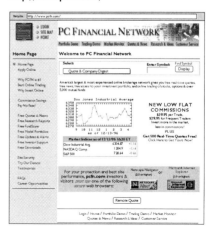

You've been hearing about mutual funds for years. Get with the times online

YOU'VE GIVEN UP on the little luxuries. You don't take cabs. You keep the tab down when you eat out, and you tip to the penny. You bargain hunt. You buy in bulk. Pat yourself on the back—at last, you are a little closer to financial stability. But for all the effort you put in, your money is probably snoozing in a bank account when it could be made to work as hard as you. Remember that article in *Time* magazine that described **Fidelity Investments** (the mutual-fund leviathan that manages $450 billion worth of other people's money) as "The Money Machine"? Perhaps you should have some of your

The Feeling is Mutual

money in that machine, or one like it. Interested? You should be. And if you're interested in mutual funds, you're interested in the Internet. The Net's financial sites, which run both broad and deep, contain mutual-related resources that rival those available from professional financial advisors. Can you go from mutual novice to expert investor in no time at all? That all depends on how well you use the Net.

Mutual Fund Basics

With a mutual fund, your money is invested in a portfolio of stocks or bonds. The objective is to offset the price fluctuation of any stock or bond in particular. You don't bet the farm on AOL shares for example, or Apple, or Wired Ventures (even if you could). Instead, each mutual fund is administered by fund managers who trade on their understanding of the markets and their long-term vision. While a stockbroker might look for a ten-day turnaround on a groovy new issue, a mutual fund manager bets on the stocks that will best take advantage of the sustained growth of the market. In other words, they're safer.

Another easy entree into the realm of Net Asset Values and no-loads, Peter W. Johnson's **Green Jungle** takes the form of a hypertext-enhanced walk-through of the mutuals process. From introduction (links take you to a dictionary that offers clear explanations of terms like "Net Asset Value" and "no-load") to purchase (which companies specialize in mutual funds), Johnson volunteers a fund of the month with a breezy, but nevertheless impressive, performance analysis. Compare past winners, and become familiar with terminology that was once as mysterious to you as the inner logic of the Cabala. And then put some real money to work.

Decide What You Can Afford

As a rule, your mutual funds investment should cut into the butter money; only invest as much as you can afford to forget about for a few years. As get-rich schemes go, mutual funds are more tortoise than hare. Don't expect quick returns. In addition, when you need money for an emergency, this is not the pool you want to be dipping into. Why? One word: penalties. Touching your mutual money before the agreed-upon time (it can be anywhere from five to ten years) will cost you big.

Consult the Mutual Fund Experts

The **Mutual Funds Homepage** should be the next step on your path to mutual fund wisdom. Haven't yet been

America's on a mutual funds high
America Online *keyword* mutual funds

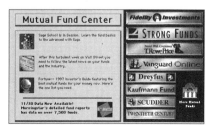

CASH REGISTER

Fidelity Investments
WEB http://www.fid-inv.com/

Green Jungle
WEB http://www.greenjungle.com

Mutual Funds Homepage
WEB http://www.brill.com

John Waggoner
WEB http://www.usatoday.com
/money/waggon/colwag1.htm

Barron's
WEB http://www.barrons.com/

Worth
WEB http://www.worth.com/

The Wall Street Journal
WEB http://www.wsj.com/

"On Choosing a Financial Newsletter"
WEB http://pawws.secapl.com/Mfis
_phtml/nl06.shtml

Mutual Funds Center
AMERICA ONLINE *keyword* mutual funds

Fidelity
WEB http://www.fidelity.com/

Vanguard
WEB http://www.vanguard.com

Dreyfus
WEB http://www.dreyfus.com/

Merrill Lynch
WEB http://www.ml.com/

Mutual Fund Company Directory
WEB http://www.cs.cmu.edu/~jdg
/funds.html

USENET misc.invest.mutual-funds

Netsite: http://www.ml.com/

Journey to Financial Success

Follow the bull on the road paved with gold
http://www.ml.com/

able to work out why anyone would pay the extra for a load over a no-load? Still not sure when's the best time to buy? Here, wisdom flows freely, at least from the page's experts, a formidable array of financial pros who, for the most part, share their knowledge lucidly. If anyone can help you part with your hard-earned wages, these guys reckon they can. *USA Today* also publishes a weekly online column that features the advice of mutual guru **John Waggoner**. And publications like **Barron's**, **Worth**, and **The Wall Street Journal** (subscription required) deliver seasoned analyses of the market and specific funds. Of course, you could always take your chances with an online newsletter dedicated to guiding investors in making their decisions, but you'll first need some advice on choosing the right newsletter (Mark Hulbert's helpfully titled **"On Choosing a Financial Newsletter"** may be of some assistance). If you're a member of AOL, the **Mutual Funds Center** pulls everything together in one forum: introductory explanations of funds, quotes, Morningstar ratings, mutual fund games, discussion boards (a topic for each fund), newsletters (The Sage Scoop, for instance), and reports from *Investors Business Daily*, not to mention online centers for major fund companies.

❝ How do you start a fund? What's better, an index fund or a specialized fund? Did you hear what Peter Lynch said about mutual funds? ❞

Talk to Other Mutual Fund Investors

As you begin to master the terminology, and become familiar with the large mutual fund companies like **Fidelity**, **Vanguard**, **Dreyfus**, and **Merrill Lynch**, you may want to ask questions, get recommendations, or even just talk about about your investments. The newsgroup **misc.invest.mutual-funds** is an active forum for experienced and novice investors alike. How do you start a fund? What's better, an index fund or a specialized fund? Did you hear what Peter Lynch said about mutual funds? You can join the debates, ask the questions, or check in periodically to see which funds Net investors are excited about this week.

Compare Mutual Funds

Before you actually invest, you will want to compare different funds. The large mutual fund companies have set up Web sites with extensive information for personal investors. Fidelity, for instance, lets investors search for data on their funds, track portfolios, sign up for a quarterly newsletter with insights on Fidelity's Select Portfolios, and retrieve detailed performance figures. For a list of mutual fund companies, see the **Mutual Fund Company Directory** which features contact information, including Web sites when available, for funds all over the world.

A worthwhile site
http://www.worth.com/

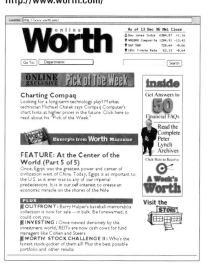

But as you examine funds, what kind of performances should you expect? According to the **Rogue's Perspective on Mutual Funds** (which is part of the ever-entertaining investment forum, The Motley Fool), mutual funds invariably underperform the S&P 500, a list of 500 of the top performing companies. All that means, of course, is that you're not going to make a quick killing. You do, however, want to do as well as you can. How can you find out enough about the differnt funds to make a decision? Unless you choose to rely on the gossip and theorizing at misc.invest.mutual -funds or the wisdom of, say, the **Sage** on America Online, you have a fair bit of legwork ahead of you.

One of the most straightforward ways online to find out how a fund compares with the competition is to use the **NETworth** site. Dip into the Fund Atlas where you will find a selection of Fund Families. Choose one at random. Let's say, Janus Funds. Select one of the funds from the family—for consistency's sake, make it Janus Fund. Learn that the fund's Wall Street symbol is JANSX, and that the average return on the fund over the last decade is a healthy 16.46 percent. If you want, research the fund's holdings (tobacco? technology?). Do this with as many funds as you feel you need to before making a decision. If you want to restrict your research to funds that have earned a five-star rating from the well-respected **Morningstar** Mutual Fund report, you can do this at Networth as well. For $5 a pop, Morningstar will also give you a report on the mutual funds you're considering.

Invest in a Mutual Fund

Once you have made the decision to invest in a particular fund, there are several houses which will broker the transaction for you (most will require a minimum;

expect to invest more than $1,000). Consider larger brokers like **Charles Schwab**, **E*Trade**, and **PC Financial Network**. The last offers a beguiling demo program which shows you how to buy funds as easily as if you were sending email. As a bonus, there are no transaction fees on purchases over $5,000, nor on retirement accounts over $1,000.

> **" And if that egg looks as though it may be going rotten, don't sell before you have consulted Fund Alarm. Who knows? Your fund may yet turn out to be golden. "**

But the question remains: If all you are doing is buying into a mutual fund (which you are unlikely to want to change more than once over the course of a year), why pay a broker's fees at all? Back at NETworth, you can download a prospectus of the fund you're interested in, and buy directly—if not always online—from the company itself.

Track Your Investments

Sites like the **InvestorGuide to Mutual Funds** and **The Mutual Funds Investors Center** are packed with enough resources to make mutual fund watching a full-time hobby. If you don't want to devote that much time to your investments, though, you can still keep tabs on your funds. One of the fastest ways to check up on your nest egg is to get a quote from one of the many quote services online, like **CNNfn's Quote Service**. And if that egg looks as though it may be going rotten, don't sell before you have consulted **Fund Alarm**, a site dedicated to notifying investors when a fund is in trouble. Who knows? Your fund may yet turn out to be golden.

▼ Mutual funds

FundLink Jam-packed with information about mutual funds, this page gives netsurfers an easy way to answer virtually any mutual fund question. There is a helpful introduction to mutual fund investing, including a glossary of terms, a mutual fund checklist, and an FAQ. Delve deeper into the site and you'll find the latest news about fund performance and brokerage research. And, in the unlikely event that you exhaust the information at FundLink, there are plenty of links to take you to other mutual fund resources on the Internet.
WEB http://www.webcom.com/~fundlink

Fundwatch Online by Money Magazine Sift through more than 4,500 mutual funds and find those that match your investment philosophy. The funds are classified according to criteria like investment objective, return over time, dividend yield, risk ratings, and so on. The service has detailed reports on most of the funds listed, with performance information and sector and portfolio holdings updated monthly.
COMPUSERVE *go* fundwatch

The full spectrum of risk
http://networth.galt.com/www/home/mutual/I00

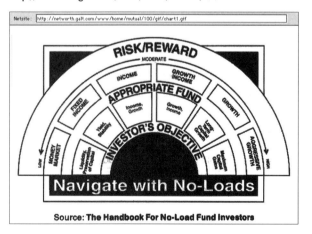

Netsite: http://networth.galt.com/www/home/mutual/100/gif/chart1.gif

Source: The Handbook For No-Load Fund Investors

misc.invest.mutual-funds Are load funds better in the long run? Can currency funds serve as an inflation hedge? And what about those infomercials for Fidelity funds? Sometimes the postings at this newsgroup get very specific—one man wants to know if his wife's company, a small nonprofit whose 403(b) plan is invested in a family of loaded mutuals, is paying too much to its administrator. But if you like to talk about annuities and no-load mutuals, the fund—er, fun—will never end.
USENET misc.invest.mutual-funds

Are load funds better in the long run? Can currency funds serve as an inflation hedge? And what about those infomercials for Fidelity funds?

Morningstar Mutual Funds The best-known independent company in the business of tracking mutual funds, Morningstar follows the performance, operations, and analytical methodology of more than 5,000 mutual funds. These are ranked by more than 30 investment objectives, including Top 25 Overall Mutual Funds, Aggressive Growth, Speciality-Natural Resources, and Municipal Bond-Single State. You can search most of the funds that Morningstar tracks. For real-time discussions, you're welcome to drop by the Lounge, but the bulk of mutual-fund talk happens on the message boards, which feature more than 50 topics, including Retirement and Load vs. No-load Funds.
AMERICA ONLINE *keyword* morningstar

Mutual Fund Company Directory This simple but helpful site is a comprehensive list of mutual fund companies around the world. The list includes telephone numbers and URLs (when available), and lists information on unit investment trusts and variable annuity companies structured like mutual funds.
WEB http://www.cs.cmu.edu/~jdg/funds.html

Mutual Fund Investor's Center The Mutual Fund Education Alliance's free-access Web site is a great starting point for new mutual funds investors. In addition to describing a variety of investment plans—for college, retirement and portfolio building—the site furnishes resources for individual investors. One of the more interesting features is the Fund Quicklist, which lists almost 1,000 companies offering mutual funds and comes complete with daily quotes. If you want translations for the occasional investment jargon that peppers this and other Web sites, the glossary should help you along. Fund news is updated regularly.
WEB http://www.mfea.com

Mutual Funds Interactive MFI has been lauded for its Web site by just about every organization that has a prize to give away. Having said that, the site is so comprehensive that it's somewhat intimidating. You'll need some time just to figure out your first step. Do you really want sports and global-weather information next to advice on mutual funds? The savvy investor very well may. MFI offers that and a whole lot more.
WEB http://www.brill.com/funds.html

Mutual Funds Made Simple The name says it all. This Web site delivers the ABCs of investing in mutual funds from annualization through yield. Find out what types are available, how you can make money from them, and when you should sell. Best of all there's an interactive Q&A for in-depth assistance. If only the

SOME JUST LIKE TO TALK FIRST

I still prefer to pick up the phone and talk to a live broker and ask about his opinion on certain stocks or the general market, before trading. I would imagine that the current phenomenae of online trading (I use **ETRADE**) is a testing of the waters. It is inevitable, however, foregoing any complete collapse of the global society, that online trading—along with online banking, online shopping, and online everything else, become as sophisticated as "visiting the Mall" became in the mid '70s. Society is evolving into an 'online organism'—possibly too rapidly for most folks to comprehend in the context of this ruling generation. By the second generation from now, however, (three decades or so), most people are going to be locked into their individually created small asocial environments where all outside interaction transpires over some future form of the net via the home terminals. Interactive TV is only the next step in that direction. Online trading will be only a miniscule part of this new lifestyle.

—from misc.invest.mutual-funds

rest of investing were this easy.
WEB http://members.aol.com/plweissl/mfunds.htm

No-Load Mutual Fund Council Now here's a great beginner's guide to no-load mutual fund investing, complete with a glossary of terms and definitions. You'll also find an intelligent introduction to the advantages of no-load investing, and links to investment companies that offer 100 percent no-load funds. Be warned—that qualifier means some of the biggest companies (like Fidelity) are conspicuously absent.
WEB http://networth.galt.com/www/home/mutual/l00

WHAT TO DO WITH $3,000 TO INVEST

Hi all, I have $3,000 to invest. What should I do? I think the stock market is probably heading for a correction sometime soon. Even if it is not, I think most stocks are overpriced. So, I'd like a fund that should go up in a time of correction and which I can cash out of when bargains exist after the correction. Which funds do you think I should consider if that is what I wanted to do? Alternatively, tell me what you would do if you are starting out with $3,000 in your hands? Thanks all!

First of all... it seems likely that you are going to have a negative experience... At any rate, with the vast information you provided I would suggest you apply your $3,000 to your highest interest credit cards or other obligations before you do anything else. Most people can get a guaranteed I5 percent to 20 percent just by doing that... tax free too! First, get your financial house in order. Pay off any and all consumer debt (credit cards, loans, etc) then figure out what your plans are for the future. Are you looking at long time investment or will you need the money soon? I don't know your whole situation but there is more to consider.

If you want to bet on a correction, Rydex Ursa is the fund to use, but I believe their minimum investment is higher than $3,000. But just for the sake of argument, keep in mind that if you bought a fund like this, it would be more speculation than investment, and you'd lose money if the market continues to rise. I think your best bet is to find a fund whose strategy is consistent with your objectives and risk tolerance, and set up an automatic investment program to allow you to dollar-cost average into the fund.

—from misc.invest.mutual-funds

The Investors Website The best thing about visiting the Investors Website is the opening investment trivia question. Stories on companies and investment articles make up the body of information, as do the usual investor's links. Articles can be submitted by anyone, so heed the site when it warns, "Take any advice at your own risk." Programs for investors are a thoughtful gesture, as is the suggestion box, which cries out for content.
WEB http://www.cyberuniverse.com/investor/trader.htm

The Mutual Funds Home Page The name sounds a bit over-ambitious, especially when they underline the word "The," but this independent home page comes pretty close to living up to its claim. It includes articles designed to appeal to the fund novice as well as the more experienced investor. There's a discussion page (they call it a "moderated newsgroup") that people actually use to discuss fund issues, such as the best way to calculate total return if you're investing a small amount in a fund each month. The site also publishes original interviews with mutual-fund managers.
WEB http://www.brill.com

User's Guide to Mutual Funds Twelve pages worth of abbreviations and definitions, from NAV (net asset value) to average weighted maturity. Handy for anyone starting to peer below the surface of mutual funds.
AMERICA ONLINE *keyword* morningstar→Mutual Fund User's Guide

▼ Publications

Mutual Funds Magazine Online It's never too early to start planning for the future as far as the editors of Mutual Funds Online are concerned—recent cover stories include an article explaining how to get your children, and even your grandchildren, started in funds. The reproduced letter from Matt and Nick

Schurk, 12 and 9 years old, who begin their missive, "My brother and I love money," qualifies the mag's confidence in its story. Meat-and-potatoes stuff, the emag includes an archive of articles from this individual investor-oriented magazine, but registered users can also get a free weekly personalized email newsletter that includes news and statistics about the funds they own. Paying subscribers also get access to a database covering 7,000 funds.
WEB http://www.mfmag.com

You're never too young to start investing
http://www.mfmag.com

▼ Stock & fund checkers

NETworth: The Internet Resource for Individual Investors With tie-ins to financial analysis firms like the Chicago-based Morningstar, the service allows users to download no-load mutual fund marketing information, prospectuses, and financial newsletters. With free quotes on over 5,000 mutual funds, as well as educational forums and industry news, the service provides a solid entry into the world of mutual funds. The Equities service offers Free Quotes, a personal Portfolio, and graphing of stock prices.
WEB http://networth.galt.com

You have stocks or funds you want to check out? Type in the symbol and seconds later, up comes your 20-minute delayed price.

NYU EDGAR Development Site If you have the smallest knowledge of funds or stocks, the FAQ at this NYU project will help you with everything from introductory material on how the site works to an explanation of how to find all the 8-ks filed last week for all companies. Also on offer are corporate SEC filings, and prospectuses and semi-annual reports for major mutual funds. The Mutual Fund databases is a little ropey for the time being but perhaps when there are a few more respondents to the request for assistance in financing these "noble efforts," as they regard them, then this will improve.
WEB http://edgar.stern.nyu.edu/

StockMaster Get stock information on command. Claiming to be the Web's first stock service, StockMaster is part of an experimental market data project at MIT which was designed to provide clear, long-term price graphs for selected mutual funds. You have stocks or funds you want to check out? Type the symbol or part of the name into the boxes on the home page and seconds later, up comes your 20-minute delayed price, followed by performance charts. You then have the opportunity to take part in a survey. Guess how well you believe your stock will do over the next three months and you are rewarded with a survey that incorporates your personal confidence/doubt into a chart.
WEB http://www.stockmaster.com/

Find out how to cash in, cash out, and get rich quick!

NITIAL PUBLIC OFFERINGS. The concept seems simple: Take a start-up company, value it at a modest $10 to $12 a share, advertise it to the right people, and then bask in the aftermarket glow as the stock price doubles or triples within hours or even minutes of its debut. Ever since Yahoo! went public and made its owners poster boys of the **Internet Millionaires Page**, Wall Street has had IPO fever something awful. In fact, the number of companies going public this year is nearly double that of last year, leaving the individual investor anxious to find out how to cash in, cash out, and get rich.

The 411 on IPOs

Unfortunately, if you're one of the anxious, you may be dismayed to discover that high-profile IPOs may be out of your reach. If you know anything about how companies are taken public (read **Everything About IPOs** for a quick tutorial), you know you can't just call up your personal broker and ask for a hundred shares in the latest hot stock offering. Unless you have a long-standing account with Goldman Sachs (or an investment banker friend who owes you a big favor), you're going to be left out of the loop.

Enter the Internet, which is slowly but surely promising to make IPOs more accessible to the average Joe with a few thousand bucks to gamble. Not only will the mouse-powered investor be able to catch wind of new issues as soon as they file with the SEC, but small companies looking to raise capital will be able to do so much more cheaply. While you're still not likely to get in on this week's highly publicized, high-tech IPOs—and with *Wired* balking twice, why would you want to?—you may find a diamond in the rough through a growing number of online channels that offer everything from news to investment advice to brokerage services. Some sites even allow investors to participate in IPOs directly over the Net. Be aware, however, that Web-based IPOs are still undergoing the usual media skepticism and SEC scrutiny. A few recent headlines

An attractive interface for IPOs
http://www.ipocentral.com

The ideal WebIPO candidate should have the following characteristics:

1. A company with a proven, experienced management team that can lead the company to success.

2. A company with a product or service that is unique, relatively protected from competition (eg, patents) and would benefit from Internet exposure.

3. A company that can achieve gross sales levels of $50-$100 million in five to ten years.

4. A company that can achieve break-even within five years.

Ready, set, IPO!
http://www.webipo.com

on *Money Daily* cautioned that **"Despite promise of fairness and accessibility, investors should be wary of Internet-based IPOs"**, and reported on **"Market regulators stepping up online enforcement"**. So while the details of this new investing venue get straightened out, it might be best to feed your IPO fever only with information. After you learn the basics from IPO hubsites such as Hoover's **IPO Central** or the **IPO Network**, do your homework and go for broke online.

Internet-based IPOs

▶ **IPOnet** This affiliate of W.J. Gallagher & Company advertises public offerings and private placements on the Web. Read the FAQ, find out if you're a qualified investor (do you have at least two years' investment experience and a minimum of $10,000 liquid capital?), then learn how to become a millionaire in minutes by participating in the IPO frenzy.
WEB http://www.zanax.com/iponet

▶ **WebIPO** Based in Southern California, WebIPO has a two-fold mission: to offer small companies the means to raise capital via the Web and to offer investors the chance to profit from new issues. For small companies, "Are You Ready For an IPO?" lists the characteristics necessary for a business planning to go public. For example, your company should be able to achieve gross sales levels of $50 to $100 million in five to ten years and should be "clean of any contingent liabilities" (i.e. pending lawsuits). Investors can read a guide to the basics and link to free IPO reports.
WEB http://www.webipo.com

▶ **Direct Stock Market** Launched in April, 1996, the DSM promises investors "an equal opportunity at the potential venture-capital-type returns enjoyed by insti-

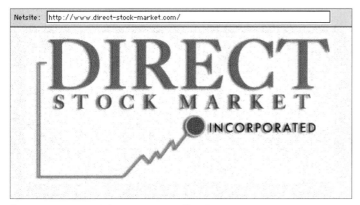

Small companies don't have to mean small profits
http://www.direct-stock-market.com/

tutions and wealthy individuals." Access comprehensive and up-to-the-minute information about small businesses and participate in their direct public offerings from this central location. Subject to regulatory approval, the stock of the companies involved may not be actively traded on the conventional stock markets, which means if you buy stock here, you may be left holding the bag.
WEB http://www.direct-stock-market.com

▸ **INVBank** Another young hopeful in the world of Internet-based IPOs. This one would like to provide you with your own corner office on the Wall Street of cyberspace, even promising its own IPO Financial Forum to replace the "road show" that is traditionally used by investment bankers to drum up interest in a new issue. Theoretically, the forum will allow investors to interact and negotiate directly with companies by email and online video conferencing. Register as a "Savvy Investor" or as part of the "INVestor's Circle" to get in on the game of IPOs and private placements. To access the inner circle, you must first have a net worth of $1 million.
WEB http://www.invbank.com

Learn about road shows
http://www.invbank.com

▼ Starting points

Internet Millionaires Page If you still don't believe there's a way to make money on the Internet, check out this site's list of public Internet companies and their millionaire owners, updated every 15 minutes. Get in on the action by taking a look at the list of "upcoming Internet IPOs and their wannabe millionaires." If *Wired* ever does go public, Louis Rossetto would be worth more than $65 million. In a section called Companies We Want to See Go Public, analyst Mike Walsh touts his stock picks in a refreshingly colloquial fashion: "Healtheon—Jim Clark of Netscape fame is bored. Talk about Attention Deficit Disorder. So what does he do—start another company to put the medical industry on the Net. Why not! Everyone needs a hobby." http://www.pulver.com/million/

IPO Central Leave it to Hoover's and Edgar's Online to provide this attractive interface for such a potentially dry and sometimes scary topic. If you don't know much about IPOs,

Darren Chervitz, looking pensive
http://www.dbc.com/cgi-bin/htx.exe/newsroom/iponder.html?source=core/dbc

Location: http://www.dbc.com/cgi-bin/htx.exe/newsroom/iponder.h

I.P.O.nder

By Darren Chervitz

... a look at new stock offerings

I.P.O.nder Daily | IPO Spotlight | Other IPO News
Recent Filings | Aftermarket Performance | IPO Links

check out the Beginner's Guide, which has an overview of the concept, definitions of investment terminology, and articles about how to profit from them. Once you get your feet wet, the Insider section has news on IPO trends. Then you can check out the latest IPO filings (updated daily), browse the more extensive IPO Directory, and a weekly listing of IPOs in Review. You can also read the company profile of one featured IPO per week and track the stock quotes of IPOs that have already gone public. Before you pull out of this station for IPO information, refer to Destinations for more investment links.
WEB http://www.ipocentral.com

IPO Network In 1993/94, IPOs created more wealth than lotteries, casinos, and Fortune 1,000 companies combined. This membership organization is dedicated to networking investors with IPOs. Sign up for the mailing list and learn how to take advantage of the IPO Network's do-it-yourself resources.
WEB http://www.ipo-network.com

▼ News

Cal Law IPO Watch A weekly update on IPO registrations of California-based corporations, including lists of new issues, new registrations, the best and worst performers, and the year's biggest IPOs. A special section on Internet IPOs contains a performance table on the IPOs of California's hottest Internet-related companies such as CyberCash, Yahoo!, and IDT.
WEB http://www.callaw.com/ipo/ipo.shtml

Capital Markets Financial Center The home of the *IPO Insider*, a semi-monthly newsletter. The investing spirit here is to "keep on dancing with the one who brought you to the party." That is, if you start with a $1,000 investment, don't quit when you think you've realized a large enough gain. Keep investing and reinvesting for the biggest gains and remember that you started out with just $1,000. With that light-hearted attitude, learn a bit about the business of IPOs by following the irresistible hyperlinks titled, "How to Pick a Hot IPO Stock" and "5 Secrets for Super Stock Picking." If you're not satisfied with the cornucopia of information available for free, subscribe to the IPO Insider newsletter ($195 for one year if you order via the Web). A link to E*Trade is conveniently provided.

WEB http://www.capmarkets.com

 Cyberstocks Business analysis is a tricky business, and something best left in the hands of capable financial professionals like Hoover's, the creators of this useful site dedicated to making sense of the perilous new world of Internet investing. Originally published as a book, the Cyberstocks site not only holds the complete text of the Internet investment manual, but also up-to-date Net investment news, Hoover's trademark analysis, and columns by experts on industry issues from IPOs to firewalls. The basics are here as well-from a cyberspace glossary to the financials on top Internet-related businesses. Cyberstocks is well on its way to being the premier online forum for Internet investment research and is making the most of this interactive medium with a well-attended discussion center for trading investment tips and prognoses.

WEB http://www.cyberstocks.com

I.P.O.nder Investment advice always seems so much more palatable when its comes from a real person. Of course, "Nothing in I.P.O.nder is intended to be investment advice," if you read the disclaimer. In any case, the IPO "ponderer" here is Darren Chervitz, an online editor and

writer for the Data Broadcasting Corporation NewsRoom, and he muses daily on IPOs, including recent filings and aftermarket performance reviews in his thought stream. Current and upcoming offerings are rated on a scale of five lightning bolts ("killer concept") to one ("use other people's money").

WEB http://www.dbc.com/cgi-bin/htx.exe/newsroom /iponder.html?source=core/dbc

Interactive Nest Egg's IPO Center Concise information on IPOs. The breezy IPO diary has snippets of the week's IPO action, with quotes from industry analysts. At a glance, find out who's going public, who's gone, and the best and worst performers over the past two months. One look at the IPO 100 chart, which details the aftermarket performance of the 100 most recent IPOs, and you realize that big names don't always spell success. A few weeks after its initial offering, the watchmaker TAG Heuer International was trading at less than 20 percent of its offering price.

WEB http://nestegg.iddis.com/ipo/

Renaissance Capital IPO Calendar and Profiles
The self-described IPO experts provide market intelligence, IPO ideas, picks of the week, upcoming IPOs and priced IPOs that you can look into immediately by linking to the company's Web site.

WEB http://www.ipo-fund.com

US IPO News Hot off the electronic press, read all about the latest IPO pricings, filings, and commentary—courtesy of Reuters newswire. The info is current but out of context. Visit for ideas, then do your homework elsewhere.

WEB http://biz.yahoo.com/reports/ipo.html

USA Today Weekly IPO Update A minimum of information about selected IPOs scheduled for the current week. Includes the company

and underwriter name, a brief description of the company, the number of shares being sold, the expected price range and the first-day premium rate.
WEB http://www.usatoday.com/money/mipo.htm

▼ Reports

Alert IPO For less than the price of a decent haircut, you can subscribe to a year's worth of advance notification on impending IPOs. Every email report contains detailed summaries about the companies that have filed that week for initial public offering with the SEC. Subscribers then have 40 to 60 days to do their homework and decide if they want to participate in the IPO. With the money you could make, you'll be able to afford a really good haircut.
WEB http://www.ostman.com/alert-ipo

IPO Data Systems At no cost, you can read more than 1,000 company profiles for 1996 IPOs. For $15 a month, you can get a recap of the day's IPO filings and offerings, weekly reviews of prior IPOs, and a listing of IPOs set to go public. A variety of other reports is also available.
WEB http://www.ipodata.com

IPO Maven "Let us not get caught up with what happens during the first hours of trading." So says investment strategist Manish Shah, who points out that sometimes the buy-and-hold approach will yield better returns with IPOs. IPO Maven offers extensive pre- and post-IPO coverage on equity public offerings larger than $10 million and publicly traded small capitalization companies. If you've got Adobe Acrobat software, you can download information ($3 for the summary, $25 for the full report) on the companies. Free services include a list of all the IPOs in registration with the SEC (start

monitoring them now) and two weekly IPO calendars provide up-to-date profiles of IPOs that are coming up in the current week, as well as performance reviews of the past week's deals.
WEB http://www.investools.com/cgi-bin/Library/mavn.pl

IPO OnLine Home Page For less than $30 a month, investors can access the IPO OnLine database which contains reports on upcoming IPOs of common stock as well as information on those that have already occurred.
WEB http://www.ipo-source.com

IPO Retriever It won't bring you the newspaper and your slippers in the morning, but if you're looking for the hidden secrets of corporate insiders, this site will do just fine. Savvy investors should comb through the documents of past IPOs for valuable insights. Use the Prospex IPO Retriever to fetch the full text of a sampling of 1995 IPOs and FO (follow-on) prospectuses for free, and then find out how to order reports from the entire Prospex library of IPO prospectuses dating back to 1989. But knowledge doesn't come cheap. Hard copies of past and current IPO documentation cost about $50 for a single report; a year's worth of IPO prospectuses on CD-ROM costs a hefty $4,000.
WEB http://prospex.com/IPOs.html

IPOs Online A penny shy of $30 (that's $29.99, for those who don't have their calculators handy) gets you a month's worth of savvy, unbiased information about IPOs. Subscribers will find three tiers of investment info, including Deals in Registration, a comprehensive listing of new issues expected for the following two to three weeks; the Bullpen, a listing of IPO deals set to open the following day; and Today's Deals for the daily dose of new issues hitting the market.
WEB http://www.ipos-online.com

PART 5

Finance Your Life

F IT'S NOT ONE THING it's another, but that's what makes life interesting. Whether you need a plan for life insurance or retirement, the Net makes the process simpler. If you want to buy a car, a computer, or a house, you've got to plan your purchases wisely or you'll end up right back where you started—in debt. We'll show you just how to avoid the perils of reckless spending, while getting exactly what you want. You'll also learn how to earn your degree without paying for it for the rest of your life, and find out how to get married on a shoestring. And then, if and when you have kids, you'll be able to teach them everything you know!

Teaching kids about money takes more than telling them it doesn't grow on trees

PARENTS JUST DON'T UNDERSTAND. But when it comes to money, neither do kids—unless you teach them. Just like study habits, table manners, and cleanliness, fiscal habits are primarily learned. If parents are constantly in debt, for example, it's likely that children will have a hard time managing their finances—especially once

How to Turn the Tykes

they figure out that money doesn't exist solely to purchase toys.

So what should you teach your little ones? How can rugrats who get a dollar a week for allowance learn to save any money? And should they be getting that allowance in the first place? The experts are divided—but fortunately, they're on the Internet to help you decide which side of the divide makes sense. A great place to start looking for ideas is **Kids' Money Web Resources**—or simply follow our suggestions below.

The first, and most prevalent kind of help you'll find online is articles written by financial and childhood experts. One great one is **When the Kids Scream "I Want"** from *Worth Magazine*. The author, Neale Godfrey, suggests an allowance starting at age three, which is connected to the performance of chores. A system of savings jars, in which kids are required to deposit one-third of their allowance, rounds out Godfrey's simple earn-and-save method. You'll find other excellent suggestions in articles like **Teach Your Children About Money** and **Spare Change**.

Into Tycoons

CASH REGISTER

Kids' Money Web Resources
WEB http://pages.prodigy.com/kids money/lists.htm

When the Kids Scream "I Want"
WEB http://www.worth.com/articles /Z9406AIO.html

Teach Your Children About Money
WEB http://cnnet.com/syoung/young 5.htm

Spare Change
WEB http://family.starwave.com/ex perts/leach/archive/ygcI00796.html

No parents allowed
http://www.lsttech.com/kidsclb/

CASH REGISTER

Street Cents
WEB http://www.halifax.cbc.ca/street
cents/

EduStock
WEB http://tqd.advanced.org/3088/

Get Fiscal
WEB http://www.ingenius.com/pro
duct/cyberhd/youth/fred/fred.htm

Lemonade Stand
WEB http://www.fn.net/~jmayans
/lemonade/

Summit Safari Club
WEB http://www.summitfcu.org
/summit/kids/

Kids Club
WEB http://www.lsttech.com/kidsclb/

Also on the Web are sites written just for kids and teens, like the Canadian **Street Cents**, which is a sort of *Consumer Reports* for young people based on a popular TV show. (Unfortunately, *Zillions, Consumer Reports'* excellent kids' magazine, is not online.) Kids can find simple explanations of the stock market, and find out about how to control spending habits. Free stock simulations such as **EduStock** shouldn't be missed. **Get Fiscal**, written by a grown-up investor, is another great place to learn lots of information about a wide variety of financial topics, although it's written with an annoyingly insincere enthusiasm that may grate on parents and older children. In America, free enterprise doesn't discriminate against race, religion, or age. Start the kids early with the basics of profit and outlay via the classic **Lemonade Stand**.

If Junior has some money saved up, it's definitely a good idea to start teaching him about banking. Most banks have some kind of children's savings program, and family-oriented banks like the Summit Federal Credit Union in Rochester, New York, set up entire sections of their Web sites just for kids. Check out the

COOL FACTS ABOUT COLD CASH

Kids ages 8 through 17 average slightly more than a dozen shopping trips per month and average about $25 spending per trip. So who spends the most, boys or girls? Those who think it's girls are right... but not by as much as one might believe. Girls average $25.58 while boys shell out an average of $24.44.

—from USA Today Snapshot

Believe it or not, banks will actually pay you to keep your money in their bank. The payment is called "interest." Here's how it works: People pay a fee, called interest, to make use of your money. When someone (and this includes kids like us) puts money in something called a savings account in a bank, the bank pays them interest for the use of their savings.

—from Get Fiscal

It's the '90s—you can start charging more than a nickel
http://www.fn.net/~jmayans/lemonade/

Summit Safari Club pages or First Technology's **Kids Club** for ideas—then ask your bank to create a similar program if one doesn't already exist. Remember, there's nothing a bank likes better than handing out lollipops to future depositors, whether offline or on the Web.

Consumer Reports recently noted that companies target 30,000 commercial messages to youngsters every day. The pre-teen audience is a significant one. Consumer experts note that the nearly 40 million children ages 5 to 14 purchase $16.7 billion worth of food, drinks, toys, and videos each year and influence another $165 billion in sales. The children's market for consumer goods has increased by 20 percent in the past seven years.

—*from The Real Deal*

A stock is a certificate that shows that you own a small fraction of a corporation. When you buy a stock, you are paying for a small percentage of everything that that company owns: buildings, chairs, computers, etc. When you own a stock, you are referred to as a shareholder or a stockholder. In essence, a stock is a representation of the amount of a company that you own.

—*from EduStock*

▼ For parents

Kids' Money Finally, advice for parents on the subject of money. Kids' Money was created by David McCurrach, a 20-year veteran working with financial institutions, in an effort to help parents raise children with responsible money management habits. Help Kids' Money has a variety of resources, but the flagship is the list of the top ten financial principles any good parent will want to impress on kids. You'll get advice about allowances (to give or not to give, and if so, how much to give) from people like Liberty Financial to *Good Housekeeping* to Dr. Spock. Need advice? There's a question-and-answer section written by other readers. For bedtime reading, check the book list, the links to other money sites, and even the Kid's page (written by and for the little ones).
WEB http://pages.prodigy.com/kidsmoney

Kiplinger: Kids & Money A super bunch of advice columns by noted *New York Times* columnist "Dr. Tightwad," a.k.a. Janet Bodnar. Parents write to Dr. Tightwad with a sur-

---

It's never too early to start learning about money
http://www.finitycorp.com/

prising array of tyke-related financial issues. Should kids be allowed to sell things door-to-door? How should Santa and the Tooth Fairy respond to childrens' outlandish requests? Do those checks from Grandma really have to go straight to a savings account? Dr. Tightwad not only replies with wonderful advice, but also relates the wonderful advice of other parents.
WEB http://www.kiplinger.com/drt/drthome.html

misc.kids.consumers Though this newsgroup's name conjures up images of allowance management symposia—"The Nickel: Don't Spend it All in One Place"—it's actually a candid forum designed to address the financial needs of parents. And as the newsgroup proves, whether it's discussing the cost of biodegradable diapers or rating pull sleds, kids may be small, but they're not cheap.
USENET misc.kids.consumers

Parenting Library: Kids and Money Parent Soup's "goddess of money," Neale Godfrey, has conducted several chat sessions with parents on the subject of kids and dollars. These are the transcripts, and though they are a bit messy to read, they are full of answers to perplexing questions. For example, Godfrey feels that college kids need a credit card of their own, but not one that drains Mom and Dad's pockets. She also weighs in on giving kids money for their birthday and allowances.
WEB http://www.parentsoup.com/library/mon003.html

Raising Money-Smart Kids Children imitate their parents, this article is quick to state, so if you're financially responsible, chances are good that they will be, too. Even if you're drowning in debt, you can still begin to instill good habits. Simply read this article, chock-full of math activities and advice for raising Frugal Franks and Frannies. Then follow through on the suggestions—and while you're

at it, balance your darn checkbook.
WEB http://www.kqed.org/fromKQED/Cell/flg/kids.html

▼ For kids

Get Fiscal A cheerful character named Fred Fiscal explains financial matters to middle schoolers at this site in such a clear manner that some adults might benefit from a read themselves, especially if the tiny ones are beginning to ask persistent questions about money. The articles range from the topical (the question "why will Disney programming be showing up on ABC?" is used to illustrate principles of corporate ownership) to the more general (there's a good general piece about the stock market). All in all, a great introduction to money matters and why they matter to youngsters.
WEB http://205.168.70.2/product/cyberhd/youth/fred/fred.htm

Kids & Money: A Newsletter for Young People The title says it all, and although this Web newsletter by the North Dakota State University Extension Service is without further introduction, the articles contained within are valuable sources of advice for both parents and children. The newsletters are arranged by month, with each month devoted to a single topic. Sample topics include "Kids and Money Goals" and "Cash, Checks and Credit."
WEB http://ndsuext.nodak.edu/extnews/pipeline/d-parent.htm

Lemonade Stand The classic computer game Lemonade Stand has come to the Web, and it's perfect for elementary schoolers who need to learn simple concepts of profit and loss, as well as the rudiments of running a business. Determine how many cups of lemonade to make for the day, and what to charge for them, and watch the money roll in or out. Remember, weather affects the success of the lemon-

ade stand, as does advertising expenditure. The game is free, fun, and positively addictive.
WEB http://www.fn.net/~jmayans/lemonade

Money KaZAM Do your kids think money grows on trees? Worse yet, do they think it comes from a small, plastic card? Money KaZAM may be the answer to your prayers. It's a kit to help very young children begin to develop concepts of fiscal responsibility. For $12.98, it includes a story book, parents' guide, a money book for kids to use as a ledger, and some other gadgets. Finity, the company that makes it, was founded by the same man who founded Sterling Wentworth. The Web site even includes a section here for kids, but beware—there's a brazen marketing ploy intended to collect children's names that may leave some parents nonplussed.
WEB http://www.finitycorp.com/

Do your kids think money grows on trees? Worse yet, do they think it comes from a small, plastic card?

Young Consumer Publications The Federal Trade Commission is interested in protecting American youth from fraud; at the same time the commission acknowledges the incredible onslaught of advertising directed at those very same youngsters. This small collection of pamphlets helps kids and young adults develop good consumer habits. The fanciest, an activity booklet called *The Real Deal*, was released with some hype as a cooperative effort between the FTC and the National Association of Attorneys General in early 1996.
WEB http://www.ftc.gov/bcp/conline/pubs/young/young.htm

Chapter 18
Going to College

Higher education doesn't have to mean high financial anxiety

YOU'RE SMART. You're a good kid. You always thought you'd go to college. But according to **The College Board**, tuition bills are rising at a rate of 5 percent to 6 percent above inflation every year. Can you and your family afford it?

The financial aid maze can make even a brave family feel like nervous rats, unsure if they're going to receive a tasty pellet or a shock when they arrive at the end of the tunnel. The financial aid game, though, is not arbitrary. The harder you work and the more you learn, the better chance you'll have of getting the money you need for school. On the other hand, financial aid is not exactly a science. An expensive private school can sometimes cost a student less than a cheaper state school, because the private school can afford to give

Get Your Degree

more aid. One private school may offer a student a scholarship that another school won't. One school might calculate aid differently than another. If you're going to try and navigate the financial aid maze, do it with the Web. There are no sure-fire guarantees of scholarship riches online, but the Web provides free financial aid information, worksheets, advice, and scholarships databases. The government even makes it possible to fill out the proper forms online. In short, you can't lose.

Don't Know Much About Financial Aid?

Begin with a basic primer called **Financing College**, which is sponsored by the Princeton Review. In a few paragraphs, the site explains forms such as the Free Application for Student Aid (FAFSA) and the particulars of government loan programs. To reduce confusion, keep a financial aid glossary handy at all times, such as the ones from **The College Board Financial Aid Services** or **Peterson's Education Center: Financing Education**. Well-armed with knowledge after exploring these sites, you'll be ready to hunt big game at **FinAid**, the largest financial aid site of them all.

Debt-Free

How Much Can Your Family Afford?

Unfortunately, you don't decide how much you can afford. The colleges who review your application make this determination. To help estimate what you'll get in aid, you need to figure out your "magic number," otherwise known as the Expected Family Contribution (EFC). Although many grants, loans, and scholarships

CASH REGISTER

The College Board
WEB http://www.collegeboard.org/press/html/960925.html

Financing College
WEB http://www.review.com/faid/college_faid.html

The College Board Financial Aid Services
WEB http://www.collegeboard.org/css/html/students/indx00l.html

Peterson's Education Center: Financing Education
WEB http://www.petersons.com/resources/finance.html

FinAid,
WEB http://www.cs.cmu.edu/afs/cs/user/mkant/Public/FinAid/finaid.html

CASH REGISTER

Mark's Financial Aid Calculators
WEB http://www.finaid.org/finaid
/calculators/finaid_calc.html

Financial Aid Estimation Form
WEB http://www.finaid.org/finaid
/calculators/estimate.html

ExPan: Expected Family Contribution
WEB http://www.collegeboard.org/efc
/bin/efc-init.cgi

**DCB&T Financial Planning Calculator
College Savings Planner**
WEB http://www.dcbt.com/FinCalc
/College.html

Office of Postsecondary Education
WEB http://www.ed.gov/offices/OPE
/index.html

FAFSA Express
WEB http://www.ed.gov/offices/OPE
/express.html

The Money Online College Guide
WEB http://pathfinder.com/money
/colleges/article/rankindx.htm

Best Values Ranking
WEB http://www.usnews.com/usnews
/fair/bvr_main.htm

**"Cutting a Deal: Your Best College for
the Best Price"**
WEB http://pathfinder.com/money
/colleges/article/bestdeal.htm

**University Financial Aid Office Web
Pages**
WEB http://www.finaid.org/finaid
/fao-web.html

Federal Direct Loan Program
WEB http://www.ed.gov/offices/OPE
/DirectLoan/

Purdue's Loan Counselor
URL gopher://oasis.cc.purdue.edu
:2525/II/student/cnslr

are based on number, it is in no way binding. Colleges may award a student more or less aid than the EFC estimates. Still, it's a good place to start. Gather your family's financial info (especially old tax returns) and turn to **Mark's Financial Aid Calculators**. The **Financial Aid Estimation Form** is particularly useful. When you're done, get a second opinion from **ExPan**. If you have younger siblings, fill out the **DCB&T Financial Planning Calculator College Savings Planner** to find out how close your family is to meeting college costs for all members of the family. Even if the news isn't terrific, most families feel much better knowing how the FAFSA assessment is likely to turn out. The FAFSA is used to apply for the Pell Grants awarded by the government and for all other need-based aid (usually awarded by colleges). To learn more about applying for government aid online, start exploring the **Office of Postsecondary Education**'s site, then download the **FAFSA Express** program, which enables Windows users to modem their financial aid applications to the Department of Education painlessly and paperlessly.

Get smart about college finance
http://www.collegeboard.org

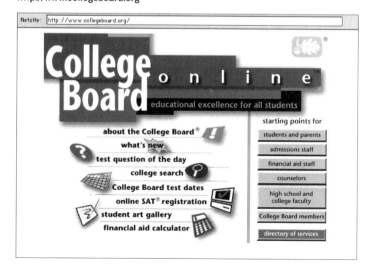

Bargain Hunting: The Best College Deals

Start comparison shopping with **The Money Online College Guide**'s annual list of Best Buys. *U.S. News & World Report Online* also publishes an annual **Best Values Ranking**. Supplement the lists with articles like **"Cutting a Deal: Your Best College for the Best Price,"** which describes bargaining techniques (Hint: A college's word on aid packages may or may not be final). Or try the Web sites of colleges you're considering, where most online financial aid offices are contained within the admissions section of a college site. For one-stop shopping, the **University Financial Aid Office Web Pages** collects electronic addresses for financial aid offices on a single page.

There's a scholarship out there just for you
http://www.student-loans.com/

> ❝ **When it comes to college loans, a student's best friend is a character named Bill, the namesake of the 4-year-old Federal Direct Loan Program.** ❞

Looking for Loans in Cyberspace

When it comes to college loans, a student's best friend is a character named Bill, the namesake of the 4-year-old **Federal Direct Loan Program**. After a student files the FAFSA with the Department of Education and is accepted by a college, the chosen school's loan office (**Purdue's Loan Counselor**, for instance) determines how much money the student will need in order to meet costs. The loans come directly to the student from the government, eliminating the bank as middle man. The repayment terms vary, but are generally kind.

Of course, it is still possible to borrow through a regular old bank, with the government guaranteeing the

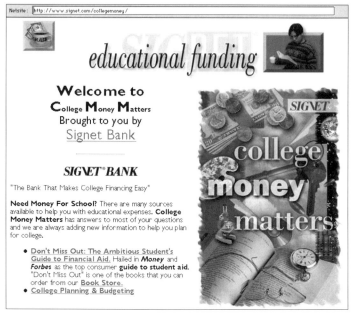

You shouldn't have to work to be able to study

http://jerome.signet.com/collegemoney

loans. In fact, some of the most elaborate financial aid Web sites are sponsored by banks. Loan applications, contests, background information, and much more are on the **Crestar**, **Signet**, and **PNC Bank** sites. In fact, these sites are often so helpful that anyone considering college financial aid should visit. And don't forget to pay a call to **Nellie Mae** and **Sallie Mae**—these are the grand old ladies of nonprofit college loan providers.

> **❝ Don't forget to pay a call to Nellie Mae and Sallie Mae—these are the grand old ladies of nonprofit college loan providers. ❞**

Tracking Down Scholarships

Tracking down a specialty scholarship can be just as challenging as negotiating other types of financial aid.

Everything that makes a student unique, including race or sex, talent, athletic ability—even place of residence—is grounds for a scholarship somewhere. Signet has lists of specific scholarships offering **Money for Minorities and Women**, **Money Because You Have Brains and Talent**, **Money Because You are an Athlete**, and **Money in Your Community**. But an efficient search should begin with **fastWeb**, where filling out several screens of data yields a tailor-made list of scholarships from a database containing more than 180,000 different sources of aid. Athletes may find the **All-Sport**'s recruiting site useful, and minorities should visit the amazing **MOLIS Scholarship Search** site. Depending on where you live, regional information can be invaluable—for example, the **California Student Aid Commission** site, or the **Ohio Board of Regents Financial Aid** page, point students to the local money.

Parents should start saving while their kids are still in the womb
http://www.merrill-lynch.ml.com/personal/college/collegecalc.html

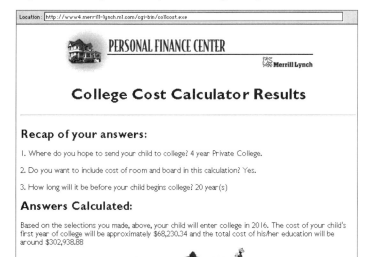

Location: http://www4.merrill-lynch.ml.com/cgi-bin/collcost.exe

PERSONAL FINANCE CENTER

Merrill Lynch

College Cost Calculator Results

Recap of your answers:

1. Where do you hope to send your child to college? 4 year Private College.

2. Do you want to include cost of room and board in this calculation? Yes.

3. How long will it be before your child begins college? 20 year(s)

Answers Calculated:

Based on the selections you made, above, your child will enter college in 2016. The cost of your child's first year of college will be approximately $68,230.34 and the total cost of his/her education will be around $302,938.88

INVESTOR LEARNING CENTER · PERSONAL FINANCE CENTER · BUSINESS PLANNING CENTER · FINANCIAL NEWS & RESEARCH CENTER · Home

---

CASH REGISTER

Crestar: Student Loans
WEB http://www.student-loans.com/

Signet: College Money Matters
WEB http://jerome.signet.com /collegemoney

PNC Bank: Education Loan Center
WEB http://www.eduloans.pncbank .com

Nellie Mae Loan Link
WEB http://www.nelliemae.org

Sallie Mae
WEB http://www.salliemae.com

Money for Minorities and Women
WEB http://jerome.signet.com /collegemoney/ch22.html

Money Because You Have Brains and Talent
WEB http://jerome.signet.com /collegemoney/ch18.html

Money Because You are an Athlete
WEB http://jerome.signet.com /collegemoney/ch19.html

Money in Your Community
WEB http://jerome.signet.com /collegemoney/ch15.html

fastWEB
WEB http://www.fastweb.com/

Allsport
WEB http://www.irc-coordinator.com

MOLIS Scholarship Search
WEB http://www.fie.com/molis /scholar.htm

California Student Aid Commission
WEB http://www.csac.ca.gov

Ohio Board of Regents Financial Aid
WEB http://www.bor.ohio.gov/progs /obrprog3.html

CASH REGISTER

College Cost Calculator
WEB http://www.merrill-lynch.ml.com
/personal/college/collegecalc.html

ParentSoup: Money/College
WEB http://www.parentsoup.com
/library/mon002.html

The Tuition Challenge
WEB http://www.fleet.com/abtyou
/inveduc/tuition.html

USENET misc.invest

USENET soc.college.financial-aid

Location: http://www.eduloans.pncbank.com/

School loans you can bank on
http://www.eduloans.pncbank.com

Advice for Parents: Start Early

You've heard the horror stories of how tuition costs will mount. You know what? They're all true. Merrill-Lynch's **College Cost Calculator** can help parents estimate how much four years at a private school will cost them in, say, the year 2001: more than $109,000. Parents should start saving for their children's college education as soon as they can. Many banks, brokerages, and financial advisors promote services to help parents make the investments needed to meet college costs. **ParentSoup: Money/College** furnishes one of the best online guides to investing for college; **The Tuition Challenge** details the ins and outs of meeting costs; and **misc.invest** and **soc.college.financial-aid** let parents discuss saving for college with other parents. With luck and careful planning, your children will graduate from college debt-free.

▼ Starting points

FinAid: The Financial Aid Information Page Just remember that time is money. Allot yourself plenty of the former while checking out this site if you want to score lots of the latter for college. Some of the resources available here include a form for electronically submitting questions to financial aid advisors; a glossary of financial aid terms; and calculation tools for determining how much your family will be asked to contribute to college expenses and how much aid you'll need. This site also links to other financial aid resources on the Web, including sources of scholarships, fellowships, grants, loans, and tuition payment plans. Links are further cataloged according to special interest groups (i.e., students with disabilities, students from minority backgrounds, older students). A good place to start at this comprehensive site is "Mark's Picks," a selection of the best and most popular financial aid sites.
WEB http://www.finaid.com

Financing College A primer from the Princeton Review, starting with an explanation of the financial aid process. Also included: general information on grants and scholarships, explanations of state and federal loan and grant programs, and a Q&A covering such queries as "Will applying for aid jeopardize my chance of admission?" and "Should I hire a professional to help me fill out the forms?"
AMERICA ONLINE *keyword* princeton→College→ Financing College
WEB http://www.review.com/faid/college_faid.html

The Money College Guide '97 Money's famous Best Buys are cataloged here, along with an incredible interactive search engine which collects your preferences and churns out the schools that are perfect matches for you. Read about each potential alma mater—1,105 in all—in great detail, and then consult more general articles on searching for scholarships or cutting a deal with the evil financial aid office.
WEB http://pathfinder.com/money/colleges/index.htm

Peterson's Education Center: Financing Education Peterson's has the financial aid scene down to a science. Besides a general description of types of aid and a glossary of useful terms, there's a month-by-month college admissions calendar for both high school juniors and seniors who may be so consumed with thoughts of the prom and yearbook, that they forger to file their FAFSA. At this site you can also read up on other financial aid sources— including, of course, Peterson's own guide Paying Less for College.
WEB http://www.petersons.com/resources/finance.html

T@P Schools & Money Shopping at thrift stores, buying and freezing day-old bread, and not gambling are just three ways to exhibit financial prudence. There are others, though, that relate more specifically to educational issues. Not exclusively about budgeting, this site has

---

A guide to higher educational value
http://pathfinder.com/money/colleges/index.htm

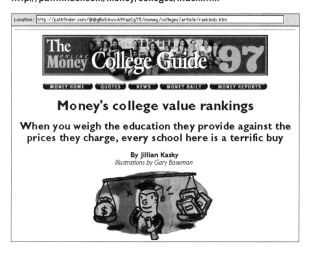

THE FAMILY THAT PAYS TOGETHER

Q. Are parents penalized for saving money for college?

A. No. As a matter of fact, families that have made a concerted effort to save money for college are in a much better position. For example, a student from a family that has saved money may not have to borrow as much in student loans, which are part of most financial aid packages. Also, when the parental contribution is calculated for federal aid, less than 6 percent of the parents' assets are entered in the calculation, and none of their home equity is included. Thus a parent who saved $40,000 for college expenses will have $2,240 counted as part of the parental contribution. When students have assets in their names, 35 percent of those assets count toward the calculated family contribution. The reason for the difference is that the student will be the direct beneficiary of the college education.

—from Peterson's Education Center: Financing Education

an online book exchange, and articles on financial issues relating to students.
WEB http://www.taponline.com/tap/higher.html

U.S. News College Fair Forum The equivocal financial status of middle-class kids may be the most prevalent theme of discussion in this forum, but it's not the only topic in the air. When a divorced parent asks for advice about filling out financial aid applications, others in similar situations respond. And, when someone asks for ideas for funding a Russian exchange student, the forum is flooded with responses. U.S. News has staff online to help answer financial aid questions and provide information on grants and scholarships. The magazine will also point you in the direction of more detailed sources. All options are explored here, from gaining "independent status" to staying in-state for payment breaks.
COMPUSERVE *go* usncollege→Browse Messages→Financial Aid

▼ Step-by-step

Don't Miss Out The handbook, subtitled *The Ambitious Student's Guide to Financial Aid* from Signet Bank, takes would-be students step-by-step through the quest for college funding, from defining monetary needs through acquiring successful financing. Included are tricks of the trade for tilting the financial aid process in your favor, like reducing the family contribution or increasing the cost of education in order to up your award.
WEB http://www.infi.net/collegemoney/tocl.html

Education Planning A simple but informative introduction (in the form of an FAQ, articles, and message board) to legal gift-giving to children, trust funds, and tax shelters. Learn the nitty-gritty of college savings as parents try to grapple with the most pertinent question of all: How much is enough? The feature also carries a link to the message board "Ask the College Board," where anxious students and parents get advice directly from the College Board, along with a link to the 2,500 institutions profiled in the searchable version of the *College Handbook*.
AMERICA ONLINE *keyword* your money→Education Planning

Parent Soup: College Planning One of the best guides to financial planning of a college education, whether you have six years or six months to go. Parent Soup's site answers

questions like, "What if You Come Up Short?" and provides both detailed and general advice about investment strategies, including scholarships and grants, setting up an investment plan, and how students can help pay their own way.
WEB http://www.parentsoup.com/library/mon002.html

▼ Scholarships & loans

fastWEB! (Financial Aid Search Through the Web)
Fast it's not. This financial aid search requires you to give up screen after screen of personal info before providing you with information about scholarships and loans. However, it pays off, with a personally tailored search that lets you check for updates (according to the site, approximately 1,200 awards are added to the database each day, and additions matching your profile are added to your online mailbox). Best of all, it's free.
WEB http://www.fastweb.com

Questions about how to finance your education? Ask your Uncle Sam.

The Loan Counselor At the Loan Counselor, you'll get all the benefits of a trip to the financial aid office without the impertinent student receptionists, long lines, and curt counselors. Purdue's site provides prospective students with loan counseling, ways to manage educational loan debt before your payments begin, and alternative financing options. And you don't have to attend the Indiana school for the information to be applicable.
URL gopher://oasis.cc.purdue.edu:2525/11/student/cnslr

Minority Scholarships and Fellowships No matter what kind of educational program you're

headed for, if you're a member of a minority group, you're probably eligible for some form of financial aid. Search financial aid opportunities by school, state, degree program, or sponsoring institution.
WEB http://web.fie.com/htbin/cashe.pl

Scholarships and Grants A gateway to educational funding sources, including the Grant Getters Guide, the Catalogue of Federal Assistance, and FEDIX. For science scholars and researchers, the site links to the National Institutes of Health, the National Science Foundation, and the Science and Technology Service. The online version of *The Scientist* is also available here.
URL gopher://riceinfo.rice.edu:70/11/Research

▼ The government

ASKERIC The federally funded Educational Resources Information Center (ERIC) is an immense clearinghouse for educational information. ASKERIC, its online version, is a helpful virtual library that points fund-seekers in the direction of relevant information, publications on education, and discussions of college testing and admissions.
WEB http://eryx.syr.edu

The Student Guide from ED Have questions about how you're going to finance your education? Ask your Uncle Sam. This is the official guide from the U.S. Department of Education's Office of Postsecondary Education, updated each academic year. General information on student eligibility for federal aid, the application process, and borrower rights and responsibilities are available. You'll also find specifics on Pell Grants, Stafford Loans, PLUS Loans, and other federal assistance programs. A glossary helps future freshmen interpret the financial aid lingo.
WEB http://www.ed.gov/prog_info/SFA/StudentGuide

Chapter 19

Buying a Computer

SIMPLESTEPS

Purchase a PC Online

IT'S A BIG PURCHASE. DON'T LET SOME SALES GUY EMPTY YOUR POCKETS. BUY IT YOURSELF ONLINE

1 **Look deep into your soul.** This first step doesn't have religious implications, but it may have important financial ones. Why do you need a computer? If you're just looking for a way to send email and print out letters, you don't need the same high-end machine as someone who's planning to design multimedia animations. Take *Computer Shopper* magazine's six-question quiz in its **Guide to Buying Direct** to help pinpoint your needs. **Dave's Guide to Buying a Home Computer** is also an excellent primer for the computer consumer just starting to shop.

Guide to Buying Direct
WEB http://www5.zdnet.com
/cshopper/content/9606/guide.html

**Dave's Guide to Buying a Home
Computer**
WEB http://www.css.msu.edu
/pc-guide.html

2 **Pick your platform: Mac or PC.** Windows PCs fill most computer-equipped offices and homes in the world. They are the standard. But some work, such as desktop publishing, is easier to do on a Mac. Apple will argue that there are other reasons to buy Mac, too—see the company's propaganda at **Why Macintosh?** If you decide to go Mac, spend some time at **The Cult of Macintosh**, a comprehensive resource for the Mac owner. On the other hand, if you find yourself leaning toward a Windows 95 machine, check out the newsgroup **alt.windows95** for advice and equipment recommendations or **alt.os .windows95.crash.crash.crash**, which is viciously named but actually supports a small community of fairly helpful (if grumpy) Win95 users. If you can withstand all of the commotion in the **comp.sys.ibm.pc*** newsgroups (such as **comp.sys.ibm.pc.hardware.systems**, **comp.sys.ibm .pc.hardware.misc**, and **comp.sys.ibm.pc.misc**) and **comp .sys.mac*** newsgroups (such as **comp.sys.mac.system**, **comp.sys.mac.hardware.misc**, and **comp.sys.mac.portables**), these may be the best places to help you decide which

Why Macintosh?
WEB http://www2.apple.com/whymac/

The Cult of Macintosh
WEB http://cult-of-mac.utu.fi

USENET alt.windows95

USENET alt.os.windows95.crash.crash .crash

USENET comp.sys.ibm.pc.hardware .systems

USENET comp.sys.ibm.pc.hardware .misc

USENET comp.sys.ibm.pc.misc

USENET comp.sys.mac.system

USENET comp.sys.mac.hardware.misc

USENET comp.sys.mac.portables

USENET comp.sys.mac.advocacy

l, 2, 3, 4, 5, 6, 7, 8 ,9... there goes another Apple
http://www2.apple.com/whymac/

In this case, hot doesn't mean stolen
http://www.compusa.com

system—and which model—you want. You can ask other computer users about the performance records and cost of the machines you're considering. The PC vs. Mac war is played out in many forums in cyberspace, but one of the most entertaining and informative is **comp.sys.mac.advocacy**. Here's where some of the best and worst arguments for owning a Mac are made.

3 **Determine how much you can afford to spend.** Don't spend less than you can. Advancements in computer hardware and software happen incredibly quickly. Today's low-end computer is tomorrow's doorstop. Spend as much as you can now and buy a quality machine or your computer will be obsolete before it's even paid for.

❝ Don't spend less than you can. Advancements in hardware and software happen incredibly quickly. Today's low-end computer is tomorrow's doorstop. ❞

Choosing a Computer
WEB http://www.cbs.cornell.edu /techconn/choosing/choosing.html

Knowing Something About Your Computer FAQ
WEB http://mbln.lib.ma.us/emrls /works.htm

ZD Net
WEB http://www.zdnet.com/

TechWeb
WEB http://techweb.cmp.com

C|net
WEB http://www.cnet.com

Yahoo! Computing
WEB http://www.zdnet.com/yahoo computing/

4 **Decide which products you need.** Cornell University's guide to **Choosing a Computer** walks you step by step through the various pieces of hardware you'll need, decoding the jargon along the way. **The Knowing Something About Your Computer FAQ**, from the Eastern Massachusetts Regional Library System, is another excellent resource. **ZDNet** and **TechWeb** are the online homes of two of the country's largest computer magazine publishers, Ziff-Davis and CMP. Use their Web sites to search for reviews of the hardware and software you're considering buying. **C|net** and **Yahoo! Computing** also review computer products. Reviews are important, but don't ignore the vast amount of information on the Net put out by computer companies like those listed in **Tile.net/Vendors**. Besides the computer itself, you'll probably want additional equipment—printer, modem, scanner, or more specialized gizmos like a camera or video board. The Net is filled with excellent buyers' guides to computer products, for example **A Multitude of Modems** or the **CD-ROM Drives Buyer's Guide**.

5 **Comparison shop for the best buys.** When you know what you want, the only remaining questions are price and reliability. **ZDNet's Company Finder** helps you find product information from more than 1,100 computer companies. **Product Search** is a great price-comparison site—it hosts search engines for several major online computer warehouses and is also searchable by type of product.

6 **Make the best buy.** Go straight to online superstores like **Insight Direct**, **CompUSA**, or **Mac Zone/PC Zone** to complete your purchase and join the computer revolution.

Looking for a product review? Look no further
http://www.cnet.com

Tile.net/Vendors
WEB http://www.tile.net/tile/vendors/

A Multitude of Modems
WEB http://www.picksys.com/articles/pw/0995bg.html

CD-ROM Drives Buyer's Guide
WEB http://www.creaf.com/wwwnew/products/mmuk/cdrombuy.html

ZDNet's Company Finder
WEB http://search3.zdnet.com/locator/

Product Search
WEB http://www.productsearch.com

Insight Direct
WEB http://www.insight.com

CompUSA
WEB http://www.compusa.com/

Mac Zone/PC Zone
WEB http://www.internetmci.com/marketplace/mzone/

▼ Comparison shopping

The Computer Price Cruncher This site lets you compare prices on all kinds of computer hardware. Whether you're looking for CD-ROM drives, modems, scanners, memory chips, monitors, printers, sound cards, or entire systems, just plug in the words describing your desired system, and this free search engine will retrieve links to the numerous mail-order companies and Bay Area vendors. This "killer app" would be truly useful if the search automatically retrieved prices as well, but for that information you must visit each retailer. Still, the database has thousands of products and companies, and with a little patience you can save enough money to get even more RAM and a really huge monitor. If you don't know quite what you're looking for, browse the Buyer's Guide for a list of products, editorials, news, and benchmark tests.
WEB http://www.killerapp.com

Price Watch Shopping for a computer and wondering if the price is right? Check with Price Watch first to get its estimated street value. DIMM chips, SIMM chips, floppy drives—street prices for almost everything, including electric fans, are here. Also listed are complete systems for those who aren't into assembling components. A simple search engine is provided to help speed through the mayhem, but more deliberate shoppers will probably want to browse through the huge alphabetical list of product categories.
WEB http://www.pricewatch.com/

Product Search With every computer site sporting its own search engine, it wouldn't take a Mark Andreessen to figure out that it would be a whole heck of a lot easier if all the product search engines were collected at one site. Search the files of Stream, CompUSA, Internet Shopping Network, Microwarehouse, Computer Discount Warehouse, Insight, First Source, and Creative Computers and make the Internet shopping a breeze. And with the site's special three-screen format, surfers can shop for special bargains, vendors, and stores simultaneously.
WEB http://www.productsearch.com

This killer app takes the bite out of prices
http://www.killerapp.com

▼ Guides

Dave's Guide to Buying a Home Computer When Dave talks about buying a PC, people listen; he knows his stuff. Ask yourself the first question listed here: "What am I going to be using the computer for?" and you'll be well on your way to purchasing the perfect 'puter for your needs. Dave, who teaches "Introduction to Home Computing" at Michigan State University, recommends, and links to, trustworthy brand names, and talks about hardware and software. When you've brought the new electronic baby home, he even offers troubleshooting tips to keep it colic-free.
WEB http://www.css.msu.edu/pc-guide.html

▼ News & reviews

CMP's TechWeb Obsessed with computing news, convinced that comprehensive reporting can eradicate ignorance, this technology site goes a long way toward closing the information gap between the technological haves and have-nots. Browse the latest computer stories, and then head for the in-depth features in CMP's digital magazines, like "click picks" and a Tech Calendar. And then peruse the electronic versions of many of the most popular computer-related magazines on the newsstands—*NetGuide, Interactive Age, Windows Magazine, Computer Retail Week, Home PC, InformationWeek*, and others.
WEB http://techweb.cmp.com

MacWorld Online Forget the bells and whistles. A small selection of articles and a large selection of freeware and shareware help make this online sampler of the print magazine a prime example of the less-is-more philosophy. MacWorld Daily will clue you in to new daily insights in the computer cult. Free registration permits you to post and receive items on their (logically enough) Mac-oriented message board, or get great new stuff from their huge and well-indexed shareware and freeware library. If you've gotta shop, stop in at MacWorld Mart for a vendor directory.
WEB http://www.macworld.com

PC/Computing Online Even the limited, online version of the magazine that brings you the best the PC environment has to offer is fairly comprehensive. Updated reviews help you to recognize and find the "1,001 best sites" as chosen by PC/Computing Online. There are also a hefty number of Internet tools and games that you can download. Articles review hardware and software and cover Internet issues and PC usage.
WEB http://www.zdnet.com/pccomp

▼ Stores

CompUSA What's at the Web site for the home technology superstore? Computers for corporate, personal, government, and general use. Almost every item has a picture and the online prices are different (although not necessarily better) than those offered at the actual store. Select from PC systems, Macintosh products, hardware, printers, multimedia, upgrades, games, compkids and all sorts of software. Use the search engine to find a specific item in the catalog and save yourself some time. CompUSA also offers technical services and training to businesses and home users, and a list of Hot Products is provided so you can keep up with what's new.
WEB http://www.compusa.com

Cyberwarehouse A bona fide computer store for smart shoppers. Choose from computers, modems, monitors, accessories, memory, multimedia, drives, printers, power protection, network, input devices, video controllers, and software. For the latest deals, check the storewide specials section. Shopping online is a pleasure here, in part because each department has such a cute little icon. Like many cyberstores, a shopping cart is provided and checkout is easy.
WEB http://www.cyberwarehouse.com

Micro Warehouse Fans of the mail order catalogs *Mac Warehouse* and *PC Warehouse* will quickly recognize the familiar logo at this Web site. Choose from several categories: computers, hardware, software, data communications, and supplies. Membership is mandatory to buy, but browsing is permitted without signing up. With so many products available, it would be silly not to include a search engine, and Micro Warehouse isn't silly. Watch out for the weekly specials.
WEB http://www.warehouse.com/MicroWarehouse

Buying a New Car Online is
SIMPLESTEPS Automatic

No more haggling with condescending car salespeople. Use the Net for a real deal

1 **Decide how much you can afford to pay for a car.** Enter your preferred loan term, rate, and purchase price and **Microsoft CarPoint Loan Calculator** will help you estimate your monthly payments. Too high? Try again. Eventually you'll find a price range that doesn't chill your blood.

Microsoft CarPoint Loan Calculator
WEB http://carpoint.msn.com
/loancalc/loancalc.asp

2 **Compare the advantages of buying a car with leasing one.** Start at **Automobile Leasing: The Art of the Deal** for a straightforward summary of the leasing process and monthly payments. According to the site, you're a good candidate for leasing if "you like having a new car every two or three years; you want to drive a more expensive car, and have lower monthly payments; you

Automobile Leasing: The Art of the Deal
WEB http://www.mindspring.com
/~ahearn/lease/lease.html

like having the option of not making a down payment; you like having a car that's always in warranty in case something goes wrong; you hate having to sell or trade your old cars, and losing money in the process; or you don't like tying your up money in depreciating assets, i.e., cars." Does this sound more or less like you? If so, get used to the idea of leasing. If not, get used to the idea of buying.

3 Find out which makes and models are in your price range.

Begin with the tried and true **Kelley Blue Book**. Just select a make and model, and the site will return a Blue Book Pricing Report. **AutoWeb Interactive** is also helpful: Enter a vehicle make and your state abbreviation and its AutoFinder service will return a free quick quote from a local dealer. **The CarCenter by**

Kelley Blue Book
WEB http://www.kbb.com

AutoWeb Interactive
WEB http://www.autoweb.com/

The CarCenter by IntelliChoice
WEB http://www.intellichoice.com

AutoExplorer
WEB http://www.intellichoice.com/ae/ae_sub_mini.html

Your new car doesn't have to cost a lot of green
http://www.kbb.com

Location: http://www.kbb.com/cgi-bin/cgi.exe?kbb+nc+gpic :SZZEKLB

1997 New Cars

Netsite: http://popularmechanics.com/popmech/auto2/9612AUNC3P.html

The 1997 Plymouth Prowler leads car design back to the future.

Wonder why it's called the Prowler?
http://popularmechanics.com/popmech/auto2/IHOMEAUTO.html

Popular Mechanics Automotive
WEB http://popularmechanics.com/popmech/auto2/IHOMEAUTO.html

Motor Trend Online
WEB http://www.motortrend.com/

Edmund's Automobile Buyers Guides
WEB http://www.edmunds.com/#New

Microsoft CarPoint
WEB http://carpoint.msn.com/

Car Place
WEB http://www.cftnet.com/members/rcbowden/

Buick
WEB http://www.buick.com/index.html

BMW
WEB http://www.bmwusa.com

Automobile Manufacturers' Web Pages
WEB http://www.autoinfocenter.com/makers.html

IntelliChoice, though, might have the most convenient approach to finding a car in your price range. If you select its **AutoExplorer** service and pick a class of cars, the site will immediately return a list of cars by price range. IntelliChoice also recommends the Best Overall Values of the Year in several price categories.

4 Compare performance reviews and learn more about the car you're considering. Some cars are gems. Others are lemons. Have you accidentally set your heart on a lemon? Find out with the Net. **Popular Mechanics Automotive** offers its yearly New Car and Truck Buyer's Guide and exclusive owners' reports. **Motor Trend Online** delivers road test reports, a buyer's guide, and driving impressions. Although not as well-financed or well-designed, **Edmund's Automobile Buyers Guides** features prices and specs for all new car models as well as his own reviews of the cars. (Edmund also keeps track of the most popular cars among Internet users.) At **Microsoft CarPoint**, a one-stop car buying resource, you can search a database of vehicles and dealers in your area, find statistics on this year's models, browse today's automotive news, read articles about the models you're considering—even get a quote from a local dealer. Finally, check in with Robert Bowden of **Car Place**, who publishes weekly reviews of the cars he test drives.

5 Visit car manufacturers online. Most manufacturers, from **Buick** to **BMW**, have Web sites packed with information. Sometimes they even offer virtual test drives of their new cars. The **Automobile Manufacturers' Web Pages** provides links to all cyber-minded manufacturers, foreign and domestic.

6 **Decide which features you want.** Many car manufacturers offer customers the ability to build their own options packages through the manufacturer's Web site. In other words, a Web site will walk you through the process of choosing the features you want in your car. You can then print out the list and bring it to a local dealer.

❝ Some cars are gems. Others are lemons. Have you accidentally set your heart on a lemon? Find out with the Net. ❞

7 **Find a local dealer.** Almost all Web sites for car manufacturers also include a dealer locator. Just click on your city or enter your ZIP code for a list of dealerships. Or, search the **AutoDealer Locator Service** by manufacturer, city, state, and ZIP code. The service will return a list of local dealers.

AutoDealer Locator Service
WEB http://www.adls.com

The key to your dream machine is online
http://www.adls.com

8 Arm yourself with facts to confront the salesman.

Conventional wisdom says that if you know how much the dealer paid the manufacturer for the car, you'll know the bottom line, and that you'll be able to cut yourself a better deal. **The Car Center** by Intellichoice sells detailed reports about all new car makes and models. Reports include dealer costs, news about rebates, vehicle specifications, information on comparably priced cars, estimates on how much it will cost new owners to maintain the car, and much more. The Web site sells complete reports for $4.95 and also offers free, abridged versions of each report.

The Car Center
WEB http://www.intellichoice.com/

9 Before you turn over the check to the dealer down the street, browse dealerships in cyberspace.

DealerNet provides links to hundreds of cybersavvy dealers worldwide. Browse the dealer Web pages and email the dealerships directly.

DealerNet
WEB http://www.dealernet.com/

10 Use automobile locator services to search the country for the best deals on the car you want.

You can use these services to purchase cars for as close to manufacturing prices as possible, and they'll do much of the haggling for you. Some services will connect customers with a dealership in their area that offers competitive prices, while others will negotiate the entire transaction. Better still, these services rarely charge unless you buy!

Is your loan on the level?
http://www.intellichoice.com/

11 Make sure you don't want to buy used.

Most people like new cars. They're status symbols and investments, and then there's that bewitching new-car smell. But used cars can be great bargains. The Internet is a haven for classified listings, and auto classifieds are far easier to browse online than the oversized pages of your local newspaper. Track down that daily rag online with a visit to **Newspapers Within the United States**. Many papers, along with other sites (like the online head-quarters for National Public Radio's car-repair show **Car Talk**), have put their classifieds online. Search by the criteria most important to you (cost, size, model).

Newspapers Within the United States
WEB http://www.newspapers.com /npcoml.htm

Car Talk
WEB http://cartalk.com/Classifieds/

❝ Most people like new cars. They're status symbols and investments, and then there's that bewitching new-car smell. ❞

I2 **Check your credit.** Before you fill out the car loan application, make sure your credit's in good standing. You can write to each of the country's three major credit bureaus and get the reports at no cost, or you can use the **Confidential Credit** service at DealerNet. For less than $50, it will write to all of them for you.

Confidential Credit
WEB http://www.dealernet.com/credit /ccredit.htm

I3 **Begin the loan process.** In your search for the best car loan terms, try **1-800-CARLOAN**, where you can even begin the loan application. Almost all major banks, and many smaller ones, have extensive Web sites with information on applying for personal loans. Visit **BankWeb** for a comprehensive collection of links to banks online.

1-800-CARLOAN
WEB http://www.carloan.com/

BankWeb
WEB http://www.bankweb.com /bankweb.html

I4 **Get rid of your old junker.** Sure, your 1972 Nova may have nostalgic value, but it's not good for much else. Sign up with **AADCO Vehicle Disposal Service for Charity** and it will haul away your useless hunk of gears and arrange to auction it off for a good cause.

AADCO Vehicle Disposal Service for Charity
WEB http://www.vector.ca/aadco/

▼ Starting points

All Things Automotive Directory When you imagine a comprehensive online car directory, you probably think of an overloaded, laboring dump truck, or an overburdened pickup at the very least. But All Things Automotive is something entirely different—a sleek, mega-horsepower semi, barreling down the information superhighway. With categories ranging from Auto Clubs to Sales and Service listed in clear alphabetical order, you'll be able to find your information quicker than you ever imagined. Car-lovers love car magazines, and online fans are no different—check out the international array of ezines. Finally, if you're sick of your gas guzzler, drive by the Miscellaneous heading for solar and electric car information.
WEB http://www.webcom.com/~autodir

 Auto Site If you can spare a few bucks from your new-car fund, register with Auto Site. It's money well spent. A high-octane server offering more than 30,000 pages of automotive statistics, guidelines, and directories, Auto Site will tell you everything about the car of your choice, from its options to its crash-test ratings. The information offered is truly all-encompassing, and the free services (maintenance references, basic buying tips) are handy as well. It's all delivered with cheery graphics and intelligible organization, so buckle up for all the automotive data you could ever need.
WEB http://www.autosite.com

Cyberspace Automotive Performance This collection of automotive links claims to be the most comprehensive server of its kind on the Net. Link to all kinds of information about making a vehicle purchase. Use the site's calculator to determine monthly car payments. Learn which cars are on manufacturer recall and why. Or read about the turbo oiler and how to install it in the Technical Guru's Corner. Links to online magazines (like *Chrysler Power Magazine* and *Racer Magazine*) make this site complete.
WEB http://www.cyberauto.com/catalogs/auto_info /index.html

Vehicle Marketplace Don't miss the super section called Resources—you'll find monthly payment calculators, tips on buying a new car, and a guide to leasing. Then return to the main page to choose the state in which you live, and get local links to information on automobile loans, leases, and manufacturer financing, as well as RV, boat, and even aircraft loans.
WEB http://www.nfsn.com/Vehicle.htm

▼ Buyers' guides

Car and Driver The premier automotive review magazine, *Car and Driver* has put the complete text of its definitive buyer's guide online,

How much without the standard brakes?
http://www.autosite.com

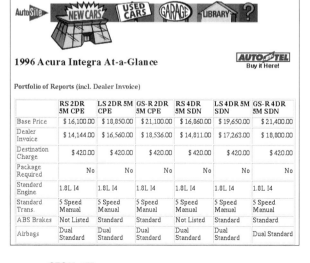

reaffirming a 40-year tradition of dependability. The next best thing to a test drive, this online guide is pleasantly easy to use. Many of the magazine's latest car reviews are here, too, in addition to a road map of links to car shows, races, and other automotive hot spots.

AMERICA ONLINE *keyword* car and driver

WEB http://www.caranddriver.com/hfm/index.html

The Car Place This page is assembled by Robert Bowden, who has test-driven more than 500 cars in his life and whose words of wisdom are updated weekly. Bowden's reviews are not written in the language of dry technical manuals; he rates the cars at between one and four "James Deans," four being as good as it gets. The Car Place covers a wide range of makes and models. Bowden also photographs cars in rather unique locales—check out his photo album.

WEB http://www.cftnet.com/members/rcbowden/

Consumer Reports: Automobiles The Car Guide and Road Test reports for virtually every make and model in all automobiledom, from the Acura Integra to the Volvo Golf. Accessories and related products are also reviewed, including repair services, motor oils, and car waxes. Plus, don't miss the articles on how to get the best deal on a new car and how to shop smart for a used car.

AMERICA ONLINE *keyword* consumers→automobiles

Edmund's Automobile Buyer's Guides You want to sound as if you know something about cars when you first step onto the showroom floor. Edmund has been helping car buyers for 30 years, and has the online goods. Pick a model and spend the next hour reading the relevant details, then peruse the solid price-haggling and negotiating tips which arm you with the knowledge of dealer's cost and other essentials. With millions of hits a month, the word is out about

PONTIAC PANIC

In my entire used car buying history, which includes a Pacer and an oil leaking T-Bird, I only correctly bought a used car once. That was my '88 Pontiac 6000. I shopped the lots of PA. I had a mechanic check it out before purchase, and I even haggled down the price some. I liked this car because it was big enough to take a dent and old enough that it wouldn't be worth stealing. Unfortunately I was wrong about that second part. A couple weeks ago it was stolen by a joy rider, abandoned the next day, and later stripped because the NYC Police Dept. didn't bother to call for a tow truck even after a good samaritan called 911 and later flagged down the police and showed them the car. The police took down my registration info and license plate number but never called for a tow like they promised (it wasn't a high priority). I really liked that car, so knowing that I could have gotten it back hurts more than the fact that my insurance didn't cover the loss.

So now, I need to find another car (while still paying off a small loan on the last one). I like the Pontiac 6000, and I've also heard good things about the Chevy Celebrity, but I don't know which years they were made better in. I figure that I'll have to find something for under $1,500.00, so I need their repair histories for 1985-89. Is there a web site that has such information? Is the Pontiac 6000 as good a car as I think or was I lucky? Are there other 4-door sedan types with good repair histories in my price range that someone could recommend? I have two small children so safety is a factor. I've also heard a lot about leasing, but I'm afraid that even if I could afford the lease, my insurance, now $1100.00 for basic liability, would be outrageously high. Does anyone know more about that or a web site I could check out on leasing options?

—from rec.autos.misc

Drive it off the cyberlot
http://www.car-link.com

the usefulness of Edmund's guides.
WEB http://www.edmunds.com

▼ Car talk

alt.autos Discuss a variety of models and makes here—from hot rods to RVs, from the building to the buying to the maintenance to the selling to the scrap heap. An awful lot of crossposting, and complaints about crossposting ("Spammers can only think of spam,

Outdeal the dealers
http://www.well.com/user/kr2

spam, spam, spam... wonderful spam"), take up a bunch of the bandwidth here, but the sheer variety of the expertise on this newsgroup makes alt.autos worth a drive-through.
USENET alt.autos

Automobile Forum What's the best used Nissan? Is the Taurus a good deal? Why does the Neon say "Hi" all the time? And why hasn't anyone invented a device to turn off a turn signal after 20 minutes of infernal blinking? One of the best online sources of general info about cars, with libraries and message boards on purchasing, performance, safety, and insurance.
COMPUSERVE *go* cars

Why does the Neon say "Hi" all the time? And why hasn't anyone invented a device to turn off a turn signal after 20 minutes of infernal blinking?

rec.autos.misc Tommy is looking for third-party replacement roll pads to give his 4-by-4 truck the "fat look." Joel wants to know if a hole in the muffler of his Mustang will hurt the car's engine (besides being loud). Two Accord owners compare their cars (one was built in Japan, one in Ohio). Automotive enthusiasts meet here for car talk of all kinds. The newsgroup's FAQ is a tremendous resource as well, answering questions from "What is this threshold breaking business?" to "How often should I change my brake fluid?"
USENET rec.autos.misc

▼ Find a car

Auto Web Interactive Ever driven by a suburban auto mile, where a seemingly endless array of new- and used-car dealers' signs pollute the horizon? This is the Internet equivalent. With comparable information, but none of the charm (read: smarm) of a real car salesman, this site will help you find the new or used car you're looking for through a dealer in your state. There's even a Web worksheet for generating new-car price quotes or figuring trade-in values. Once you've done your window shopping, you can make your purchase locally. We're sure the folks on your local auto mile will be glad to see you.
WEB http://www.autoweb.com

Car-link Used-car shoppers will find an illustrated list of hundreds of autos, listed by individuals and dealers. Because the photographs are such an essential part of this site, the people at Car-link have posted hardware requirements—jalopy computers won't do the job. Don't forget the handy calculator, here to help you compute your monthly payment.
WEB http://www.car-link.com

▼ Wheeling & dealing

Beat the Car Salesman "Congratulations. You've discovered the Internet Web site that the car salesman desperately hopes you won't visit," are the words that welcome you to this site. While this may be true, the site itself is mostly an advertisement for a book called, not surprisingly, "Beat the Car Salesman." Interestingly enough, while the book may be purchased from the site for $8.95, an complete online version is available for only $4.95. Even if you don't have a dime to spend, you can read extensive online excerpts.
WEB http://www.beatcar.com/

STICKIN' TO YOUR GUNS

In its simplest form, broken record lets you make a constant restatement of your point of view. In its more refined form, it would be a restatement of your position with a reasonable explanation added. Here is an example of a customer skillful in the use of broken record. Customer: "Yes, I know that you want to sell your car for $18,500, but I can only afford $16,500." Salesperson: "I would love to make a sale, but my boss just won't let me make a deal with almost no profit. You'll have to come up with more money. Maybe we can help you in terms of payments." Customer: "Yes, I know the deal is not great, but at $16,500 you'll still be making a profit." Salesperson: "But, we are losing money at that price." Customer: "But you will make a decent profit, and if you look at my figures, you will see that $16,500 is fair. Other dealers I know are offering the same car at $16,500." You should repeat this cycle of restating the same demands, with a new explanation each time, until a deal is reached or you, not they, leave.

—from Edmund's Automobile Buyer's Guides

CARveat Emptor Scroll, scroll, scroll past the rants and ravings of a mad genius. He's mad because car dealers are ripping people off, but he's genius enough to know how to get around it. Click on a topic—will it be A Consumer's Car Deal Repair Kit, a guide to "driving" a hard bargain, or some other way to avoid paying too much for a lemon? CARveat Emptor—let the car dealer beware the buyer who visited this site first.
WEB http://www.well.com/user/kr2

Tying the knot doesn't have to mean breaking the bank. Finance the union online—and live happily ever after

YOU'RE IN LOVE, working at a job that doesn't require wearing a paper hat, living in an apartment that isn't a fire trap, and ready to get married. But are you really ready to haggle with florists over a baby's breath pew treatment? Are you comfortable arguing with caterers about the use of peanut oil in a side salad? Are you prepared to obsess about napkin rings and cake plates? Most of all, are you man (or woman) enough to cough up the cash that will purchase the most important day of your life?

The Budget Bride

Whatever your budget, wedding organization is going to be critical. But don't bother hiring a professional wedding planner. The Net is all you'll need. **Opus' Online Wedding Resource** is a good place to start for the basic wedding plan. **WedNet** and **I Do** also make the prospect of nuptials more natural. And you'll even find a **Wedding Budget Calculator** to help manage the cost of everything from the champagne to the videographer.

When it comes to the specifics of the ceremony, you'll find something old at **Medieval and Renaissance Wedding Information** and something new at the **Sacred Rainbow**.

You can borrow some ideas from **The Wedding Exchange**, and you can beat back the wedding planning blues with the help of other newlyweds at **soc.couples .wedding** and **alt.wedding**. The newsgroups are especially helpful—not only do they serve as style consultants for prospective brides and grooms, but they function as giant etiquette books packed with anecdotes from triumphant and defeated wedding vets alike.

As the newsgroups frequently remind worried near-marrieds, having a classy wedding doesn't have to mean breaking the piggy bank. Check out **Terrific Tightwad Weddings** for two ways to wed at less than $3,000, and then visit **Weddingbells** to learn about the new, frugal trends in wedding party fashion. Be the first on your block to use children's Valentines as funny place cards, or reinstitute the tradition of a "Dollar Dance," where guests can dance with the bride or groom only if they contribute to a honeymoon fund.

And what about That Dress? Measured at cost-per-wear, it's perhaps the most expensive garment a woman will ever own. To economize, you might be tempted to purchase a **Dual-Use Wedding Gown**. But there are other ways to cut corners while still remaining in good taste. Scanned glossies of wedding dresses on the Internet are almost as numerous as pictures of *Star Trek: Voyager* characters. Window shop through the pages at **The Bridal Showroom**, which offers full-color pictures of gowns, or head directly over to

CASH REGISTER

Opus' Online Wedding Resource
WEB http://www.opuswedding.com/

WedNet
WEB http://www.wednet.com/

I Do
WEB http://www.i-do.com/

Wedding Budget Calculator
WEB http://www.ido.com/budget.html

Medieval and Renaissance Wedding Information
WEB http://paul.spu.edu/~kst/bib /bib.html

Sacred Rainbow
WEB http://www.gaypride.com /rainbow/

The Wedding Exchange
WEB http://www.nebride.com/

USENET soc.couples.wedding

USENET alt.wedding

Terrific Tightwad Weddings
WEB http://www.frugalfun.com /weddings.html

Weddingbells
WEB http://www.weddingbells.com

Dual-Use Wedding Gowns
WEB http://www.visi.com /~dheaton/bride/dual_use.html

The Bridal Showroom
WEB http://www.ramnetsys.com /apparel/bridal/

CASH REGISTER

The Bridal Search
WEB http://www.bridalsearch.com

Modern Bride
WEB http://www.modernbride.lm.com

Budget Bridal Outlet Store
WEB http://www.eskimo.com
/~stopper/dress/dressa.html

Willow Tree Lane
WEB http://www.willowtreelane.com

FTD
WEB http://www.ftd.com/

Epicurious Travel
WEB http://travel.epicurious.com/

Pariscope
WEB http://pariscope.fr/

Welcome to Venice
WEB http://www.portve.interbusiness
.it/wetvenice/wetvenice.html

Bali Online
WEB http://www.indo.com/

Location : http://www.modernbride.lm.com/

Buy online and get a discount on the dress
http://www.modernbride.lm.com

The Bridal Search, which claims to be the "world's largest bridal gown search" service. **Modern Bride** (of Pittsburgh, not the magazine) will locate the retailer or the pattern of any dress from any of the leading bridal magazines—and if you purchase it online, you can get a discount of up to 25 percent. Better yet, head to the **Budget Bridal Outlet Store**, where you can save up to 50 percent off retail prices on designer gowns, or Bridal-net, which offers advice on purchasing a wedding gown from the cheaper factory-direct outlets.

The dress is not the only thing you can get at a discount. **Willow Tree Lane** has beautiful wedding invitations for as low as $16.90 a box. And as any frugal bride can knows, the cheapest and best florists are not always "wedding florists," no more than the cheapest and best travel agents are "honeymoon travel agents." Check out **FTD** for flowers, and make your post-nuptial travel arrangements at **Epicurious Travel** or location-specific sites like **Pariscope**, **Welcome to Venice**, or **Bali Online**. The savvy couple can also take advantage of the Net for creating their ceremony, picking poems from online texts at Columbia's **Bartleby Library,** or selecting wedding music from the **Wedding Music Information Source** and **Love Songs**.

If the idea of cheap conjugality is not your cup of tea, consider joining one of the online bridal registries to augment your hope chest. Services such as the **American Bridal Registry** will organize and display your wish list for all the Web to see. Be sure to include the URL of your registry page on your print invitations—which, of course, you'll be making yourself. Going from a registry page to an online wedding album takes only a few short lines of HTML code. Sites like **Wed on Web** and **I Thee Web** are set up to provide couples with a full range of pre-wedding services such as a multimedia scrapbooks and interactive guestbooks. These sites aren't free, and some aren't even cheap, but online bridal registries and travel planning features (including local maps and lodging suggestions) can at least save you and your guests plenty of time. And, as they say, time is money.

CASH REGISTER

Bartleby Library
WEB http://www.columbia.edu/acis/bartleby/

Wedding Music Information Source
WEB http://www.nuwebny.com/wedmusic/index.htm

Love Songs
WEB http://www.st.nepean.uws.edu.au/users/mbuena/songwords.html

American Bridal Registry
WEB http://www.abregistry.com/

Wed on Web
WEB http://www.wedonweb.com/

I Thee Web
WEB http://www.itheeweb.com/

If you can't save money, at least save time
http://www.wedonweb.com/

Location: http://www.wedonweb.com/

▼ Starting points

Wedding Budget Workshop Gone (mostly) are the days where parents footed the bill for a blushing teenager's nuptials. Couples waiting until they're older to get married may also find themselves paying for their own weddings. Sticker shock, of course, ensues. The wedding budget tips offered here are in response to that trend, and include a worksheet that the lucky couple can customize to reflect the size of the wedding.
WEB http://www.vservices.com/Budget/budgettip.html

Wedding Shops Online This may be the one site you'll prefer above all others for its simple, easy-to-use trackers and planners. There's an activity timeline, so you'll know what to do with six months to go; a budget planner and payment tracker; money saving secrets; and lots more goodies to help you make the most of that special day. Wedding Shops Online really seems to have the big picture figured out. Soon, so will you.
WEB http://www.advol.com/WedShops.htm

Organization is a must for the bride on a budget
http://www.i-do.com/publicplanner.html

Location: http://www.i-do.com/planner.html

Wedding Planner

Planner

▼ Frugality tips

Budget Bridal Outlet Store One of the most costly, and least cost-effective, purchases for a wedding is the bridal gown. Surely, you've heard the refrain: "Why spend so much when you're only going to wear it once?" Why, indeed? Check out the Budget Bridal Outlet Store instead, which promises you the designer gown of your choice, factory-direct, at up to 50 percent off the retail price.
WEB http://www.eskimo.com/~stopper/dress/dressa.html

Couples waiting until they're older to marry may also find themselves paying for the wedding.

Terrific Tightwad Weddings: Two Approaches
Beautiful, simple suggestions to make an affordable wedding even more meaningful than a lavish, catered extravaganza—that's what Terrific Tightwad Weddings is all about. The site itself is strictly no-frills, but the article, taken from a book by Shel Horowitz, is well-written and encouraging. Horowitz tells the story of his own wedding and the "assigned potluck" wedding of a friend, both of which cost less than $3,000. At the end, the reader is left feeling that cheap really doesn't have to mean chintzy.
WEB http://www.frugalfun.com/weddings.html

Wedding Dollars and Sense Do you have to pay the hotel expenses for your out-of-town guests? Can you still have a beautiful wedding for less than $5,000? When it comes to any average wedding, budget spending lies halfway between etiquette and realism. This

Q&A column by Rachel Schreckengast offers plenty of specific suggestions and general comfort for budgetary nightmares. Read and digest—it's much better than rubber chicken.
WEB http://www2.wednet.com/wedsense/wedsense.asp

Wedding Frugality Deck those wedding halls with dollar-store fabric. Make your dress. Make your mother's dress. Save, save, save money with Rachel's ramblings on Wedding Frugality. This long article offers hundreds of suggestions for financing a glorious wedding with less cash. Buy a cubic zirconium ring. Bake the cake yourself. Make your own invitations. Find out if your relatives can cut you a deal. Martha Stewart would be so proud.
WEB http://www.achiever.com/freehmpg/rachel/wedding.html

▼ Budget calculators

The Bridal Guide Budget Calculator Enter your target spending range in the blank for each of the major wedding expense categories, and this calculator will list them and add them up for you. Unimpressed? It's understandable. You could probably do it yourself. But the tips and guides for keeping your wedding within your budget are helpful to financially challenged families of the engaged.
WEB http://www.bridal-guide.com/budget.htm

I Do Wedding Planner An excellent set of calculators. First, a timeline calculator schedules your wedding plans from today until your wedding day, with each step given a specific date. Second, a spreadsheet of sorts helps you plan your budget, and enter actual expenses along the way to keep careful track of how close you're sticking to your target expenses. Both are little helpers no "father of the bride" should be without.
WEB http://www.i-do.com/publicplanner.html

SET YOUR SITES

The key to saving money when choosing a ceremony and reception site is to have both the ceremony and reception at the same location. In addition to not having to pay for an additional site, you save the cost of transportation from one site to the other. When choosing the most economical and appropriate site for your ceremony and reception, list every club, organization, even college, that you and your fiancée and your respective families are affiliated with to see if they may offer you a site at a reduced cost. For example, many churches will charge their members less money to use their sites.

You may also wish to consider the following locations for a ceremony and reception:

- Restaurant
- Social Club
- Country Club
- Community Center
- Winery
- You or Your Parents' Home or Mansion
- College or Military Chapel
- City Sites
- Anywhere outdoors. Most locations such as your parents' home or garden, can be available for free or for a small fee. However, make sure that you have an alternate location in case you need one for bad weather.

Another good resource for a location would be if your family, relative or friend owned a location such as an Inn in the mountains, a yacht, or a mansion. You could ask if they would let you use the facility as their wedding gift to you. Also, local historical societies can provide you with a list of free or economical locations within the area.

—*from Wedding Shops Online*

Finance Your Dream Home Online

SIMPLESTEPS

SEARCH FOR SHELTER ONLINE, AND SAVE ENOUGH TIME AND MONEY TO SPLURGE ON FURNITURE

Top Ten Tips for First Time Home-buyers
WEB http://www.mortgagealmanac.com/TMA/articles/article2.htm

Consumer Information Catalog
WEB http://www.gsa.gov/staff/pa/cic/housing.htm

Your Homebuying Questions Answered
WEB http://www.realtorads.com/consumer/buyer.htm

HomeWeb: Buying a Home
WEB http://www.us-digital.com:8080/consinfo/buyingco.html

Interactive Homebuying on the Web
WEB http://www.maxsol.com/homes/steps.htm

I **Take a crash course in home-buying.** What kind of realtor do you need? How can you get a mortgage? How does a house closing take place? What should you look for when you visit a home? Get an overview of the whole process and prepare for many of the decisions you'll have to face. Begin with **Top Ten Tips for First Time Home-buyers**, then head to the **Consumer Information Catalog**'s selection of housing pamphlets (such as "How to Buy a Home with a Low Down Payment" and "The HUD Homebuying Guide") the National Association of Realtor's **Your Homebuying Questions Answered**, or the exhaustive **HomeWeb: Buying a Home**. For another survey course, take a peek at **Interactive Homebuying on the Web**, which outlines the basics of buying a house, from identifying your needs to closing the deal.

2 **Learn the lingo.** The homebuying process involves plenty of confusing terms, many of them related to finance. Before you get started, remember to keep a few glossaries at hand, such as the helpful **Mortgage Terms** or the comprehensive **Real Estate Dictionary**. The government can help, too, with HUD's **Home Buyer's Vocabulary**.

Mortgage Terms
WEB http://yournewhouse.com/mtgterms.html

Real Estate Dictionary
WEB http://www.homeowners.com/dictionary.html

Home Buyer's Vocabulary
WEB http://www.windermere.com/user.html/buy/gov.docs/buyers.vocab.html

3 **Compare cities' quality of life.** First stop: *Money* magazine's **Your Best Places** search engine. You can search the living conditions of 300 cities in America by any combination of 63 factors, including weather, economy, and culture. The search, based on *Money*'s yearly survey, will even map the suggested regions for you. Visit **City.Net** and the **USA CityLink Project** for information about the schools, attractions, and businesses in the cities that you're considering.

Your Best Places
WEB http://pathfinder.com/money/best-cities-96/seaindex.htm

City.Net
WEB http://www.city.net/

USA CityLink
WEB http://usacitylink.com/

Make yourself at home on the Web
http://www.us-digital.com:8080/consinfo/buyingco.html

Location: http://www.us-digital.com:8080/homeweb/

HomeWEB
The Internet's Most Comprehensive Real Estate and Relocation Source

Home Search
Real Estate Professionals
Relocation Service Providers
Consumer Information
Corporate Relocation Managers
HomeWEB Membership Information
What's New?!

US Digital

4 **Consider the cost of living in different cities.** The 1996 Home Price Comparison Index compares the cost of homes in different locations. It may cost more to live in certain cities, but keep in mind that the salaries are often higher, too. Use *Money* magazine's **Cost of Living Comparator** to find out what a potential salary might mean in a new location. For example, if you are considering moving from a $40,000 salary in Charlottesville, Va. to a similarly paid position in Los Angeles, you'll see a decrease in purchasing power of 35.96 percent. In other words, you'd need to make almost $63,000 to have an equivalent lifestyle. In New York City, you'd need to make more than $87,000.

1996 Home Price Comparison Index
WEB http://www.coldwellbanker.com /hpci/hpci2.html

Cost of Living Comparator
WEB http://cgi.pathfinder.com /cgi-bin/Money/col.cgi

5 **Decide whether you should buy or rent.** There are often financial advantages to owning a home, especially if you're planning to be in the area for a long time. But sometimes, renting is a better option. Compare the costs of purchasing a home equivalent to the one you currently rent with the **Rent vs. Buy Analyzer**. For the most accurate comparison, you'll need to know the **National Average Mortgage Rates**, your income tax bracket, the property tax rate in your area, expected appreciation of homes in your area, and an estimate of your current rental's purchase price.

Rent vs. Buy Analyzer
WEB http://www.homefair.com /homefair/sept95/frrent.html

National Average Mortgage Rates
WEB http://www.interest.com/ave.htm

" If you are considering moving from a $40,000 salary in Charlottesville, Va., to Los Angeles, you'd need to make almost $63,000 to maintain an equivalent lifestyle. "

Affordability Analyzer
WEB http://www.homefair.com /homefair/sept95/frafford.html

 Figure out how much you can spend on a house. Here's where it gets a little tricky. The **Affordability Analyzer**

will return a ballpark figure of how much house you can afford. But according to **H.O.M.E. Housing Costs**, there's a catch: It's hard to know how much you can afford until you already have a down payment and mortgage in mind.

Decide which type of mortgage is best for you. The **Intelligent Mortgage Agent** will help you evaluate mortgage plans. Although this is probably the best mortgage tool available from the **Homebuyer's Fair Mortgage Finance Resources,** there are other handy utilities there. Crestar's mortgage tools offer several calculators for the home buyer so you can **Know How Much House You Can Afford Before You Start Looking**—there's even an interactive mortgage application. For a complete overview of the mortgage process, try **Mortgage-Net**.

Get pre-qualified or pre-approved for a mortgage. It's best to be pre-qualified or pre-approved for a

H.O.M.E. Housing Costs
WEB http://www.homefair.com /homefair/article1.html

Intelligent Mortgage Agent
WEB http://www.homefair.com/home fair/cmr/premium.html

Homebuyer's Fair Mortgage Finance Resources
WEB http://www.homefair.com /homefair/mortgage.html

Know How Much House You Can Afford Before You Start Looking
WEB http://www.crestar.com/borrow /cbbo_ub_banker.html

Mortgage-Net
WEB http://www.dirs.com/mortgage/

Get moving online
http://www.crestar.com/borrow/cbbo_ub_banker.html

mortgage before you fall in love with a house that costs too much. And, in a competitive real estate market, your pre-approved financing is worth as much to a seller as a cash bid. You can obtain pre-qualification online from most major lenders. **American Mortgage Online** is one place to start looking for a lender—you can search by state and pre-qualify with one of the many participating lenders using a single online form.

American Mortgage Online
WEB http://amomortgage.com
/index.htm

9 **Start searching for a house by browsing the real estate hub-sites.** The big real estate sites include listings from real estate agencies across the country. Typically, they allow you to search by price range, number of bedrooms, and other criteria. Color photos of homes are usually available, and the realtor's name, phone number, and email address are listed. One site, **Cyber-Homes**, even offers street-level mapping so you can see your new neighborhood. And while this service isn't as national as it pretends to be, it does cover several U.S. regions. Almost half a million homes in 37 states are listed at **Realtor.com**, which is sponsored by the National Association of Realtors. **Real Estate Xtra!** and **HomeWEB** are also highly recommended databases of house listings. Looking for more than just relocation services and real estate listings? At **America's HomeNet**, you can search for house listings, but you can also get information about schools, businesses, realtors, and lenders in the area. The huge **Internet Real Estate Directory** has its own classified section, along with real estate advice columns and thousands of links to the pages of real estate agents worldwide. And **Realty Links** has a nationwide listing of real estate agents.

CyberHomes
WEB http://www.cyberhomes.com/

Realtor.com
WEB http://www.realtorads.com/

Real Estate Xtra!
WEB http://207.120.59.133:80/

HomeWEB
WEB http://www.us-digital.com:8080
/homeweb/

America's HomeNet
WEB http://www.netprop.com
/homenet.htm

Internet Real Estate Directory
WEB http://www.ired.com/

Realty Links
WEB http://wwwl.infowest.com
/realnet/links/

IO **Visit the Web sites of specific realtors.** Many of the big national realtors have great Web sites—for example,

Netsite: http://www.coldwellbanker.com/index.html

This Iowa mansion is equivalent to a Manhattan studio apartment
http://www.coldwellbanker.com/index.html

Coldwell Banker, **RE/MAX**, and **Century 21** (which links to local agencies). But there are also hundreds of regional and local realtors with helpful sites online. Several sites (in addition to major search engines like **Infoseek**) collect links to local and regional realtors, including **America's Real Estate Connection**, **1 Real Estate Road**, and the **FractalNet WWW Real Estate Server**.

II Hunt for a house in the classifieds. Don't overlook the real estate information in your newspaper. It's cheap, efficient, and timely. With the Web, you can now search the real estate classifieds by the criteria important to you. In other words, you no longer have to plod through the real estate listings in the **Los Angeles Times** and the **New York Times**, circling the best listings with a pen. Instead, you can enter preferences like location and price in these newspapers' search forms, and the sites will return relevant listings. Locate a newspaper in your area at **Newspapers Online**, which has links to everything from the *Anchorage Press* to the *Washington Post*.

Coldwell Banker
WEB http://www.coldwellbanker.com
/index.html

RE/MAX
WEB http://www.remax.com/

Century 21
WEB http://www.c2lrealty.com/

Infoseek: Real Estate
WEB http://guidep.infoseek.com
/Business/Real_estate?tid=433&lk=
noframes

America's Real Estate Connection
WEB http://www.millionaire.com
/realestate/arec/

1 Real Estate Road
WEB http://www.1realestate.com/

FractalNet WWW Real Estate Server
WEB http://www.fractals.com
/realestate.html

Los Angeles Times Real Estate Classifieds
WEB http://www.latimes.com/HOME
/CLASS/REALEST/

New York Times Real Estate Classifieds
WEB http://search.nytimes.com
/classified/reres.html

Newspapers Online
WEB http://www.newspapers.com
/npcoml.htm

▼ Starting points

Consumer Mortgage Information Network The best aspect of the Consumer Mortgage Information Network is its impartiality. Of course, the network would like you to download (and pay for) a shareware version of its mortgage planning software QualifyR (the full version is $30.) Aside from that, though, the site's information is free from bias toward any lender or real estate agent. A long list of articles is indexed in the File Library. Unfortunately, these articles are unformatted FTP links to sometimes outdated government sites. Once consumers are done reading these thousands of pages, the housing market will have collapsed entirely and all housing will be free. Or, if that's not the case, they can at least link to what seems like an endless number of realty links from around the country.
WEB http://www.pacificrim.net/~proactiv/cmin/first.html

Homebuyer's Fair Welcome to the Fair, and to listings in the Washington, D.C., area, including a clickable map that allows you to specify smaller geographical areas for property searches. But the Homebuyer's Fair is a whole lot more than real estate listings, containing some of the

best calculators and most helpful articles of any other real estate site. There's an "Intelligent Mortgage Agent," a Rent vs. Buy analyzer, and much more, all contained under the mortgage finance resources page. Don't miss the terrific section for first-time buyers.
WEB http://www.homefair.com/

International Real Estate Directory It's simply a megalist of links to every type of real estate offering, but the International Real Estate Directory, or IRED, is a treasure. Looking for realtors in your town? How about government agencies? Direct lenders? An apartment in Tuscany? The only thing you won't find at IRED is a missing link. Even tangentially related resources for real estate and real estate financing have been included.
WEB http://www.ired.com/cgi-bin/ssi.cgi/dir/index.html

Real Estate Center AOL's Real Estate Center is a busy area designed to help people buy, sell, rent, finance and invest in real estate. Both seasoned real estate pros and those who are still renting are welcome, and you'll find all levels of expertise in the message boards. Fortunately, true experts give answers, advice and comments in several boards designed for a Q&A format. Don't miss the MLS section where you can list properties for sale or exchange at no charge. Mortgage Rates from 60 lenders are available. The ever-present host of the forum, Peter G. Miller, a.k.a. "Ourbroker," is also the author of several real estate books and a media darling.
AMERICA ONLINE *keyword* mls

▼ Mortgages

American Mortgage Online How do I prequalify? How can the Federal Housing Administration help me? And what the heck is all this talk about arms? Find out the answers to all of these questions here, referring to the glos-

Buying a new house can be a roller coaster ride
http://www.homefair.com/

Netsite: http://www.homefair.com/home/

Welcome to the Homebuyer's Fair!

Popular Exhibits

The Salary Calculator (TM)
The Moving Calculator (TM)
Intelligent Mortgage Agent (TM)
Mortgage Qualification Calculator
The Relocation Wizard (TM)

Main Booths

Mortgage Finance Resources
First Time Buyer Info
Buying a Home
Relocation Information
Apartments
FREE SERVICES

HOME BUYER'S fair

sary when you run across an unfamiliar term (ARMs stands for adjustable rate mortgage) and then link to a small database of realtors and lenders. Lots of forms enable you to request more information about refinancing, your credit history, and prequalification. Thinking of taking out a second mortgage? Don't look here—that page, although it's linked from the home page, was nowhere to be found when we visited.
WEB http://amo-mortgage.com/index.htm

HomeOwners Finance Network HomeOwners Finance is a California-based mortgage broker offering fast qualification for consumers in 43 states—just fill out the Rapid Approval Form and find out if you're loan-worthy in less than one business day. While you're waiting, look around this super site. First, learn the most recent interest rates for every kind of mortgage, plus a daily rate analysis. Use the mortgage calculator stored in the Tools box, or subscribe to RateWatch, a mailing list designed to keep you informed about trends in loan rates. A searchable glossary, a mortgage FAQ, and a directory of realtors make this a darned good, if biased, site.
WEB http://www.homeowners.com/

HSH Mortgage Information If you're thinking of buying a house, this is worth a look. HSH Associates, Financial Publishers, is the nation's largest publisher of mortgage and consumer loan information. It conducts surveys of mortgage lenders—so there's no advertising onsite. Aside from the daily National Average Mortgage Rates, you can send away for more detailed surveys, like the comprehensive list of local lenders that's available for $10. And don't forget the free information onsite, such as the ARM Check Kit and Refinancing Guide. Download the free shareware to help you get the best mortgage for your needs or use one of their many finan-

ALL ABOUT APR

APR stands for "Annual Percentage Rate." It is also one of the most misunderstood numbers people find when applying for loans. As consumer loans, and mortgages in particular, turned more complicated it became necessary to help regulate the way lenders advertise and notify the potential borrower of their interest rates. The attempt was to help people compare similar loans from different lenders and to explain the ultimate cost of credit.

The APR is defined as the cost of credit to the borrower in relation to the amount borrowed expressed as a yearly rate. This is required by the federal Truth in Lending Act, Regulation Z. When you apply for a mortgage the Federal Truth in Lending Disclosure form will be sent. At the top of the page you will see lots of numbers. Two of those numbers are the Note Rate (the actual rate used to calculate your monthly payments) and the Annual Percentage Rate (APR). The Annual Percentage Rate will most always be slightly higher than the note rate because the APR includes other items associated with obtaining a mortgage.

Did you need an interest rate to get a mortgage? Of course. But you also needed some other things. Origination fees, points, mortgage insurance premiums, inspections, prepaid interest and other items may also be required to obtain a mortgage. If so, these things need to be included when calculating the APR.

Why is the APR useful? I'll give you an example. Great Big Bank offers a 30 year fixed mortgage for 8 percent. Really Small Bank offers a 30 year fixed mortgage for 7 percent. Easy choice, right? Maybe. Before lenders and mortgage brokers were required to state the APR it was hard to tell.

—*from Mortgage Rates*

MORTGAGE MARK-UP

How much profit should your mortgage company make? In the case of direct lenders, it's hard to figure how much profit they are making on a given transaction. This is because the lending process is complex. In some cases the lenders may portfolio the loan, in other cases the lender may sell the loan to an investor. Mortgage brokers on the other hand have a clearly defined wholesale price. This price is marked up to produce a retail price. The question is what is a reasonable profit margin? Remember—pricing and profit margins are always set by supply and demand. Every company has a different pricing strategy. Some companies want to be the "Price Club" of the industry and some want to be the "Saks Fifth Avenue." Also price is not everything—quality service is even more important.The average markup for good credit quality borrowers ("A" Paper) is between I to 2 points. The markup may be higher for smaller loans under $100,000 and lower for jumbo loans over $207,000. Just because one mortgage broker has a lower markup than another—this does not mean that their final rate will be lower—because the brokers' wholesale rates might vary too!! If this is too confusing—remember if your mortgage company publishes their rates on the Internet every day—all you care about is the final rate, and not what the wholesale is. Do business with mortgage companies that publish their rates on the Web.

—from Mortgage-Net

cial calculators to help figure what's affordable for you. You can also link to *Money* magazine's "best mortgage rates" and the Consumer Mortgage Information Network.
WEB http://www.hsh.com

Mortgage Market Information Services The MMIS updates on mortgage rates and trends appear in more than 300 newspapers nationwide. Now you can get them on the Web. They've got a daily update on what's happening in the mortgage market and listings of mortgage rates offered by various financial institutions, organized by state. Click on the name of the one making the offer and jump straight to their home page, if they have one. Companies pay to be included in the database. The site also has advice columns.
WEB http://www.interest.com

Mortgage Mart It wouldn't be overstating the case to say that the Mortgage Mart is the most organized, easy-to-navigate hubsite of its kind on the World Wide Web. Pleasantly colorful, peppy graphics, and a system of pull-down menus makes this site a joy to use. The information is at least as good as similar mortgage hubsites. You'll find pretty much anything you can imagine—calculators, news, industry trends, government programs, articles, the works! A small database of lenders, current rates, and loan applications seal the mortgage deal.
WEB http://www.mortgage-mart.com/

Mortgage Rates A brief introduction defines the types of mortgages—30-year fixed, 15-year fixed, jumbo (more than $203,150), negative amortization (deferred interest), and adjustable rate mortgages (ARMs). Specialized loan programs like those from the Veteran's Administration and the FHA are also detailed. With this information in hand, prospective home buyers can begin to explore the individual bank listings, which are updated on a daily basis. Each bank involved furnishes the current rate on most or all types of mortgages, contact information, and details on its lending program.
AMERICA ONLINE *keyword* mortgage→Mortgage Rates

Mortgage-Net Brave mortgage shoppers, enter here to learn the sordid details that mortgage lenders don't want you to know. The requisite links to calculators and small directories of mortgage brokers and direct lenders—not to mention the ubiquitous glossary—obscure the real gem here. It's a special section called How to Shop for a Mortgage, which explains in crystal-clear language how the lender makes money, how much money you should allow them to make, and how to use the Internet to keep your lenders honest.
WEB http://www.mortgage-net.com/

▼ Definitions

The LoanPage Mortgage Terms "Equity: The difference between the amount owed on the loan and the current purchase price of the home or property." Plain language defines the terms in this small glossary of common mortgage lingo. Haven't you always wanted to know the meaning of "buydown"?
WEB http://www.loanpage.com/morterms.htm

▼ Number crunchers

Home Sales Line Five dollars buys a lot online—fill out a simple form here, and Home Sales Line will return the results of one of three kinds of searches. First, you can receive all sales information on a single property for the past five years. Second, you can choose to order a report on the 15 most recent sales on a single street. The final search option is to request up to 15 homes that have most recently been sold in your town at the price you select. This can help you find a fair price for the house you're selling yourself, learn if you've been offered a fair price, or merely attempt to keep up with the Joneses in the 700 block of Easy Street.
WEB http://www.insure.com/home/Sales/

Mortgage and Financial Calculators A simple homemade page that does lots of not-so-simple math. Various calculators will figure out car-leasing payments, how much house you can afford, and whether a balloon-convertible mortgage might make sense for you. Also offered is a collection of mortgage and personal finance software ready to download.
WEB http://ibc.wustl.edu/mort_links.html

Your New House Mortgage Information Can you really afford that half-a-million-dollar home? Don't let the real estate agent convince you; do some number crunching of your own. This page will ask you the three big questions when buying a home: How much down? How much a month? And can you qualify? You're given some practical scenarios that will educate you about topics like hidden expenses, where you might have to pre-pay some property tax and hazard insurance. You can also calculate back ratios and front ratios if you know your gross salary. It's all in plain, easy-to-understand terms which will help you comprehend just what it takes to buy a home.
WEB http://yournewhouse.com/mortgage.html

Don't let a heavy mortgage cart away your hopes for a new house
http://www.mortgage-mart.com/

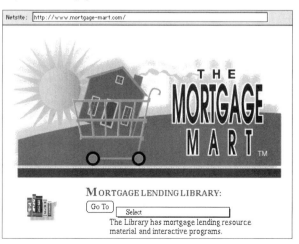

The virtual home shopping network
http://www.homes.com/

▼ Step-by-step

How to Buy a House "A realtor is to home buying what a conductor is to an orchestra," enthuses the author of this article. Three guesses what her occupation is—yup, she's an orchestra conductor. You'll be able to follow along the realty score after reading this insider's guide to purchasing a home. It's written for the first-time homebuyer, and walks the reader through the process from choosing a realtor to closing the deal after the final loan is approved.
WEB http://www.rtis.com/nat/com/accesscb/howtbuyl.htm

▼ The government

Fannie Mae Online Some think Fannie Mae was the name of Harry Truman's favorite cow. Others think it's a recent hit country song. Wrong. It's the Federal National Mortgage Association—the Congressionally created, shareholder-owned lending institution that targets low- to middle-income home buyers. Several Fannie Mae programs are described here, like those promoting rural home owner-

ship, home buying for the self-employed, and community living for disabled adults.
AMERICA ONLINE *keyword* fannie mae
WEB http://www.fanniemae.com

Freddie Mac Freddie Mac is a 30-year-old quasi-governmental company designed to support homeownership and rental housing. The corporation acts behind the scenes to puchase mortgages made by lenders nationwide and then sells them as securities, thus lowering costs to homebuyers. This site answers some of the most frequently asked questions about Freddie Mac, discusses news and new legislation, and links to the site where foreclosed Freddie Mac homes are for sale.
WEB http://www.freddiemac.com/

You finally cut your piece of the American pie—you bought a home of your own. Now what do you do?

Homes and Real Estate You finally cut your piece of the American pie—you bought a home of your own. Now what do you do? The FTC has a series of publications designed to help homeowners (and those who would be homeowners) manage their debt and equity. For first-timers, there is a "Home Financing Primer," filled with suggestions about how to choose your lender, what different types of mortgages mean in interest, points, and principle. Second-stage owners should check out "Home Equity Credit Lines" and "Refinancing Your Home," which clearly explain the financial meat behind the fluffy TV spots promising to end payment worries with a second mortgage. Worksheets

are included to help figure out if refinancing is the best solution. Senior citizens with plenty of house but no cash to speak of might be fascinated to learn about "Reverse Mortgages," which allow them to gain monthly stipends, credit lines, or lump sums by taking an uninsured reverse mortgage. Pay it off at death or sale... or finance forward in a regular mortgage again.
COMPUSERVE *go* consumer's forum→Banking and Credit Libraries
WEB http://www.ftc.gov/bcp/conline/pubs/homes /homes.htm

▼ The perfect house

Coldwell Banker Finding the right home is complicated, but Coldwell Banker helps frustrated home buyers with this virtual real-estate agent. A specialized search engine, now common on real-estate sites, lets customers enter the desired location, price range, and minimum number of bedrooms, and the program responds with a semi-illustrated list of available properties. Plus, an assortment of articles weighs in on buying or selling a house, and a calculator determines how much your current castle would sell for in another city.
WEB http://www.coldwellbanker.com

Home Online If imagination is not your strong suit, you can download the most popular home plans at this site, and find out which manufacturers provide the best materials for your future castle. You can also pick the brains of other readers for money-saving tips, or meet them in real-time online events. The message center covers a variety of issues, from listings of the best sources of Victorian and Celtic wallpaper designs to discussions of synthetic building materials, environmentally conscious design solutions, and cost-efficient solar energy.
AMERICA ONLINE *keyword* home design

Homes & Land Yes, this is the same free magazine you can pick up in the foyer of your local diner or supermarket. But don't let that discourage you; the searchable listings for sales and rentals are extensive—*Homes & Land* claims to have the largest online database of available properties, with more than 200,000 retrievable listings. Another option is to search for the names of local real estate agents. But there are other nifty gizmos to entertain you, such as software to track your mortgage, a personal relocation guide, and more than a dozen home finance calculators.
WEB http://www.homes.com/

RE/MAX Real Estate Network Up, up, and away goes that RE/MAX hot air balloon, just like in the commercials on television. And off you go from this attractive home page to get a smattering of mortgage information, tips on choosing a realtor, and a giant database of home listings from all over the country via HomeWEB. Search by location and price range—most homes have a picture, and you can contact the agent right on the page.
WEB http://www.remax.com/

Get real estate online
http://www.remax.com/

Chapter 23
Buying Insurance

Apply for insurance online and you'll never have to bother with door-to-door agents again

AMERICANS SPEND MORE than $11 trillion a year on individual life insurance coverage, according to the American Council of Life Insurance. The average amount of life insurance per household has risen from $5,000 to $111,600, with 78 percent of Americans holding policies. The Life and Health Insurance Foundation for Education projects that more than $200 billion will be paid out to policy holders by life insurance companies during 1996.

Improve Your Quality

Only one problem: Close to 100 percent of individual life insurance policies are sold by commissioned, life insurance agents—those pesky, sorry-to-bother-you-again-at-dinner types. The solution? Cyberspace. Simply supply the Web with the same information you'd divulge to an agent, get quotes on policies, and apply for insurance online.

A year ago, commissioned agents were the only choice available to consumers shopping for life insurance. There simply were no easy alternatives to the brief-case-wielding salesman. In the spring of 1996, however, the Supreme Court ruled that banks could compete with traditional insurance companies and offer policies to their customers. Hundreds of banks took the court up on its offer. Investment brokers like Charles Schwab also began to sell life insurance directly to customers, bypassing commissioned agents. Many of these institutions and third-party rating systems put free information about life insurance policies on the Web. The Net-savvy insurance buyer is now free to go online, get quotes, and compare policies from different providers.

CASH REGISTER

LIFE-Line
WEB http://www.life-line.org/sitel.cgi

The 60-Second Selector
WEB http://www.insuremarket.com/basics/life/ltql.htm

Allstate Needs Analysis Worksheet
WEB http://www.allstate.com/evergreen/needs/life/analysis.html

# of Life Insurance

You should first learn how to find a policy that meets your needs at **LIFE-Line**, which has a calculator to help you determine how much insurance you should be buying. Then you can locate a premium in your price range using any of the online quote services and apply for and purchase the life insurance, often at the same site. The entire transaction can't be done online — urine and blood samples as well as signed documents are often required, but the process provides a faster turn-around (no scheduling meetings with agents) and more privacy. Remember: Just as there are shifty salespeople offline, there are also insurance scams online. Before you buy, make sure the agent is reputable.

Whole or term life?
http://www.life-line.org/site1.cgi

The bulk of insurance offered over the Internet is term life, a relatively straightforward type of life insurance providing only a death benefit (no cash-in options) and good for only a specified period of time. Term life, as opposed to the popular whole life policies which can be carried indefinitely and build up a cash value, is recommended by many consumer groups because it offers a lot of coverage for little money. There's also an online advantage to buying term life: It requires little or no consultation, so you'll be able to complete much more of the process online. If you're not sure what kind of insurance to buy, try **The 60-Second Selector** for a quick answer, then consult the in-depth explanations at any of the many insurance sites on the Web.

❝ What's next? How about a new kind of agent—the software, not the human kind? ❞

What's next? How about a new kind of agent—the software, not the human kind? The insurance industry is waiting for (and developing) agenting technology sophisticated enough to learn about a customer, then recommend policy options; or anticipate a customer's confusion, then explain the issues in language that the customer understands. These programs will take to a whole new level the worksheets, such as the **Allstate Needs Analysis Worksheet**, that now ask the customer a few questions about their life insurance needs and then return recommendations for how much life insurance they should purchase. For now, though, individuals can save money and time by using the free online life insurance quote and information services that follow.

▼ Starting points

Insurance and Risk Management Central's Advice for Consumers Page It's not the prettiest site, and some links are outdated, but the variety of the insurance choices here make this an extremely worthwhile stop on an Web insurance safari. Find out how long you'll live with the Longevity Game, learn about living wills, life insurance, and other fun stuff.
WEB http://www.irmcentral.com/persadvi.html

Insurance Marketplace Click on the name of your state, and the type of insurance you want (choose from everything from auto to viatical) and get a list of online insurers. It's that simple, and although the lists of insurers are never long, the smoothness of the process is what makes this site worth a visit. If you're interested in other financial matters such as consumer credit or securities, just dig deeper into the National Financial Services Network hub.
WEB http://www.nfsn.com/Insure.htm

Insurance News Network Operating on the theory that more information is always better than less, the editors of Insurance News Network are committed to providing overwhelming amounts of content on every kind of insurance. An insurance glossary, frequent news updates, consumer-oriented features, and plenty of information organized by state is just the appetizer at INN. For dinner? Try Standard & Poor's reports on major insurance policy providers, with an insurance-links sundae for dessert.
WEB http://www.insure.com

LIFE-Line The Life and Health Insurance Foundation for Education has created an online introductory guide to insurance. You can consult the glossary, use the calculator to figure out how much insurance you should be buying, learn what to look for in an insurance agent (assuming you're going to buy your insurance offline), and even link to sites created to help keep you healthy.
WEB http://www.life-line.org/site1.cgi

NerdWorld Insurance This A to Z of insurance links is mostly made up of smallish, state-level policy providers, but the fairly detailed descriptions of the sites are more helpful than many similar indexes. Still, for real content and substance, seek elsewhere. NerdWorld neither has, nor claims to have, anything but links.
WEB http://www.tiac.net/users/dstein/nwl83.html

Quicken's Insuremarket Insurance made sweet and simple. Quicken's well advertised site walks you through the decisions you'll need to make when buying insurance (what types, how much, how costly). Visitors can take advantage of the site's free calculators, insurance explanations, links to pages for major insurance companies

Quicken's done it again!
https://wwws.insuremarket.com

FEEL THE EARTH MOVE

Do I need earthquake coverage? How can I get it? Direct damages due to earthquakes are not covered under the standard homeowners insurance policy. However, unless you live in an area that is prone to earthquakes, you probably do not need this coverage. If you do live in a part of the country with high earthquake activity you may want to consider adding an earthquake endorsement to your homeowners insurance policy. This endorsement will cover damages due to earthquakes, landslides, volcanic eruptions and other earth movements.

—from Homeowners Insurance Questions

like MetLife, real-time quotes on insurance policies, policy information, and purchase options.
WEB https://wwws.insuremarket.com

The Chubb Corporation: Insurance Library One of the top five largest insurance companies in the world has provided this handy little library of articles and links on all aspects of insurance. The articles are less about types of insurance, like those of other sites, and more about preventive measures consumers can use to keep insurance costs down and property safe. Topics range from "Is Your Home Alone? Loss Prevention In Your Absence!" to tips for businesses wishing to prevent theft (presumably, that would be all businesses).
WEB http://www.chubb.com/library.html

▼ Definitions

The Complete Glossary of Insurance Coverage Explanations This is a site with an overcompli-

cated title and a not-for-the-dopey-consumer glossary. Many of the defined terms are clauses that appear in standard insurance policies, like "debris removal" or "selling price." Now you'll know just what it is that you're signing.
WEB http://www.lcgroup.com/explanations/

▼ Health insurance

Health Care Financing Administration This federal agency, part of the Department of Health and Human Services, is responsible for the administration of the Medicare and Medicaid programs. These government health insurance programs benefit 72 million recipients, and it can be nearly impossible for those recipients to keep up with changes in the programs. The HCFA Web site is designed for both consumers and health care providers, and contains handbooks, legal and regulatory updates, and statistics and data with both audiences in mind.
WEB http://www.hcfa.gov

Medical Expense (Health) Insurance Questions What's a copayment for? How do you know what's covered under your health insurance plan and what isn't? What if there's a gap between what's covered and your costs? Find out answers to questions like these by reading this FAQ.
WEB http://www.insweb.com/main/07-faq/hea-qu.htm

▼ Home insurance

Homeowners Insurance Questions Insurance, like philosophy or differential calculus, is one of those topics that gets more confusing the more you learn about it. This FAQ on homeowners insurance answers all of the questions a confused insurance shopper might have. Learn how to lower your homeowners policy costs, and all about the different clauses and

subclauses you're bound to run into.
WEB http://www.insweb.com/main/07-faq/iho-qu.htm

The Insurance Information Institute The collected publications of the Insurance Information Institute seek to boost the public's understanding of property and casualty insurance—not only the economic theory behind the risk industry, but the legal regulations confining insurance companies. Consumers can read general brochures on such topics as "Home Security Basics" and "Insurance for Your House and Personal Possessions," as well as find out about an insurance helpline.
WEB http://www.iii.org/consumer.htm

Six Ways to Save on Homeowner's Insurance This is a super, must-read article, part of Pathfinder's Money Online. If you aren't already following the numerous suggestions outlined here, you should be. For example, remembering not to overinsure your home is important. Sale value is not what you should go by, since the land is a large part of the value and is virtually indestructible by fire. More seemingly obvious tips will make you say, "Why didn't I think of that?"
WEB http://pathfinder.com/money/saveon/1996/homeins.html

▼ Life insurance

BudgetLife Looking for term life insurance? BudgetLife provides the insurance-purchasing public with a continually updated list of low-cost term life-insurance rates. For a table of annual premiums for $250,000 death benefit term life insurance, choose from preferred male, preferred female, standard male, or standard female. You'll get a free quote from any of the companies listed. There's a list of online agents who can answer your questions, and advice for selecting a life-insurance agent who can help you put together the best

possible protection plan for your specific needs.
WEB http://www.budgetlife.com

InsWeb Consumer Center InsWeb offers everything from short-term health insurance to auto insurance to wedding insurance (which protects your financial investment in that special day from everything except a change of heart). It's also one of the best places to shop for life insurance. Answer a few simple questions and InsWeb will provide you with an instant term life insurance quote from Zurich Kemper Life (not currently available for residents of Iowa, New York, New Jersey, or South Carolina). If you prefer to buy life insurance from a local company or if your state is not yet covered by Zurich, the site lets you select an agent in your area who will review the information you submit online and contact you with a quote. InsWeb also offers insurance-related FAQs, glossaries, and statistics.
WEB http://www.insweb.com/main/01-ci/default.htm

You're a good policyholder, Charlie Brown
http://www.metlife.com/

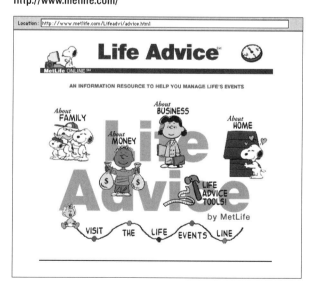

SIX BASIC POLICIES

There are six basic kinds of home insurance policies and they're pretty much the same regardless of where you live (except for Texas). They tend to be defined by the perils they cover:

- HO-I: Basic homeowner stuff. Covers your dwelling and personal property against losses from II types of perils: fire or lightning; windstorm or hail; explosion; riot or civil commotion; aircraft; vehicles; smoke; vandalism or malicious mischief; theft; damage by glass or safety glazing material that is part of a building; and volcanic eruption.

- HO-2: Basic homeowner stuff plus. Covers dwelling and personal property against II perils plus six more: falling objects; weight of ice, snow or sleet; three categories of water-related damage from home utilities or appliances and electrical surge damage.

- HO-3: Extended or special homeowner stuff. Covers I7 stated perils plus any other peril NOT specified in the policy, except for flood, earthquake, war and nuclear accident.

- HO-4: Renters coverage. Covers personal property only from I7 listed perils.

- HO-6: Condominium owner coverage. Covers personal property only from I7 listed perils.

- HO-8: Basic older home stuff. Covers dwelling and personal property from II perils. Differs from HO-I in that it covers repairs or actual cash values—not rebuilding costs. For homes where some historic or architectural aspects make the home's replacement cost significantly higher than its market value.

—*from Insurance News Network*

MetLife Online You know the drill: When you're hanging from a cliff by your fingernails, MetLife, in the form of Snoopy, will come to your rescue with rappelling gear and a friendly yodel. MetLife Online is a cartoon-filled but immensely helpful site. An FAQ for MetLife's life insurance policies, a local representative finder, and a glossary are among the offerings, along with a super page called Life Advice, for all those little milestones along your life's rocky climb. It's like your mom. Like your mom if she were an insurance company. Above all, like your mom if she always gave good advice, and carried Snoopy around with her.
WEB http://www.metlife.com/

Prudential: Life Insurance Planning Your piece of the rock can protect your family in case something happens to you—like if you're hit by a falling piece of rock, for example. Bone up on the fundamentals of life insurance here. Find out how much you need, and what kind of insurance you should get. Then hook up with a local Prudential representative. Beware biased sources, however—there's no mention here that you might not need life insurance at all.
WEB http://www.prudential.com/life/index.html

What You Should Know About Buying Life Insurance The Consumer Information Center comes through again with another great, if a little bit simple-minded, pamphlet. It will teach you everything you need to know before you begin to shop for life insurance, and while you're in the process of choosing a policy provider. What should you ask an insurance agent? What's the difference between term policies and permanent ones? One caveat: The pamphlet doesn't address the vast numbers of people for whom life insurance is a waste of money.
WEB http://www.pueblo.gsa.gov/acli/index.htm

Zurich Direct If you're healthy and support a healthy lifestyle, you may be eligible for the highly competitive insurance rates at Zurich Direct. From the company's Web site, you can read about its policies, get online quotes if you qualify, and buy the insurance.

WEB http://www.zurichdirect.com/

▼ Quotes

4 Insurance.com Here's a simple way to get quotes for the type of commercial or personal insurance you need from a number of insurance agents in your state. It's an easy click-through process, and filling out one short form can allow you to contact as many of the listed agents as you'd like for further info. A renewal reminder service will send you a note when it's time to renew your insurance, and if you sign up, you might win a free year of auto insurance. (Naturally, you can find out how much that prize might be worth here.)

WEB http://www.4insurance.com/

AccuQuote Free stuff is good. Free stuff that's really good is even better. AccuQuote is a free service that provides life insurance quotes for several hundred providers. As an insurance broker, the company hopes that you will purchase the quoted insurance policy through AccuQuote, but the quote service otherwise is obligation-free. Simply provide your vitals in an email form or call the 800 number—or spend some extra time tooling around the various FAQ's and calculators the site also provides.

WEB http://www.accuquote.com/irnindex.htm

InsuranceQuote Services InsuranceQuote Services operates a free, computerized databank of low-cost term insurance policies from better insurance companies, most rated "A+" (superior) by A.M. Best. Enter your age, sex, smoking habits, and the amount of coverage you'd

like in the online form. If you believe yourself to be in superior health and you lead a low-risk lifestyle, you can request preferred rates. Quotes will be forwarded by mail the next business day, along with company safety ratings, plan descriptions, and a guide to understanding life insurance. They promise not to hound you with high-pressure salespeople (you don't even have to give your phone number). Should you decide to purchase a policy, the issuing company pays InsuranceQuote for its efforts. Quotes are available for coverage from $50,000 to $1 million.

WEB http://www.iquote.com/IQuote/iquote.html

QuickQuote QuickQuote lets customers search a database of more than 1,500 term life plans for free. They also offer instant online quotes and comparisons of the best insurance values from top carriers. Select your preferred amount ($100,000 to $3 million), term (5, 10, 15, or 20 years), and payment plan (monthly, quarterly, semi-annually, or annually), then enter your personal data. QuickQuote will return a list of providers and quotes matching your criteria. An insurance estimator is available if you don't know how much coverage you need. You can apply for the policy at the site. Information is also available in Spanish.

WEB http://www.quickquote.com

QuoteSmith Corporation QuoteSmith offers an online service that compares policies offered by term life insurers. Choose coverage from $150,000 to $5 million and an initial rate guaranteed for 10, 15, or 20 years; answer a few questions; then instantly check the rates and coverages of more than 130 term life companies. The service lists the cheapest policies based on sex, age, and smoking status. Click on the company names returned in the search for more detailed ratings, benefit analysis, cost analysis data, and an application.

WEB http://www.quotesmith.com

Chapter 24
Planning for Retirement

You can't work till death. Here's how to plan for the carefree golden years

I T'S HARD ENOUGH to decide what to do on Friday night. Imagine how difficult it is to plan for retirement. But just about every financial advisor on earth agrees that the only way to grow old without going broke is to start saving early. And that means retirement savings plans. But working out your financial future can mean battling a dangerous alliance of acronyms, jargon, and arcana—401(k), IRA, rollover, distribution, and calculations centered around the mystical age of 59½. Conquer your fears by starting at **COMFIN's glossary of terms**, then follow our quick guide to the two most popular retirement plans—the employer-sponsored 401(k) and the generally available IRA.

Taking It With You

The 401(k): Your Employer Giveth, the IRS Taketh Away

While both 401(k) and IRA plans offer tax exemptions on the money you save, 401(k) plans have several advantages over IRAs. **A Primer on 401(k) Plans** is part of a great general guide to **Understanding and Controlling Your Finances** from Interface Technologies, Inc. Its **401(k) value calculator** (requires Netscape 2.0 or better) estimates how much you should be saving based on your salary, savings percent, and rate of return.

Fidelity Investments' Workplace Savings FAQ explains not only the 401(k) but its variations, such as the 403(b) plan for employees of non-profit organizations. If your company's 401(k) plan is managed by Fidelity, you may be able to check your account and transfer funds directly over the Internet—check with your employer for details. Stop by The Vanguard Group for hints on **Retirement Planning: Getting the Most From Your Employer's Retirement Plan**. And you wouldn't want to pick a retirement plan without getting the details from the horse's mouth; check out the IRS's **Tax Topic 425**. Topic 425 introduces the basics of 401(k) plans and links to the fine print about withdrawing your money.

Don't get backed into a corner at retirement
http://www.frontier-news.com/retire/home.htm

Location: http://www.frontier-news.com/retire/home.htm

CASH REGISTER

IRA Corner
WEB http://www.frontier-news.com
/retire/home.htm

IRA FAQ
WEB http://www.vanguard.com/educ
/lib/retire/faqira.html

Frequently Asked Questions About IRAs
WEB http://www.prusec.com/ira.htm

Tax Topic 451
WEB http://www.irs.ustreas.gov/prod
/tax_edu/teletax/tc451.html

"Is Now the Time for You to Set Up an IRA?"
WEB http://www.frontier-news.com
/retire/ciral.htm

IRA Calculator
WEB http://iddmz3.iddis.com
/smithbarney/iracalc.html

Don't Just Sit There—Invest Something!

I say Individual Retirement Account. You say Individual Retirement Arrangement. Let's put the whole thing into mutual funds. Anagrammatic disagreement aside, anyone can start an IRA, and anyone can start researching IRA options online. Frontier Business News' **IRA Corner** is a comprehensive, covering IRA basics thoroughly and introducing readers to advanced topics like rollover and conduit IRAs. The Vanguard Group, on the other hand, has a good 30-question **IRA FAQ** while the Prudential Securities site includes **Frequently Asked Questions About IRAs**, a document that reviews the ins and outs of retirement savings and taxation.

Because IRAs are more confusing than 401(k) plans—there are many more options, and picking the right plan can be difficult—you might also want to consider visiting the Internal Revenue Service's IRA resources.

> **" I say Individual Retirement Account. You say Individual Retirement Arrangement. Let's put the whole thing into mutual funds. "**

Tax Topic 451 is a straightforward summary. Once you understand IRAs, Frontier's online interview called **"Is Now the Time for You to Set Up an IRA?"** can help you decide if it's time to start saving. Even a few minutes spent in the grip of Smith Barney's **IRA Calculator** drives home the point that saving money takes time—quite a bit of time. Start now.

▼ Starting points

Life's Financial Concerns—Retirement Planning A friendly guide to the fears and concerns of all potential retirees, this site is a product of Prudential Securities. The section called "Did You Know..." explodes the not-too-prevalent myth that Social Security is a monthly retirement package buffet. Instead, the articles urge you to invest in 401(k) plans, to plan carefully in the present with an eye to the future, and to depend on nothing except the pennies you've saved.
WEB http://www.prusec.com/retrl.htm

MoneyWhiz: Retirement Planning Come here with your retirement questions. Why? Because there are articles explaining everything from the mysterious 401 (k) retirement plan to Social Security issues. Check out the Retirement FAQ before you dive into the chat forum—members have already asked and answered questions about the number of times an IRA account may be changed each year, the rules about taxing Social Security, and all about life insurance. If you still can't find what you're looking for, or you want to investigate further, visit the MoneyWhiz retirement planning bulletin board, and trade tips and concerns with other retirees and potential retirees.
AMERICA ONLINE *keyword* moneywhiz→MoneyWhiz Finance Center→Retirement Planning

Planning for Retirement: Money Online "Whether you're 25, 75, or any age in between, this package can help you plan a comfortable future," declares the opening paragraph to this large retirement area, which is part of *Money* magazine's Web site. So if you're craving a comfortable dotage, come play with the toys at Planning for Retirement, which range from editorial (articles about living comfortably on a modest income) to mathematical (a Retirement Calculator that helps figure the costs of long life).
WEB http://pathfinder.com/money/features/retire/index.htm

Retirement: T. Rowe Price Social Security is part of the answer for retirement, but not the entire solution—as any retiree knows, money saved in youth pays the greatest dividends in old age. The science of saving is only one of the topics discussed in this walk-through of retirement planning information, which is sponsored by mutual fund giant T. Rowe Price. Find out, with the assistance of some handy calculators, how much you know and how much you'll need to save. If you can't get all the information you need from the site, there's always the convenient email literature request form.
WEB http://www.troweprice.com/retirement/index.html

RetireWeb Reirement isn't the same everywhere, especially when it comes to government policies toward withheld incomes, taxes, and so forth. That's why the world needs more services like RetireWeb, which investigates the financial implications of retirement

---

It's a bit safer than stuffing money into your mattress
http://www.prusec.com/index.htm

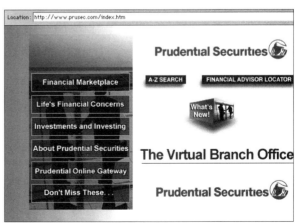

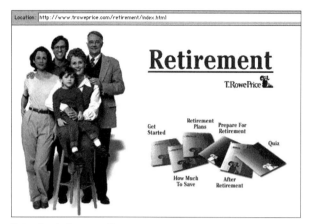

Get online before your time
http://www.troweprice.com/retirement/index.html

for Canadians. The site includes documents, links, and calculators that can help you figure out how big a nest egg you're going to need before you can start spending your weekdays on the golf course.
WEB http://www.retireweb.com

▼ Senior life

Retirement Living Forum The retirement advice in CompuServe's senior citizens forum is divided into two sections. First, there are the libraries, which contain a wealth of information for downloading, and divide those files by topic—there's the Pension Rights Center, with its files on pension plans and the Employee Retirement Income Security Act (ERISA); H&R Block's tax information for seniors; primers on Mutual Funds and IRAs; and extensive Social Security libraries filled with useful programs on benefit calculation, disability and survivor benefits, and benefit adjustments. Once you've collected the necessary documents from the library, visit the forum, in which participants post questions about retirement and are answered by online experts and other wired retirees.
COMPUSERVE *go* senior

Senior Resource Senior Resource offers advice for senior citizens on housing and lifestyle choices and how to plan and pay for them. However, the service is peppered with hidden advertisements. To avoid them, skim the top level of the site, which surveys a number of hypothetical lifestyle choices (senior day care, mobile home community, condominium, etc.). Next, move to the finance section, which is chock full of useful information on options like the one-time $125,000 Federal Exemption and Reverse Mortgages plan. Then read the insurance section for a general list of what is covered by Medicare A and B, and for things to look for when buying supplemental insurance and/or auto insurance. The site is sponsored by Barbara Krueger & Associates, an online company that markets specifically to seniors.
WEB http://www.seniorresource.com

Figure out how big a nest egg you'll need before you start spending weekdays on the golf course.

▼ Investing

Fidelity: Investing for Retirement Although this site is one long commercial for Fidelity, it manages to cover the basics about retirement investing along the way. Learn about IRAs, and how to choose the best retirement plan. Also, consider annuities, and plug some numbers into the Retirement Savings Calculator to see how your savings stack up. There's also a special section for the self-employed.
WEB http://personal.fidelity.com/decisions/invest _retirement.html

Investor Education Just when you think the whole Web is a useless TV commercial, you find a site like this. Sure, it's corporate, sponsored by the Vanguard Group. But the breadth and depth of the resources will have you wondering why "corporate" was ever a dirty word. Set yourself on the road toward silver-haired solvency with a series of online courses from the Vanguard Online University, offered in topics like mutual funds and taxation and retirement investing. Browse the giant online library of articles and in-depth guides, which run the gamut of investment topics. Then hole up in the Vanguard Online Laboratory, where you can play for hours with the Java-based retirement calculator.
WEB http://www.vanguard.com/educ/inveduc.html

▼ Taxes

ComFin It's never too early to start saving for those all-important retirement years, and ComFin gives clear and useful advice on beating the taxman through the marvelous scam—er, "shelter"—of tax-deferred savings plans. Did you know that by enrolling in a 401(k) plan, you can save $100 with an outlay of only $72 in income (that's presuming you're in the 28 percent tax bracket, of course). Learn this—and much more—at ComFin, and make sure that when you're an old bird your nest is properly feathered.
WEB http://www.comfin.com/

The Copeland Companies Visit Copeland for this invaluable library of tax and retirement planning articles. You won't find many bells and whistles here, just good information culled from a variety of reliable news sources. Article titles include "Childhood Stories Shape Your Savings Habits" and "Investing Strategies To Stretch Your Retirement Income."
WEB http://www.copeland.com/retnews.htm

Depression Babies

If you were born in the 1930s, you may have the time, and the money, to spend freely on yourself and your grandchildren—but tend to be a heavy saver. A conservative upbringing may make you wary of risk. With Social Security benefits, widespread pension plans and your savings, you have bright retirement prospects. Including stocks and mutual funds in your portfolio can help guard against inflation—and leave you with plenty to bank on for the future. Baby Boomers—many of you were blessed with your parents' prosperity and developed a strong sense of individualism. You were raised in an era of economic growth and increased expectations.

If you are one of the Boomers whose savings are straggling, invest in your TSA and other long-term vehicles. This tax-deferred investing is a great way to jump-start your savings and decrease your current taxable income to the federal government.

—*from The Copeland Companies*

▼ Organizations

American Association of Retired Persons The American Association of Retired Persons, one of the nation's most influential lobbies and a powerful voice on behalf of the elderly, isn't only concerned about money, but the organization recognizes that money is never far from the minds of retired persons. On the AARP's AOL bulletin board, seniors discuss the difficult business of surviving on a fixed income in the '90s. In the Finance section, a middle-aged man warns others about an investment scam that bilked his mother out of her hard-earned savings. Elsewhere, a retiree wants to stay active, and asks if remaining employed will reduce his Social Security payments. The

SECURITY BLANKET

Q: I will be 62 on August 2 of this year and that's when I plan on retiring. Will my first benefit check be for the month of August or September?

A: Since you were born on the first or second day of the month, you will be eligible the month you were born—August. But, in most cases, Social Security retirement benefits do not begin the month the person reaches 62; benefits usually begin the following month. To receive retirement benefits, you must be at least age 62 for the entire month. But, the law says that you "attain" your age the day before your birthday. Since you were born on August 2, you legally attain your age on August I; therefore you're eligible for benefits for August because you're considered 62 for the entire month.

Q: My neighbor, who is retired, told me that the income he receives from his part-time job at the local nursery gives him an increase in his Social Security benefits. Is that right?

A: People who return to work after they start receiving benefits may be able to receive a higher benefit based on those earnings. This is because Social Security automatically recomputes the benefit amount after the additional earnings are credited to the individual's earnings record.

Q: I think Social Security is a rip off compared to a private retirement plan I have. Can I drop out?

A: No. Social Security coverage is mandatory. But consider this: Unlike your private plan, Social Security provides disability and survivors coverage in addition to retirement benefits. And Social Security generally offers greater protection for family members than private pensions.

—from Social Security Online

American Association of Retired Persons's Web site is quite similar in content to the AOL forum, although it relies more on informative documents and resources than on interactive chat.

AMERICA ONLINE *keyword* aarp
WEB http://www.aarp.org/

Social Security Online The Social Security Administration furnishes a good deal of information about its programs at this site. To keep on top of Congress' constant adjustments of benefits, the government publishes a news summary with details of all cost of living increases, along with the complete text of all Social Security legislation, such as the Social Security Domestic Employee Reform Act of 1994 (remember Nannygate?). After you've reviewed the documents and requested your Personal Earnings and Benefits Estimate Statement (PEBES) online, don't forget to peruse the SSA's newsletter, which is filled with research articles on all aspects of retirement in America.

WEB http://www.ssa.gov

▼ Software

Retirement Planner Software What software will help you plan your retirement? Not the latest shoot-'em-up game, certainly. But this piece of software can help you feather your future nest, primarily because it's concerned less with shooting armored enemies, and more with developing a savings strategy for your 401(k) plan. You can use a simplified version of the program right on the Web; input the financial details about your current retirement arrangement, click a button, and instantly find out whether you're saving enough to meet your retirement goals. If you're not, the program offers helpful suggestions for changing your savings habits.

WEB http://www.torrid-tech.com/retire/

PART 6
Spend Your Money

YOU'VE WORKED HARD for your money. You know where every penny is being spent, and your taxes are a manageable burden. Maybe you even made a killing on the market. It's time to go buy yourself something nice. Avoid the crowded malls and shop online. You'll find all the brand names you want, plus unique items available only on the Web. Go ahead and charge up a storm. If you use your credit card, a federal act protects you from fraud. But if you happen to run into a shady business online, the Net's consumer resources can help you recover what's due.

Using your credit card online is safe —but not for the reasons you might think

SOME STATISTICS: In 1995, Americans spent almost $500 million shopping for goods and services on the Internet. About $200 million of that was spent shopping on commercial services like AOL and CompuServe. Last year, consumer spending online approached $1 billion, and by the year 2000 it's expected to top $6 billion. Some say it could reach $400 billion. That's a lot of zeros.

Everyone's pretty excited about shopping in cyberspace, but if you've never done it before, you may have some reservations, especially if you've been reading the latest media reports about privacy and security on the Internet.

Put It on My Web Charge

What's the Fuss About Credit Card Safety?

The incidence of credit card fraud on the Internet is only about 1.5 percent, which is significantly lower than the 4 or 5 percent fraud rate via telephone. That's probably because not many criminals have figured out how to commit credit card fraud online. What credit card companies fear most is the enormous potential for fraud, and when computers are involved, the potential increases exponentially. Just ask Kevin Mitnick, who with a few deft keystrokes swiped 20,000 credit card numbers from computer systems around the country.

This is why most credit card companies discourage consumers from sending credit card numbers over the Net: They, not you, are liable for the money lost. The exception is AT&T, which has such confidence in the demographics of the Internet—netsurfers are smarter, richer, and more educated than everyone else—that it publicly guarantees the safety of online transactions conducted with its Universal Card.

Secure Browsers

There are several methods in the works that promise to ensure the security of sensitive information sent across

CASH REGISTER

EIT's S-HTTP
WEB http://www.eit.com/projects
/s-http/index.html

Netscape SSL
WEB http://www.netscape.com/info
/security-doc.html

SET
WEB http://www.mastercard.com/set
/set.htm

MasterCard
WEB http://www.mastercard.com/

Visa Expo
WEB http://www.visa.com/

Sometimes you just want that extra bit of protection
http://www.eit.com/projects/s-http/index.html

Location: http://www.eit.com/projects/s-http/index.html

Transaction security is a critical factor in the establishment and acceptance of commercial applications on the Internet. For example, if you are using a home banking service, you want to be assured that your transactions are both confidential and untampered. Additionally, both you and your bank need the ability to verify each other's identity and to produce auditable records of your transactions.

Survey Says

According to the 2nd Study of Internet Commerce, conducted in Winter 1995-96 by Global Concepts on behalf of MasterCard International:

▶ 27 percent of those surveyed bought something online

▶ 88 percent of those who bought something paid for it by credit card

▶ 36 percent of the buyers who used a credit card sent their account info over the Internet encrypted

▶ 37 percent of the buyers who used a credit card sent their account info over the Internet unencrypted

▶ 13 percent of the buyers who used a credit card sent their account info to the merchant offline

▶ 35 percent of the buyers who used a credit card sent their account info by phone or fax

▶ 10 percent of those who bought something mailed in a check to pay for it

▶ 5 percent of those who bought something issued a check upon delivery

▶ 1 percent of those who bought something paid cash on delivery

▶ 0 percent used digital cash

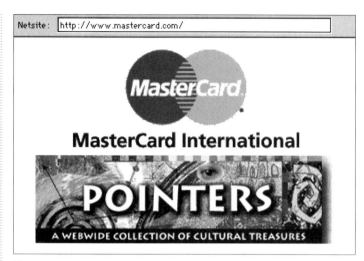

Master your credit card spending
http://www.mastercard.com

the open networks of the Internet. Two already in place are **EIT's S-HTTP**, or Secure Hypertext Transport Protocol (you know the site you're visiting provides it if the URL changes to "https://..." when you attempt to send sensitive info) and **Netscape's SSL** or Secure Sockets Layer (if it's active at the site you're visiting, the little golden key in the lower left hand corner of your Netscape browser will become unbroken).

But the world of online commerce has special needs. The major credit card companies (MasterCard, Visa, and American Express) and industry big guns (GTE, IBM, Microsoft, Netscape, SAIC, Terisa Systems, and Verisign) have joined together to work toward a standardized and even more secure protocol called **SET** (Secure Electronic Transactions), which is specifically designed to protect financial information in its online journey from consumer to merchant to financial institution. SET promises to create a safe environment for online transactions by using digital certification and 1,024-bit encryption. According to Steve Mott, senior vice-president of Electronic Commerce at MasterCard

International, "SET provides a standard system of authentication between merchants, issuing banks, and customers." It's an attempt to "duplicate the interoperability of real-world transactions." Critics say that SET is "vaporware," that the security it affords is merely a matter of perception. Others say that the SET encryption level is stronger than the code used to protect nuclear missiles, and is totally unnecessary. Clearly, there are many questions still to be answered.

Until the SET protocol is fully operational, the Web sites of both **MasterCard** and **Visa** recommend that consumers not send their credit card numbers over the Net; they suggest that you send your account info by phone or fax. Transactions conducted on the commercial services, however, are considered safe, perhaps even safer than credit card transactions over the phone, because the commercial services are password-protected private networks. The Net, on the other hand, is an open network. Anything can happen.

What the credit card companies don't say, however, is that security is more of an issue for the merchants and

It's everywhere you want to be, even on the Net
http://www.visa.com

The Ins and Outs of Internet Crime and Credit Card Fraud

▶ **Digicrime, Inc.**
The brilliance of this "full service computer hacking organization" is that it satirizes Internet vulnerabilities while imparting very real information. The employees of Digicrime find exploitable weaknesses, invent accompanying scams, and taunt users with the lucrative-sounding, all-too-real possibilities.
WEB http://www.digicrime.com

▶ **Credit Card Fraud Technique**
Getting the credit card number of an unsuspecting individual is the easy part. Ordering merchandise without overextending the credit limit and having the stuff delivered to a place where it's safe for you to pick it up is the hard part. Whatever you do, try not to order anything that costs more than $200 or you may end up going to jail for grand theft.
WEB http://www.echotech.com/ccfraud.htm

GET SET

When the other "person" is merely a blip on a computer screen, how do you know they hold a valid account? How do you know you can trust a merchant you've never actually seen? After all, the merchant's "store" may exist only on a fraudster's hard drive. And, how can a "real" merchant feel comfortable accepting a Visa card account number without some form of identification?

For electronic commerce to flourish on the Internet, all parties need a way of verifying each other's identities—and establishing trust. The new **SET** standard put forth by Visa and MasterCard address all of these issues. **SET** will make shopping via the Internet as safe and easy as using a Visa card in your local mall.

PLEASE NOTE: Until now there has been no readily available, secure way to prevent fraud or theft when giving out a Visa card number or other sensitive information over an open network, such as the Internet. For this reason, we strongly encourage consumers, merchants, and financial institutions to avoid using Visa card accounts over open networks until there is a secure transaction system in place.

—*from Visa International*

card companies than for consumers. Merchants stand to benefit most from SET, because the ability to verify customers means they're more likely to get paid. At the individual consumer level, there's not much at stake except $50 and a little inconvenience. Even Mott admits, "I personally have been buying stuff over the Net for a year and a half. But I use my Visa card."

Charge Ahead

The risks involved in transmitting your credit card information online are real. But before you put your credit card away, remember the bottom line: Regardless of whether you make your credit card purchase in person, by phone, or over the Internet, you are protected by the Fair Credit Billing Act. Specifically:

- You have the right to dispute charges on your credit card statements if you believe the charge was made illegally or in error (for example, if the merchant charged the wrong amount or you were dissatisfied with the service or product received).

- As long as the charge is in dispute, you don't have to pay it and you will not incur finance charges for it. However, your credit card company will usually make you put your complaint in writing and work with the merchant to resolve the dispute.

- The Fair Credit Billing Act protects you from credit card fraud. In the event that your card number is lost or stolen, you can be held liable for only up to $50 of any unauthorized charges that are made. And if you report the card before it is used, you won't be liable for any of the charges at all.

▼ Malls

Access Market Square Access Market Square helps you feel the mall-ness of it all with little pictures of a hypothetical futuristic mall scattered here and there. This is a low-rent, low-concept kind of mall that hosts about 100 stores, all of them small, independent retailers. But you'll find selections in a full range of categories, from art to music to toys. A few monthly giveaway contests liven things up a little.
WEB http://www.icw.com/ams.html

The American Cybermall You won't find frilly merchandise at the American Cybermall, aside from some nifty American flags waving in the cyberwind. (Zen koan: Is the flag moving, or is the wind moving? The Java is moving.) Though it's not very aesthetically appealing, the Cybermall is a functional, efficient site that brings together an eclectic group of online stores in categories that include Aviation, Pets and Animals, and Travel and Tourism. The real problem here? Half the categories are still empty, or contain only one or two sites. Maybe in a few months, Cybermall will put some meat on those bare bones.
WEB http://www.usacm.com

Anet Virtual Mall There's nothing particularly special about the Anet Virtual Mall, but there's nothing especially wrong with it, either: It has links to more than 100 of the bigger names in Web commerce, minus the flashy graphics usually associated with them. Anet tries to make itself a little more full-service by sponsoring some extra features—personal ads, classifieds, and a Help Wanted section—but so far, nobody's really using them. Online shopping has never been so uninteresting.
WEB http://aconnection.com/anet/index.html

Branch Mall The Branch Mall claims to have been the first mall on the Internet, which seems unlikely, but who's keeping track? In any case, it hasn't aged gracefully: The site is little more than a list of about 100 merchant links, mostly retail with a few random additions, such as non-profit groups, thrown in for seasoning. But there are some truly unique finds to be uncovered by the persistent shopper, like the one and only, unbeatable Burp Gun and the About Me! personalized books.
WEB http://server.branch.com

Dream Shop It's "The anywhere place." Time Warner's Dream Shop is a high-concept, nicely designed mall that features about 25 of the sort of "better" shops found in almost any shiny upscale suburban mall: Eddie Bauer, The Sharper Image, the Bombay Company, Williams-Sonoma—you get the picture. You can also get brand-name workout gear from Crunch, "insider authentics" (use your imagination) from *Sports Illustrated,* and gourmet tea from Stash. There are some great gastronomical delights, including the Mozzarella Company. Spend-

This mall's open 24 hours a day
http://www.icw.com/ams.html

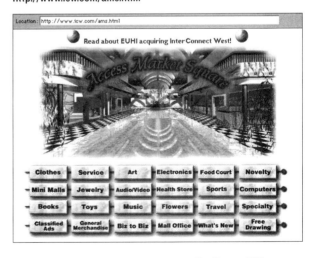

A highly acclaimed set of shops
http://www.internet-mall.com

thrifts can take advantage of the Dream Deals, such as six filet mignon steaks from Omaha Steaks for less than $30.
WEB http://www.dreamshop.com

The Electronic Mall One thing about big companies: They like to hang out together. CompuServe has assembled an impressive array of upmarket merchants, like Brooks Brothers and J.C. Penney, any two or three of which would probably be enough to anchor your average offline mall. But once you've clicked your way through the mall to the actual store in which you're interested—say, Hammacher Schlemmer—you'll find that most of the items featured in the catalog don't actually come with pictures, just pithy descriptions along the lines of what you'd get in a catalog. In some cases you're given the option to view the company's Web site instead, which may have pictures, but then, what are you paying CompuServe for? True, you get access to occasional promotions and giveaways, and the selection is far better than in most malls, on or off the Net, but unless you know precisely what you want, it's hard to get the information you need to make your choices.
COMPUSERVE *go* mall

Empire Mall There's no obvious reason why the Empire Mall should be called the Empire Mall, but it is, and it's a nicely designed, if rather glitzy, online shopping site. The approximately 50 stores gathered here are an interesting, eclectic lot scattered over a handful of hyped-up categories—look for books and music under Media World, for example. On the other hand, not every mall offers designer windsocks for sale.
WEB http://empiremall.com

iMall I, Claudius. I, Robot. And now iMall, a serious mall for serious shoppers: tons of stores, tons of features, a nifty search engine, and a no-nonsense approach to secure transactions. It's hard to tell exactly how many stores there are at iMall, but suffice it to say that if they were in a real mall, that mall would have its own ZIP code. What keeps iMall's sheer size from getting overwhelming is the "Power Shopping" feature: Most malls let you search the names of stores, but with "Power Shopping" you can actually look for a particular item in a single search covering the inventories of all the stores in iMall, plus classifieds and the iMall newsletter. Drop by the Deals of the Day page to see what's going cheap.
WEB http://www.imall.com

The Internet Mall At last, a mall that knows what it's doing. Dave Taylor, the author of several books about computers and programming, put this site together, and it's become one of the largest, oldest, and best-designed shopping malls on the Web. Eschewing in-your-face color schemes and computer-crashing animation, the Internet Mall consists primarily of links to each of its more than 15,000 constituent stores, including brand names like L'eggs and Spiegel, which are divided into sensible categories and sub-categories, including an

adults-only section for sexually oriented products. At times the sheer number and variety of the stores can be daunting, but unlike many malls, this one gives you paragraph-long descriptions of each one, so you can look before you link. And for wacky online shopping fun, it's hard to beat the splendor of the one-of-a-kind RAND-O-MALL, a special feature that automatically selects 25 stores at random from the Internet Mall.
WEB http://www.internet-mall.com

Internet Plaza Is it just another online mall, or just another online mall that bills itself as "Not Just Another Online Mall?" You be the judge. Internet Plaza has a somewhat cutesy facade, with homey illustrations (PlazaTown looks like something left over from "The Prisoner") and fancy titles for its different shopping areas (Gourmet Lane, etc.), but there are links to some of the biggest names in online commerce here: Amazon.com, L'eggs, and Planet Reebok. More a collection of shopping links than a real mall, you won't find the hundreds of smaller and sometimes more interesting stores that crowd other shopping sites here. Internet Plaza also maintains its own magazine, Zone Interactive, a snappy roundup of Web comics and zines designed to amuse and inspire you.
WEB http://internet-plaza.net

iShops Visiting iShops is a calmer, more comfortable experience than you'll get at most online shopping sites, perhaps because there are only about 35 shops here. But they're great stores, including lots of well-known name brands, such as Dean & DeLuca and International Male. Links are laid out in a no-nonsense design that doesn't flash or move or otherwise promote eye-strain. Viaweb, the company behind iShops, has taken charge of the design of each store, rather than letting the clients do it

themselves, resulting in a uniformly pleasing and functional look. The site also explains its security precautions in plain and reassuring language.
WEB http://www.ishops.com

The Marketplace This is one of the premier shopping destinations on the Net. The 80 to 90 stores that sell their wares in AOL's online mall are for the most part reliable, tasteful, and reputable brand names—a random sampling might turn up Eddie Bauer, FAO Schwartz, Tower Records, and the Nature Company. The products are nicely illustrated, and the ordering process, while fairly lengthy, is clear and easy to follow. Some of the snazzy extra services include regular specials, an incredibly useful gift consulting page (gifts for teens, five novel gift-wrapping ideas, anniversaries...), and free gift wrapping.
AMERICA ONLINE *keyword* marketplace

MegaMall It's frame-tastic. MegaMall gets you all revved up to shop with a cheesy sci-fi intro about "the lights of Internet City," then bogs you down with an overly complex frame-based design, but if you can forgive them all that, you'll notice that the selection here is

---

It takes a village of commerce
http://internet-plaza.net

---

really quite good. More than 200 shops offer you golf books, gifts, gewgaws, and everything else you'd expect from a real mall, along with those ever-popular "adult" services. MegaMall also offers a newsletter that informs subscribers of new stores and promotions, and the Personal Shopper service informs you by email of events related to your shopping preferences.

WEB http://infotique.lm.com/megamall.html

More than 200 shops offer you golf books, gifts, and everything else you'd expect from a real mall, along with those ever-popular "adult" services.

Microsoft eShop It used to be just eShop until Microsoft devoured it, along with eShop Plaza. You would have thought that this would create a massive online shopping conglomerate, but so far there are only eight shops here, although they are among the highest-profile merchants online: Spiegel, Tower Records, Insight, L'eggs, Avon, etc. Microsoft's high-tech savvy will be reflected in the software these shops will use to accept online payments, although at the moment those features aren't in place yet.

WEB http://www.eshop.com

MSN Mall MSN's mall goes for quality over quantity—fewer stores, but bigger names, such as QVC, FTD Online, Omaha Steaks, Columbia House. If you were putting together an ideal mall, there are worse tenants you could choose. However, you can't do much comparison-shopping here. None of the stores compete with each other for the same product. There are also a few special MSN services that specifically deal in gifts—one for MSN-related items, one for gourmet food items—and giveaways (five weeks of the *Wall Street Journal*—free!). There's also a link to Microsoft's eshop.com, which houses Avon, Tower, and L'eggs, among others.

COMPUSERVE *go* mall

NetMarket On AOL and CompuServe, this site is known as the Shopper's Advantage, but you can just think of it as... the Price Club of cyberspace. Shop from over 250,000 brand-name products protected by a two-year warranty and a low-price guarantee. What's the catch? You've got to pay to play. Annual dues are about $49, but you can sign up for a three-month trial membership for only $1 (and receive a baby boom box for free). If you're not skittish about sending your credit card number over the Internet (and the site won't let you if your browser isn't secure), NetMarket can be a pleasant experience. Choose a room from an architectural floor plan and select from a category in the room. For example, the Master Bedroom lets you browse categories like fashion, flowers, and fragrances.

AMERICA ONLINE *keyword* compustore *or* shopper's advantage

COMPUSERVE *go* sac

WEB http://www.netmarket.com

Shops.Net About 150 shops, mostly on the smaller, specialized side, organized by categories from Automotive to Videos. Some categories suffer from a paltry selection (only one flower shop is listed), but the site has a search engine to find products by keywords or concepts. The most distinctive feature of Shops.Net is a software innovation that allows shopkeepers to update their inventory listings whenever they like, so presumably the product selection is more accurate than at other malls.

WEB http://shops.net

ShopUSA ShopUSA claims to be a multilingual cybermall, but the only language here besides English is Japanese, and frankly, we hope their Japanese is better than their English. Still, there's a small but dependable selection of stores here, from the Crafters Source to Lands' End, plus a great bike store called Cycle Path.

WEB http://www.globalstrategies.com/shopusa

Specialty Shops Yes, they're special. Specialty Shops consists of only five stores, but they're very distinctive stores, and the site presents them with a great deal of style and design savvy. The colors are soothing, the frames are intelligently constructed, and visitors can choose to shop either by individual store or by product category. The shops include Seckinger-Lee, a gourmet food store, the Common Pond, a company that manufactures high-quality recycled products, and Heritage Outdoor Furniture, for deck furniture to die for. Yes, these places are on the expensive side. A registration process is required, but it's relatively painless.

WEB http://www.specialtyshops.com

21st Century Plaza Internet Mall A mall just isn't a mall without pastel colors, and 21st Century Plaza has brought them to the Web. This excessively mauve-and-beige site hosts more than 100 stores, and although it's low on brand names, the selection is impressive— this is where you'll find those quirky, clever little items you expect when you shop online. One of 21st Century Plaza's special gimmicks is its 45 "Anchor Merchants," which offer special deals and discounts every day.

WEB http://www.worldshopping.com/direct.html

The Price Club of cyberspace
http://www.netmarket.com

Web Warehouse Its utilitarian name aside, Web Warehouse does what it can to keep in step with those crazy kids by including links to sites like Geek Girl, Armani Exchange, and MTV Online. What do those three sites have in common, aside from a desire to be considered hip? They don't actually sell much of anything. Drop by here if you want a quick tour of online trendiness, but don't expect to come away with an armful of Christmas presents. Ironically, Web Warehouse presumptuously bills itself as "The Only Place to Shop on the Internet." As if.

WEB http://www.webwarehouse.com/index.shtml

World Wide Mall Although the people behind the World Wide Mall boast of their willingness to talk to potential advertisers in Finnish, the stores here are almost exclusively American, so it doesn't particularly fulfill its promise of being an international venue. It also doesn't distinguish itself in the field of selection or design, but give it time: Malls like this one have a lot of potential as a means of contacting foreign retailers.

WEB http://www.olworld.com/olworld/mall/mall_us/index.html

Get funky in cybertown
http://www.cybertown.com

Worldshop Although cyberspace knows no political boundaries, the stores in online malls tend to be American, and mall administrators are aggressively wooing retailers from other countries. Worldshop is doing a better job than most. Although the actual percentage of international stores here is low, there are a few gems, which tend to be on the artsy-crafty side. There are gifts from Ireland and Hungary, and a firm called Abercrombie & Kent offers tours of Africa.
WEB http://www.worldshop.com

▼ Virtual communities

Cybertown Mall Won't you take me to... Cybertown. Cybertown is a kind of virtual community, a massive Web site organized like a real-life town, including of course, a mall. Everything in Cybertown has an aggressively "futuristic" (not our future, we hope) look and feel, including lots of shiny fake buttons that don't do anything when you click on them. The stores here are small retailers and mail-order houses covering quite a few categories—the Boulevard St. Michel carries an

interesting (and cheap) line of fake (faux, darling) jewelry. Note the Cybertown ATM feature: Registering with Cybertown earns you 100 free credits (you can earn more), which you can use toward discounts on purchases that you make through the mall.
WEB http://www.cybertown.com/

Downtown Anywhere It's not just a mall, it's a sociological experiment! Downtown Anywhere takes the high-concept road to online shopping, and in fact shopping is only one of the features of this mega-site, which attempts to give some structure to the chaos of the Web by organizing it into the form of a virtual city—the shopping areas are, of course, Main Street and Fifth Avenue. The actual number of stores featured here is low, a couple dozen at most, but they're an interesting group, featuring Amish crafts, exotic pet supplies, gourmet fruit, and the endlessly fascinating Speak to Me Catalog. Plus, Downtown Anywhere takes a special interest in providing state-of-the-art secure transactions, so unlike some real downtowns, you stand a decent chance of not getting mugged.
WEB http://www.awa.com/index.html

Virtual Town Unlike *Our Town*, there's no Stage Manager stepping in to offer comments, and unlike your town, there's no fast-food drive-thru. Like Cybertown and Downtown Anywhere, Virtual Town is a mega-site structured along the lines of a real-world community, and like any American community deserving of the name, it has a mall. The Virtual Town mall is made up of about 50 sites, including large retailers like CD Connection as well as small, independent stores. There's a disproportionate number of bookstores and sci-fi and fantasy-related stores here.
WEB http://wwwcsif.cs.ucdavis.edu/virt-town/welcome
.html

▼ Specialized malls

DigiCash Cybershop It's new, it's cosmopolitan, it's... Ecash! Although it looks a little scary, Ecash actually sounds like it might be a pretty good idea. It's an all-electronic currency that allows for easy, risk-free online transactions (the Ecash home page explains the whole idea), and the Cybershop is a set of links to stores on the Net that accept it. Most of the stores here deal in information, rather than actual concrete goods—music, images, text, even personalized encryption software—but the selection is absolutely wild: These are some of the funkiest, weirdest stores you'll see anywhere on the Net. If you can't get your mind around CyberBucks, a few shops still accept real dollars.
WEB http://www.digicash.com/shops/cybershop.html

Direct to Retail Are you fascinated by the Contour Mattress Pad, the Instant Flower Garden, and all those other products "As Seen On TV"? When the commercials interrupt your favorite programming, are you frustrated that you can't write down the ordering information fast enough? The inexorable convergence of TV and Web has produced Direct to Retail, where you can order the nationally advertised AB Roller Plus and Vanna White's Perfect Smile toothpaste online. If you really want to, you can join the Buyer's Club and get hefty discounts on most of these products, but so far there aren't all that many products up on the page, and it might not be worthwhile until the selection fills out a little more.
WEB http://pwr.com/dtrtv

First Virtual InfoHaus So what's an InfoHaus? Well, it's a mall. First Virtual is one of the larger digital cash enterprises, and this is a complete set of links to their sellers, which are an eclectic bunch (there are about 150 of them), running from Education to Games to

Spend your green on eco-friendly products
http://www.igc.apc.org/GreenMarket/

Children's Items. These enterprises deal mostly in information and services (consulting, education, that sort of thing), with a few goods (like some yummy-sounding brownies) sprinkled here and there. If you shop online regularly, and you're interested in exploring a more advanced and potentially more convenient way of paying for your plunder, this might be a good place to start.
WEB http://www.infohaus.com/

Green Market "Green Market's goals are twofold: education and product promotion." Green Market showcases companies with products that benefit—or at least don't harm—the environment and that usually replace products that do. Putting this eco-friendly online shopping center on the Net makes perfect sense; the savings on paper alone must count for something. The message at this mall isn't to go out and live on blue-green algae or anything (although you can order a batch here), but a Sun Pipe would brighten up anybody's bedroom and save a little power at the same time.
WEB http://www.igc.apc.org/GreenMarket/

New York Style—Shopping Is it the essence of style not to have a style? New York Style,

which is also an online magazine, tries very hard to simply ooze Manhattanite sophistication, and it ends up doing a pretty decent job. The site is quite beautiful, and the products featured here tend to be upscale and high-concept, not to mention expensive: artsy photographers, fruitiers, a ceramic artist billing himself as the "Ace of Vase." Lots of great gifts here, including tons of earrings, crepe trapeze dresses, and for the person who can't get enough caffeine, tea-infused chocolates from Burdick's.
WEB http://www.nystyle.com/shopping/shoptxt.htm

Don't download the shopping music, unless you're really hankering for some of that down-home Muzak.

The Malls of Canada Cyberspace is relatively free of national boundaries, but the friendly folks at the Malls of Canada give their site a dash of nationalistic pride anyway. It's strictly no-frills, though, and the larger Canadian merchants are not included (not that Americans would recognize them even if they were). The stores here are mostly independent retailers. But if you've been looking for that distinctive North-of-the-border shopping experience, the Malls of Canada will suffice.
WEB http://www.canadamalls.com

▼ Shopping directories

The All-Internet Shopping Directory Don't download the shopping music, unless you're really hankering for some of that down-home Muzak. Despite its terminal unhipness, the listings on the All-Internet Shopping Directory are quite extensive, highlighting new

sites and those that have won Top Shopping Site awards. Most sites have a few words of explanation (read: hype) next to their links. Note that this directory is pretty much at the mercy of its advertisers, and the prominently featured entries with big green check marks next to them are singled out because they're sponsors, not because they're good sites.
WEB http://www.webcom.com/~tbrown/welcome.html

Internet Mall Listings Regional, local, specific, and private malls are featured among the listings, from the Branch Mall (which claims to be the Internet's first Web mall) to the Transportation Mall (for all types of vehicles).
WEB http://www.opse.com/mallistings

Internet Shopping Directory Whoever put this directory together decided to err on the side of completeness. In a good way, that is, but keep in mind that not all these sites allow for actual online purchasing: The Lego site features tons of nubbly fun, but you can't actually buy anything there. Sites are organized by category (Sports, Entertainment, Kids Zone, etc.) and presented without commentary. The Free Stuff category is bursting with all kinds of giveaways and promotions, although that rotating dollar sign may give you motion sickness if you stare at it too long.
WEB http://www.isdirectory.com

Mall of Malls A plain, graphics-free, hypertext index of hundreds of malls. It might be hard to decide between visiting the Global Mall and the Global Shopping Mall based on a name alone, but hey, no one ever said the spending life was going to be easy.
WEB http://www.westcomm.com/westpgl0.html

Mall Retailer Directory All the brand name stores you know and love. Border's Books & Music, Burlington Coat Factory, Clothestime, The Disney Store, Computer City, the Home

Depot, Staples, Lenscrafters, and even KFC (that's Kentucky Fried Chicken for those who live under a rock). Even if you don't live in the 'burbs, you can still shop as though you do.
WEB http://www.ecola.com/ez/retail.htm

Nerd World—Shopping Nerd World is a benevolent site that just wants to make the Web easier for everybody, and its shopping directory certainly stands a fair chance of doing just that. It's intelligently designed (well-used frames are a rarity these days), which is a good thing because it's quite large: There must be thousands of stores listed. Most of the store listings have short blurbs that describe what they sell. Pocket protectors aren't prerequisites to shop here.
WEB http://www.nerdworld.com/nwl53.html

ShopInternet Global Shopping Centre The Global Shopping Centre is run by a group called Renaissance Internet Services, and its goal is to become the definitive shopping list of the Net. If shiny buttons count for anything, it's well on its way. The listings here are a respectable size, but its major virtue is the brief description of each site that follows the link. Most shopping directories let the site write its own blurb, or just borrow its ad copy. The descriptions are short and pleasantly free of hype.
WEB http://www.ro.com/ShopInternet

The Shopper At least when it comes to services and design, this directory has 'em all beat. Search by product or site name and The Shopper's database returns a list of online shops or malls that include it. Each mall has a comparatively lengthy description next to it, which specifies the number of sites the mall contains. The Shopper also includes lists of best sites and five-star sites (there is a difference), a gift guide, and tips for merchants. All

You don't have to brave New York to shop here
http://www.bloomingdales.com

the bells and whistles tend to make you forget that The Shopper has serious limitations—it lists only malls, not individual sites—but it's definitely worth a visit.
WEB http://www.shoppingdirect.com

WWW Shopping Directory Order Turkish coffee, South African wine, and an Irish breakfast in bed—without ever leaving your bed. This is the sort of languorous fantasy life cybershopping affords the average individual with some electronic cash and an Internet connection. From this site, link to hundreds of shopping malls and specialty shops from around the world, including Australia, Canada, Italy, Ireland, Japan, South Africa, and the United States.
WEB http://www.worldshopping.com/director.html

▼ Department stores

Belk Department Store Shop for sports gear or some designer perfume at the site. Otherwise, email the Belk personal shoppers with a request and they'll get back to you in a few days. A bonus: The betrothed can sign up on Belk's bridal registry.
WEB http://www.infi.net/foto/belk

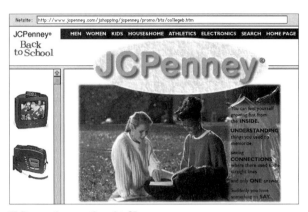

"A Penney for your thoughts?"
http://www.jcpenney.com

Bloomingdale's This site isn't fully online yet, but the previews are snazzy, especially if your browser works with the Shockwave plug-in. The only thing you can order right now is a limited-edition CK Barbie, billed as "The Most Unique Barbie Ever." With her denim jacket and Calvin Klein T-shirt, she looks like plenty of other trendoid teens, but that's beside the point. She's a doll.
WEB http://www.bloomingdales.com

Interactive QVC Quality, value, convenience—and interactivity. Shop online for the usual QVC "bargains," at a site that's surprisingly tasteful, given the purposeful tackiness of the show's sound stages. You won't have to wait around for Today's Special Value to come around, but you will miss the mesmerizing spokesmodels of middle America found on the cable TV show. The indexed product listings need help in keeping up to date. It's hard to believe that QVC has no sterling silver maracasite jewelry in stock.
WEB http://www.iqvc.com

J.C. Penney Whether you're shopping to buy, window-shopping, or just surfing the Web at random, J.C. Penney online rates a visit as an example of beautiful design work, although to

the untrained eye it might looks like someone got a bit too busy with a scissors and a J.C. Penney catalog. The site doesn't feature everything J.C. Penney sells, but there are more than 600 products to choose from, divided into men's, women's, and children's clothing, plus housewares and electronics. So what if the fashion police give you a warning if you start walking around flaunting your Arizona jeans? There are plenty of other products here, many discounted, lots of snazzy pictures, and even a well-thought-out frame-based design. Web designers should take notes.
WEB http://www.jcpenney.com

Kmart Take a look at a selection of items from the latest Kmart circular—the Denise Austin Trim Rider, only $79.99! With these and other deals rendered resplendent on the Web, the cybersavvy homemaker can now shop for a blue-light special online.
WEB http://www.kmart.com

May Department Stores The May department stores—Lord and Taylor, Hecht's, Filene's, and others—use their Web site to publish financial reports about the company. More corporate information is promised for the future, but if it's online shopping you want, you'll have to get in your car and drive.
WEB http://www.lordandtaylor.com

Nordstrom Online shopping at Nordstrom works a little differently. Instead of browsing a catalog online, customers can personally contact Nordstrom by email, through a service called Personal Touch America. You inform Nordstrom of your shopping interests, and a Personal Shopper then selects items that they think might appeal to you and emails you descriptions of them. Then, if your interest is sufficiently piqued, you can order. Sounds a little cumbersome, but if personal

attention is your thing, they'll give it to you.
WEB http://www.nordstrom-pta.com

Spiegel "The most extraordinary catalog on the Web," if they don't say so themselves. Spiegel's site has a beautiful color scheme, classy little drawings, lots of helpful product information, and so many cute little features it's hard to keep track of them all. The site is extremely ornate, but it comes in five basic parts, Work, Play, Home, Learn, and Shop. The first four sections showcase various special products in the context of a chatty article featuring one of their spokesmodels. The serious shopping gets done in the aptly named Shop area, which features the entire product line of housewares, electronics, Barbie products, and men's, women's, and kids' clothing. The search engine is convenient and helpful, and there's a range of payment options, tailored to your technical prowess and security concerns.
WEB http://www.spiegel.com

Target Target, a huge discount store with more than 600 locations (customers can use the online store locator to find a Target near them), hits the bull's eye for new parents with its energetic Web page that offers support and advice for beginning families. Target describes its popular Lullaby Club, a baby registry program that parents can sign up for at one of the stores, and follows up with helpful hints for first time Moms and Dads heading toward baby shower time. The site even includes a checklist of baby items that parents can use to figure out what they need. To assist parents with that all-important decision—what to name the little one—Target solicits favorite baby names from Web site visitors and posts them online. Fluba May? Tyisha Laprice? Wellington Hung? Take your pick of these and more. The Target site isn't just selling baby supplies; although it positions

the store as a family outfit, the site runs a fashion column and other features to appeal to its childless customers.
WEB http://www.targetstores.com

Upscale Wholesale "Buy a little or a lot!" Of what? Of computer gadgets, pet accessories, automotive merchandise, personal professional security items, and outdoor and indoor recreation products. Customers can order one NV100 Night Vision Scope or 500 Australian Kuranda Trampoline Dog Beds, or whatever their whim. Great presentation and a ridiculous array of products will keep visitors checking back for new oddities they never new they needed.
WEB http://www.upscale.com

Wal-Mart Wal-Mart Online is a little defensive about its community policies. But all politics aside, it has everything you'd find at an offline Wal-Mart, as well as the usual price-matching policies, discounts, and deals. To actually purchase those tempting Wal-Mart products you have to register, but there's no charge.
WEB http://www.wal-mart.com

Shopping at the speed of your Web browser
http://www.spiegel.com

Hit the bull's eye with your browser
http://www.targetstores.com

▼ Classifieds

American Internet Classifieds The downside: You have to pay to post an ad. The upside: That may weed out some of the more frivolous entries. Another feature that works in this site's favor is that it prints pictures, which can make you feel a whole lot more comfortable about buying something from a total stranger. This service doesn't support quite as vast a volume of ads as some others, but if you really want it, whether it's a car, a computer, or a house, it's probably here.
WEB http://www.bestads.com

AmericaNet.Com Classifieds Sure, it's hideous: AmericaNet.Com's color scheme is based on red-and-blue banner headlines on a background of what appears to be yellowing newsprint. Who cares? It's got the ads, thousands of 'em, in more categories than we care to count.
WEB http://www.americanet.com/Classified

Classifieds CompuServe's classifieds aren't much fun to look at, but they're functional

and easy to use. The volume of posts on these board isn't overwhelming, but there's good stuff up there: The fact that it costs money to post an ad tends to winnow out needless posting. Replying to an ad is easy: Just hit the reply button and fill out the form. No personals here, but there are employment ads, as well as a special section for U.K. classifieds.
COMPUSERVE *go* classifieds

The Cyber Garage Sale The URL is a little bit daunting, but the Cyber Garage Sale is a helpful and free service. All kinds of characters show up here to hawk their wares, which include motorcycles, original computer games, waterbeds, you name it. There's also a separate category for people who aren't into the whole money scene and would rather barter.
WEB http://205.219.200.4/want_ads/index.htm

LinkAGE Online Free Classifieds As the sign says, mister, they're free. LinkAGE—an international corporate Internet provider—has put together this nicely arranged frames-based service, which puts you in touch with that one guy out there who desperately wants to buy all your old Rick Wakeman CDs, so don't be shy. These classifieds include personal ads as well, under the coy name "Friendship Connection." Otherwise, this is simply a well-put-together, tasteful service, with few bells and whistles.
WEB http://www.hk.linkage.net/classified.html

misc.forsale.non-computer For a newsgroup with such a vague-sounding title, misc.forsale.non-computer sure sees a lot of action. It's hard to think of anything that isn't either FS (For Sale) or WTB (Wanted To Buy) on this one: synthesizers, kitschy things, condos, phone systems, computer game platforms, cars, Barbie dolls... It's almost better not to go there looking for anything in particular: Sooner or later everything in the world will come floating by.

USENET misc.forsale.non-computer

Online Classifieds This area comes with a bunch of handy statistics telling you how great and useful it is, and some of them are pretty persuasive: These are the most active boards on AOL, with tens of thousands of posts weekly, and they're more "active" than the entire misc.forsale heirarchy on Usenet. This is an all-round excellent resource, well-organized and easy to use. The ads come in eight categories, including Employment, Real Estate, and People as well as the commodities; the General Merchandise section covers things like tickets, musical instruments, and even bridal wear. You can't search these boards by keyword, but you can sort through them according to how recently the ads were posted. Reply to ads by sending email to the poster.

AMERICA ONLINE *keyword* classifieds

Recycler Classifieds Recycler Classifieds is a free service that exists as both a Web site and a paper publication. Part of the beauty of the system is that ads posted online go into the paper edition as well. It costs nothing to post an ad, which might have something to do with the fact that there are more than 170,000 of them here, arranged by category and then alphabetically by city. The database is fully searchable, and it's updated every Saturday morning.

WEB http://www.recycler.com/htm/home.htm

Trader's Connection Size isn't everything, but if that's what you're into, Trader's Connection's got it: 1.7 million ads, all told. Trader's Connection is a service that gives you access to classified ads from a whole flock of print and electronic

Baby needs an old pair of shoes...
http://www.bonk.com/auctions/auction.html

publications, everything from the Charlottesville Blue Buck Saver to Montreal Boat Book. The service requires registration, and you have to keep track of your log-in code, but most of the features are free, including photographs of the items for sale, and a rather impressive "intelligent agent" called AdWatch, which searches ads as they appear for what you're looking for, even when you're not logged on.

WEB http://www.trader.com

▼ Auctions

Auction Gallery The site auctions off art, antiques, glassware, and collectibles. Bids may be made by phone, email, or in person, and a 10 percent premium is charged. Auctioned items are listed on the site and bidders can click on them for a phone number and the current bid.

WEB http://www.bonk.com/auctions/auction.html

Auction.Net Auction.Net designs home pages for auctioneers, maintains a state directory,

Rolling stock gathers no moss
http://www.whatever.com

and last but not least runs a service called Electronic Auctions, which runs online liquidation sales of furniture and office equipment. The company provides the site for auctions but is not involved in the transactions.
WEB http://auction.net

AuctionLine The site has set up an online auction house and a place where registered users can browse merchandise on the block and make a bid. Auctions are scheduled regularly.
WEB http://www.auctionline.com

Auctions On-Line The name of this service is a bit misleading because the auctions in question don't actually take place online. The site, a boon to both collectors and auction houses, lists auctions around the world, links to the Web sites covering them, and is a huge repository of catalogs for past and forthcoming auctions.
WEB http://www.auctions-on-line.com

AuctionWeb Going once. Going twice. Soooooold, to the bidder in cyberspace. Popular, easy to use, and free to most customers, AuctionWeb boasts 1,000 new items daily and a 75 percent success rate

(that is, three quarters of the items it lists get sold). How does the site work? People can list merchandise (free for items under $100) and set a bidding schedule (usually one or two weeks). At the end of the bidding, they are then given the names and email addresses of the highest bidders. Since the site merely facilitates these auctions and doesn't get involved in the actual transactions, the person auctioning items must contact the bidders directly. In addition to the standard auctions, the site also runs Dutch auctions. Forums allow people to air their experiences with online auctions. Contains rules, registration information, schedules, current listings, and even a personal shopping service that alerts bidders by email when items they might be interested in are being auctioned.
WEB http://www.ebay.com/aw

If you see one you like, just sign yourself up by checking a box. No fuss, no muss: Your mailbox need never be empty again.

Government Asset Sales Explore the weird world of government auctions. Every once in a while the federal and the 50 state governments find themselves with a wee bit too much stuff on their hands, whether it's extra office supplies or jewels left in old safe deposit boxes or speedboats confiscated from drug dealers. So what do they do? They auction it off to you, the people. This frames-heavy site makes for some difficult navigating, but once you get the hang of it, you can find just about everything under the sun. Drop by the Defense Reutilization and Marketing Service site for some mili-

tary equipment, and you might be tooling around in a Hummer in no time.
WEB http://pula.financenet.gov/sales.htm

▼ Catalogs

Advanced Catalogs Advanced Catalogs is the ultimate resource if you're interested in online catalogs. Unlike other such sites, this one only lists catalogs that allow online ordering, which makes this a lot more useful than most, and it's a great shopping resource in itself. The sites listed here give you exceptionally complete information about the products they're offering for sale.
WEB http://www.advcat.com

Catalog Link Catalog Link is arranged in two categories, one for consumer catalogs and one for business-to-business catalogs (industrial, office, and other supplies). If you head to the link for a particular catalog you can have it sent to you, and if the company has a home page you have the option of linking to it. Great for sending embarrassing catalogs to your so-called friends!
WEB http://cataloglink.com

Catalog Mart Going strictly by numbers, Catalog Mart probably has access to more catalogs than any other site on the Web—more than 10,000, distributed over more than 800 categories. But it works a little differently than other catalog sites. Instead of requesting a particular catalog, you fill out the address form, then choose as many areas of interest as you want. Based on this information, Catalog Mart decides which catalogs you will receive. Requires a small leap of faith.
WEB http://catalog.savvy.com

Catalog Select OK, you can't really shop online here, but this service is just too cool to leave out. Browse through hundreds of catalogs,

and if you see one you like, just sign yourself up by checking a box. No fuss, no muss: Your mailbox need never be empty again.
WEB http://www.pathfinder.com/CatalogSelect

The Catalog Site The complete resource for the catalogaholic. The Catalog site has reviews of catalogs, a gift center, a catalog of the week, a search engine, order forms for gift certificates, even catalog dish (gossip and news related to catalogs). Whew. Maybe the most useful feature here for the online shopper is the collection of links to online catalogs, complete with point-and-click ordering.
WEB http://www.catalogsite.com

Mall of Catalogs This meta-catalog has an excellent selection and a couple of features that distinguish it from some of the other catalog sites. If a particular company is running a special offer or a promotion, you can check a box when you're ordering its catalog to participate. There's also a list of the most-requested catalogs, if you simply have to know who's hot and who's not.
WEB http://www.marketeers.com/marketeers/mall ofcatalogs/

If you're hot for catalogs, surf here
http://www.catalogsite.com

Chapter 26

Consumer Resources

SHOPPING ONLINE SEEMS so convenient and easy. Click a little, type a little, cross your fingers a little, and voila!—a purchase, a home delivery. But while encryption and purchase protection calm most security fears, "caveat emptor" still applies, and it's awfully easy for the buyer to get burned.

You'll find more than one Ralph Nader on the Net

Consider the case of Jennifer, an enthusiastic online consumer who purchased a rare CD box set (she had been searching for it for years) from a very professional-looking Web site. It arrived in fine condition

Don't Get Mad,

except for one thing—there were only four CDs instead of the five the box set was supposed to contain. There was no receipt in the package, and when Jennifer tried to return to the Web site, it had disappeared. She realized, to her dismay, that she had no mailing address for the company. What should you do if something like this happens to you?

First, try to contact the company. Legitimate operations—even those that have gone out of business— usually attempt to keep customers happy. Go back to the Web site—you bookmarked it, right?—and copy down all the information there. That way, if the company's Web site vanishes, you'll have some kind of record of the company's full name and physical location. If the site has already disappeared, analyze the URL for clues to its whereabouts. Small businesses often lease space on a server; if you can figure out who runs the server, they might have information about the company you're seeking. Try entering just the first portion of the URL into the browser's location field to see if you can find out who's leasing the space. On the other hand, if the offending company had its own

Get Online

domain name, it may be possible to find out information about the company by searching in one of the domain name lookup services, like **FourII**, which allows you to find email addresses and geographic locations for that domain name.

Next, suggests attorney **Richard Alexander**, "Think about what you would accept as a reasonable resolution of your complaint. Do you want your money back, or would a store credit suffice? Would you accept a replacement item? Can the product be

CASH REGISTER

FourII
WEB http://www.fourII.com/

Richard Alexander
WEB http://seamless.com/alexander
law/txt/complain.html

Better Business Bureau
WEB http://www.bbb.org

BBB Online
WEB http://www.bbbonline.org/

Web Watchdog
WEB http://www.webwatchdog.com/

CyberCop
WEB http://www.ucan.org/

"Ten Tips for Preventing Information Highway-Robbery"
WEB http://www.ucan.org/neighbor
.htm#tips

Spy on those who done you wrong
http://www.fourII.com/

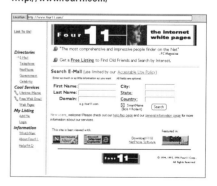

CASH REGISTER

USENET misc.consumers

National Fraud Information Center
WEB http://www.fraud.org/

The Open Text Boycott
WEB http://freethought.tamu.edu
/~Emeta/rs/ot/

I Hate Sony Page
WEB http://ernie.bgsu.edu/~Eadavoli
/jb/ihate/sony.html

Multi-Level Marketing Schemes
WEB http://gnn.com/gnn/meta
/finance/feat/archives.focus
/pyramid.html

repaired? Think through your goal." Gather any correspondence you had with the company, including email, receipts, credit card bills, and packaging. Email, call, or write to the company and demand satisfaction of your problem.

If you still have a grievance about online commerce after contacting the company, there are plenty of places to complain online, publicize your bad experience, and possibly get your problem resolved:

The first of these places is the familiar **Better Business Bureau**, a consumer interest group of offline businesses pledging to be held accountable to ethical standards. You can search for a branch of the BBB closest (geographically not cyberspatially) to the company with which you have a problem, and file a complaint online. Several of the local BBB's Web sites offer satisfaction reports for companies with online operations. Also, the Better Business Bureau is about to launch a watchdog site called **BBB Online**, which will be specifically focused on online consumer protection. Major

The place to whine online
http://www.bbb.org

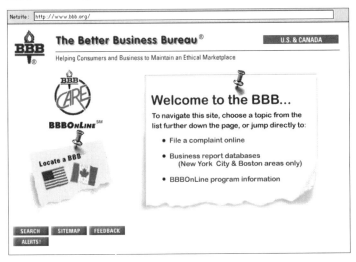

corporate support for this venture is strong. The Better Business Bureau is expected to institute stricter standards for online commerce than those currently in effect. The organization will launch officially early this year.

Meanwhile, several other operations are cracking down on con artists and irresponsible businesses. The most familiar name in the game is **Web Watchdog**, whose logo appears on many Web stores' pages. Members of Web Watchdog must prove that they conduct business, and promise to respond to customer complaints within ten business days, among other criteria. The "doghouse," which was empty when we checked, lists companies that have not resolved consumer complaints satisfactorily. A search engine aids consumers in finding the sites of member companies, and any disgruntled customer can file a complaint online.

Consumer crime-watch for the online community
http://www.ucan.org/

❝ The 'doghouse', which was empty when we checked, lists companies that have not resolved consumer complaints satisfactorily. ❞

CyberCop—sponsored by UCAN, a nonprofit consumer group in California—is more than a Better Business Bureau wannabe. It's also a grassroots movement toward self-policing of online commerce. Consumers can file a complaint or report suspicious activity, view a list of complaints, and join the Internet Commerce Activity Network (ICAN), a group of consumers on the lookout for Internet fraud. There is also plenty of reading material for consumers, including an excellent pamphlet called **"Ten Tips for Preventing Information Highway-Robbery."**

Had enough of fraud? Fight back
http://www.fraud.org

If you still feel dissatisfied, you haven't completely exhausted your options. You can take the complaint to the public yourself. The Usenet newsgroup **misc .consumers** is filled with gripes about irresponsible companies—the posters name names and don't mince words. In addition, the National Consumers League, which closely cooperates with the Federal Trade Commission, has set up a great Web site for its **National Fraud Information Center**. The NFIC handles individual consumer complaints, refers them to the government, and offers plenty of legal advice, including an online daily report on Internet fraud activity. If you prefer the frontier method—taking the law into your own hands—you may wish to join the dozens of ordinary folks who have set up protest Web pages. For example, **The Open Text Boycott** details some possibly unethical business practices by a popular search engine, the **I Hate Sony Page** reveals a customer service nightmare, and **Multi-Level Marketing Schemes** rants against the familiar perils of Amway and pyramid schemes. Setting up a protest page is a recourse of last resort for the supremely disgruntled—here's hoping you're not among them.

Personally, we love Sony!
http://ernie.bgsu.edu/~Eadavoli/jb/ihate
/sony.html

Starting points

Consumer Alert: Technology and Telecommunications A collection of seven or eight articles on Internet privacy, safety tips for online consumers, and child safety. More articles are added at infrequent intervals. The information here is much more in-depth and thorough than what's found at many online consumer resources, although the selection of topics is limited.
WEB http://www.his.com/~calert/issues/telecom /index.htm

Consumer Forum Like many of the forums run by the commercial Internet providers, the Consumer Forum contains an enormous amount of information, much of which is fluff. But try browsing the Library, where other users have uploaded an amazing collection of articles and resources, including old columns from David Horowitz's "Fight Back" feature [the new ones are at *go* fightback], which keep track of, among other things, federal efforts to regulate Internet commerce without violating everybody's inalienable rights. If you pick your topics carefully, the message area can be a rich source of wisdom from your fellow shoppers.
COMPUSERVE *go* conforum

Consumer World Look in the dictionary under megasite: Consumer World should be there. This is strictly a links-only site, but what links! If, the creator of Consumer World has erred at all, it's on the side of thoroughness; the site includes hundreds of consumer agencies and information sources, organized by product and locale, when applicable. You're sure to find info here about anything you've ever bought. The links are frequently updated, and some are accompanied by brief descriptions of their contents.
WEB http://www.consumerworld.org

The Internet Advocacy Center For now, this well-meaning site is a little scatter-brained: gobs of information and links flying everywhere, mixed in with headlines and pretty graphics. You'll find links to other advocacy sites here, along with reporting on pending consumer legislation, libraries of Internet terminology, mailing lists, brochures, information about company policies... it's enough to make your head spin. More is on the way. When it gets organized, this will be one of the best consumer resources online. For now, give it a look, but get ready to do a little digging for what you want.
WEB http://www.consumers.com

The authorities

Better Business Bureau The BBB brings its helpful consumer publications to the Web, offering advice on avoiding scams, resolving disputes with businesses, and more. If you're thinking of using a company's services, the BBB in your area may be able to tell you if the company has a good reputation. The bureau provides publications for businesses too,

Consumers rule the online world
http://www.consumerworld.org

The Hazards of Online Classified Ads

We have received complaints about an online auto classified listing service that sold classified ads much like those in the Sunday paper. For a flat fee of $399, Internet Classified Listings (ICL) would add a brief description of the customer's auto to a Web page. ICL even provided a money-back guarantee that the vehicle would sell within 90 days.

However, ICL evidently did nothing to ensure auto sales other than put the classified ad on a Web site. Several customers have complained to the Florida Attorney General that the 90-day period expired, their car did not sell, and they could not locate ICL reps to receive their money back. The Web site in question has since closed down.

Similar scams may appear in other parts of the country. Consumers should be skeptical of "money-back guarantees" when solicited for any type of online classifieds, and should thoroughly check out online merchants before paying any money.

—*from Cybercop Precinct House*

including material on the ethics of advertising.
WEB http://www.bbb.org/

Cybercop Precinct House "Keeping cyberspace safe for consumers." This swaggering, six-gun-packin' site is maintained by ICAN, the Internet Consumers' Action Network (its offline half is the Utility Consumers Action Network). Cybercop Precinct House receives and catalogs information and personal complaints relating to unfair business practices

online, and posts that information for public consumption. It does quite a good job of both. The site features an excellent set of links to consumer resources and consumer law sites online. Note, however, that Cybercop is not a law enforcement agency of any kind; it's made up of good, solid private citizens such as yourself.
WEB http://www.ucan.org

FTC Consumer Brochures Don't get scammed. Here's the full text of more than 100 consumer brochures issued by the Federal Trade Commission's Office of Consumer and Business Education. Find out consumer facts, laws, and regulations about everything from shopping for eyewear to separating factual from fictitious health claims.
WEB http://www.webcom.com/~lewrose/brochures.html

Internet Business Information Registry The IBIR attempts to provide a basic directory listing of reputable businesses in cyberspace. It provides a perfunctory factual profile of companies that register with it, offers its services in resolving disputes related to online business transactions, and publicizes news of online scams. Relatively few companies have signed up yet, but the infrastructure looks promising.
WEB http://quebec.ie.utoronto.ca/IBIR/ibir.html

NetCheck The NetCheck Commerce Bureau was created "to promote ethical business practices worldwide and to increase consumer and corporate confidence in purchasing products and services on the Internet." It's essentially an institution created to assist companies in allaying any concerns their customers might have about buying by modem. Companies that join it get to display the NetCheck logo and have their site listed at NetCheck, presumably as proof that they play nice with their clients, although it's not clear how closely NetCheck monitors its members. Visi-

tors can file either compliments or complaints about companies that sell online, and they can also report copyright violations and any unsolicited email they might have received. In turn, NetCheck offers its services as an arbitrator or mediator in resolving disputes.
WEB http://www.netcheck.com

Privacy Rights Clearinghouse The PRC is a nonprofit group associated with the University of San Diego's Center for Public Interest Law. Its stated mission is to education consumers about issues of personal privacy. Essentially, it offers guidelines on how much and how little you need to tell people with whom you do business, and how to avoid telling them more than you intend to. PRC's helpful brochures, the texts of which are online, cover topics such as "How Private is My Credit Report?" and "Privacy in Cyberspace: Rules of the Road for the Information Superhighway."
WEB http://www.acusd.edu/~prc/index.html

WebWatchdog The Web Watchdog is the leader in a growing group of well-meaning organizations that are attempting to keep track of the madding crowd of businesses stampeding onto the Internet, and to separate the on-the-level from the not-so-legit. It's a win-win proposition: Businesses benefit, because quality control brings more shoppers to the Net, and consumers benefit when the crooks are weeded out. Of course, the screening process isn't very rigorous; the only way for a business to be listed as a Watchdog site is for consumers to complain about them directly to Watchdog. Still, it's better than taking your chances elsewhere, and Watchdog's listings are larger and better-organized than any other group's. You can search the Watchdog database for a specific business, or you can search by category to get listings of legitimate companies providing a specific product or service. When a

Check the Doghouse for errant businesses
http://www.webwatchdog.com

complaint is filed and verified, the offending company is placed in the Doghouse.
WEB http://www.webwatchdog.com

▼ Product information

Consumer Electronics Forum The electronics industry turns over so quickly that this year's hot product is often next year's doorstop. With the Consumer Electronics Forum, you can find out which speakers put the most boom in your bass, which VCRs have the best clarity, and which CD-ROM players will enable you to meet the future head-on. The forum includes product descriptions and online technical support from such manufacturers as Videonics and Sennheiser.
COMPUSERVE *go* cenet

Consumer Reports The online, full-text version of the country's premier source of consumer information rates everything from toasters to sports cars, always with an eye toward affordability, performance, and reliability.
AMERICA ONLINE *keyword* consumer
COMPUSERVE *go* consumer

THE ELTON JOHN JACKET SCAM

I sent $250 to this company called Staritems located in Arizona for an Elton John tour jacket. I found them through advertisements they placed in music-oriented Usenet newsgroups. They will not send my order. I have since heard from five other people who have also been taken for considerable sums of money and expect to hear from more. Does anyone have any suggestions how we can handle this situation?—Kim

Kim, if you were smart enough to pay by credit card, then send the card company a letter and dispute the charge. (See your statement for instructions.) Otherwise, call your local post office. Ask for the address for the postal inspector. File a mail fraud complaint. (If you sent a check, you did use the U.S. Postal Service, right?)—Bob

—from misc.consumers

FDA Info and Policies The service includes news releases, product approval lists, and summaries of investigations by the Food and Drug Administration, which is charged with certifying all food products and pharmaceuticals before they hit the market. There are also selected full-text articles from the FDA Consumer magazine, and resources about toxicology, radiology, and biologics.
WEB http://www.fda.gov

misc.consumers "Super-glue warning." "The best liquid drain opener?" "Geico sucks." This newsgroup reads like one huge whine cellar, with hundreds of consumers complaining about airfares, lamenting the scourge of telemarketers, and discussing credit policies.

While attitudes vary wildly, everyone shares the desire to illuminate the often shadowy world of consumer spending—in short, to put their mouths where their money is.
USENET misc.consumers

U.S. Consumer Products Safety Commission This government agency issues alerts when toys or other products turn out to be potentially dangerous. Check out their latest press releases or ask to be put on the agency's electronic mailing list for new announcements. The CPSC Publications folder has safety tips for power tools and backyard pools.
URL gopher://cpsc.gov/

▼ Scams & frauds

National Fraud Information Center The NFIC has extended its long arm into the online world, fielding reports of shady schemes and posting up-to-date information to their simple but effective Web site. If you've been the victim of a scam, you can report it here, and get tips on what kinds of actions you can take; if you're just trying to educate yourself, there are tips for spotting fraudulent offers, as well as warnings about shady deals going down.
WEB http://www.fraud.org

Online Scams A concise document containing helpful hints for recognizing and avoiding online frauds and scams. The repertoire of online con jobs is fairly limited, and this page outlines the most common strategies for separating you from your hard-earned wages.
WEB http://www.ftc.gov/bcp/scams01.htm

Scams & Ripoffs Complain about getting fleeced. The Warnings/Scams library archives Federal Trade Commission documents on a wide variety of bunco jobs.
COMPUSERVE *go* confor →Browse Messages→Scams & Ripoffs

Appendix

INDEX

A

B

The Bag Lady's Cart Full of Abe Pinching Links, 81
Bali Online, 257
Bank of America, 53
banking, 48-63
   banks online, 53-59
   bill-paying software, 59
   digital payment, 60-63
Banking and Credit Library, 74
BankNet Electronic Banking Service, 54
bankruptcy, 71-74, 157
Bankruptcy Alternatives, Debtor's Options, 71
Bankruptcy is a Ten Year Mistake, 74
Bankruptcy Tax, 157
BankWeb, 249
bargains, 78-92
   college, 231
   wedding, 258-259
Barron's Online, 99, 180, 205
Barron's Online Business Dossiers, 193
Battern Family Tightwadding, 83
Baybank Online, 54
BBB Online, 309
Be Sure You Get the Credit You Deserve, 45
Beat the Car Salesman, 253
Beginner's Investment Checklist, 15
Belk Department Store, 301
Ben's Progressive Counter-Culture Pages, 87
Benetta's Refunding Resource, 88
Best Jobs in the USA Today, 97
Better Business Bureau, 309, 313
BigBook, 115
bill-paying software, 59

bit.listserv.museum-l, 103
BIZ*FILE, 196
biz.jobs.offered, 113
biz.marketplace.discussion, 124
BizWeb, 115
Bloomberg Personal, 18
Bloomingdale's, 302
BMW, 246
Bonehead Finance, 18
The Boston.com Stock Portfolio, 175
Branch Mall, 293
The Bridal Guide Budget Calculator, 259
The Bridal Search, 256
The Bridal Showroom, 256
Bridalnet, 256
Britton & Koontz Electronic Banking Center, 54
brokerages (online), 200-203
Browse the Federal Tax Code, 162
Budget Bridal Outlet Store, 256, 258
BudgetLife, 277
budgets, 12-23, 78-92
Buffett, Warren, 175
Buick, 246
business, 116-131
   advice, 123-125
   directories, 115
   franchises, 126
   government resources, 126-129
   organizations, 130
   software, 129-130
   taxes, 157-158
Business@Home, 117
Business Resources on the Web: Small Business, 131
Business Tax Information, 157
Business Taxes, 157
Buying Equipment Now Can Net Tax Gains, 157

C

Ca$h In, 88
Cal Law IPO Watch, 218
calculators
   car loan, 244
   net worth, 47
   personal finance, 23
   real estate, 262, 269
   tax refund, 147
   wedding budgets, 259
California Student Aid Commission, 234
Campbell Harvey's Futures and Options Glossary
Can SOHO Entrepreneurs Really Compete with Big Corporations on the Web?, 117
Canadian Stockwatch, 197
Capital Bank, 54
Capital Markets Financial Center, 218
Car and Driver, 250
The Car Dealer, 248
The Car Place, 251
Car Place, 246
Car Talk, 249
Car-link, 253
The CarCenter by Intelli-Choice, 245
Career Mosaic Resume Services, 112
Career Shop, 115
CareerPath.com, 97
Careersite, 115
cars, 244-253
   buyers' guides, 250-251
   classifieds, 253
   dealers, 247
   loans, 244, 249
   manufacturers, 246
CARveat Emptor, 253
Catalog Link, 307
Catalog Mart, 307
Catalog Select, 307
The Catalog Site, 307

S

S&P Online, 195
Sacred Rainbow, 255
Sage, 206
Salem Five Cents Savings
    Bank, 57
Sallie Mae, 233
Sample Credit Repair, 66
savings, 12-23
    coupons, 88-89
    eating cheap, 89-90
    free stuff, 90-92
    household hints, 84-85
    kids, 222-227
    lifestyle, 92
    See also **investment,
    personal finance**
**SBA (Small Business
    Administration), 126-
    127**
SBA Online's Women's Busi-
    ness Ownership, 117, 127
SBA: Small Business Admin-
    istration Home Page, 127
Scalable, Secure Cash Pay-
    ment for WWW
    Resources with the
    PayMe Protocol Set, 63
scams, 316
Scams & Ripoffs, 316
scholarships, 232-233, 237
Scholarships and Grants, 237
sci.electronics.repair FAQ, 85
sci.research.careers, 103
Scoring for Credit, 66
Secure Electronic Transac-
    tions, 289
security
    **consumer resources,
    308-315**
    Internet, 288-292
Seeking Shelter with Munis,
    160
Senior Resource, 284
seniors
    See **retirement**

SET Mailing List, 289
shareware, 37-39
ShopInternet Global Shop-
    ping Centre, 301
The Shopper, 301
Shopper's Advantage
shopping, 288-307
    auctions, 305-306
    bargain, 85-86
    cars, 244-253
    catalogs, 307
    classifieds, 304-305
    computers, 238-243
    **consumer resources,
    308-316**
    coupons, 88-89
    **department stores, 301-
    303**
    digital payment, 60-63
    directories, 300-301
    malls, 293-298
    security, 288-292
    software, 32-33
    **virtual communities,
    298-299**
The Shopping Wizard, 86
Shops.Net, 296
ShopUSA, 297
Signet Bank, 58
Signet: College Money Mat-
    ters, 233
The Simple Living Journal,
    92
The Simple Living Network
    Home Page, 92
Simply Money, 35
Simply Tax, 148
SimTel, 38
Six Ways to Save on Home-
    owner's Insurance, 277
The 60-Second Selector, 273
Small and Home Based Busi-
    ness Links, 131
small business
    See **business**
Small Business Administra-
    tion (SBA), 117
Small Business Advancement
    National Center, 130

The Small Business Advisor,
    122
Small Business Forum, 121
Small Business Foundation of
    America, 130
Small Business Innovation
    Research Program
    (SBIR), 127
Small Business Resource
    Center, 122
Small Business Software
    Library, 130
SmallbizNet, 131
SmartBiz: Doing Business on
    the Internet, 122
Smith Barney Financial Man-
    agement Account, 58
So... Where's My Refund?,
    142
So You Want to Start an
    Investment Club, 185
soc.college.financial-aid, 234
soc.couples.wedding, 255
Social Security Online, 286
software
    bill-paying, 59
    business, 129-130
    **Kiplinger's Simply
    Money 2.0b, 24-25**
    Managing Your Money,
    26-27, 30-31
    **Microsoft Money97, 27-
    28, 30-31**
    online stores, 32-33
    personal finance, 24-39
    Quicken Deluxe, 28-31
    retirement planning, 286
    reviews, 35-36
    shareware libraries, 36-39
    support, 34-35
    **tax preparation, 143-
    144, 147**
Software Clearance Outlet, 33
$Software Net, 33
Software Plus, 33
**SOHO (Small Office/
    Home Office)**
    See **business**
SOHO America, 117

U

V

W

XYZ

NOTES

NOTES

WOLFF NEW MEDIA

Wolff New Media is one of the leading providers of information about the Net and the emerging Net culture. The company's NetBooks series includes titles such as *NetGuide, NetGames, NetChat, NetMoney, NetTrek, NetSports, Net-Tech, NetMusic, Fodor's NetTravel, NetTaxes, NetJobs, NetVote, NetMarketing, Net-Doctor, NetStudy, NetCollege, NetSpy, NetSci-Fi, NetShopping, NetKids,* and *Net-Love*. In the coming year the series will add new titles such as *NetTravel USA, NetOut, NetWine, NetFix-It, NetInvesting,* and *NetRoots*. The entire NetBooks Series is available on the companion Web site YPN—Your Personal Net (**http://www.ypn.com**). And *Net Guide*—"the *TV Guide®* to Cyberspace," according to *Wired* magazine editor Louis Rossetto—is now a monthly magazine published by CMP Publications.

The company was founded in 1988 by journalist Michael Wolff to bring together writers, editors, and graphic designers to create editorially and visually compelling information products in books, magazines, and new media. Today, the staff consists of some of the most talented and cybersavvy individuals in the industry. Among the company's other projects are *Where We Stand—Can America Make It in the Global Race for Wealth, Health, and Happiness?* (Bantam Books), one of the most graphically complex information books ever to be wholly created and produced by means of desktop-publishing technology, and *Made in America?*, a four-part PBS series on global competitiveness, hosted by Labor Secretary Robert B. Reich.

Wolff New Media frequently acts as a consultant to other information companies, including WGBH, Boston's educational television station; CMP Publications; and Time Warner, which it has advised on the development of Time's online business and the launch of its Web site, Pathfinder.